BOYS LOVE MANGA AND BEYOND

BOYS LOVE MANGA AND BEYOND

HISTORY, CULTURE, AND COMMUNITY IN JAPAN

Edited by Mark McLelland, Kazumi Nagaike,
Katsuhiko Suganuma, and James Welker

University Press of Mississippi • Jackson

www.upress.state.ms.us

The University Press of Mississippi is a member of the Association of American University Presses.

An earlier version of "'The Evolution of BL as 'Playing with Gender': Viewing the Genesis and Development of BL from a Contemporary Perspective" was originally published as Fujimoto Yukari, "Shōnen'ai/yaoi, BL: 2007-nen genzai no shiten kara" (*Shōnen'ai, yaoi,* and BL: From the perspective of 2007]), *Yuriika* 39, no. 16 (December 2007): 36–47.

An earlier version of "Representational Appropriation and the Autonomy of Desire in *Yaoi*/BL" was published as Ishida Hitoshi, "'Hottoite kudasai' to iu hyōmei o megutte: Yaoi/BL no jiritsusei to hyōshō no ōdatsu" (On the declaration "Please leave me alone": The autonomy of *yaoi*/BL and the appropriation of representation), *Yuriika* 39, no. 16 (December 2007): 114–23.

First printing 2015
∞
Library of Congress Cataloging-in-Publication Data

Boys love manga and beyond : history, culture, and community in Japan / edited by Mark McLelland, Kazumi Nagaike, Katsuhiko Suganuma, and James Welker.
pages cm
Includes bibliographical references and index.
ISBN 978-1-62846-119-0 (hardback) — ISBN 978-1-62846-120-6 (ebook)
1. Young gay men—Comic books, strips, etc.—Japan. 2. Romance comic books, strips, etc.—Japan. 3. Women cartoonists—Japan. 4. Young women—Books and reading—Japan. 5. Girls—Books and reading—Japan. 6. Sex in popular culture— Japan. I. McLelland, Mark J., 1966– editor. II. Nagaike, Kazumi, editor. III. Suganuma, Katsuhiko, editor. IV. Welker, James, editor.
PN6714.B69 2015
741.5'952—dc23   2014029775

British Library Cataloging-in-Publication Data available

CONTENTS

ACKNOWLEDGMENTS

Most chapters in *Boys Love Manga and Beyond* were first presented at the workshop "Glocal Polemics of Boys Love: Production, Circulation and Censorship," organized by Kazumi Nagaike and Katsuhiko Suganuma at Oita University in January 2011. The workshop was cosponsored by Oita University's Center for International Education and Research and the University of Wollongong's Institute for Social Transformation Research. We would like to thank the discussants, Romit Dasgupta, Vera Mackie, Paul McCarthy, Sharalyn Orbaugh, Ulrike Woehr, and Taimatsu Yoshimoto, as well as all the presenters and attendees who contributed to the success of this event. The current volume brings together the papers delivered at that workshop that focus on Japan, along with translated essays by Fujimoto Yukari, a well-known *shōjo* manga (girls' comics) critic, and by Ishida Hitoshi, a scholar who has written extensively on BL. A separate edition of papers from the workshop that examine the transnational dimensions of boys love fiction was published as "Transnational Boys' Love Fan Studies," volume 12 (2013) of the journal *Transformative Works and Cultures*, edited by Kazumi Nagaike and Katsuhiko Suganuma.

A NOTE ON JAPANESE NAMES AND TERMINOLOGY

Throughout the text we have reproduced Japanese names in the natural Japanese order, that is, surname first, except in reference to scholars who normally publish in English. Note that among the contributors to and editors of this volume, only Fujimoto Yukari and Ishida Hitoshi publish predominantly in Japanese, and thus their names are written in Japanese order.

Japanese text uses neither capitalization nor italicization, and the use of these features in Romanized Japanese is always problematic. We have tended to limit the use of capitalization to Japanese personal and place names. Japanese terms that have not found their way into common English usage are italicized when mentioned in the text, as are Japanese book titles. Macrons designating long o and u sounds in Japanese have been used when transliterating Japanese terms except in those commonly rendered into English, such as place names.

BOYS LOVE MANGA AND BEYOND

AN INTRODUCTION TO "BOYS LOVE" IN JAPAN

MARK McLELLAND AND JAMES WELKER

If you walk into a typical bookstore in Japan today, somewhere on the shelves you are likely to find various books depicting romantic and sexual relations between beautiful, stylish male characters. These male homoerotic stories might be found in the form of manga—the name for Japan's globally known narrative comics—or in the form of "light novels" (*raito noberu*)—a local label for lowbrow, highly disposable prose fiction. If the store you're wandering around is large enough, you might find these texts occupying an entire shelf, floor to ceiling, or even multiple shelves. In fact, it's quite possible that the bookstore will have one section for manga and a separate section somewhere else for light novels, all depicting male–male romance. You may be able to find these sections by searching for a sign reading "*bōizu rabu*" in the phonetic *katakana* script or perhaps even "Boys Love" spelled out in English. The sign might also just say "BL."

If you pull one of those BL books off the shelf and start reading, more likely than not you'll find that those beautiful male characters within the book do not think of themselves as "gay." What's more, while the widespread availability and relatively high visibility of BL narratives might give the impression that it's easy to be openly gay in Japan, if you examine not the stories themselves but the context of their creation and consumption, you'll learn that BL is only tangentially connected with the lives of actual gay men. To the contrary, in Japan BL is generally assumed to be created and consumed by heterosexual girls and women. The fact that this widely held assumption is not altogether accurate is one of the many points about BL upon which the contributors to this volume shed light.

As its title makes clear, *Boys Love Manga and Beyond: History, Culture, and Community in Japan* examines various aspects of the BL phenomenon in Japan. Written by scholars working in diverse fields including anthropology, cultural studies, history, literature, and sociology, the twelve chapters that follow address a number of key questions about BL, such as: Under what cultural and historical circumstances did adolescent girls and young women in Japan begin creating and consuming narratives about beautiful adolescent boys and men? What genres of BL have emerged in the course of its more than forty-year history? What is the significance of the differences between these genres? What kind of girls and women actually create and consume BL works, and what kinds of pleasure do they derive from reading and writing about male–male romantic and sexual interactions? What kinds of bonds among readers are fostered by a shared interest in such narratives? Do boys and men read BL too? Are they gay? If not, why do they enjoy BL? What do the boyfriends or husbands of BL readers and artists think about their girlfriends' and wives' interest in BL? How is the BL phenomenon received in Japan in general? The answers to questions such as these will be explored in depth in the chapters that follow. First, however, a brief introduction to BL is in order.

As we note above, BL narratives focus on male–male romantic and sexual relationships. They first drew the attention of publishers and the public in the form of *shōjo* manga (girls' comics). *Shōjo* manga is a category encompassing a wide range of comics that ostensibly target female readers from preadolescence to almost adulthood—though many *shōjo* manga works have had an actual readership that includes male readers and older readers.[1] While BL narratives featuring original characters and storylines have had a strong fan base since they first were published in *shōjo* manga magazines in the early 1970s, derivative works based on the characters and plots of existing manga, anime, films, television shows, and literature, as well as works narrating imagined experiences of actual celebrities and athletes have also long been very popular. BL narratives are produced and distributed through both commercial and non-commercial channels. In the commercial sphere, manga and light novels are most common, both of which are often first serialized in BL magazines before being reprinted in bound volumes. BL narratives are also produced and distributed commercially as anime, audio dramas, video games, live-action films, and stage plays, among other media. As with other genres, particularly popular works may be recreated across a range of media.

Outside the commercial sphere, the most common media form for the sharing of BL narratives remains "*dōjinshi*," zine-like publications of highly varied quality. While most closely associated with original and derivative manga, *dōjinshi* may also contain text-based narratives, non-sequential illustrations, essays, and other musings. *Dōjinshi* are created and distributed by small "circles" (*saakuru*) of "*dōjin*," that is, like-minded individuals. These circles are often *very* small; in practice, they can consist of even a single individual. Some circles produce *dōjin* webcomics, video games, and anime.

Although most chapters in *Boys Love Manga and Beyond* are primarily focused on the creation and consumption of BL manga found in commercially published books and magazines as well as *dōjinshi*, some chapters give attention to other media as well.

A number of terms have emerged to label and categorize BL media over the past four decades. Although these categories overlap and the terms' meanings have shifted over time, four have been predominant:

- *shōnen'ai*—This term combines "boy" (*shōnen*) and "love" (*ai*) and has been most widely used in reference to commercially published *shōjo* manga from the 1970s into the 1980s. It is sometimes used retrospectively today to describe these works, but the term, now more closely associated in popular discourse with pedophilia, has largely fallen out of favor.
- *JUNE*—This word comes from the title of a commercial BL magazine published from the late 1970s to the mid-1990s and has been used to refer to the kinds of manga appearing in the magazine. It has also been used in reference to works produced and consumed outside commercial channels, particularly original rather than derivative works.
- *yaoi*—An acronym for *yama nashi, ochi nashi, imi nashi* (which might be translated as "no climax, no point, no meaning"), this self-mocking label was coined in 1979 and disseminated by an influential *dōjinshi* circle. It became popularized in the 1980s in reference to BL works that have not been published commercially, but it is sometimes used to encompass both commercial and non-commercial works.
- **boys love**[2]—Pronounced "*bōizu rabu*" and usually written in the *katakana* script, this term first appeared in the commercial BL sphere at the beginning of the 1990s. It is most frequently used as a label for commercially published manga and light novels, but it can also be used as a label for non-commercial works. It is often abbreviated "BL."

In addition to their overlapping usage in Japan, note as well that the common use of "*shōnen'ai*," "*yaoi*," and "boys love" in English and other languages among fans outside Japan often differs from the meanings given above.[3] (The emergence of these categories and distinctions between them are discussed at length in chapters by James Welker, Fujimoto Yukari, and Kazuko Suzuki.) For the sake of simplicity, in this volume we generally use "BL" as shorthand to encompass all of these categories, alongside more specific terms reflecting the context. Because the meaning of these terms varies by contexts, however, chapter authors often offer their own more specific definitions.

Other key terms used in the BL sphere in Japan not exclusive to BL culture include "*tanbi*" (aesthete or aesthetic), "*aniparo*" (short for "anime parody"), "*sōsaku*" (original work), "*niji sōsaku*" (derivative work), and "*sanji sōsaku*" (derivative work based on a derivative work).

While in contemporary Japan, appreciation for "beautiful boys" (*bishōnen*) in general and BL narratives specifically are most closely associated with adolescent girls and women, the depiction of the "beautiful boy" (*bishōnen*) has long been a romantic and sexualized trope for both sexes and commands a high degree of cultural visibility today across a range of genres from kabuki theater to pop music, anime, and manga. The celebration of youthful male beauty in Japanese culture arguably stretches back at least to the Heian period (794–1185), when prominent female authors celebrated the charms of aristocratic young men in texts such as the eleventh-century *Tale of Genji* and Buddhist priests penned "tales about beautiful boy acolytes" (*chigo monogatari*) for the reading pleasure of other Buddhist priests.[4]

It is not until the Edo period (1603–1868), however, that we see the development of a self-conscious literary tradition devoted to extolling the charm of youthful male beauty. This is associated particularly with famous novelist Ihara Saikaku, author of *The Great Mirror of Male Love* (1687), which contains love stories featuring relationships between older and younger samurai and rich townsmen and young kabuki actors. Homoerotic themes were also prevalent in the kabuki and puppet theater of the times.[5] During the Edo period the valorization of male–male love in the literary canon was also reflected in actual practice with many high-status individuals, including several shoguns, being renowned for their appreciation of youthful male beauty. Stories depicting male–male relationships (as well as such male–male relationships themselves) were described at this time as *nanshoku* (male–male eroticism), within which there were several categories, including the samurai-oriented *shudō*, or the "way of youths," a term that also named the norms which these relationships were expected to follow.

Yet, to speak of a tradition of "boys love" in Japan would be misleading since the historical and cultural contexts in which images of youthful male beauty have occurred differ widely over time and have been assigned often contradictory meanings. Furthermore, a history of boys *love* in Japan cannot be reconstructed without also attending to the changing nature of ideas about love itself in the Japanese context. In a compelling study of romantic love in Japanese and European literature, Takayuki Yokota-Murakami advances the provocative notion that romantic love as it was elaborated in European novels at the end of the nineteenth century was a concept unknown in Japan prior to the influx of Western culture beginning in the mid-nineteenth century.[6] He notes that "the 'equality' between male and female lovers or spouses described in Western literary discourse was often quite incomprehensible to . . . intellectuals" in the Meiji period (1868–1912).[7] There were no terms in Japanese at the time that could adequately express the fusion of spiritual and physical love that underlay Western notions of romantic love. Moreover, Confucian morality, which became increasingly influential in the latter half of the Edo period, saw women as inferior, sometimes evil, and certainly not as suitable objects of admiration.[8] To the extent that anything similar to the Western concept of "romantic love" existed in Japan prior to the Meiji period, it had been explored in the context of tales of "devoted male love" between older and younger samurai.[9]

The absence of a native Japanese term approximating the English word "love" is conspicuous in early Japanese translations of Western novels where it was sometimes simply transliterated as "*rabu*." Yet, as Leith Morton notes, "there is no doubt that by mid-Meiji a revolution was underway in regard to notions of love, marriage and the status of women."[10] By this time the notion of "romantic love," connoting elements of spiritual attraction between men and women, was being expressed in the newly coined compound "*ren'ai*," which combines the meaning of physical love contained in "*koi*" (also pronounced *ren*) with "*ai*," whose meaning had begun to encompass the wide range of feelings indexed by the English term "love." This "shocking new perspective" became an important talking point in the Japanese media and was popularized via women's literature and magazines and via Christian educators at private girls' schools.[11] Despite the misgivings of many social commentators, the discourse of romantic love had an enormous impact upon culture generally, especially upon literature. As Jim Reichert has pointed out, lacking indigenous examples, Japanese novelists had to find convincing ways to develop "new literary languages [and] new approaches toward characterization and plot" in order to realistically depict romantic heterosexual relationships.[12] One casualty of this process was that male–male erotic relationships, that is, *nanshoku* and *shudō*, both of which had been well represented in the literature of the previous period, were excluded from the new category.[13] Their association with the now discredited "uncivilized" and "feudal" practices of the Edo period further placed male–male eroticism outside the bounds of civilized morality.

By the late Meiji period, the uptake in Japan of Western sexology that pathologized homosexuality, alongside the developing hegemony of heterosexual romantic love, had led to a narrowing of sexual identification and practice. Male homoeroticism did continue as a minor theme in Japanese literature, but as Jeffrey Angles points out, those authors who specialized in this type of fiction had to resort to a range of strategies to disguise their interests.[14] No longer could the "love of youths" be valorized as an ennobling experience or a cultural ideal.

It is at this point chronologically that chapters in this volume begin to examine the prehistory of BL with Barbara Hartley's discussion of Taisho-period artist Takabatake Kashō. The Taisho period (1912–1925) saw significant economic growth and technological developments in Japan that resulted in major advances in the living standards of the urban population and in educational advances for both girls and boys. A vibrant literary culture developed, especially around popular monthly magazines aimed at differing readerships such as housewives, businessmen, and boys and girls. Kashō was one of the best-known illustrators of the period and created beautiful illustrations of both girls and boys used as cover art and to illustrate the content of leading boys' and girls' publications. In boys' magazines, Kashō tended to represent boys as young, beautiful, and sometimes effeminate-looking male figures that, as Hartley points out, "project an air of homoeroticism." Indeed, as Hartley, citing well-known Japanese cultural critic Takahara Eiri, remarks, many of the scenarios featuring these beautiful boys also featured depictions of older men, thus referencing the *chigo* (boy acolyte) tradition of Buddhist iconography discussed above. Kashō's illustrations of boys reflect the homosocial environment of the early twentieth century and in many of his pictures "there are no girls or women in sight." Given that contemporary accounts suggest that all male environments such as boarding schools and military barracks were sites for homosexual activity, it would be reasonable to assume that the homoeroticism of many of Kashō's beautiful-boy figures inspired interest and desire in the eyes of some male readers.

It is to a potential audience of female readers that Hartley draws attention, however. She notes that many girls would have had access to these images through brothers and other male relatives who subscribed to the magazines. Whereas girls' magazines offered depictions of women and girls in training for "respectable domesticity," boys' magazines focused on an outdoors' lifestyle of exploration and adventure, with boys often seen fighting and dying alongside their male comrades. These male figures—inflected with an oblique and therefore perhaps all the more thrilling sexuality—no doubt attracted interest among female readers. Noting that such images could also be featured in girls' magazines, such as *Shōjo no tomo* (Girls' friend), Hartley suggests that it was precisely the absence of women in the frame of these pictures—and hence their homoerotic charge—that may have attracted girl readers. Hartley speculates that the girl viewers of Kashō's illustrations may have interpolated themselves into the pictures and thereby the scenarios they represented in an attempt to discover "something beyond the flower girl aesthetic that characterized much narrative for girls." Hartley proposes that the homosocial world of Kashō's beautiful boys anticipates in some ways the cross-gender identifications that later come to characterize BL.

James Welker's historical overview of BL manga also stretches back to this period. Referring to a growing body of scholarship charting the prehistory of *shōjo* manga, Welker draws attention to the role Kashō and his male contemporaries—as well as to the *shōjo* literature they were illustrating—in creating the aesthetic foundation for *shōjo* manga in the postwar. The predominantly male artists creating *shōjo* manga in the 1950s and 1960s would pick up and further develop the images of delicate girls with large twinkling eyes, providing a portal into the illustrated girls' psychological state and inviting identification by viewers. In the 1970s, the creation of *shōjo* manga was taken over by a new generation known as the Fabulous Year 24 Group (*Hana no nijūyo'nen-gumi*), or just the Year 24 Group, as most of them were born around the year Showa 24, that is, 1949. In English, they might more fittingly be called the "Fabulous Forty-Niners." Building on such developments in manga and borrowing elements from foreign and domestic literature, film, history, and folklore, the Fabulous Forty-Niners invigorated *shōjo* manga with lavish illustrations and complex narratives. These new works were appreciated for their literary qualities by a readership well beyond the targeted audience of *shōjo* manga magazines.

It is also at this time that some Fabulous Forty-Niners began creating narratives featuring romantic—and eventually sexual—relationships between beautiful adolescent boys. While they were not the first women writers to show an interest in male homosexuality, nor the first artists to create *shōjo* manga with male protagonists, this new "*shōnen'ai*" manga arguably set the stage for the emergence of diverse genres of manga and other media that would depict male–male romantic and sexual relations in subsequent decades, continuing to the present. Welker traces the historical development of these BL genres from the first manga published in commercial magazines in the early 1970s to a highly diverse market combining commercial and noncommercial production and distribution channels, with an estimated annual domestic size approaching $25 million. He draws attention to key sites of creation and consumption, particularly commercial magazines and "spot sale events" (*sokubaikai*) for *dōjinshi*. In tracing the emergence of these genres as well as the etymologies of the labels "*shōnen'ai*," "*yaoi*," and "boys love" (*bōizu rabu*), Welker suggests points of overlap in the development of the genres themselves that may account for their frequent conflation in popular and critical discourse on BL.

Well-known and frequently cited *shōjo* manga critic Fujimoto Yukari addresses this conflation in a chapter revisiting some of the arguments she made about *shōnen'ai* and *yaoi* more than twenty years ago.[15] Fujimoto argues that, while "*shōnen'ai* first emerged as a mechanism offering an escape from the social realities of gender suppression and the avoidance of sex(uality)," the development of *yaoi* "made it possible for girls to 'play with sex(uality)' (*sei o asobu*) and opened up possibilities for them to shift their own point of view from passive to active engagement." A central aspect of this play is directed by what she calls the "*seme–uke* rule," that is, the norms whereby characters in a relationship are determined to be the "*seme*"—the "attacker," that is, the dominant and insertive sexual partner—and the "*uke*"—the "receiver," that is, the passive and receptive sexual partner.

In the modern period, sexuality emerged as a difficult terrain for girls to navigate, burdened as they were with state-sanctioned demands to be pure and chaste (see McLelland's chapter in this volume). Hence, some early commentators on BL—including those relying on Fujimoto's criticism—argued that through imagining a male homosocial world without girls, and through focusing on "forbidden" relationships that took place exclusively between male bodies, girls were able to explore issues of sexual attraction and desire in a safe environment. However, Fujimoto critiques this position since she feels that it diminishes girls' agency as readers. Instead, she puts forward the argument that through the *yaoi* genre in particular, which is frequently a parody of existing texts created by and for male readers, women's re-appropriation of these characters in a homosexual setting is an example of girls' agency in imagining sexual scenarios, including sadomasochism and rape, that have traditionally been considered the preserve of male sexual fantasy.

In a related vein, in her chapter Kazuko Suzuki points out how the proliferation of different terms referring to genres of male–male romance in Japanese makes it difficult to make generalizations about either authors or readers without attending to specific terminology. She argues that much closer attention should be paid to various subgenres in academic writing about BL in order to facilitate "more refined historical, cross-national, and comparative analyses encompassing empirical research." Based on interviews with professional BL writers, Suzuki works to establish how those most closely associated with the production of male–male romance stories understand the various terms used to label it. While from the outside the categorization of narratives into subgenres may seem a purely esoteric pursuit—most suitable perhaps for caffeine-fueled late-night debates among fans—Suzuki demonstrates that these categorical distinctions are quite significant to the artists who create these texts as they point to fans' expectations and, thereby, delimit narrative possibilities.

In discussing the categories "*shōnen'ai*," "*tanbi*," "*JUNE*," "*yaoi*," and "BL," Suzuki's interviewees stress both chronological and narrative (content) differences between these terms. For instance, they associate the traditional term *shōnen'ai* with the pioneering manga by the Fabulous Forty-Niners, an important influence on most of the artists she interviewed. Many of these artists also cite as influential "*tanbi*" (aesthetic) literature most associated with themes explored by "aesthetic" authors such as Thomas Mann and Oscar Wilde in Europe, as well as Tanizaki Jun'ichirō and Mori Mari in Japan—though the term "*tanbi*" has sometimes been used to refer to male–male romantic narratives in this sphere. The groundbreaking commercial magazine *JUNE*, published between the late 1970s and mid-1990s, sought to combine elements of highbrow *tanbi* culture with pornography and popular entertainment, and "*JUNE*" has come to be treated by some as a genre in its own right. While sharing with earlier *shōnen'ai* and *tanbi* stories an obsession with tragedy and unhappy endings, *JUNE* also developed more explicit sexual scenarios between the characters. It is the introduction of more explicit reference to sexual behavior between men that leads some BL writers to identify *JUNE* as the foundation of contemporary BL. BL has inherited the formal *seme–uke* distinction established in the *yaoi* genre, but unlike *JUNE* stories, which were often tragic, there is the expectation that BL stories will have happy resolutions. The picture Suzuki's research paints is complicated, however, by the fact that the terms are not used consistently within Japan, as well as that, as Suzuki notes, their meanings have also shifted as they have been taken up in Western fandoms.

Contrasting to varying degrees with Fujimoto, and Suzuki, in their chapter Kazumi Nagaike and Tomoko Aoyama "avoid . . . drawing clear borderlines" among BL genres since the genres are so "thematically intertwined," a sharp delineation between them has never been universally accepted, and because in Japan "many BL researchers use 'BL' . . . as an umbrella term, without clearly delineating these subgenres." It is this BL research and criticism in Japan that is their focus. Central in their overview of Japan BL studies is Nakajima Azusa, known for her early writing on *shōnen'ai* and her contributions to the magazine *JUNE*, including both critical writing under that name, as well as male homoerotic fiction she penned under the name Kurimoto Kaoru. In 1991, Nakajima expanded the horizons of Japanese BL studies with her influential book, *Communication Dysfunction Syndrome* (*Komyunikēshon fuzen shōkōgun*), arguably "the first full-fledged critical analysis of Japanese

BL."[16] Nagaike and Aoyama attempt to clarify and elaborate on certain aspects of her analysis, and, in so doing, trace the historical development of the discourse surrounding Japanese BL studies over a period of twenty years.

They begin with an examination of the initial stage of BL studies, in which scholars generally took an essentially psychoanalytic approach to these narratives. Later, other BL scholars explored a wider variety of theoretical frameworks, including media studies, minority discourse, author–audience studies, gender studies and queer studies, literary studies, and so forth. This historical and analytical overview reveals that Japanese BL studies have provided an analytical space for the cultivation of such interdisciplinary approaches. However, Nagaike and Aoyama also investigate a number of potential future paths in Japanese BL studies, such as transnational research concerning BL developments, both in Japan and abroad.

The concept of fantasy as a dominant force that characterizes the male homosexual narratives created by women is shown in the psychoanalytic approaches taken by several early BL critics, such as Matsui Midori, Tanigawa Tamae (later known as Mizuma Midory), and the aforementioned Nakajima Azusa. In order to explore the prevailing circumstances of female subconscious desires and repressions, these critics have discussed the framework of female fantasies of male homosexuality as an identity-creating process in terms of the psychoanalytic domain. In her chapter, Rio Otomo offers a different model for reading BL as fantasy, interrogating BL narratives as feminist—or more precisely, feminist-utopian—pornographic fantasies. Otomo looks at feminist theories of how fantasy works in women's pornography in order to challenge the common perception that pornographic imagery is necessarily degrading or demeaning. To highlight this reading, Otomo contrasts the essentially narcissistic autoeroticism of Modernist writer Mishima Yukio's obsession with three-dimensional male bodies with female BL artists/readers' fascination with the flat, two-dimensional bodies of fantasized male BL characters. The absence of female characters in the BL text entails the negation of their own female bodies, and thus enables the "floating away from a fixed identity" and an erotic autonomy that is not tied to any specific viewpoint or sexual identity. In this way, Otomo alerts us to potentially liberatory readings of BL as autoerotic female pornography.

This stress on women's agency as both readers and (re)creators of BL texts has gained ground in recent academic scholarship, in part in recognition of the growing awareness among BL consumers that they represent a particular subgroup or community. Around 2000, the word "*fujoshi*" emerged as a term of mocking self-reference among avid fans of male–male romance on the notorious BBS *2-channel*. The term itself is a homophone of a word meaning "girls and women," but, in this case, BL fans have replaced a *kanji* character to create the neologism "rotten girls." *Fujoshi* have emerged in media discourse as a specifically female equivalent of the male *otaku* (obsessive fan or nerd), whose preoccupations sometimes include *rorikon* (Lolita complex) fantasies about the sexuality of or sex with precocious girls. In the case of *fujoshi*, rather than attempting to evade confronting or problematic aspects of female sexuality through fantasizing about love between boys, these girl readers actively embrace their "rottenness" and accept that their preoccupation with BL is not socially acceptable.

Patrick W. Galbraith, in his contribution to this volume, offers a fascinating glimpse into the *fujoshi* world. Galbraith's work is particularly important for its ethnographic approach. Rather than speculate about the possible motivations and desires of girl consumer-creators of BL products, Galbraith follows a group of *fujoshi* over a period of a year. His female interviewees allowed him access to their "rotten friendships" with other girls and young women who share their interests in the transgressive potential of male–male desire. Galbraith reinforces Fujimoto's critique of the "escapism" argument accounting for the development of the BL genre, noting how his informants characteristically divided their emotional energy between physical partners and fictional characters, with affective responses to the latter expanded in intimate communication with *fujoshi* friends. Galbraith highlights the importance of sharing *moe* chat among BL fans. "*Moe*," a term literally meaning "to bud," has come to refer to the erotically charged interest that manga and animation fans feel for fictional characters. It is now used more broadly throughout various fandoms to refer to any kind of scenario, fictional or otherwise, that evokes (erotic) desire on the part of the viewer. Galbraith notes how his *fujoshi* informants are constantly on the lookout for *moe* moments inspired by real and fictional people and events, and the shared nature of these moments means they are transforming the relations they see in the world around them.

Whereas Galbraith's chapter offers ethnographic insight into the workings of the *fujoshi* subculture, in his chapter Jeffry Hester looks at the emergence of the *fujoshi* as a controversial and contested figure in popular culture. As Hester notes, the *fujoshi* is not necessarily in control of her own image, and a variety of discourses have emerged in the media seeking to comprehend and explain these "rotten" women. As he observes, *fujoshi* are read as a kind of *otaku*, but until the emergence of the *fujoshi* in popular discourse, female *otaku* were only ever "a derivative and misty presence." In recent years, however, the *fujoshi*, characterized by her interest in male homoerotic relationships, has, through online and print media coverage, been given "a solid and accessible social presence without precedent."

Hester focuses his analysis on three popular multimedia narratives, *Fantasizing Girl, Otaku-Style* (*Mōsō shōjo otaku-kei*), *My Neighbor Yaoi-chan* (*Tonari no 801-chan*), and *Fujoshi Girlfriend* (*Fujoshi kanojo*), two of which are authored by men and narrated from the perspective of male characters, and all three of which involve *fujoshi* as their main protagonists.[17] As Galbraith points out in his chapter, many *fujoshi* are in their everyday lives involved in intimate relationships with ordinary men, and the three texts that Hester looks at each focus on the male partners of *fujoshi* women who are bemused (and sometimes feel abused) by their partners' obsessive interest in male homoerotic possibilities. Once again, Hester's work highlights the agency that women readers and creators of BL products exercise, an agency that actually has transformative effects on material culture. He points to the way in which women's economic power has given rise to "female-dominated spaces" of consumption where "heterosexual men . . . are excluded or rendered uncomfortable or irrelevant." The male partners of the *fujoshi* women in these narratives, rather than imagining themselves as the "central pillar" of familial relationships as has traditionally been their role, now feel themselves to be sidelined or marginal to this fantasy world of female desire. The male narrators are bewildered by their girlfriends' activities and interests and although they "may come to understand, to some degree, indulge, or accommodate" these desires, the *fujoshi* community remains something they "can never call their own."

This last point—that heterosexual men are somehow *necessarily* excluded from the female-dominated economy of desire that circulates around the BL subculture—must, however, be reconsidered in relation to research highlighted by Kazumi Nagaike's contribution to this volume. Nagaike draws attention to how, in the past several years, a range of male viewers/readers has emerged who are not afraid to declare an interest in BL. The term *"fudanshi"* (rotten men) has emerged to describe them. Although it might be assumed that it is primarily *gay* men who are interested in these homoerotic narratives, as Nagaike points out, gay men have had a sometimes problematic relationship with these texts. As early as 1992 a *"yaoi* debate" (*yaoi ronsō*) emerged in feminist media wherein some gay spokesmen criticized women writers for appropriating and misrepresenting gay relationships and desire. However, as Nagaike explains, *fudanshi* does not clearly map onto any specific sexual orientation (just as *fujoshi* does not). In fact, in questionnaire surveys, self-identified *fudanshi* readers declare a range of sexual orientations, including gay, straight, bisexual, and even asexual.

Concerning the motivations of *fudanshi* for engaging with BL texts, we can discern a curious return to early explanations for women's interest in the genre, to the extent that the escapist potential of the texts are emphasized. However, in the case of male readers, it is an escape from the bounds of conventional masculine identity and desire that are enabled through identification with the "feminized males" of the BL world. As Nagaike shows, for many male readers what is enjoyable about BL characters is their freedom to express vulnerability and passivity. The beautiful boys of the BL world frequently "fail" to perform the tough image demanded by the codes of conventional masculinity. Hence, it is not so much the sexual orientation of the BL characters that is of interest to *fudanshi* men, but rather their embodiment of characteristics that have traditionally been gendered feminine and thus undervalued when expressed by male bodies. As Nagaike concludes, what BL offers to some men is "a subversive space, in which *fudanshi* can re-view traditional Japanese images of masculinity and learn to acknowledge, accept, and ultimately love such elements of maleness as weakness, fragility, and passivity."

Given that BL deals in stories of male–male romance and sexuality, it might be supposed that gay men in Japan are also a key audience for these texts. As Ishida Hitoshi makes clear in his chapter, however, there has been a fraught relationship between BL creators and some spokesmen from the gay community.[18] This dispute goes back to a 1992 article penned by gay critic Satō Masaki, who argued that BL represented a kind of misappropriation or distortion of gay life that impacted negatively upon Japanese gay men. Various BL fans and writers responded both that BL creations were pure fantasy and not meant to be about, or refer to, actual gay men or their lives and that fantasy should be unrestrained. In fact, as Ishida observes, the protagonists in male–male romance in many BL stories often deny or repudiate homosexuality since it is important for the female readership that these characters experience an exclusive attraction to each other (that is, they are not attracted to men in general). So, despite engaging in male–male romance, these characters still reject homosexuality and are often troubled by feelings of guilt or repulsion, as if same-sex love were a bad thing. In so doing, Ishida argues, the male characters in BL texts are actually repeating and reinforcing the prejudices against homosexuality that exist in Japan in real life. Hence, in BL texts, despite their core theme of male–male romance, gay men themselves are still repudiated and excluded from the narratives.

However, despite these criticisms, it can be argued that women's intensive engagement as both producers and consumers of male–male romance stories over the past four decades of BL culture has had a cumulative effect in transforming images of masculinity in Japanese popular culture more widely.

Indeed, these days, when thinking of representative masculine role models, it is not the "corporate warrior" salaryman (*sarariiman*) that first comes to mind. Rather, Japanese popular culture is dominated by images of "soft" masculinity as embodied in fabulously successful boy bands such as SMAP, and in particular, SMAP lead singer and actor Kimura Takuya, whose beautiful face and slender, defined torso have been ubiquitously displayed throughout Japanese media for over two decades. To this extent, mainstream representations of masculinity have begun to incorporate some of the characteristics that previously were associated with gay men.

Tomoko Aoyama, in her contribution to this volume, looks at three popular manga series by female artist Yoshinaga Fumi which are centered on such "soft" male characters. These stories all feature male characters somehow associated with the world of cooking—and it seems relevant here to note that SMAP also have had their own long-running TV cooking show. All the texts discussed by Aoyama began as manga, and some have gone on to become books, TV dramas, anime series, and even a film, suggesting their widespread appeal. As Aoyama notes, only the 1994 *The Moon and the Sandals* (*Tsuki to sandaru*) can be described as a BL work, the others—the 1999 *Antique Bakery* (*Seiyō kottō yōgashiten*) and the 2007 *What Did You Eat Yesterday?* (*Kinō nani tabeta*), are mainstream media products (the last being serialized in one of Japan's best-selling men's manga magazines, *Morning*).[19] Yet, as Aoyama demonstrates, BL conventions play a strong part in the representation of masculinity in all these manga, rendering them transgressive spaces in which conventional masculinity is subjected to scrutiny and critique.

Although the association of men with cooking might seem feminizing (and arguably is so in the case of SMAP), as Aoyama notes, there is a long tradition in Japan (as in the Anglophone world) of representing "cooking men" as virile mavericks who reject "domestication and formality," relying on their own intuition and skill as opposed to cookbooks. Cooking men have often been represented as promiscuous wanderers, not constrained by any cuisine or cooking style, but adventurously trailing all over the world in search of new culinary challenges. The cooking men in Yoshinaga's manga, however, "transgress just about every characteristic of . . . male chefs and gourmand protagonists" represented elsewhere in Japanese culture. Yoshinaga's cooking men are not maverick wanderers but focused on the domestic and use their culinary skills to express love and care for their (sometimes same-sex) partners. Through representing these BL-ized males in nurturing and caring roles, Yoshinaga is thus able to "convey feminist ideas and messages in the commercial media."

In the final chapter in this collection, Mark McLelland addresses cultural responses to BL texts, including both manga and light novels, in the context of broader conservative critiques of manga, anime, and related popular culture. McLelland points out how manga have often been targeted by moral campaigners across the late twentieth century. Since the late 1980s, following on from a moral panic occasioned by the serial killing of four infant girls by avid manga collector Miyazaki Tsutomu, manga and anime content has increasingly been governed by a code of industry self-regulation, but this does not apply to the self-published *dōjinshi* scene, which includes many BL writers. Until recently most public debate has been over the sexual and violent content of boys' manga but in recent years girls' manga, too, have come under scrutiny. McLelland's chapter focuses on two recent incidents in Japan: the 2008 furor over the large number of BL titles available for loan in a library district in Osaka, and the 2010 debate in Tokyo over the "Non-Existent Youth" Bill aimed at using zoning laws to restrict the sale of erotic manga. McLelland suggests that the enhanced scrutiny paid to girls' popular culture, and BL specifically, by conservative commentators in Japan needs to be read in the context of an ongoing moral panic over "gender-free" education and social-inclusion policies. Some politicians, most notably former Tokyo governor Ishihara Shintarō, imply there is a connection between women's reading habits and their increasing reluctance to marry. These conservative commentators also worry that the declining birthrate is also attributable to the "gender confusion" occasioned by the decline of traditional gender roles, in which BL plays a role.

McLelland also argues that until recently debate about manga content in Japan was largely about protecting children and young people from harmful adult themes. However, due to growing international pressure, the debate has now shifted to the supposedly harmful depictions of children and young people in manga themselves. Given that BL is a genre that specializes in the sexualization of its youthful characters, this chapter concludes with the prediction that BL is likely to come under increasing attack from conservative lobbyists in Japan and overseas.

In spite of such criticism and censure, male–male romantic and sexual narratives have been expressed in various ways and contexts in Japanese culture for centuries and are still very much alive in various popular cultural contexts today. This stands in stark contrast to the current situation in many Western cultures. As prominent feminist scholar Germaine Greer points out in her study of "the boy" in Western art, despite a long tradition of representing the charms of adolescent male beauty in classical and Renaissance art, in the late twentieth century fears about pedophilia resulted in a "criminalization of awareness of the desires and charms of boys" in Western societies.[20] A major contribution of this volume has been to draw attention to the many different meanings that youthful male beauty has attracted in Japan and to provide a foundation for understanding the spread of BL narratives elsewhere, including, increasingly, Western nations.[21]

As we have detailed above, there is not a singular "tradition" of boys love in Japan. The styles, contexts, and meanings associated with the love of boys and young men have been radically transformed over time. When accounting for this process of transformation it has been necessary to look at the way in which love and intimate relationships have been conceived in the Japanese tradition. Ironically, in the period directly preceding Japan's opening to the West in the mid-nineteenth century, the love expressed by older men for male youths was the closest exemplar of the spirituality and equality that underlay Western notions of "romantic love." However, as husband–wife relationships were reimagined as central to the new nation-building project of the Meiji State, male–male love was sidelined and came to be regarded as an exemplification of a "feudal" and uncivilized past. But the new stress on the primacy of heterosexual relations as part of the nation-building project had the effect of subsuming personal feelings under national goals. Women, in particular, were constrained by these new ideologies, which exhorted them to be pure and chaste until the time of marriage, when their duty was to become good wives and wise mothers. It is not surprising, then, as Hartley illustrates, that in the early twentieth century some girl readers looked on enviously at the freedom and passion that boy characters were able to express in their exciting lives outside the confines of the home. At a time when patriarchal, heterosexual norms were increasingly stressed for both men and women, it is also not surprising that some readers were attracted by new kinds of transgressive relationships that could be imagined between men.

Although from the late Meiji period on, male–male sexual relationships came to be represented as base and carnal in mainstream discourse, the very domestication of male–female relationships in the interests of the State enabled a radical reimagining of male–male romance as somehow outside or beyond the demands of the family system. For some readers, male–male lovers became exemplars of what Anthony Giddens calls "pure relationships," that is, relationships that are driven entirely by the sentiments of the two people involved and which do not depend on any exterior support or motivation.[22] In the postwar period, particularly with the emergence of *shōnen'ai* and subsequent BL genres, male–male love once again becomes an exemplar of true romance, especially for female readers whose own lives were often circumscribed by expectations of childbirth and domestic duties. Yet, as the contributors to this collection show, women have never been passive readers in relation to BL narratives. Not content with interpolating themselves into existing representations of male–male love, over the last four decades women readers have become creators of BL culture. Not only have some women appropriated and recreated existing characters from traditional boys' genres in their *dōjinshi*, but, as Galbraith argues, they have come to view all of culture through their "rotten filters," constantly on the lookout for homoerotic interpretations of otherwise everyday situations and events.[23] In their radical reimagining of the potentialities of affection between men, Japan's rotten girls *avant la lettre* have opened up new spaces for the exploration of masculinity and femininity for men and women alike.

Notes

1. While often translated into English as "girl," as many others have observed, the term "*shōjo*" does not convey the same meaning. A succinct discussion of the category "*shōjo*" within the context of Japanese culture in general and *shōjo* manga specifically can be found in Jennifer S. Prough, *Straight from the Heart: Gender, Intimacy, and the Cultural Production of* Shōjo Manga (Honolulu: University of Hawai'i Press, 2011), 7–10.

2. While sometimes written with an apostrophe ("boys' love" or "boy's love"), we have chosen to omit the apostrophe to keep the meaning of the term more open-ended.

3. The encyclopedia on the popular website *Anime News Network*, for example, repeats a distinction between "*shōnen'ai*" and "*yaoi*" commonly made in English. The former, it says, focuses on romance and love, while the latter points to sex. See the respective terms in "Lexicon," *Anime News Network*, last accessed January 16, 2013, http://www.animenewsnetwork.com/encyclopedia/lexicon.php.

4. Paul Atkins, "Chigo in the Medieval Japanese Imagination," *Journal of Asian Studies* 67, no. 3 (2008).

5. Earl Jackson, Jr., "Kabuki Narratives of Male Homoerotic Desire in Saikaku and Mishima," *Theater Journal* 41, no. 4 (1989).

6. Takayuki Yokota-Murakami, *Don Juan East-West: On the Problematics of Comparative Literature* (Albany: State University of New York Press, 1998).

7. Ibid., 36.

8. This can be seen, for instance, in the idea of *danson johi*, or "respect men, despise women."

9. Leith Morton, "The Concept of Romantic Love in the *Taiyō* Magazine, 1895–1905," *Japan Review* 8 (1997): 82.

10. Ibid.

11. Michiko Suzuki, *Becoming Modern Women: Love and Identity in Prewar Japanese Literature and Culture* (Stanford, CA: Stanford University Press, 2010), 9.

12. Jim Reichert, *In the Company of Men: Representations of Male–Male Sexuality in Meiji Literature* (Stanford, CA: Stanford University Press, 2006), 227.

13. Watanabe Tsuneo and Iwata Jun'ichi, *Love of the Samurai: A Thousand Years of Japanese Homosexuality*, trans. D. R. Roberts (London: Gay Men's Press, 1989).

14. Jeffrey Angles, *Writing the Love of Boys: Origins of Bishōnen Culture in Modernist Japanese Literature* (Minneapolis: University of Minnesota Press, 2011), 22–24.

15. Fujimoto's chapter is a substantially revised version of an article that appeared in a special issue of the Japanese literary journal *Eureka* (*Yuriika*) on "BL Studies." See Fujimoto Yukari, "Shōnen'ai/yaoi, BL: 2007-nen genzai no shiten kara" [*Shōnen'ai, yaoi*, and BL: From the perspective of 2007], *Yuriika* 39, no. 16 (December 2007).

16. Nakajima Azusa, *Komyunikēshon fuzen shōkōgun* [Communication deficiency syndrome] (Tokyo: Chikuma shobō, 1991).

17. Konjoh Natsumi, *Mōsō shōjo otaku-kei* [Fantasizing girl, otaku-style], 7 vols. (Tokyo: Futabasha, 2006–2010); Kojima Ajiko, *Tonari no 801-chan* [My neighbor Yaoi-chan], 5 vols. (Tokyo: Ohzora shuppan, 2006–2010); Pentabu, *Fujoshi kanojo* [Fujoshi girlfriend], 2 vols. (Tokyo: Enterbrain, 2006–2007).

18. Ishida's chapter is a substantially revised version of an article that appeared in a special issue of the Japanese literary journal *Eureka* (*Yuriika*) on "BL Studies." See Ishida Hitoshi, "'Hottoite kudasai' to iu hyōmei o megutte: Yaoi/BL no jiritsusei to hyōshō no ōdatsu" [On the declaration "Please leave us alone": The autonomy of *yaoi*/BL and the appropriation of representation], *Yuriika* 39, no. 16 (December 2007).

19. Yoshinaga Fumi, *Tsuki to sandaru* [The moon and the sandals] (Tokyo: Hōbunsha, 1996); Yoshinaga Fumi, *Tsuki to sandaru 2* [The moon and the sandals 2] (Tokyo: Hōbunsha, 2000); Yoshinaga Fumi, *Seiyō kottō yōgashiten* [Antique bakery], 4 vols. (Tokyo: Shinshokan, Wings Comic, 2000–2002); Yoshinaga Fumi, *Kinō nani tabeta?* [What did you eat yesterday?], 7 vols., ongoing (Tokyo: Kōdansha, Morning KC [Kodansha Comic], 2007–).

20. Germaine Greer, *The Boy* (London: Thames and Hudson, 2003), 10.

21. On the spread of BL to the West, see Antonia Levi, Mark McHarry, and Dru Pagliassotti, eds., *Boys Love Manga: Essays on the Sexual Ambiguity and Cross-Cultural Fandom of the Genre* (Jefferson, NC: McFarland 2010).

22. Anthony Giddens, *The Transformation of Intimacy: Sexuality, Love and Eroticism in Modern Societies* (Cambridge: Polity Press, 1992).

23. Patrick W. Galbraith, "Fujoshi: Fantasy Play and Transgressive Intimacy among 'Rotten Girls' in Contemporary Japan," *Signs* 37, no. 1 (2011).

A GENEALOGY OF BOYS LOVE

The Gaze of the Girl and the *Bishōnen* Body in the
Prewar Images of Takabatake Kashō

BARBARA HARTLEY

Introduction: Gender Hegemony and Boys Love

As Teresa de Lauretis observes, "the cultural conceptions of male and female as two complementary yet mutually exclusive categories" is a common denominator that applies across cultures.[1] These categories are the basis of "a gender system . . . that correlates sex to cultural contexts according to social values."[2] While often construed as a categorical imperative, "gender" is, to borrow de Lauretis's term, a "representation" only, which, while having "real implications . . . for the material life of individuals," is ultimately no more than a fantasy construct.[3] While mutually exclusive gender categories often serve the interests of hegemonic social elements, the very need to impose these categories confirms both their instability and their susceptibility to subversion. This is because the norms that support privilege are often contradictory or, as Lauren Berlant and Michael Warner note, "garbled."[4] Gender, concludes de Lauretis, is more than "the effect of its representation;" it is also "its excess," which is able to "rupture or destabilize" the very hegemonic systems that it supports.[5]

I use de Lauretis's comments to preface the following discussion of what I argue are the boys love images of Taisho and early Showa era artist, Takabatake Kashō (1888–1966), in order to consider boys love as an element of the "excess" that is outside the hegemonic discourses that construct gender and/or sexuality. Boys love images belong to the domain that, referencing Rio Otomo's chapter in this collection, permits agency, a critical gaze and a resistance to "the authority of a singular narrative." In the discussion that follows, I will invoke a number of elements of queer analysis, an approach that is ideally suited to discussing "non-normative expressions of gender" and "non-straight expressions of gender and sexuality."[6] My principal aim is to demonstrate that the work of prewar commercial artist Takabatake Kashō— hereafter referred to as Kashō—belongs to a genealogy of modern-era visual texts that precede the current longing among girl readers and viewers for material that focuses on the homoerotic desires of *bishōnen*, that is, beautiful young men. Rather than analyzing reader reception, my discussion will probe the capacity of Kashō's images to obliquely collapse gender norms— and thereby to evoke the destabilizing realm of gender "excess"—within the social context at the time of production.

In a discussion of Kashō's illustrations that appeared on the front covers of the magazine *Nihon shōnen* (Japanese boys) between 1925 and 1933, Kajita Yuichirō argues that this series of images was a cultural representation of the ideal boy of Japan.[7] Reverberating beneath this ideal, however, Kajita notes an ambivalent passivity (*shizukesa*), fragility (*zeijakusa*), empherality (*hakanasa*), and softness (*yasashisa*).[8] It is these qualities, I would argue, that assist in eroticizing—in classic boys love style—the images of Kashō's ideal Japanese boys, ostensibly represented as cultivating their bodies for the nation through the sport, adventure, historical heroics, and military activity which Kajita identifies as the categories of illustration featured on the magazine's covers.[9] While the *bishōnen* images that are the subject of my discussion appeared contemporaneously, it is important to note that in some instances these were also produced specifically for circulation in *Shōjo no tomo* (Girl's friend), a popular magazine for girls. We shall see, however, that the images that Kashō constructed for the viewing of girls feature equally pervasive elements of eroticism—a quality that Takabatake Asako provocatively argues was present even in the artist's images of children.[10]

Kashō's unrivalled ability to produce seductive images of boys and young men was a function of both his aesthetic training and perhaps, given the occasional references to his "homosexual sensibilities," of his own sexuality.[11] Privileged at the height of his popularity to live a sumptuously baroque lifestyle funded by the fortune assured by his artistic talents, Kashō produced some of the most pervasive cultural imagery of *bishōnen* of the prewar era. In addition to this work, the artist also produced a sizable corpus of images of girls and women.[12] Born in Ehime in 1888, Kashō first studied art in Kyoto before moving to Tokyo in 1908 where his talents were quickly recognized by leading magazine publishing houses. By the 1920s the artist was one of Japan's most famed commercial illustrators producing images of boys and men and also of girls and women. While a selection of Kashō's material from this era depicts traditional Japanese themes, the artist also produced images with modern settings. In a review of contemporary artist Tagame Gengoroh's compilation of postwar Japanese gay erotic art, Mark McLelland comments on the "pathologizing framework" that limited the prewar expression of overt homosexual imagery.[13] Kashō's material is certainly a far cry from the "sadomasochistic fantasy world populated by hypermasculine characters" that McLelland points out feature in Tagame's collection.[14] There are, nevertheless, reverberations of material of this kind in Kashō's representations of the male body with various young men bound, wounded, or (arousingly) subject to the threat of violence. My particular interest is in how these reverberations ensure that, while complying with prewar hegemonic norms, Kashō's images can simultaneously elicit in girl viewers a boys love-type response.

In spite of (or perhaps because of) persistent official attempts to inscribe hegemonic gender and sexual practices on the subjects of imperial Japan, the time of Kashō's dominance was also an era of *ero-guro-nansensu*, a popular term derived from the English words "erotic," "grotesque," and "nonsense."[15] One expression of this genre was the circulation of perverse, or *hentai*, publications, often presented as pseudo-medical texts.[16] There are examples of Kashō's material, too, which flirt with this subterranean upheaval of gender and sexuality norms, so that as noted above a clear erotic charge resonates through much of his work. I repeat, however, that my particular interest is in material that, while appearing to adhere to the conservative standards promulgated by mainstream publishing houses, nevertheless has an alluringly sexual edge that blurs the boundary between the modest image approved for public consumption and the "erotic, grotesque nonsense" seen in more explicit material of the time. It is the tension between this compliance with and disruption of hegemonic norms that, I would argue, contributes to the sense of the *bukimi*, or the uncanny, that Takabatake Sumie argues can be a feature of Kashō's work.[17]

Kashō's fame peaked in 1925 with the publication of illustrations accompanying Ikeda Kikan's serialized novel, *Song of the Bandit* (*Bazoku no uta*). Although he continued to produce images throughout the ensuing decade, by the mid-1930s the artist's influence had declined as his interests shifted to more conservative genres, such as *Nihon-ga* or Japanese-style visual art that followed traditional artistic convention. In addition, magazine readers and viewers increasingly sought inspiration in the work of a new generation of illustrators, such as Nakahara Jun'ichi (1913–1988). While he remained active until his death in 1966, Kashō's popularity—and, it might be noted, the brilliance of his production—continued to wane after the war.

The Genre

Although boys love is now a well-established international genre, Japan is generally acknowledged as the site at which texts that feature male homoerotic encounters were first produced by girls or women for mass circulation and consumption by other girls and/or women. Kazuko Suzuki discusses boys love as a feature of *shōjo* manga produced by the canonic *Nijūy'nengumi* (Year 24 Group) artists—women who were born in the year of Showa 24, that is, 1949—while Tomoko Aoyama notes the importance of acknowledging the contribution of novelist Mori Mari (1903–1987).[18] In spite of Mori Mari's protests at being labeled a forerunner of boys love, Aoyama argues that this writer was one of the few literary women who produced male homoerotic material, although not necessarily for the specific consumption of women.[19] Further discussing the manner in which women writers in Japan had incorporated male homosexuality into their writing, Aoyama perceptively notes both the rejection by girl writers and readers in the 1980s of "persistent variations on the Cinderella theme" and "a desire to explore masculinity or androgyny as opposed to the worn-out image of femininity."[20] Suzuki, moreover, argues that although early boys love manga were replete with complex and difficult-to-follow "philosophical and abstract musings," it was this very complexity that focused reader attention on "the figure of the male protagonist and how he acted in homo-social relations, particularly sexually."[21] While Aoyama and Suzuki provide valuable insights, they nonetheless confine their discussions to postwar cultural production. Both Fujimoto Yukari and Mizuki Takahashi, however, note how postwar *shōjo* manga had its antecedents in the prewar era, particularly in the so-called *jojō-ga*, or dreamy romantic images, of artists such as Kashō and a number of his contemporaries.[22] I would argue that a longing for boys love is also apparent in the prewar era and that Kashō is a key figure in this genealogy. I earlier suggested that queer theory provided a helpful filter through which to view the artist's work. While Alexander Doty notes how some commentators regard the representation of "queerness" as only occurring in "non-mainstream" contexts, through his engagement with the commercial publishing industry Kashō does this from the heartland of the capitalist enterprise that funded the activities of imperial Japan.[23]

In strict terms of its contemporary definition, boys love refers to material that is produced by a girl or woman artist or writer for the readership or viewership of other girls or women. How, then, can images produced by a Taisho/early Showa-era male commercial artist have significance in this context? Firstly, we must remember that, in addition to there being few published women writers in the prewar era, there were even fewer women artists. It took the energy of the Year 24 Group to create a space in which women could become active in this way. Kashō, I would argue, was one prewar artist who had the ability to engage with an aesthetic which, based on the passivity, fragility, ephemerality, and softness identified above by Kajita,[24] created male figures of great beauty that could appeal to women and girls as much as to men and boys. We must also remember, as will be further detailed below, that Kashō produced illustrations of male figures specifically for consumption—through girls' magazines—by girls. Furthermore, Nagamine Shigetoshi's 1997 analysis of prewar surveys that included figures on the reading practices of factory girls, working girls, and schoolgirls, gives evidence of cross-reading by at least some girls, especially schoolgirls, in the Taisho and early Showa eras. This was precisely the time during which Kashō's popularity was at its height. Nagamine's discussion demonstrates how, while few factory girls appeared interested in reading material for boys, significant numbers of schoolgirls were reading *Shōnen kurabu* (Boys' club) and *Nihon shōnen* (Japanese boys) in addition to other publications published specifically for boys.[25]

Girls Who View or Read as Boys

While Kajita's discussion focuses on Takabatake Kashō's ideal image of the Japanese boy, the artist was equally active as an illustrator for magazines for girls and women. The girls' magazine *Shōjo no tomo*, for example, featured illustrations by Kashō in almost every edition from June 1922 to December 1926. In some editions Kashō's material occupied in excess of one fifth of the total pages of the magazine. The images presented included advertisements, inset images (intended for readers to remove and frame), illustrations for romantic material such as poetry and reflective prose (sometimes composed under Kashō's own name), and illustrations for action novels. Predictably, for publications targeting *shōjo* readers, Kashō often specialized in representations of dreamily demure girls. However, in addition to these aestheticized *shōjo*, there is also a plethora of male figures that, on first glance, might be regarded as produced for the readership of boys. These latter include a host of the taut and often semi-naked bodies of beautiful boys who project a decided air of homoeroticism. This homoeroticism is often achieved through the depiction of the boy under dire threat, pushed to a state of *in extremis* that conflates with sexual rapture. A similar effect results from Kashō's inscribing on his *bishōnen* what Takahara Eiri notes is the insecurity coupled with the contradictory arrogance of the *chigo*—boy companions of medieval monks—who, while feeling a sense of menace at being the property of a dominant man, are simultaneously elated by the knowledge of their own beauty as a means to attract power.[26]

Aoyama Ōshū's novel, *The Whirlpool of Flames* (*Honoho no uzumaki*), serialized in *Shōjo no tomo* during the late Taisho era, provides a range of illustrations of these obliquely sexualized boys. The November 1925 installment features the image of the unconscious form, eyes closed, of a beautiful boy washed up on a seaside shore.[27] With the lower part of his body lying parallel to the wave line while his upper body turns to the left, the boy appears to be writhing—and perhaps moaning. His neck is arched back in a pose of ecstasy, while his right arm dangles across his back creating the captivating vision of a bared shoulder. Some way behind the boy, a group of local peasants—perhaps they are farmers or fishermen, lumpen workers in contrast to the grace and dignity the boy displays even in such a state—dash across the sand to examine the unconscious body over which the waves gently wash. Although it is likely that the background figures will rescue the boy, the possibility also exists that these approaching males present a threat. What is certain is that there are no girls or women in sight and the encounter will almost certainly be a homosocial one. Whether this will progress to a sexual level depends on the limits of the reader's imagination. The first page of the April 1926 installment of *The Whirlpool of Flames* has a small head and shoulder insert of the protagonist, similarly naked and vulnerable with a provocatively slender neck, set against a background that could be a roaring sea or rushing wind, a small dagger clutched between his teeth.[28] In spite of various cues that suggest danger and tension—a subtitle reads "the eerie laugh" (*kikuwai na waraigoe*)—this image is strangely passive, almost postcoital in its lack of strain or energy.

I argue that these obliquely sexualized *bishōnen* images produced prolifically by Kashō for girl readers of girl magazines contributed in a powerful way to the development of the boys love genre, as did the images that were replicated in the boys' material that many girls undoubtedly sought out to read. The overt beauty of the unconscious form on the beach transgresses the usual heterosexual image of the male upon whom the *Yamato nadeshiko*, the feminine flower of Japan, can depend. The postcoital state of the boy in the second image is not that of the male who has "taken" a woman in usual heterosexual style, but one who has himself been ravished. And both—the one unconscious after a shipwreck and the other with a dagger between his teeth—are clearly in dialogue with danger and possibly death. Canonical girl studies scholar Honda Masuko has identified a preoccupation with death on the part of girl readers.[29] It is images of young men liminalized by their confrontation with a threat to life and limb that will be the focus of the textual analysis of the images that follow. However, I precede this analysis with specific background information on the social conditions in Japan at the time during which Kashō engaged in textual production and a number of more general comments on the restrictive social conditions that impede the expression of women's sexuality in Japan and elsewhere.

Kashō's Japan

A feature of Kashō's prewar Japan was the violent control that often led to the virulent erasure of women's sexual identity. Koyama Shizuko, for example, has pointed out that according to the prewar hegemonic feminine norm of *ryōsai kenbo*, or good wife and wise mother, sexual expression on the part of modest women was anathema, being the province of prostitutes and hysterics only.[30] Furthermore, until the 1956 Anti-Prostitution Law outlawed such practices, the bodies of women in modern Japan were, literally, commodities for sale. Yukiko Tanaka has noted how this situation not only constrained the circumstances of the daughters of the impoverished families facing starvation who were sold in this way, but of every woman in the land.[31] In the postwar era, a number of commentators have famously remarked on the reluctance of girls to accept adult responsibility.[32] However, given the often hostile potency of the male gaze directed towards women—and especially towards girls as "unspoiled" women—we can surely understand the resistance of girls and young women to accepting a role that made them either the sexual objects of men or instruments to continue the family line, regardless of the prewar status that might have accrued to this.[33] With these limited options, it is little wonder that the girl of the time demonstrated a preference for withdrawing to a reading and viewing "room of her own." Within that room, girls from all walks of life were free to indulge in the fantasies generated, for example, by Kashō's beautiful boys. Although Mizuki Takahashi correctly notes that the concept of *shōjo* was largely a bourgeois creation, we have seen above that the Taisho-era girls with varied social backgrounds engaged in acts of reading.[34] Nagamine—while cautioning against the assumption that because some factory girls read magazines all girls who worked in factories must have been great magazine readers[35]—nevertheless gives the example of a factory girl who, having left school following the death of her father, encouraged six other workmates to pool their meager resources to buy a magazine that could be shared. This they did rather than going to the movies.[36]

In the same way that, as de Lauretis noted, gender binaries feature across cultures, we might argue that the hostility of the male gaze is expressed in heterosexual relations in every society structured around male violence. Discussing *Histoire d'O* (*Story of O*), for example—a text that features an accelerating sequence of sadistic sexual acts against the eponymous O— Leo Bersani suggests that "at the moment of a spectacular male triumph," referring (in his words) to the moment at which O engages in "passionately willing performances of male desires," the supremacy of the woman over whom the male has triumphed is also "just as spectacularly asserted."[37] This insistence on pain and humiliation as an imperative for sexual expression by women, however, surely was—and still is—unpalatable to many girls and women. While the story of O may postdate the period during which Japan's putatively "innocent" *shōjo* indulged themselves in the pleasure of Kashō's visual texts, Honda's research suggests that these girls instinctively sensed the ominously oppressive fate that awaited them in marriage and maternity.[38] Viewing material resistant to this ideal, such as Kashō's images, permitted girls to experience the heightened pleasure of the sexualized text and thus contest Japan's prewar hegemonic gender system which proscribed the brutal suppression of feminine sexuality.

Discussing the emergence of a community of girl readers in the late Meiji era, I have noted with Aoyama the way in which magazine editors originally published their offerings for boy readers only.[39] Once editors and publishers, however, recognized the market potential of girls, they enthusiastically promoted publications targeting this group. Hiromi Tsuchiya Dollase discusses how editors in Japan initially sought a didactic role for magazines, an attempt that duplicated efforts around the globe to discipline socio-sexual behavior, especially the behavior of women.[40] Commenting on the putative threat of "contamination" presented by "queer domesticity"—that is, any form of the family that did not conform to the male head of a household model—to nineteenth-century United States society, Nayan Shah argues that

> respectable domesticity enabled the proper moral and biological cultivation
> of citizen-subjects necessary for American public life to flourish. . . . Modern
> healthy society was conceptualized as a series of heterosexual married couples
> and their families, who, as middle-class families, perpetuated the race and
> enriched the nation.[41]

If we substitute "Japanese" for "American," Shah's words become directly applicable to the official discourse of imperial Japan. The girls who viewed Kashō's images were subjects in training for the "respectable domesticity" demanded of the women of the empire. However, in the "rooms of their own" in which they engaged with magazine text and imagery, girls resoundingly rejected being burdened with the overt preparation required to successfully assume these roles.

Even when editors relinquished an overtly didactic role, however, the guiding hand of the hegemon remained arguably present in magazine content. The popularity of Yoshiya Nobuko's deliciously ornate and highly influential *Flower Stories* (*Hana monogatari*), serialized between 1916 and 1924 when the reception of Kashō's material was reaching its peak, was in one sense a triumph for the subversive readership of girls. We might equally argue, on the other hand, that editors were happy to concede ground and permit the circulation of these ostensibly disruptive tales, which, in actual fact, promoted a culture of refined consumerism that matched the aspirations of conservative business interests. Yoshiya's narratives undoubtedly contested feminine gender roles and offered readers a world in which, to use Takahara Eiri's words, anything was "imaginable."[42] Nevertheless, in comparison, for example, with the alcohol consuming, cigarette smoking, and (putatively) sexually predatory modern girls of the 1920s who terrified authority by displaying themselves on the streets of the metropolis, Yoshiya's flower girl protagonists were positively reactionary.[43]

I have noted above Honda's theorizing the affiliation of girls with the theme of death. Yoshiya's material, too, referenced death. However, this was often a limpid fading away that evoked saccharine European narratives, such as *Little Lord Fauntleroy*, or the lingering notes of an Italian piano wafting *sotto voce* in the background. Although this narrative template satisfied many modest Taisho-era *shōjo*, others sensed further possibilities in a different sort of text and accompanying illustrations, including narratives and images of beautiful boys. Although we cannot be certain whether his material was a deliberate response to reader demand or a felicitous intersection of the artist's own desires with those of his readers, Kashō was one illustrator who satisfied that longing with his discreetly eroticized boys love images.

The Male Body and Intimations of Boys Love

There is a long genealogy of the representation of the male body in Japanese visual art across a range of genres. Some of the most well-known of these feature ferocious samurai, dolorous religious men, scholars, public figures such as lords and other powerbrokers, near-naked Edo workmen, and, of course, the *iki*, or stylish, Edo man frequenting the pleasure quarters in *flagrante*

delicto with either a Yoshiwara beauty or a young male lover at the wildly ex-
aggerated height of pleasure. As Japan entered the Meiji era and came under
the thrall of Western norms, however, stirring images of samurai epics gave
way to static Westernized military scenes of the Sino-Japanese and Russo-
Japanese wars, while sexually repressive Judeo-Christian influences removed
explicit material from public circulation. Jim Reichert, for example, discusses
how the Meiji authorities subjected those under their control to a stringent
civilizing process, which included, moreover, condemning *nanshoku*, a term
commonly used in the Edo period to refer to "male to male sexual desire,"[44]
as "the most grievous of these 'evil customs of the past.'"[45] Kashō, however,
judiciously adopted elements from earlier indigenous models, a number of
which—including the handsome young men of the Heian era (794–1185)
classic, *The Tale of Genji* (*Genji monogatari*), the Kamakura era (1185–1333)
chigo boy companions of older monks, and Muromachi era (1337–1573)
samurai youth—are discussed by Nakamura Keiko in her 2003 *Handbook
of Showa Era Beautiful Boys* (*Shōwa bishōnen techō*).[46] The artist then over-
laid the resulting pastiche with a Western visual aesthetic to produce *shōnen*
images fitting for a twentieth-century Japan that yearned to take its place
among the international great powers. This material displayed the heroism of
the young male ready to sacrifice all for a modern nation state characterized
by an expansionist military policy. While sufficiently indigenous to be recognizably Japanese, Kashō's work is nonetheless devoid of any pre-modern
"indulgences," such as visible genitalia, that might have "debased" Japan in a
world order largely operating under a puritanical Protestant ethic. Nevertheless, the skillful manner in which the artist's eye and brush fell lingeringly
over these representations of the wholesome young subjects of the emperor
infused the images with an implicit and therefore perhaps all the more
breathtaking sexuality that resonated with many young boy reader/viewers
and that also attracted the eye of the girl.

For a more specific understanding of how the homoerotic representation
of beautiful boys permitted—and continues to permit—girls to express their
emerging sexual identities without the need to confirm to the oppressive hegemonic paradigms of sex and gender, we might consider Kazumi Nagaike's
discussion of Matsuura Rieko's novel *Reverse Version* (*Ura baajon*). Discussing a male homoerotic fantasy in which one of the narrative's protagonists,
Chiyoko, engages after being betrayed by her boyfriend, Nagaike observes:

> Here Chiyoko's male homosexual fantasies . . . function as the primary medi-
> um that endows her with power. An ironic reversal of the established gender

hierarchy can be seen here as the female obtains a privileged position through the act of "playing" with her male "puppets."

In this way, Matsuura Rieko clearly articulates her thematic intention of using male homosexual fantasies to subvert the established gender hierarchy. The author herself has commented as follows: "For example, in Chapter 10 several homosexual fantasies known as '*yaoi*,' occur. If it can be said that men have colonized women, women can also colonize men through their images. I purposely wrote in terms of such a consciousness."[47]

Nagaike concludes by rejecting any notion of negativity around feminine fantasies of male homoeroticism, arguing instead for the "subversive possibilities" inherent in the "free play" that characterizes these modes of cultural expression.

Reverse Version is a narrative of storytelling characterized by a series of texts within texts within texts and the trebled instability that this implies. Kashō's images, on the other hand, are static, two-dimensional works and therefore, it might be argued, offer little capacity for the "free 'play' with male homosexual characters" that Nagaike argues is available to Matsuura's characters. Sharalyn Orbaugh's discussion of the active reworking by amateur manga artists of the *Harry Potter* narratives for the 2004 Tokyo Comic Market, however, confirms that reading/viewing is a highly creative process and that many readers and viewers subvert an author's original text and make it their own.[48] While, unlike Matsuura, Kashō may not have written with the sexual colonization of boys and men by girls and women consciously in mind, his images at least suggest such possibilities. This becomes apparent when we make a close viewing of a selection of the artist's texts.

Kashō's Images

The first image considered here is that of the tattooed body of a boy that appears on the cover of Nakamura's 2003 collection of beautiful boy images referred to above, *Handbook of Showa Era Beautiful Boys*.[49] This image, the date and source of which are unknown, is given the title "Tattoo," and features the rear view of the fully and exquisitely tattooed body of a beautiful young man sitting cross-legged, wearing only a *fundoshi*, a Japanese style loincloth. The boy looks quizzically although impassively—yet another of the many Kashō figures characterized by an air of passivity—across his shoulder, while a disheveled kimono lies on the floor beneath him. Has he disrobed? Been forced to disrobe? Entering from the left of the frame as a phallic threat is two-thirds of the blade of a long samurai-type sword. The young man, who has the distinctive Kashō facial features that appear in the artist's illustrations of both women and men—we might recall Ikeda Shinobu's commentary on the manner in which all figures in Heian art had similar, if not identical, facial features—has clearly been unexpectedly disturbed.[50] The reader shares his disquiet. What will befall this boy? Will he perhaps be the target of an attack? There is a sexual tension in the image deriving, in addition to the naked form, from the boy's taut buttocks, tensed as he turns in surprise. Perhaps he is about to leap to his feet in order to protect himself from the unseen intruder. With the sword aimed directly at the boy's upper body—possibly even his throat—the threat of mortal conflict is clear in this tension-laden amalgamation of Eros and Thanatos.

The second image discussed was produced specifically for the viewing of girls and appeared as an illustration accompanying the serialized novel discussed above, *The Whirlpool of Flames*, in a 1926 edition of *Shōjo no tomo*.[51] The image features a young man tied to the mast of a ship in the driving rain of a storm. Mishima Yukio may have ostensibly monopolized postwar intertextual commentary relating to the image of the martyred Saint Sebastian.[52] Nevertheless, in the prewar era Kashō, too, had a penchant for young men who were restrained, occasionally suspended, and beatific in pain. The young man's face here, turned at ninety degrees from his torso, grimaces with the effort to withstand the onslaught of the elements to which he has been exposed. While the hairstyle indicates that the figure is Japanese, the clothing is in tatters. In spite of this, a kimono shape can be discerned, a shoulder and underarm bared. An upper thigh is also exposed, as the shredded fabric intended to conceal the body is whipped by the wind. The angle of the image indicates that the ship is listing while the strain on the face of the boy suggests he can scarcely endure much more. Will the ship sink? Can the boy break free? In spite of—or perhaps precisely because of—his *in extremis* situation, the boy's body strains against the ropes that bind him, creating a sense of his torso twisting and turning beneath his bonds. Needless to say, even without the threat of death, this boy is beautiful. We might recall Karatani Kōjin's discussion—and that of Susan Sontag—of the sexualized significance of ill health and suggest that there is a similar sexual element to any depiction of the body facing threat.[53]

It is useful to consider just what it is about this beautiful young man featured in a magazine for ostensibly heterosexual girls that suggests homoeroticism or boys love rather than more hegemonic sexual appeal. Could such

Figure 2.1 "Tattoo" (*Shisei*,
date unknown)—a
beautiful tattooed boy in
Japanese-style loincloth.

an image not be a representation of conventional heterosexual attraction—a
case of girl loves sweet-looking boy? In order to answer this question we can
consider images of another beautiful boy, the incomparable Uehara Ken
(1909–1991), voted by readers of the February 2008 edition of the widely
read social commentary magazine *Bungei shunjū* as the second most attractive man (*bidan*) of the Showa era.[54] In stills from his early acting career, Uehara is almost unfailingly accompanied by a girl or young woman who either
gazes adoringly at the actor or leans securely again his protective shoulder,
arm, or other body part.[55] Images now circulating online in various film blogs
also often feature a Rudolf Valentino look-alike Uehara gazing longingly at—
with a suitably muted suggestion of lust—and almost making contact with
various young women who enthusiastically return his attentions. Both the
reciprocal gaze (women gaze at Uehara, Uehara gazes at women) and body
language of the women mark the male characters so portrayed as indelibly

Figure 2.2 Untitled 1926 illustration from the serialized novel *The Whirlpool of Flames*—beautiful boy tied to the mast of a ship listing in a storm.

"straight." Furthermore, in these early works at least, the actor is rarely under serious threat. Death does not repeatedly stalk the young Uehara Ken as it does Kashō's figures. While Uehara's characters might be roguish, moreover, they are wholesomely so (although "wholesome" is not necessarily a term that one might apply to the actor's later activity). With their intimations of decadence, Kashō's creations are certainly erotic, even if the grotesque and/ or nonsense element is largely elided by the artist's superb aesthetics. And while the heroes of Kashō's texts can, like Uehara Ken, often be seen partnering a girl, both hero and girl are generally committed to the task of trouncing evil. Romantic love between a girl and a boy—expressed through reciprocal gazing or codependent body contact—is, as Takabatake Sumie notes, "completely absent" from the artist's work.[56] Girls who appear with boys in Kashō prints often themselves, in fact, challenge the gender norms of the time.

The third image considered, another 1926 *Shōjo no tomo* illustration that also accompanied the serialized novel, *The Whirlpool of Flames*, introduces the theme of exoticism into the mix of the artist's illustration corpus. As noted above, Kashō had a penchant for Western aesthetics and this illustration references the "Tarzan" and "wild Africa" themes that swept international popular culture in the 1920s and 1930s. Here, the well-defined figure of a young man, naked except for a leopard skin loincloth that swings precariously across the top of his groin, arms raised, fiercely swinging a sword horizontally back across his head, defends himself against attack.[57] As with the tattooed boy in image one, weapons enter the frame of the illustration from the left, this time two swords and an African spear, the latter passing beneath the boy's groin at knee level. The boy's body, at the height of its youthful beauty, is scored by wounds that stream with blood. The background appears to be a cloud of smoke—is the boy defending a burning house or village? It would appear impossible that he can hold out against his attackers much longer. I referred earlier to my interest in material that enters the mainstream as apparently "inoffensive" yet which reverberates with strong undertones of sexuality. While this and similar images appear to be on first viewing an expression of "pure" youthful energy, the pose of the body, the way in which the movement of the loincloth almost reveals too much, the wounds, and the likelihood of impending attack all evoke an intoxicating appeal that transcends the boundaries of adolescent narrative and gives the material clear links with more overtly sexual images that circulated for clandestine adult consumption. And all this is for publication in a commercial girls' magazine produced by Jitsugyō no Nihon-sha, a highly successful publishing house that entrenched its position in the market by developing a widespread sales network in the provinces where the readership was putatively much more conservative than in urban centers.

The final image, taken from a 1936 issue of *Shōnen kurabu*, was not produced specifically for the consumption of girls. However, recalling Nagamine's study, we know that some girls at least had a habit of reading material published for their brothers. This illustration depicts two young men steering a flat-bottomed boat through raging waters.[58] Each wears only a traditional Japanese loincloth and *hachimaki* headband. One crouches and turns, actions that highlight the definition and tone of his slender muscles and chest. The other gazes earnestly into the middle distance as he determinedly strains to hold the rudder against the flow of the current and crash of the waves around the boat. The artist has particularly emphasized the sinewy outline of this figure's naked buttocks, lower abdomen, and waist area, while a discreet

Figure 2.3 Untitled 1926 illustration from the serialized novel *The Whirlpool of Flames*—
semi-naked and wounded boy
swinging a sword at unseen
attackers.

nipple is visible on the boy's chest. Again these young men are risking their lives. Will they triumph over the natural forces of nature? Will they be swept away? There is a tension that fills the frame and that undoubtedly excited the sensibilities of the girls, as well as the boys, who viewed the image. Furthermore, as with many of Kashō's "pair" illustrations, that is, images featuring two figures, there is mystery surrounding the relationship between the boys. Could they be brothers? Perhaps best of friends? While there is nothing overt to suggest a sexual liaison in the way that is clearly evident, for example, in contemporary boys love genre pairs, this mystery, in fact, creates a space for reader imagination to play with such a possibility. As iconic manga artist Takemiya Keiko noted during a round-table discussion commemorating the 120th year of the artist's birth, Kashō clearly inscribed on his *bishōnen* pairs a sense that said to viewers, "Now we will sleep together."[59]

水天彷彿 「日本少年」(実業之日本社) の挿絵原画

Figure 2.4 "Between heaven and the open sea" (*Tensui hōfutsu*, 1936)—pair of semi-naked boys perilously navigating boat through rough water.

Conclusion

This chapter has argued that the images of Takabatake Kashō are part of a genealogy of boys love that runs through modern Japanese visual and print narratives. In addition to girls cross-reading the *bishōnen* images produced by Kashō for boys magazines, the artist produced material specifically for publication in material such as *Shōjo no tomo* that included demure girls and eroticized boys. The taut bodies of Kashō's young men, often bound and confined or under mortal attack, were one set of materials that satisfied the expanding viewing and reading desires of Taisho and early Showa era girls. Referring to the work of Gayle Rubin, Robert J. Corber, and Stephen Valocchi observe that "in certain historical periods when sexuality is highly contested and overtly politicized, sexual acts become burdened with an excess of meaning, and individuals are divided up according to a 'hierarchical system of sexual value.'"[60] This effect certainly functioned for women and girls in imperial Japan. However, girls could escape this hierarchical system by entering a realm of excess in which they viewed and played imaginatively with the artist's beautiful boy images. In this way, prewar girls were able, albeit briefly and in a fantasy space only, to "rupture and disrupt"—recalling de Lauretis—the hierarchical system of sexuality and gender while also reveling in the pleasure of Kashō's boys love text.

Notes

1. Teresa de Lauretis, *Technologies of Gender: Essays on Theory, Film and Fiction* (Bloomington: Indiana University Press, 1987), 5.

2. Ibid.

3. Ibid.

4. Lauren Berlant and Michael Warner, "Sex in Public," in *Queer Studies: An Interdisciplinary Reader*, ed. Robert J. Corber and Stephen Valocchi (Malden, MA: Blackwell, 2003), 170.

5. de Lauretis, *Technologies of Gender*, 5.

6. Alexander Doty, "Queer Theory," in *Film Studies: Critical Approaches*, ed. John Hill and Pamela Church Gibson (Oxford: Oxford University Press, 2000), 146.

7. Kajita Yujirō, "Taishō kara Shōwa shoki no aida ni oite no risō no shōnen imeeji no keisei: Takabatake Kashō no te ni yoru *Nihon shōnen* no hyōshie kara" [The formation of the ideal image of the boy from Taisho into the early Showa era: From the magazine covers of *Nihon shōnen* (Japanese boys) drawn by Takabatake Kashō], *Kyōto Seika Daigaku kiyō* 37 (2010): 110.

8. Ibid., 111.

9. Ibid., 119.

10. Takabatake Asako, "Takabatake Kashō no kodomo e ni tsuite no ikkō: Arisu to no dōshitsusei o megutte" [Thinking about Takabatake Kashō's images of children: Concerning similarities with Alice], *Bigaku bijutsu shi ronshū* 19 (March 2011): 432.

11. Nakamura Keiko, *Shōwa bishōnen techō* [A handbook of Showa beautiful boys] (Tokyo: Kawade shobō, 2003), 127.

12. Barbara Hartley, "Performing the Nation: Magazine Images of Women and Girls in the Illustrations of Takabatake Kashō," *Intersections: Gender and Sexuality in Asia and the Pacific* 16 (2008), http://intersections.anu.edu.au/issue16/hartley.htm.

13. Mark McLelland, Review of *Gay Erotic Art in Japan (Vol. 1): Artists from the Time of the Birth of Gay Magazines*, compiled by Tagame Gengoroh, with English translation by Kitajima Yuji, *Intersections: Gender and Sexuality in Asia and the Pacific* 10 (2004), http://intersections. anu.edu.au/issue10/mclelland_review.html, para. 6.

14. Ibid., para. 1.

15. For more on *ero-guro-nansensu*, see Miriam Silverberg, *Erotic Grotesque Nonsense: The Mass Culture of Japanese Modern Times* (Berkeley: University of California Press, 2007).

16. Mark McLelland, "A Short History of 'Hentai,'" *Intersections: Gender History and Culture in the Asian Context* 12 (2006), http://wwwsshe.murdoch.edu.au/intersections/issue12/mclelland.html. See particularly paras. 8–12.

17. Takabatake Sumie, "Takabatake Kashō to narushishizumu: Kashō sakuhin no seishin bunsekiteki shiron" [Takabatake Kashō and Narcissism: A psychoanalytic discussion of Kashō's work], *Taishō imajurii* 3 (2007): 153.

18. Kazuko Suzuki, "Pornography or Therapy: Japanese Girls Creating the Yaoi Phenomenon," in *Millennium Girls: Today's Girls Around the World*, ed. Sherrie A. Inness (Lanham, MD: Rowman and Littlefield, 1998), 250–51; Tomoko Aoyama, "Male Homosexuality as Treated by Japanese Women Writers," in *The Japanese Trajectory: Modernisation and Beyond*, ed. Gavan McCormack and Yoshio Sugimoto (Cambridge: Cambridge University Press, 1988), 191.

19. See, for example, Kaoru Nakata, "The Room of Sweet Honey: The Adult *Shōjo* Fiction of Japanese Novelist Mori Mari (1903–1987)" (MA thesis, The Ohio State University, 2004), 62. Here Nakata cites Nakajima Azusa's discussion of Mori's influence on her own work: "I believe Mori Mari dislikes being called the progenitor of so-called 'June novels,' and she would insist that her rigorous aesthetic world has nothing to do with them. . . . However, it was she who bore 'us.'"

20. Aoyama, "Male Homosexuality," 184.

21. Kazuko Suzuki, "Pornography or Therapy," 250–51.

22. Mizuki Takahashi discusses this point with specific reference to Takabatake Kashō in Mizuki Takahashi, "Opening the Closed World of *Shōjo Manga*," in *Japanese Visual Culture: Explorations in the World of Manga and Anime*, ed. Mark Wheeler MacWilliams (Armonk, NY: M.E. Sharpe, 2008), 115–19; Fujimoto Yukari notes how Takahashi Macoto bridges old and new forms of representation in Fujimoto Yukari, "Takahashi Macoto: The Origin of Shōjo Manga Style," trans. Matt Thorn, *Mechademia* 7 (2012); see also James Welker's chapter in this volume.

23. Doty, "Queer Theory," 147.

24. Kajita, Taishō kara Shōwa shoki no aida ni oite," 111.

25. Nagamine Shigetoshi, *Zasshi to dokusha no kindai* [Magazines and readers in the modern era] (Tokyo: Nihon editaa sukūru no shuppanbu, 1987). See especially the tables on pp. 174–78. A 1940 study on the reading pattern of United States adolescents conducted by Robert L. Thorndike and Florence Henry also found a significant gender crossover of readership with girls especially seeking out material published for boys. See Robert L. Thorndike and Florence Henry, "Differences in Reading Interests Related to Differences in Sex and Intelligence Level," *Elementary School Journal* 40 (1940): 755–56. For boys or men in the West cross/reading or viewing as women, see Alex Webb, "Publishing for Love's Sake," *BBC News On-line*, February 14, 2002, http://news.bbc.co.uk/2/hi/entertainment/1817921.stm, which discusses men who read Mills & Boon novels, and Anna Catherine Prescott, "Male Viewers of Soap Operas," April 1998, http://www.aber.ac.uk/media/Students/acp9601.html, on men viewing the soap opera, a television genre constructed specifically for women.

26. Takahara Eiri, "The Consciousness of the Girl: Freedom and Arrogance," in *Woman Critiqued: Translated Essays on Japanese Women's Writing*, ed. Rebecca Copeland (Honolulu: University of Hawai'i Press, 2006), 190–91.

27. Takabatake Kashō, untitled illustration from Aoyama Ōshū's serialized novel *The Whirlpool of Flames, Shōjo no tomo*, November 1926, 75.

28. Takabatake Kashō, untitled illustration from Aoyama Ōshū's serialized novel, *The Whirlpool of Flames, Shōjo no tomo*, April 1926, 216.

29. Honda Masuko, *Ofiiria no keifu: Arui wa shi to otome no tawamure* [The genealogy of Ophelia; Or, playing at death and the maiden] (Tokyo: Kōbunsha, 1989).

30. Koyama Shizuko, *Ryōsai kenbo to iu kihan* [The standard of good wife and wise mother] (Tokyo: Keisō shobō, 1991).

31. Yukiko Tanaka, *Women Writers of Meiji and Taisho Japan: Their Lives, Works and Critical Reception, 1868–1926* (Jefferson, NC: McFarland, 2000), 55–56.

32. See, for example, John Whittier Treat, "Yoshimoto Banana Writes Home: *Shōjo* Culture and the Nostalgic Subject," *Journal of Japanese Studies* 19, no. 2 (Summer 1993).

33. Drawing on the work of Sabine Frühstück, Mark McLelland points out that, unlike their pre-modern sisters, women in the modern era had "active agency in reproduction."

Mark McLelland, *Queer Japan from the Pacific War to the Internet Age* (Lanham, MN: Rowman and Littlefield, 2005), 37. While this is certainly correct, this agency nonetheless did not extend to sexuality.

34. Takahashi, "Opening the Closed World of *Shōjo Manga*," 116.

35. Nagamine, *Zasshi to dokusha no kindai*, 158.

36. Ibid., 182–83. This anecdote is cited from a reader contribution to one of the many magazines of the time. It is useful to note that Nagamine also cautions about the possibility of editorial interference in the selection and even production of reader contributions to prewar magazines for girls and women. See ibid., 158–59.

37. Leo Bersani, *A Future for Astyanax: Character and Desire in Literature* (New York: Columbia University Press, 1984), 298.

38. Honda Masuko, "The Genealogy of *Hirahira: Liminality and the Girl*," trans. Tomoko Aoyama and Barbara Hartley, in *Girl Reading Girl in Japan*, ed. Tomoko Aoyama and Barbara Hartley (London: Routledge, 2009), 36.

39. Aoyama and Hartley, "Introduction," in Aoyama and Hartley, *Girl Reading Girl in Japan*, 2.

40. Hiromi Tsuchiya Dollase, "Ribbons Undone: The *Shōjo* Story Debates in Pre-War Japan," in Aoyama and Hartley, *Girl Reading Girl in Japan*, 80–91.

41. Nayan Shah, "Perversity, Contamination and the Dangers of Queer Domesticity," in Corber and Valocchi, *Queer Studies*, 121.

42. Takahara, "The Consciousness of the Girl," 193.

43. For a discussion of the modern girl see Miriam Silverberg "The Modern Girl as Militant," in *Recreating Japanese Women, 1600–1945*, ed. Gail Lee Bernstein (Berkeley: University of California Press, 1991); and Elise K. Tipton, "Pink Collar Work: The Café Waitress in Early Modern Japan," *Intersections: Gender History and Culture in the Asian Context* 7 (2002), http://intersections.anu.edu.au/issue7/tipton.html.

44. Jim Reichert, *In the Company of Men: Representations of Male–Male Sexuality in Meiji Literature* (Stanford: Stanford University Press, 2006), 2.

45. Ibid., 13.

46. Nakamura, *Shōwa bishōnen techō*, 116–21.

47. Kazumi Nagaike, "Matsuura Reiko's *The Reverse Version*: The Theme of 'Girl-Addressing-Girl' and Male Homosexual Fantasies," in Aoyama and Hartley, *Girl Reading Girl in Japan*, 116.

48. Sharalyn Orbaugh, "Girls Reading Harry Potter, Girls Writing Desire: Amateur Manga and Shōjo Reading Practices," in Aoyama and Hartley, *Girl Reading Girl in Japan*.

49. Takabatake Kashō, "Tattoo" (*Shisei*), date and publication unknown. See the cover illustration of Nakamura, *Shōwa bishōnen techō*. The image is also reproduced on p. 15 of Nakamura.

50. Ikeda Shinobu, "The Image of Women in Battle Scenes: 'Sexually' Imprinted Bodies," in *Gender and Power in the Japanese Visual Field*, ed. Joshua Mostow, Maribeth Graybill, and Norman Bryson (Honolulu: University of Hawai'i Press, 2003), 45.

51. Takabatake Kashō, untitled illustration from Aoyama Ōshū's serialized novel *The Whirlpool of Flames*, *Shōjo no tomo*, October 1926, 177. Also reproduced in Nakamura, *Shōwa bishōnen techō*, 21.

52. This is a reference to the famed image of writer Mishima Yukio (1925–1970) reenacting one of the iconic images of the martyrdom of Saint Sebastian produced originally around 1616 by Italian master, Guido Reni.

53. Karatani Kōjin, *Origins of Modern Japanese Literature*, trans. Brett de Bary (Durham, NC: Duke University Press, 1993)—see specifically the chapter, "Sickness as Meaning," 97–113; and Susan Sontag, *Illness as Metaphor and AIDS and its Metaphors* (New York: Doubleday, 1990)—see specifically the first chapter on the conflation of illness and sexuality, 5–9.

54. *Bungei shunjū*, "Shōwa no bidan besuto 50" [The 50 most handsome men of the Showa era], February 2008, 159.

55. For a wide selection of images of a young Uehara Ken with, for example, an equally young Tanaka Kinuyo, see Ishiwari Osamu and Maurō Toshirō, *Tanaka Kinuyo: Nihon no eiga joyū* [Tanaka Kinuyo: Japanese movie actress] (Tokyo: Waizu shuppan, 2008).

56. Takabatake Sumie, "Takabatake Kashō to narushishizumu," 152.

57. Takabatake Kashō, untitled illustration from the serialized novel *The Whirlpool of Flames, Shōjo no tomo*, 1926. Also reproduced in Nakamura, *Shōwa bishōnen techō*, 21.

58. Takabatake Kashō, "Between heaven and the open sea" (*Tensui hōfutsu*), from *Japanese Boys* (undated).

59. Takemiya Keiko, Ishida Minori, and Shimamoto Kan, "Takabatake Kashō tanjō hyaku nijū shūnen kinen kōdan" [Commemorative Lecture Marking the One Hundred and Twentieth Anniversary of Takabatake Kashō's Birth], *Taishō imajurii* 4 (2008): 56.

60. Robert J. Corber and Stephen Velocchi, "Introduction," in their *Queer Studies*, 8.

A BRIEF HISTORY OF *SHŌNEN'AI, YAOI,* AND BOYS LOVE

JAMES WELKER

Introduction

Originating in Japan, manga, anime, "light novels," video games, live-action films, and related media and goods depicting beautiful adolescent boys or young men in same-sex romantic or sexual relationships have become an increasingly global phenomenon over the past two decades or so. Created for and, largely, by adolescent girls and women, this visual and narrative phenomenon first began to materialize in Japan around 1970 within the rapidly transforming sphere of *shōjo* (girls') manga, an expansive category of manga targeting readers from preadolescence to not quite adulthood.[1] Over time, this phenomenon has been referred to by a number of terms I will explore below; these include "*shōnen'ai,*" "*yaoi,*" and "boys love" (pronounced *bōizu rabu* in Japanese), the last of which is often abbreviated "BL." For the sake of simplicity, I collectively refer to all post-1970 manifestations of this phenomenon as "BL media." At the heart of these media is "BL manga."

In this chapter I trace the history of BL manga produced and distributed via both commercial and non-commercial channels. In the process, I draw attention to shifts in the terminology used among artists, consumers, and critics to label BL media, and, at times, to indicate distinctions in chronology, content, and format. As this history illustrates, however, to emphasize such distinctions belies a great deal of overlap across the commercial and non-commercial production and distribution of BL manga, as well as BL media in general. This history also demonstrates that BL manga has from the beginning been composed of a shifting mix of elements from high and low culture from Japan, Europe, America, and, increasingly, elsewhere.

Setting the Scene

While a limited amount of manga were included in magazines aimed at *shōjo* (girl) readers prior to the Pacific War, *shōjo* manga's emergence as a distinct category has frequently been linked to the publication of *Princess Knight* (*Ribon no kishi*, first serialized 1953–1955) by the tremendously influential male manga artist Tezuka Osamu (1928–1989).[2] Inspired in part by the all-female Takarazuka Revue and its many cross-dressing performers, this gender-bending manga narrative depicts the adventures of Princess Sapphire gallivanting around a Disney-esque European setting, all the while dressed as a prince.[3] Prominent manga critic and historian Yonezawa Yoshihiro, for instance, describes Tezuka's *Princess Knight* as the first *shōjo* "story manga" (*sutōrii manga*), and credits Tezuka with introducing novelistic elements into manga aimed at *shōjo* readers.[4]

Art scholar and curator Mizuki Takahashi has argued, however, that Tezuka's influence on the development of *shōjo* manga in the postwar era was "secondary" to that of the *jojō-ga* (lyrical illustrations) of the 1920s and 1930s, drawn by male artists such as Takehisa Yumeji (1884–1934), Takabatake Kashō (1888–1966), and Nakahara Jun'ichi (1913–1983), the last of whom got his start in the 1930s and then revived and reinvigorated the *jojō-ga* style after the war.[5] The girls depicted in this early to mid-twentieth century style were lithe and delicate in form, with large sparkling eyes, and an "empty, wandering gaze," an appearance which drew on representations of girls and girlhood in the prewar *shōjo* literature that *jojō-ga* were used to illustrate. After the war, such illustrations of girls were set against flowery backgrounds, which "reflect[ed] their inner personality."[6] Such seemingly random cascades of flowers and twinkling saucer-shaped eyes were carried on into the *shōjo* manga of the 1970s thanks in no small part to the influence of Takahashi Macoto (1934–), a male illustrator and manga artist who helped introduce visual elements of *jojō-ga* into the manga format in the mid-1950s.[7] Building on the *jojō-ga* aesthetic sense, Takahashi and other artists prior to the 1970s incorporated close-ups of characters' faces with wide, sparkling eyes that revealed characters' "inner psychology," encouraging readers to identify with them.[8] Critic Fujimoto Yukari demonstrates that Takahashi is also responsible for the introduction and proliferation of "style pictures" (*sutairu-ga*), large full-body portraits outside the narrative panels that generally convey mood rather than advance the plot, a visual move that disrupted "the established grammar" of dividing pages into panels.[9] While Tezuka is well-known for his innovative graphic techniques that advanced the plot and evoked emotive responses in readers, the internal psychology of female characters was of little interest to Tezuka but became a central element in the *shōjo* manga of the 1970s, sometimes referred to as *shōjo* manga's "golden age," when a new generation of young women artists took over its creation from the predominantly male artists who had previously been responsible for its production.[10]

In the 1970s, these artists, including Ikeda Riyoko (1947–), Hagio Moto (1949–), and Takemiya Keiko (1950–), expanded on those visual conventions developed in *shōjo* manga in prior decades, including further experimentation with the layout and shape of panels, which were sometimes dispensed with altogether. The effect was a continued emphasis on the development of the thoughts and feelings of the characters.[11] At the same time, this new generation also introduced a greater diversity of themes along with narratives with more complex plots and characters. They also borrowed widely from foreign and Japanese literature, film, history, and myth. Such characteristics garnered a new appreciation from older female and male readers and helped lead to the treatment of some *shōjo* manga works as high literature.[12] Ikeda, Hagio, Takemiya, and other young women artists who thus narratively and graphically revolutionized *shōjo* manga in the 1970s came to be called the Fabulous Year 24 Group (*Hana no nijūyo'nen-gumi*) on account of most of them having been born around the year Showa 24, that is, 1949—hence in English, they might more appropriately be called the "Fabulous Forty-Niners."

One innovation made by the Fabulous Forty-Niners was the development of a genre of *shōjo* manga that early on came to be labeled "*shōnen'ai*" (boys love). These often highly literary manga narratives—printed in mainstream *shōjo* manga magazines in wide circulation—featured male protagonists in same-sex romantic and sometimes overtly sexual relationships. The first of these narratives were placed in romanticized European settings and populated with beautiful adolescent European boys. While certainly remarkable, the *shōnen'ai* genre was not entirely groundbreaking. As with the visual style common to 1970s *shōjo* manga, the *shōnen'ai* genre built on developments in- and outside *shōjo* manga.

The borrowing and adaptation of elements from translated fiction have been a staple of girls' fiction (*shōjo shōsetsu*) for much of modern Japanese history, and have played a central role in the development of *shōjo* culture more broadly.[13] Foreign settings and characters were frequently used by both male and female manga artists of the 1950s and 1960s, including, as noted above, in Tezuka's *Princess Knight*. Interest among women in male homosexuality was also already evident. Articles by women expressing such an interest, for instance, were appearing in popular women's magazines by at least the 1950s.[14] And at the beginning of the 1960s, Mori Mari (1903–1987), daughter of well-known male writer Mori Ōgai, penned several novellas with male homosexual protagonists, beginning with *A Lovers' Forest (Koibitotachi no mori)* in 1961, works which have been positioned as part of the (pre)history of *shōnen'ai* manga.[15]

Moreover, the mature themes related to sexuality and race that would find their way into later *shōnen'ai* narratives could be found in manga targeted at older—and more sexually knowledgeable—*shōjo* readers by the late 1960s in magazines such as *Seventeen (Sebuntiin,* 1968–) and *Funny (Fanii,* 1969–1970, 1973), the latter produced by Tezuka's production company. Just prior to the first of the *shōnen'ai* narratives, Mizuno Hideko (1939–), an influential female manga artist who had debuted professionally in the mid-1950s, penned for older *shōjo* readers a narrative with candid depictions of sex among young rock musicians in Detroit. *Fire! (Faiyaa!),* serialized in *Seventeen* for nearly three years beginning in January 1969, also included early depictions of racism and violence, as well as passing reference to homosexuality.[16] More pertinently, in spite of its female target audience, this narrative had a protagonist who was both male and eroticized for readers' visual pleasure— each a groundbreaking move within *shōjo* manga.[17] Appearing in the second issue of *Funny* later that same year, another rock-themed work, Minegishi Hiromi's single-episode manga "Crossroads" *(Jūjika),* crossed both racial and sexual barriers by featuring a male homosexual relationship between two young men, one white and one black (figure 3.1).[18] While both of these manga works, as well as Mori's novellas, bear aesthetic and narrative similarities with male homosexuality depicted in amateur and commercial texts that began to appear by the late 1970s and 1980s, they were in many ways a world apart from early *shōnen'ai* manga, which featured younger, sometimes barely pubescent boys inhabiting romantic, historical European settings.[19]

The Development of "*Shōnen'ai*" Manga Narratives

Although they failed to garner widespread public attention in the 1970s, *shōnen'ai* manga were anything but marginal within the *shōjo* manga sphere. These narratives were penned by a number of prominent professional female artists during this period and were, visual studies scholar Ishida Minori asserts, central to the radical transformation of *shōjo* manga that decade.[20] As exemplified in this volume in the chapter by Fujimoto Yukari and discussed in greater detail in the chapter by Kazumi Nagaike and Tomoko Aoyama,

Figure 3.1 Aida walks in on her husband, Eric, in bed with his drummer, Leroy, in Minegishi Hiromi's "Crossroads."

critics and scholars have long argued that the beautiful boy in *shōnen'ai* serves as a locus of identification for adolescent girl readers, and that the use of male (rather than female) characters, as well as homo- (rather than hetero-) sexual relationships, placed in a foreign setting, provides female readers the means for vicarious circumvention of gender and sexual norms.[21] (While some of the same artists who penned *shōnen'ai* texts also experimented with female–female romance, in contrast with *shōnen'ai* manga narratives, few of those early, frequently dark narratives were popular at the time.)[22] Any liberatory effects are arguably mitigated, however, by the fact that the male–male couples in such narratives have generally been comprised of a more masculine and dominant partner paired with a more feminine and passive one, thus roughly reproducing the male–female binary. In recent years, these relative positions within a couple in the newer genres of *yaoi* and boys love have been referred to as the *seme* (attacker) and the *uke* (receiver), respectively, in reference to sexual positions the more masculine and feminine partners generally assume.

The emergence of *shōnen'ai* manga is most closely associated with Hagio Moto and Takemiya Keiko. In the December 1970 issue of *Bessatsu shōjo komikku* (Girls' comic extra), Takemiya published the short narrative "Snow and Stars and Angels and . . ." (*Yuki to hoshi to tenshi to*), later reissued as "In the Sunroom" (*Sanrūmu nite*), a narrative that might be considered the very first example of the new manga genre.[23] Hagio followed eleven months later in the same magazine with "November Gymnasium" (*Jūichigatsu no gimunajiumu*).[24] Both works feature schoolboys in romantic relationships with other schoolboys in historical European settings. These were not their debut pieces, however. Takemiya had published her first work while still a high-school student in 1967 and Hagio in 1969. Their earlier manga had been good enough to catch the attention of editors, but the works themselves were neither memorable nor groundbreaking. Neither initially had set out to create narratives about homosexuality, and both would go on to create many other kinds of narratives, including science fiction, mysteries, and heterosexual romance narratives—a diversity typical of *shōjo* manga artists of their generation. But those first two *shōnen'ai* narratives, as well as the pair's wildly popular later *shōnen'ai* works, Hagio's *The Heart of Thomas* (*Tōma no shinzō*, 1974) and Takemiya's *The Song of the Wind and the Trees* (*Kaze to ki no uta*, 1976–1984) (figures 3.2 and 3.3), would help pave the way for a *shōnen'ai* manga boom in the 1970s and beyond, as well as the emergence of amateur works toward the end of the decade and the flourishing of the commercial boys love genre since the 1990s.[25]

The fact that Takemiya and Hagio both produced male–male romance narratives less than a year apart from each other and would go on to pen two of the most influential *shōnen'ai* works was no coincidence. The pair were roommates for several years, having moved in together right around the time Takemiya published "Snow and Stars and Angels and. . .," when Hagio came to help Takemiya meet a deadline on another project. They lived in a small apartment "surrounded by a cabbage patch" in Ōizumi, in Tokyo's Nerima Ward. Their neighbor was Masuyama Norie (1950–), who was soon thereafter to become Takemiya's producer, roommate, and muse—or, in Takemiya's words, her "brain" (*bureen*).[26] Under the guidance of Masuyama, Takemiya and Hagio's apartment became the "Ōizumi Salon," where up-and-coming *shōjo* manga artists, assistants (generally aspiring artists themselves), and others would gather and work, eat, or chat, sometimes staying over for extended periods.[27]

Figure 3.2 Juli's angst is highlighted in a full page from
Hagio Moto's *Heart of Thomas*.

Masuyama introduced the pair to some of her favorite books and played a
pivotal role in the development of the *shōnen'ai* genre. Although she was not
a visual artist herself, Masuyama was an avid consumer from childhood of
highbrow literature, classical music, and film. While she was a fan of manga
as well, as she explains, her disappointment with *shōjo* manga instilled in her
a desire to elevate *shōjo* manga from its lowly position as a frivolous distrac-
tion for girls into a more serious, literary art form. Drawn to the talents of
Takemiya and Hagio, Masuyama recommended to the pair various works
of highbrow music, cinema, and literature in the hope of inspiring them to
incorporate elements of these into their own art.[28]

Among the works Masuyama suggested to Takemiya and Hagio were
German novelist Herman Hesse's *Beneath the Wheel* (1906), *Demian* (1919),
and *Narcissus and Goldmund* (1930). All three novels feature adolescent

Figure 3.3 Gilbert and
Serge have sex in a scene in
Takemiya Keiko's *Song of the
Wind and the Trees.*

male protagonists in school environments in Germany. While none of the
three depict overt homoeroticism—in fact, romantic or erotic relationships
with female characters help drive their plots—their narratives all revolve
around strong bonds between the protagonist and another youth or, in the
case of *Narcissus and Goldmund,* a young teacher. Masuyama never directly
suggested that Takemiya and Hagio make a manga version of one of these
novels, yet the texts played a pivotal role in the development of *shōnen'ai.*[29]

Drawing on her own interviews with Masuyama and Takemiya, as well
as existing essays and commentary by Takemiya and Hagio, Ishida shows
that these novels proved vital source material for key early *shōnen'ai* works,
helping to inspire the boarding school settings common in early works, the
focus on the psyches of the protagonists, and the relative balance between
the more masculine and the more feminine protagonists.[30] Ishida further
argues that Takemiya in particular draws on latent romance and eroticism

between some male characters in Hesse's writing, "emphasiz[ing] a tendency in Hesse's works."[31]

From the opening scene of two adolescent boys having sex, the overt eroticism of Takemiya's *The Song of the Wind and the Trees* goes far beyond anything possibly read into Hesse's novels, however. This can in part be traced to the eroticized beautiful boys celebrated in the writing of Inagaki Taruho, which reached its climax in his *Aesthetics of Boy Loving (Shōnen'ai no bigaku)*, the work which almost certainly inspired the name of the new genre.[32] As Takemiya recalls, by the time she finished reading Taruho's book, around 1969, she had developed a clear idea about what she wanted to depict in the manga that would eventually become *The Song of the Wind and the Trees.*[33] British public schools are frequently referenced in *Aesthetics of Boy Loving*, "so the first thing I decided was to make a public school-like place the setting for *The Song of the Wind and the Trees.*"[34] Yet, it merits noting, the manga's setting is not a British public school, nor an early-twentieth-century German one, as depicted in Hesse's novels, but a boarding school in nineteenth-century France.

Hagio, on the other hand, did set her two early *shōnen'ai* narratives in German boarding schools. And yet she credits the 1964 French film *Les amitiés particulières (These Special Friendships)*, first shown in Japan in 1970, as the inspiration for *The Heart of Thomas*, which she had begun working on before "November Gymnasium."[35] Based on a semi-autobiographical novel by Roger Peyrefitte, the film depicts two boys in a Catholic boarding school who fall in love and ends with the suicide of one of them.[36] This suicide that would be echoed by the titular character in *The Heart of Thomas*, whose name is given a Japanese pronunciation—"Tōma"—based on the French, not German, version of the name Thomas. Takemiya was also inspired by cinema with homoerotic themes. She recalls being initially most influenced by the films of Italian director Luchino Visconti, including *Death in Venice* (1971), based on Thomas Mann's early-twentieth-century novel. This film had many fans among *shōnen'ai* readers as well and was frequently mentioned in correspondence from young female readers printed in the *shōnen'ai*-related magazine *Allan*.[37] In this Occidentalist blurring of all things European, Hagio, Takemiya, and other artists borrowed freely from settings, characters, and plot elements, transfiguring into the new genre of *shōnen'ai* the often nostalgic depictions of intimate friendships, as well as romantic and erotic relationships between beautiful European boys in translated literature and film, and in Taruho's writing.

While, particularly in English, Takemiya and Hagio are frequently mentioned in reference to the *shōnen'ai* genre, we must remember that, as noted

above, they also created many other kinds of *shōjo* narratives with little connection to their *shōnen'ai* works aside from the almost invariably beautiful
protagonists, male and female. Nevertheless, these early *shōnen'ai* works—
particularly *The Heart of Thomas* and *The Song of the Wind and the Trees*—
were clearly very popular among *shōjo* manga readers, as indicated to editors
and artists via postcards included in the magazines in which they were first
serialized, as well as by fan letters sent to the artists, the contents of which
were sometimes printed in the magazines.[38] This popularity almost certainly
helped foster increasingly diverse male–male romance narratives within the
broader *shōjo* manga genre from the mid-1970s onward by artists who, like
Takemiya and Hagio, created *shōnen'ai* works alongside other kinds of manga.

Although the earliest works were set in Europe, some *shōnen'ai* narratives
were set in Japan, albeit often in a romanticized past rather than the present.
Such works include those by other Fabulous Forty-Niners, notably Kihara
Toshie's *Mari and Shingo* (*Mari to Shingo,* 1977–1984), set in prewar Japan,
and Yamagishi Ryōko's *Emperor of the Land of the Rising Sun* (*Hi izuru tokoro no tenshi,* 1980–1984), set in pre-modern Japan.[39] Still other artists, some
of whom had apprenticed with members of the Forty-Niners, created works
set in the present day, sometimes in a not so idealized United States, sometimes addressing the kinds of social issues foregrounded in Mizuno's *Fire!*
(discussed above). These works frequently included one or more Japanese
or half-Japanese characters, linking the narratives to their Japan-based readers. Prominent among these are Yoshida Akimi's *Banana Fish* (1985–1994),
a hard-boiled detective narrative set in New York, and Akisato Wakuni's *Tomoi* (1986), which features a "gay"-identified protagonist whose boyfriend
had died of AIDS.[40] For want of labels to distinguish them, works such as
the latter two of these have been grouped with earlier manga by Takemiya,
Hagio, and others.[41] It is clear, however, that they are distinct from earlier
works in terms of the ages of the characters, setting and mood, and the style
in which they are drawn. Retrospectively, however, we can see some such
texts have more in common with 1990s texts that would come to be labeled
"boys love" than with 1970s *shōnen'ai* manga.

As Masuyama recalls, when the early male–male romance narratives were
being created and published, she, Takemiya, and Hagio first labeled these
male–male romance narratives with the term *"kunaaben riibe,"* a transliteration of the German term *Knabenliebe,* which means "boy love" and which
is often translated into English as "pederasty." Taruho used this German
word alongside *"shōnen'ai,"* the latter of which was to become the dominant label for male–male romance narratives in the 1970s.[42] The ambiguity
of the term *"shōnen'ai"* served the new genre well, as it can simultaneously

indicate the boys as the subject of affection, that is, "a boy loves (someone)" or "(someone) loves a boy." Outside of the *shōjo* manga sphere, however, the term still pointed to pederasty or pedophilia, a meaning that continues to the present. In addition, there was blurring in some readers' minds between the "*shōnen'ai*" in *shōjo* manga world, and the real world of adult male homosexuality in Japan represented in commercial publications then known as "*homo*" magazines, as is clear in some correspondence written by young female *shōnen'ai* fans to magazines such as *Barazoku* (Rose tribe, 1971–) in the 1970s. While some fans and artists, as well as critics and scholars, still use "*shōnen'ai*" in reference to these commercially published manga narratives in the 1970s and into the 1980s, among fans and artists the term was largely replaced by other terms in the 1980s and 1990s, as will be discussed in subsequent sections of this chapter.[43]

A related label in wide use in the 1970s was "*bishōnen*"—beautiful boy—manga, referring to *shōjo* manga with beautiful young male protagonists. In addition to including *shōnen'ai* manga, which was naturally populated with beautiful boy characters, *bishōnen* manga was also used as a label for narratives such as Hagio's highly popular *The Poe Clan* (*Pō no ichizoku*, 1972–1976) about beautiful boy vampires named Edgar and Allan, who were intimate friends but not romantically involved with one other.[44]

A third label, "*tanbi*"—often translated as "aesthete" or "aesthetic"—has been circulating in the BL sphere since at least the 1980s. Fusing together beauty, romance, and eroticism, along with at least a dash of decadence, the use of "*tanbi*" to describe BL media plays on the term's broader application as a label for works of highbrow literature that are aesthetically appealing and subtly erotic—rather than blatantly sexual—including works by writers such as Mishima Yukio, Tanizaki Jun'ichirō, and Kawabata Yasunari.[45] The term's meaning and usage in the BL sphere has been rather idiosyncratic, and, while it has primarily functioned as a label for prose fiction, it has also been used to describe manga and other visual art. For some, *tanbi* is a genre in its own right, albeit one whose boundaries have never clearly been established. Within the pages of early commercial magazines aimed at fans of the *shōnen'ai* genre, discussed below, the term "*tanbi*" was applied to BL fiction by professional and amateur writers alike, as well as to literature depicting or insinuating male homosexuality such as by European writers like Oscar Wilde, Jean Cocteau, and André Gide, along with domestic writers such as Mishima Yukio and Shibusawa Tatsuhiko.[46] "*Tanbi*" has appeared most often in the phrases "*tanbi shōsetsu*" (aesthete fiction), "*tanbi bungaku*" (aesthete literature), and "*tanbi zasshi*" (aesthete magazines), the latter of which was applied to these *shōnen'ai*-related magazines.[47] In the early-1990s collection, *Guidebook to Aesthete Fiction and Gay Literature* (*Tanbi shōsetsu, gei bungaku bukkugaido*), Kurihara Chiyo observes that the term can be used in scare quotes to point specifically to "fiction (*shōsetsu*) about romance between males written by women"—ranging from the novellas of Mori Mari to fiction created by amateur authors and circulated more informally.[48] Such prose fiction is part of a larger sphere of creation and consumption of narratives about male–male romance and eroticism by and for adolescent girls and women which in the 1970s began to develop into a rich culture of its own largely outside the commercial media.

Fan Engagement and the Creation of *Yaoi*

In December 1975, a year after Hagio's *The Heart of Thomas* was published and while her *Poe Clan* was still being serialized, the first "Comic Market" was held at a public hall in Toranomon in Tokyo's Minato Ward. In spite of what in retrospect seems like a very modest turnout that day—there were just thirty-two circles disseminating their self-produced manga- and anime-related materials and around 700 regular attendees—organizers were pleased with the event's success.[49] Since then, the Comic Market has grown exponentially. From 1996 onward, it has been held over three days each August and December at the massive Tokyo Big Sight convention center. In recent years, organizers have accepted 35,000 out of the over 50,000 circles applying each time to set up a one-day sales booth. And since the mid-2000s, attendance has ranged from 120,000 to 210,000 on *each* day, and total attendance has exceeded 500,000 over each three-day event.[50] Regular attendees are referred to as "general participants" (*ippan sankasha*), a term used by the organizers to emphasize that those who take part are not "customers" but—together with "staff participants" (*sutaffu sankasha*) and "circle participants" (*saakuru sankasha*)—collective participants in the experience of sharing circle-produced media.[51]

Among the earliest events of its kind, the Comic Market—referred to in Japanese as Komikku Maaketto (often abbreviated as Komiketto and Komike)—was first organized by Yonezawa Yoshiro and a handful of others, primarily young men, as an inexpensive means for the distribution and exchange of diverse, self-produced manga. It quickly became synonymous with the buying and selling of *dōjinshi* (coterie magazines) of wildly diverse quality and content, variously including original and parodic manga and prose fiction, as well as criticism about manga, anime, and, eventually, video games. The Comic Market has provided amateur and even established professional artists a "place" (*ba*) for creative expression outside the restrictions of the commercial publishing world—although the event has also been used by commercial publishers to recruit new talent and has become increasingly commercialized over its forty-year history.[52]

In the beginning, adolescent girls accounted for the vast majority of regular participants, with female participants comprising around 90 percent of those original 700 attendees at the first event, initially billed a "manga fanzine fair" (*manga fanjin fea*).[53] These early attendees were predominantly middle and high school students enamored with works by Hagio, Takemiya, and fellow Fabulous Forty-Niner Ōshima Yumiko (1947–), with the former two artists outranking even Tezuka in a survey on favorite artists conducted that day.[54] In particular, Hagio's early manga works—which, as noted above, were by and large not *shōnen'ai*—had also attracted many fans among the young men involved in organizing the Comic Market.[55] One way the significance of such new developments in *shōjo* manga was recognized by male organizers was the choice to promote early Comic Market events in *Bessatsu shōjo komikku*, as well as local event magazines—though not in a *shōnen* (boys') manga magazine.[56] Another way *shōjo* manga was foregrounded was in the screening of a dynavision anime version of Hagio's "November Gymnasium," produced by both male and female fans of the artist.[57]

In the first several years of the Comic Market, quite a number of *shōjo* manga-related circles participated, including those who were fans of a particular artist (figure 3.4), as well as those which displayed in their art an interest in glam and hard rock musicians associated with beauty and, in some cases, homosexuality, particularly those from the UK, such as David Bowie, T.Rex, Queen, and Led Zeppelin. (This interest in male rock musicians also echoes their objectification in Mizuno's *Fire!* several years earlier.) While early *dōjinshi* by the circle Queen (*Kuiin*) and similar *shōjo* manga circles did not include overt representations of homosexuality, they did contain ample imagery of beautiful and naked males.[58] Before long, however, some *dōjinshi* circles did start creating works with more overt homosexual narratives, drawing perhaps on some combination of rumors about the lives of the rock stars, commercially published *shōnen'ai* narratives, and the homosexuality represented in *homo* magazines. For instance, a mimeographed *dōjinshi* called *Island*, published around 1979 by a group called Abnorm, sits somewhere between the eroticization and homoeroticization of male rock stars.[59] It contains drawings and photographs of some of the musicians above, including a two-page spread on one side of which is a photograph of David Bowie on stage in a jock strap and the other drawings of clothing that might be used to dress him up like a paper doll. Elsewhere is a drawing of

Figure 3.4 Cover of
Sunroom (Sanrūmu), no. 6
(June 1977), produced by
Takemiya Keiko's official fan
club, Sunroom (Sanrūmu).

Led Zeppelin's Jimmy Page and Robert Plant, respectively holding a guitar and a microphone, kissing each other (figure 3.5).[60]

By the early 1980s, the term *"yaoi"*—in recent years a truly global label for male homoerotic manga and anime—was beginning to be used in the amateur comics sphere to name these amateur homoerotic works.[61] The word is an acronym for *"yama nashi, ochi nashi, imi nashi,"* or, roughly, "no climax, no point, no meaning," an apt description of the relatively plotless original narratives and parodies replete with implied or roughly depicted male-on-male sex. Its coinage and initial use had little specifically to do with the genre, however. As recalled by Hatsu Akiko (1959–), once a frequent guest at Takemiya and Hagio's Ōizumi Salon, the term emerged organically at the end of the 1970s among the members of the popular Ravuri (Lovely) manga circle as a general, self-deprecating assessment of all types of *dōjinshi.*[62] Playing on the new term, Ravuri member Maru Mikiko created a male homoerotic manga which she titled *"Yaoi,"* writing the term in *kanji* characters meaning "chasing the night." At the time Hatsu felt that "it's true that this manga

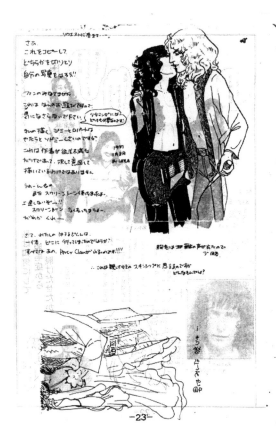

Figure 3.5 Drawing of Led Zeppelin's Jimmy Page and Robert Plant kissing, from *Island* (ca. 1979), produced by the circle Abnorm, as imagined by a contributor to the *dōjinshi*.

has no climax, no point, and no meaning. But there's something—what's going on between these guys?" So, in December 1979, she, Maru, and a small group of others collectively compiled a *dōjinshi* full of male homoerotic narratives based on the concept that "even if there's no climax, no point, and no meaning, there's eros." This *dōjinshi*, titled *RAPPORI: Special Yaoi Issue* (*RAPPORI: yaoi tokushū gō*), in effect narrowed the definition of the term.[63] It has subsequently been given alternative readings within the community to highlight the sometimes—but by no means universal—pornographic content of these *dōjinshi*, including "*yamete, oshiri ga itai*," that is, "stop, my butt hurts," and "*yaru, okasu, ikaseru*," or "do (him), rape (him), make (him) cum."[64] While "*yaoi*" took a number of years to become established—competing with "*shōnen'ai*," "*tanbi*," and "*JUNE*" (discussed below)—the term continues to have a great deal of currency in reference not just to such non-commercial homoerotic *dōjinshi* but BL media in general.

The parodying of existing manga and anime in *dōjinshi*—often broadly referred to as "*aniparo*"—circulating at the Comic Market took off in the 1980s. While an abbreviation of "anime parody" (*anime parodi*), the "*aniparo*" can be used in reference to any *dōjinshi* parodies, regardless of what or who is being parodied.[65] Although anything can be parodied, among female *dōjinshi* artists, *shōnen* manga and anime have been a major source of material for male homoerotic parodies. Pride of place goes to the magazine *Shōnen Jump* (*Shōnen janpu,* 1968–), observes *dōjinshi* researcher and manga critic Misaki Naoto. Popular manga series in *Shōnen Jump,* many of which have been made into TV anime, have been at the heart of homoerotic *aniparo* from the beginning and, Misaki estimates, are the source for around a third of such works today.[66] Most prominent in histories of homoerotic *aniparo* is Takahashi Yōichi's extremely popular *shōnen* manga and anime series *Captain Tsubasa* (*Kyaputen Tsubasa*), whose first iteration was serialized in *Shōnen Jump* from 1981 to 1988.[67] While the narrative about enthusiastic soccer player Ōzora Tsubasa, his teammates, and his rivals was not the first target of homoerotic parody, it was the first to overwhelm the Comic Market.[68] The Tsubasa "genre" (*janru*)—a label used in the *dōjinshi* sphere to indicate source texts—dominated the Comic Market for several years in the mid-1980s and was at the forefront of successive surges in popularity of homoerotic *aniparo* based on narratives serialized in *Shōnen Jump* and made into anime, including *Saint Seiya* (*Seinto Seiya,* 1986–1990) and *Slam Dunk* (1990–1996) in the 1980s and 1990s, and *One Piece* (1997–), *Naruto* (1999–), and *Prince of Tennis* (*Tenisu no ōjisama,* 1999–2008) since 2000, as well as based on other *shōnen* manga and anime including the still-popular *Samurai Troopers* (*Yoroi den samurai torūpaa,* first broadcast in Japan 1988–1989; it was later released in English as *Ronin Warriors*).[69]

The Tsubasa genre was not the first time for *shōnen'ai* or male homoerotic narratives in *dōjinshi* to be set in Japan and feature Japanese characters, yet its incredible popularity might be seen as part of a noteworthy shift away from the dominance of foreign settings and characters in *shōjo* manga depicting male homoeroticism. Critic Nishimura Mari proposes that the original text was one that middle and high school students in Japan could easily relate to.[70] The 1980s also saw the height of Japan's economic bubble and increasing recognition that Japan was a global economic power, perhaps helping to unsettle the high status given to the blonde, blue-eyed knight on a white horse ideal in *shōjo* manga.[71] Yonezawa suggests a link between parodies of Japanese celebrities and reader-contributed content in the 1980s BL-related commercial magazines *Allan* and *Gekkō* (discussed in the following section),

Figure 3.6 Cover of *Hi Five Boogie* (2008), a *dōjinshi* homoerotic parody of the band Arashi by the circle Walnuts.

which served as a site for gossip on, as well as photographs and illustrations of, real celebrities.[72]

Beyond the *shōnen* genre specifically, anime, manga, and, recently, web-comics (*uebukomikku*) targeting broader audiences have also been frequently parodied. Particularly popular as a subject of *aniparo* in recent years is *Axis Powers Hetalia*, a satirical webcomic (later adapted as a manga and anime series) by Himaruya Hidekaz that began around 2006 in which countries that fought in World War II have been reimagined as people, a majority of whom are attractive young men and adolescent boys.[73] Concrete and abstract objects that have been personified (*gijinka*) are also currently very popular both in general and among *yaoi* creators (see Galbraith this volume). Among *dōjinshi* on sale at the August 2013 Comic Market were manga pairing department stores, universities, convenience stores, train lines, and even Internet search engines reimagined as handsome young men. Popular films, television programs, video games, and other media have also served as source material for *yaoi* parodies, as have real celebrities and athletes. While British and American rock musicians were popular among girls and women at the Comic Market in the 1970s and 1980s, male musicians and other entertainers as well as athletes from Japan were and are also parodied in male homoerotic *dōjinshi*.[74] Boy bands, comedy duos, and sports teammates have long provided ample material to arouse speculation about romantic or sexual relationships, such as among the members of the 1980s beautiful boy band Hikaru Genji, as well as the contemporary band Arashi (figure 3.6), and popular Korean bands in the past decade.

In addition to distribution at existing large and small *dōjinshi* "spot sale events" (*sokubaikai*) around the country, of which the Comic Market is the largest and most prominent, *dōjinshi* are also sold by circles via advertisements in specialty magazines and, since the 1990s, online. What have come to be called "only events" (*onrii ibento*) feature fan-made media focused on "only" a specific theme or work, sometimes only on a popular "coupling" (*kappuringu*) of characters within a work.[75] While contemporary *dōjinshi* often include a "prohibition" against resale, they are frequently resold at specialty shops, which also generally sell *dōjinshi* online, and by individuals via online auction and other resale websites. Finally, since at least the 1980s, *aniparo* and original *yaoi dōjinshi* manga have been compiled into anthologies and sold commercially.[76]

The Commercialization of Amateur BL Media: "*JUNE* Things"

The commercially published anthologies in the 1980s were not, however, the first effort by publishers to commercialize these amateur works. Already in 1978, riding on the early wave of enthusiasm for beautiful young men at the Comic Market and for *shōnen'ai* manga, Sagawa Toshihiko (1954–), then working part time at San shuppan, a publisher of magazines with erotic themes aimed at adults, including the *homo* magazine *Sabu* (1974–2002), convinced the company to produce a "mildly pornographic magazine aimed at females."[77] At least at the time this is how he framed the project that became *JUNE* (pronounced "ju-nay"; 1978–1979, 1981–1996), the first commercial magazine for adolescent girls and young women featuring beautiful boys and young men in romantic and sexual relationships with one another.[78] Reflecting on the magazine's content three decades later, Sagawa explains, somewhat more equivocally, that what the Fabulous Forty-Niners produced was not "porn" but rather something between literature and pornography, with both being important aspects of the genre's appeal.[79] Sagawa was a young man who, like many other men at the time, was taken in by works by the Fabulous Forty-Niners, the artists he hoped would contribute to this new magazine. He was, however, certain that even if he was unable to get Takemiya and her cohort to draw for the magazine, he could get amateur *dōjinshi* artists to do so.[80]

Figure 3.7 Cover of the first issue of *JUNE*, then called *Comic Jun* (October 1978).

JUNE, called *Comic Jun* for the first two issues, became a mix of both (figure 3.7).[81] Takemiya contributed immeasurably to both the content and the tone of the magazine in its early years. Another central contributor to *JUNE* was Kurimoto Kaoru/Nakajima Azusa (1953–2009), a writer who published prose fiction in the magazine as Kurimoto and critical essays as Nakajima.[82] The combined presence of Kurimoto/Nakajima and Takemiya shaped the spirit of *JUNE*, which Ishida describes as a "site of collaboration" between the two women. Readers, primarily ranging from adolescent girls in their late teens to young women in their early twenties, contributed a significant portion of the content in the form of letters and drawings as well as manga narratives and short stories, the latter of which could respectively be submitted to Takemiya and Nakajima for critique in their respective columns dedicated to teaching the crafts of manga artistry and fiction writing.[83] In reaction to the popularity of the works of prose fiction in the magazine, in 1982 *Shōsetsu JUNE* (*JUNE* fiction; 1982–2004) was created.

Figure 3.8 Cover of *Allan*, no.
6 (October 1982), featuring
David Bowie.

When disappointing sales figures forced *JUNE* to suspend publishing
in 1979, the temporary gap was quickly filled by Nanbara Shirō, working at
Minori shobō, publisher of *Out* (*Auto*, 1977–1995), a magazine focused on
anime and *aniparo*.[84] Nanbara founded *Allan* (*Aran*, 1980–1984) (figure 3.8),
which was named after handsome French actor Alain Delon, but for reasons
of design, spelled on the cover in Roman letters like the middle name of
American author Edgar Allan Poe and one of the beautiful boy protagonists
in Hagio's *The Poe Clan*.[85] While at first attempting to tap into the same interests as *JUNE*, *Allan* was more textual and less visually oriented than its
predecessor and devoted far more space to reader-contributed content. In
1984, Nanbara left the publisher over a difference of opinion on the direction
of the magazine, which he took with him. He rechristened it *Gekkō* (Moon-
light, 1984–2006). While *Gekkō*—also referred to as "Luna" (*Runa*)—was
similar in content and tone to *Allan* for the first year or so, it eventually
became far more focused on bizarre and dark themes, such as suicide, death,

espionage, and the supernatural, in keeping with Nanbara's own interests.[86] It did, however, continue to provide a space for discussion of homosexuality, that of celebrities as well as of the magazine's readers.

Both *Allan* and *JUNE*, which was revived in 1981, functioned as a bridge in the 1980s between commercial and non-commercial worlds of *shōnen'ai* manga. While focused on beautiful males, the two magazines reflected a broad range of tastes from the beautiful early teen boys in the works of Takemiya and Hagio and the innocent-looking members of the Vienna Boys Choir to the glam and heavy metal rockers mentioned above. Editorial content as well as contributions from readers also introduced and discussed foreign and domestic literature and films depicting *homo* or gays and, particularly in *Allan*, lesbians. Starting in its second year, *Allan* even ran a personal column, called "Lily Communications" (*Yuri tsūshin*) first identified as being "for lesbiens only [*sic*]," although the number of advertisers who understood themselves as "*rezubian*" is questionable.[87] In addition, artists like Kimura Ben (1947–2003) and Hayashi Gekkō (also known as Ishihara Gōjin, 1923–1998), who produced often gorgeous erotic illustrations for *homo* and other magazines, also created erotic illustrations of beautiful adolescent boys and young men for *JUNE* and *Allan*, further linking *shōnen'ai* and *homo* aesthetics. (It is worth noting that well before the appearance of *JUNE*, Masuyama brought a copy of the *homo* magazine *Barazoku* to the Ōizumi Salon, though Hagio recalls that, in contrast with Takemiya and Masuyama, the magazine had no appeal for her.[88]) Extending this aesthetic connection further, in 1988 *JUNE*'s publisher created *Roman JUNE*, featuring content from the *homo* magazine *Sabu*, published once or twice a year through the late 1990s. Connecting fantasy to reality, the lives of actual gays and lesbians abroad, as well as in Japan, were also referenced and sometimes discussed more extensively in letters and articles in both magazines. Ishida Hitoshi argues that given the crossover readership, overlapping content, and cross-referencing between the various *JUNE* magazines and *Sabu* all four represent a "queer contact zone" (*kuia na kontakuto zōn*) between *shōjo* readers and the *homo*/*gei* community.[89]

Whether due to the magazine's aesthetic and narrative broadening from early *shōnen'ai* or just a reflection of the popularity and central role of *JUNE*, the label "*JUNE-mono*" (*JUNE* things; generally spelled out in capital Roman letters) came to be applied by the 1980s to original homoerotic works that evoked the aesthetics of the magazine (see Fujimoto in this volume). While as a category the term has largely been supplanted by "*yaoi*" and "boys love," it lives on in the "original *JUNE*" (*sōsaku JUNE*) genre code at the Comic Market and via regular J.Garden (the "J" stands for *JUNE*) spot sale events, originally organized in conjunction with the magazine around 1996.[90]

The availability of *JUNE* and *Allan*, sold in bookstores around the country and by subscription, gave countless readers not just access to homoerotic narratives by established and emerging professional manga artists, but also the opportunity to participate in the production and consumption of such narratives beyond commercial channels—which would have otherwise been impossible outside of venues like the Comic Market. Both ran ads from readers seeking others to join in their manga circles and help produce *dōjinshi* as well as promotions for the *dōjinshi* themselves, either as announcements or as advertisements; *Allan* even gave away issues of popular *dōjinshi* via a promotion in its premier issue.[91] These magazines, particularly *JUNE*, along with the commercially published *dōjinshi* anthologies and—even more importantly—the phenomenal popularity and proliferation of amateur BL media at the Comic Market and in other fora in the 1980s, helped pave the way for the commercial boom in the 1990s and the current prosperity of the BL market.

New Commercializations of BL Media: The "Boys Love" Boom

The commercial flourishing in BL media that began in the 1990s and continues to the present represents an extension and expansion of the *yaoi dōjinshi* of the previous decade. Not only was the financial viability of BL publications made possible by the prior existence of a large group of readers interested in such narratives, many artists producing popular *aniparo* and original *dōjinshi* were recruited to create manga for the new commercial magazines.[92] The 1990s saw an explosion of such commercial magazines, including serial "*mūku*" (short for "magazine book"), many of which were issued as different versions of the same title, with one focused on manga and the other on prose fiction, for instance. While some of the *mūku* began as, in essence, anthologies of original *dōjinshi*, even publications formatted as magazines sometimes reprinted manga that had originally been distributed as *dōjinshi*.[93] Among the first of this new wave of BL periodicals were *Kid's (Kizzu)* in 1989, *Gust (Gasto)* in 1990, and *b-Boy (Biibōi)* and *Image (Imaaju)* in 1991 (figure 3.9). These were quickly followed by fiction (*shōsetsu*) versions of the latter two magazines—*Shōsetsu Image* and *Shōsetsu b-Boy*—in 1992. Each of the following two years saw a handful of new titles, including *Magazine Be x Boy (Magajin biibōi), Reijin* (Beautiful person) in 1993, then *Charade (Shareedo), Hana oto* (Flower sound), *Chara (Kyara), Asuka Ciel (Asuka shieru)*

Figure 3.9 Cover of premiere issue of *Image* (December 1991).

in 1994, while around ten new titles appeared in 1995.[94] In sum, at least thirty new magazines focused on BL manga—that is, in addition to those primarily containing BL fiction—appeared in the first half of the 1990s, though many were short-lived.[95]

In contrast with *shōnen'ai* narratives serialized in *shōjo* manga magazines, and reflective of shifts in the *yaoi dōjinshi* sphere in the 1980s, by the time this new wave of magazines appeared, the clear preference for narratives set abroad and peopled with foreign characters had disappeared. While some popular titles have continued to be set abroad, sometimes featuring Japanese or half-Japanese protagonists—such as Matoh Sanami's *Fake* (1994–2000), set in New York and including the half-Japanese character Ryō—the majority of recent commercially published BL narratives have been set in Japan and populated with Japanese characters.[96] Another point in common with early commercial *shōnen'ai* is that many popular narratives serialized in manga magazines have been reprinted in paperback form, with dozens upon dozens of BL manga paperbacks published monthly. In addition, many are released as drama CDs (on which voice actors perform the narratives), anime, prose fiction (often described as "light novels"/*raito noberu*), and other media products. In the middle of the 1990s, bookstores began to include sections focused on BL manga and fiction.[97] A limited number of shops focusing on BL media gradually appeared as well, and in the 2000s, "Otome Road" (Otome rōdo; English: maiden road), a whole street full of shops featuring BL media, materialized several blocks from Tokyo's Ikebukuro station.[98] The surge in commercial magazines and paperbacks, as well as the appearance of BL sections in bookstores may help explain the increase in scholarly and critical attention to BL media that also began in the 1990s, as Nagaike and Aoyama note in their chapter in this volume. This new visibility has also attracted severely negative attention. For instance, as Mark McLelland discusses in his chapter in this volume, in the latter half of the first decade of the 2000s, members of the public and conservative politicians began to attack the acquisition and display of BL novels by public libraries.

Like other kinds of magazines, some of the new BL serials sought to distinguish themselves with a tag line. This, in fact, began well before the 1990s. In 1978, *JUNE* first declared on its cover that the magazine was about "now, opening our eyes to dangerous love" (*ima, kiken na ai ni mezamete*), while in 1980 *Allan* began by identifying itself as "an aesthete magazine for girls" (*shōjo no tame no tanbi-ha magajin*), making use of the term "*tanbi*" (aesthete) that, as noted above, had come to be associated with *shōnen'ai* manga and literary representations of male homosexuality in this sphere. A decade later, *Kid's* labeled itself as a "naughty girls' comic" (*ikenai onna no ko komikku*) magazine, while *Gust* flagged itself as a "YAOI COMIC" (in capital Roman letters) magazine, the latter again highlighting the connection between the new wave of commercial publications and their *dōjinshi* roots. Toward the end of 1991, *Image*, another of the BL periodicals at the forefront of this wave, debuted with "BOY'S LOVE ♥ COMIC [*sic*]"—almost certainly a transfiguration of the 1970s term "*shōnen'ai* manga"—spelled out across the top of its cover (figure 3.9). The following year, the sister publication *Shōsetsu Image* came out similarly adorned with "BOY'S LOVE NOVELS" on its own cover.

Whether because of its connection with an existing term or because of the way it resonated with readers and creators or for some other reason, "boys love" caught on as a generic label over the course of the 1990s, and the term was eventually rendered into *katakana* as "*bōizu rabu*" and shortened to "BL." Early on, however, it continued to compete with terms like "*yaoi*," "*tanbi*," "*JUNE*," and "*shōnen'ai*"—though the latter term was falling into disuse by the 1990s. For instance, among the magazines appearing in 1993, *Reijin* ran on its cover the catchcopy "a challenge to taboos . . . a revolutionary adult aesthete (*tanbi*) comic" (*tabū e no chōsen . . . kakumeiteki adaruto tanbi komikku*) and *Mauris* (*Mōrisu*) first described itself as a "*yaoi* COMIC" (with "*yaoi*" in the phonetic *hiragana* script and "comic" in capital Roman letters). Opening the covers, early on, in letters from readers and the editors' responses thereto, the content of *b-Boy*, for example, was referred to as "*yaoi*" or "*JUNE*."[99] In 1994, however, *Charade* (*Shareedo*), first published in March that year by a different publisher from *Image*, described its contents "BOYS' LOVE for GIRLS [*sic*]." And in August that same year, *Puff* carried a special feature offering "A Complete Manual to Mastering Boys Love Magazines" (*BOY'S LOVE MAGAZINE* [*sic*] *kanzen kōryaku manyuaru*), which introduced a number of BL manga and fiction magazines under the rubric of "BOY'S LOVE," a term only used in the title of the feature.[100] Yamamoto Fumiko and BL Supporters, who compiled a more recent guide to boys love, argue that this feature helped establish the use of "boys love" as a generic label.[101]

While among the magazines included in this feature are *Reijin* (which described itself as *tanbi*) and *Mauris* (*yaoi*), these magazines are collectively introduced in the feature as representing "what can perhaps be called a new genre," one that is "somewhat different" (*hitoaji chigau*) from *shōnen'ai* and *tanbi*.[102] Given the diverse content of the magazines described in the feature, ranging from "bright and refreshing" (in the case of *Image*) to "hard and heavy" (*Reijin*), however, it is not clear what the compilers of this feature believe these new magazines have in common that sets them apart narratively or aesthetically from what came before.[103] Moreover, as noted above, these new magazines were closely linked to *aniparo* and original *yaoi dōjinshi*. In addition to the fact that many of the artists creating manga for the new magazines got their start drawing *yaoi dōjinshi*, many of these magazines also provided information about and, sometimes, reviews of new *dōjinshi*. This continuing overlap between commercial and non-commercial production may explain why, although "*yaoi*" and "boys love" remain in common use, the distinction in meaning between the two terms has not been settled upon. While at present, many artists, fans, critics, and scholars treat the terms as synonymous, some distinguish between "*yaoi*" and "boys love" on the basis of the former being *dōjinshi* and the latter commercially published media—a distinction that clearly reflects the history of BL manga.[104]

Conclusion: Something Is Rotten

As we have seen, the 1970s can be identified with the emergence of the literary *shōnen'ai* genre of *shōjo* manga; the 1980s with the flourishing of *aniparo dōjinshi* self-mockingly called *"yaoi"* at the Comic Market, as well as—straddling the amateur and commercial spheres—the magazine *JUNE*; and the 1990s with the explosion of commercially produced and distributed BL media. The first decade of the 2000s might be tied to the rise of the *"fujoshi,"* the "rotten girl." The *fujoshi* has quickly become an overdetermined archetype, often caricaturized in the media in recent years, as Jeffry Hester's chapter in this volume chronicles. The term *"fujoshi,"* like the term *"yaoi,"* is deliberately self-disparaging. As Patrick W. Galbraith shows, also in this volume, *fujoshi* are "rotten" because their fantasies (centered around BL media) entail male homoeroticism rather than the heteronormative romance that "common sense" dictates.

In both commercial and amateur spheres in Japan today, the BL media they produce and consume demonstrate no signs of decay, however. A recent report by the Yano Research Institute, which has for a number of years conducted extensive surveys and other research on what it calls the *"otaku* (fervent fan) market" in Japan, estimates the scale of the boys love market in 2010 alone to have been 2.2 billion yen ($24.5 million), inclusive of commercial works, drama CDs, and webcomics, as well as *dōjinshi*.[105] And that's just the market in Japan.

BL has also gone global, particularly in the past decade or so. The production and consumption by women of texts about male homosexuality is, of course, not without precedent outside Japan, such as in the fan-produced homoerotic parody genre of "slash fiction" in the Anglophone world.[106] BL media fandom and production has been more visible than its antecedents, however. Since 2001, for example, Yaoi-Con, a convention for BL media fans and creators, has been held in San Francisco, evolving into a three-day event. Also, in addition to the massive amount of fan-produced translated and subtitled versions of BL media available online in English and other languages, since the early 2000s commercial U.S. publishers already releasing other manga in English translation—including those founded for that purpose—have been publishing translated BL manga;[107] BL have also developed a commercial market in Europe and elsewhere.[108]

While BL media have yet to prove as popular or as commercially viable abroad, enthusiasm for BL both in- *and* outside Japan shows no signs of abating. It seems unlikely that Takemiya and Hagio could have predicted their experimentation with narratives about beautiful boys at the beginning of the 1970s would reach this point, but, looking back, we can see now that BL has come a long way.

Notes

Much of the research for this chapter was made possible with the support of a Fulbright-Hays Dissertation Research Abroad fellowship, a Japan Society for the Promotion of Science short-term postdoctoral fellowship, and a summer research grant from the Department of East Asian Languages and Cultures at the University of Illinois at Urbana-Champaign. I would also like to express my thanks to Patrick Galbraith for his astute feedback and suggestions that have helped me clarify important points.

1. On the category "*shōjo*" in *shōjo* manga, see Jennifer S. Prough, *Straight from the Heart: Gender, Intimacy, and the Cultural Production of* Shōjo Manga (Honolulu: University of Hawai'i Press, 2011), 7–10.

2. Tezuka Osamu, *Ribon no kishi* [*Princess Knight*] (1953–1955; Tokyo: Kōdansha manga bunko, 1999). On Tezuka's role in the development of *shōjo* manga, see Yonezawa Yoshihiro, *Sengo shōjo manga shi* [A history of postwar *shōjo* manga] (1980; Tokyo: Chikuma shobō, 2007), especially pp. 50–53.

3. On the influence of the Takarazuka Revue on Tezuka, see Matsutani Takayuki, Ikeda Riyoko, Kusano Tadashi, Kawauchi Atsurō, and Morina Miharu, "Tezuka Osamu to Takarazuka Kageki: Myūjikaru fōramu" [Tezuka Osamu and the Takarazuka Revue: A musical forum], in *Tezuka Osamu no furusato, Takarazuka*, ed. Kawauchi Atsurō (Kobe: Kobe shinbun sōgō shuppan sentaa, 1996). On Tezuka's *Princess Knight* as originator of cross-dressing, "androgynous" (*ryōsei guyū*) characters, see Fujimoto Yukari, *Watashi no ibasho wa doko ni aru no? Shōjo manga ga utsusu kokoro no katachi* [Where do I belong? The shape of the heart reflected in *shōjo* manga] (Tokyo: Gakuyō shobō, 1998), 130.

4. Yonezawa, *Sengo shōjo manga shi*, 52. See also Fujimoto, *Watashi no ibasho*, 130.

5. Mizuki Takahashi, "Opening the Closed World of *Shōjo Manga*," in *Japanese Visual Culture: Explorations in the World of Manga and Anime*, ed. Mark Wheeler MacWilliams (Armonk, NY: M. E. Sharpe, 2008), 127. See also Yonezawa, *Sengo shōjo manga shi*, 24–27. Kashō's depiction of male bodies and their consumption by female readers is discussed by Barbara Hartley in this volume.

6. Takahashi, "Opening the Closed World of *Shōjo Manga*," 117, 118, 122.

7. Ibid., 122. See also Fujimoto Yukari, "Takahashi Macoto: The Origin of Shōjo Manga Style," translated by Matt Thorn, *Mechademia* 7 (2012); and Yonezawa, *Sengo shōjo manga shi*, 78–82.

8. Takahashi, "Opening the Closed World of *Shōjo Manga*," 122–24.

9. Fujimoto, "Takahashi Macoto," 47. See also Takahashi, "Opening the Closed World of *Shōjo Manga*," 125.

10. Ibid., 128.

11. Ibid., 122–29.

12. See, for instance, the July 1981 special issue "*Shōjo* manga" in *Yuriika* (Eureka) 13, no. 9, which includes numerous articles addressing literary aspects of works from this period. *Yuriika* is a highbrow literary journal.

13. See, e.g., Tomoko Aoyama, "Transgendering *Shōjo Shōsetsu*: Girls' Inter-text/sex-uality," in *Genders, Transgenders, and Sexualities in Japan*, ed. Mark McLelland and Romit Dasgupta (London: Routledge, 2005).

14. E.g., Ikeda Michiko, "Danshokuron: Shisutaa bōi no miryoku" [On male homosexuality: The charms of sister boys], *Fujin kōron* 41, no. 11 (November 1957).

15. Mori Mari, *Koibitotachi no mori* [A lovers' forest] (Tokyo: Shinchōsha, 1961). On the connections between Mori Mari and male–male erotic and romantic relations in *shōjo* manga, see, e.g., Akiko Mizoguchi, "Male–Male Romance by and for Women in Japan: A History and the Subgenres of *Yaoi* Fictions," *U.S.–Japan Women's Journal* 25 (2003); and on the narrative connections between them, see Keith Vincent, "A Japanese Electra and Her Queer Progeny," *Mechademia* 2 (2007).

16. Mizuno Hideko, *Faiyaa!* [Fire!], 4 vols. (1969–1971; Tokyo: Asahi panorama, 1973). On the role of *Fire!* in the introduction of social problems in the U.S. to *shōjo* manga readers, see Kinko Ito, *A Sociology of Japanese Ladies' Comics: Images of the Life, Loves, and Sexual Fantasies of Adult Japanese Women* (Lewiston, NY: Edwin Mellen Press, 2010), 62–63. See also Yonezawa, *Sengo shōjo manga shi,* 198.

17. On the groundbreaking nature of having a male protagonist in *shōjo* manga, see Ishida Minori, *Hisoyaka na kyōiku: "Yaoi/bōizu rabu" zenshi* [A secret education: The prehistory of yaoi/boys love] (Kyoto: Rakuhoku shuppan, 2008), 57n30.

18. Minegishi Hiromi, "Jūjiro" [Crossroad], *Fanii* 1, no. 2 (June 1969).

19. In Takemiya Keiko's *Kaze to ki no uta* [The song of the wind and the trees], 10 vols. (1976–1984; Tokyo: Hakusensha bunko, 1995), Gilbert does have sexual relations with adult men, but the primary narrative is driven by his romantic relationship with his fellow student and roommate, Serge.

20. Ishida, *Hisoyaka na kyōiku,* 142–43.

21. The scholarship and criticism making this case, often supported by statements by the artists themselves, is extensive. In addition to the discussion offered by Fujimoto and by Nagaike and Aoyama in this volume, representative criticism in Japanese can be found in Fujimoto, *Watashi no ibasho,* particularly in the section, "Onna no ryōsei guyū, otoko no han'in'yō" [Androgynous females and hermaphroditic males], 130–76.

22. See James Welker, "Drawing Out Lesbians: Blurred Representations of Lesbian Desire in *Shōjo* Manga," in *Lesbian Voices: Canada and the World; Theory, Literature, Cinema,* ed. Subhash Chandra (New Delhi: Allied Publishers, 2006).

23. Takemiya Keiko, "Sanrūmu nite" [In the sunroom], in her *Sanrūmu nite* (1970; Tokyo: San komikkusu, 1976).

24. Hagio Moto, "Jūichigatsu no gimunajiumu" [November gymnasium], in her *Jūichigatsu no gimunajiumu* (1971; Tokyo: Shōgakukan bunko, 1995).

25. Hagio Moto, *Tōma no shinzō* [*The Heart of Thomas*] (1974; Tokyo: Shōgakukan bunko, 1995); Takemiya, *Kaze to ki no uta.*

26. Takemiya Keiko, *Takemiya Keiko no manga kyōshitsu* [Takemiya Keiko's manga classroom] (Tokyo: Chikuma shobō, 2001), 244; *Josei sebun,* "Ima sugoi ninki no shōjo komikku sakka no karei-naru shi seikatsu" [The splendid private lives of now wildly popular *shōjo* manga authors], December 3, 1975, 199; Masuyama Norie and Sano Megumi, "Kyabetsu batake no kakumeiteki shōjo mangakatachi" [Revolutionary *shōjo* manga artists in a cabbage patch], in Bessatsu Takarajima, no. 288, *70-nendai manga daihyakka* (Tokyo: Takarajimasha, 1996); Hagio Moto, "The Moto Hagio Interview," by Matt Thorn, *Comics Journal,* no. 269 (July 2005): 160.

27. Masuyama and Sano, "Kyabetsu batake," 169. Among those taking part were Sasaya Nanae (1950–), Yamada Mineko (1949–), and Yamagishi Ryōko (1948–), the last of whom produced a number of male–male romances, albeit her protagonists were often older than in typical *shōnen'ai* narratives. See ibid., 166; Hagio, "The Moto Hagio Interview," 160–61.

28. Ishida, *Hisoyaka na kyōiku*, 52.

29. Ibid., 298.

30. Ibid., 70–71, 76.

31. Ibid., 72. See also Takemiya, *Takemiya Keiko no manga kyōshitsu*, 217.

32. Inagaki Taruho, *Shōnen'ai no bigaku* [Aesthetics of boy loving] (Tokyo: Tokuma shoten, 1968). I translate *"shōnen'ai"* in this title as "boy loving" rather than "boys love" to reflect that the content is more closely connected to pederasty than is the case for the *shōjo* manga genre.

33. See Ishida, *Hisoyaka na kyōiku*, 88; and Masuyama Norie, *"Kaze to ki no uta* no tanjō" [The birth of *The Song of the Wind and the Trees*], *JUNE*, no. 36 (September 1987): 55. While *The Song of the Wind and the Trees* was not initially serialized until 1976, Takemiya had first conceived of the narrative and began to pen drawings seven years earlier, before *In the Sunroom* was published. See Masuyama, *"Kaze to ki no uta* no tanjō," 55.

34. Quoted in Ishida, *Hisoyaka na kyōiku*, 88.

35. Hagio, "The Moto Hagio Interview," 161, 163; *Les amitiés particulières*, dir. Jean Delannoy (France: Paris: Progéfi, and LUX C.C.F., 1964).

36. Roger Peyrefitte, *Les amitiés particulières: Roman* (Marseille: Jean Vigneau, 1943).

37. *Death in Venice*, motion picture, dir. Luchino Visconti (Italy: Alfa Cinematografica, 1971).

38. I base this claim on having perused hundreds of issues of *Bessatsu shōjo komikku*, *Shōjo komikku*, *Petit Flower (Puchi furawaa)*, and other *shōjo* manga magazines published in the 1970s and 1980s.

39. Kihara Toshie, *Mari to Shingo* [Mari and Shingo], 13 vols. (1977–1984; Tokyo: Hana to yume komikkusu, 1979–1984); Yamagishi Ryōko, *Hi izuru tokoro no tenshi* [Emperor of the land of the rising sun], 11 vols. (1980–1984; Tokyo: Hana to yume komikkusu, 1980–1984).

40. Yoshida Akimi, *Banana Fish*, 19 vols. (1985–1994; Tokyo: Furawaa komikkusu, 1987–1994); Akisato Wakuni, *Tomoi* (1986; Tokyo: Shōgakukan bunko, 1996).

41. For instance, Fujimoto includes *Banana Fish* and *Tomoi* in the *shōnen'ai* lineage in her important overview of gender-bending *shōjo* manga. See Fujimoto, *Watashi no ibasho*, 146, 148–49; cf. Fujimoto in this volume.

42. Ishida, *Hisoyaka na kyōiku*, 85–92, 296. As the primary term used within Taruho's *Shōnen'ai no bigaku* was *"shōnen'ai"* itself, perhaps *"kunaaben riibe"* was borrowed from the cover, which is decorated prominently with the title in German—*"Ästhetik der Knabenliebe."*

43. While some of the dozens of avid readers of the *shōnen'ai* genre in the 1970s and 1980s with whom I have spoken still use the term, either of their own volition or at my prompting, it is the pederastic meaning that has lingered in the present day. This is evident, for instance, in the lengthy Japanese Wikipedia entry, only a small section of which describes *shōnen'ai* in the context of *shōjo* manga: Wikipedia, s.v. "Shōnen'ai," last modified July 28, 2013, http://ja.wikipedia.org/wiki/少年愛.

44. Hagio Moto, *Pō no ichizoku* [The Poe clan] (1972–1976), 3 vols. (Tokyo: Shōgakukan bunko, 1998).

45. See Kurihara Chiyo, "Tanbi shōsetsu to wa nani ka" [What is *tanbi* fiction?], in *Tanbi shōsetsu, gei bungaku bukkugaido* [Guidebook to aesthete fiction and gay literature], ed. Kakinuma Eiko and Kurihara Chiyo (Tokyo: Byakuya shobō, 1993), 325.

46. See, e.g., Ishida, *Hisoyaka na kyōiku*, 206–11, 319.

47. The term is sometimes also used as a label for andro-centric heterosexual pornography to indicate eroticism even as it purports to paint the material as refined.

48. Kurihara, "Tanbi shōsetsu to wa nani ka" (What is *tanbi* fiction?), 325ff.

49. Komikku maaketto junbikai, ed., *Komikku maaketto 30's fairu* [The Comic Market files—30 years] (Tokyo: Komiketto, 2005), 32.

50. The catalogue for Comic Market 84, held August 10–12, 2013 is nearly 1,400 pages long. According to the report it provides on Comic Market 83, held December 29–31, 2010, the December event had 35,000 registered circles—who were among 51,000 who applied. 170,000 to 210,000 "participants" attended *each* of the three days. See *Komikku Maaketto 84 katarogu* (2013), 1197. Attendance has been relatively stable over the past few years. For attendance figures as well as details on participating circles for each Comic Market event from 1975 to 2005, see Komikku Maaketto Junbikai, *Komikku Maaketto 30's fairu*, passim. The most up-to-date information can be found in current catalogues and in Komiketto, "Komikku Maaketto nenpyō" [Comic Market timeline], accessed September 18, 2012, http://www.comiket.co.jp/archives/Chronology.html.

51. Komikku maaketto junbikai, *Komikku maaketto 30's fairu*, 355.

52. Yonezawa Yoshihiro, "Manga/anime no kaihōku, Komike tte nani?" [What's Komike, that space of liberation for manga/anime?], interview, in Bessatsu Takarajima, no. 358, *Watashi o Komike ni tsuretette!: Kyōdai komikku dōjinshi maaketto no subete* (Tokyo: Takarajimasha, 1998), 15–16; Ichikawa Kōichi, "Comiket," interview by Patrick W. Galbraith, in Patrick W. Galbraith, *The Otaku Encyclopedia: An Insider's Guide to the Subculture of Cool Japan* (Tokyo: Kodansha International, 2009), 46; Yonezawa Yoshihiro, "Manga to dōjinshi no sasayaka no kyōen: Komiketto no ataeta eikyō" [A small feast of manga and *dōjinshi*: The influence of Komiketto], in Bessatsu Takarajima, no. 358, *Watashi o komike ni tsuretette!*, 42. Komikku maaketto junbikai, *Komikku maaketto 30's fairu*, 354–55.

53. The tagline "*manga fanjin fea*" (manga fanzine fair) appeared on the posters for the first four events, the last of which was held at the end of 1976. It was replaced in 1977 by "*dōjinshi sokubaikai*" or "*dōjinshi* spot sale event." See Shimotsuki Takanaka, *Komikku maaketto sōseiki* [The genesis of Comic Market] (Tokyo: Asahi shinbun shuppan, 2008), 11–12; and the posters reproduced in Komikku maaketto junbikai, *Komikku maaketto 30's fairu*, 16, 32. The term "*dōjinshi*" was not new in this sphere, however. It was already being used in Tezuka's magazine *COM* in the late 1960s to refer to non-commercial publications linked to manga and anime and related media. The early use by Comic Market organizers of "*fanjin*," a word then associated with science fiction fandom, illustrates the connection between the Comic Market and other manga- and anime-related events in the 1970s with the science fiction conventions of the 1960s that can be seen as forebears.

54. On the survey taken at the first Comic Market, see Shimotsuki, *Komikku maaketto sōseiki*, 12. While the numbers have fluctuated over the years, until quite recently women have generally constituted the majority of both circle and regular participants and a minority of staff participants. A survey conducted at the August 2010 event, the most recent for which data is available, however, found that nearly 65 percent of regular participants were male, a

figure the organizers found "comparatively high." See Komikku maaketto junbikai kontentsu riisaachi tiimu, "Chōsa hōkoku" [Survey report], December 2011, p.4 http://www.comiket .co.jp/info-a/C81/C81Ctlg35AnqReprot.pdf; Komikku maaketto junbikai, "Komikku maaketto to wa nani ka?" [What is the Comic Market?], February 2008, 21, http://www.comiket .co.jp/info-a/WhatIsJpno80225.pdf.

55. Shimotsuki describes his own encounter with Hagio's work, as well as his involvement in the creation of an anime version of *November Gymnasium* in his *Komikku Maaketto sōseiki*, 21–22, 45–46, 64–68, 76–83, 96–99.

56. Ibid., 11. Advertising in *shōnen* manga magazines began with the April 1977 event. See ibid., 44.

57. Ibid., 20–21, 77ff.

58. Itō Gō, *Manga wa kawaru: "Manga gatari" kara "manga ron" e* [Manga changes: From "manga narrative" to "manga discourse"] (Tokyo: Seidosha, 2007), 215; Yonezawa, "Manga to dōjinshi," 41.

59. Abnorm, *Island* (Japan: Self-published, ca. 1979).

60. "D. Boui kisekae o-asobi" [Fun dressing up D. Bowie], in ibid., 35–36; and Layla, illustration of Jimmy Page and Robert Plant, dated November 8, 1977, in ibid., 23.

61. By 1982, "*yaoi*" could be found on the cover of the manga culture magazine *Manga no techō* [Manga handbook], no. 8 (summer 1982), to promote content on "YAOI *anime*" (with "*yaoi*" in capital Roman letters and "anime" in the phonetic *katakana* script), suggesting its use had begun to move outside the circles producing these *dōjinshi*.

62. *RAPPORI* is discussed in Hatsu Akiko, "Yaoi no moto wa 'share' deshita: Hatsu kōkai, yaoi no tanjō" [Yaoi started as a 'joke': Public for the first time, the birth of *yaoi*], *JUNE*, no. 73 (November 1993). Hatsu confirmed the appropriate transliteration of the group's name into English as "Lovely"—usually transliterated into Japanese "*raburii*" rather than "*ravuri*" (Hatsu Akiko, personal correspondence, November 19, 2012).

63. Ravuri, *RAPPORI: Yaoi tokushū gō* [RAPPORI: Special *yaoi* issue] (Japan: RAPPORI henshū jimukyoku, 1979). I write "RAPPORI" in all capital letters at the request of Hatsu, who is listed as the primary editor of *RAPPORI: Yaoi tokushū gō*. Hatsu notes that "RAPPORI" is a word she and some friends made up and that it has no particular meaning (Hatsu, personal correspondence).

64. On the various interpretations of the acronym *yaoi*, see Nishimura Mari, *Aniparo to yaoi* [Aniparo and *yaoi*] (Tokyo: Ōta shuppan, 2002), 12n3.

65. Nishimura, *Aniparo to yaoi*, 11; Itō, *Manga wa kawaru*, 222–23.

66. Misaki Naoto, "2007-nen no josei-kei parodi dōjinshi no dōkō" [Trends in femaleproduced parody *dōjinshi* in 2007], *Yuriika* 38, no. 16 (December 2007): 176.

67. Takahashi Yōichi, *Kyaputen Tsubasa* [Captain Tsubasa], 37 vols. (1981–1988; Tokyo: Shūeisha, 1982–1989).

68. Nishimura writes that after first becoming noticeable in 1984, parodies of the Captain Tsubasa series constituted half of the total sales of *dōjinshi* at the summer 1986 Comic Market. See Nishimura, *Aniparo to yaoi*, 32–33. The Tsubasa genre existed as an official "genre code" used by Comic Market organizers from at least 1987 through the end of the 1990s. See Komikku Maaketto Junbikai, *Komikku Maaketto 30's fairu*, 120ff, 384–88.

69. See Misaki, "2007-nen no josei-kei parodi dōjinshi," 176. Kurumada Masami, *Seinto Seiya* [Saint Seiya], 28 vols. (Tokyo: Shūeisha, 1986–1991); Inoue Takehiko, *Slam Dunk*, 31 vols. (Tokyo, Shūeisha, 1991–1996); Oda Ei'ichirō, *One Piece*, 71 vols., ongoing (Tokyo: Shūeisha,

1997–); Nishimoto Masashi, *Naruto*, 66 vols., ongoing (Tokyo: Shūeisha, 2000–); Konomi Takeshi, *Tenisu no ōjisama* [Prince of tennis], 42 vols. (Tokyo: Shūeisha, 2000–2008).

70. Nishimura, *Aniparo to yaoi*, 32.

71. Ibid., 36.

72. Yonezawa Yoshihiro, *Sengo ero manga shi* [A history of postwar erotic manga] (Tokyo: Seirin kōgeisha, 2010), 131.

73. The ongoing narrative is available at http://www.geocities.jp/himaruya/hetaria/.

74. Nishimura, *Aniparo to yaoi*, 22–23, 35–36.

75. Ibid., 32–33, 40.

76. E.g., the Tsubasa and Seiya anthologies *Tsubasa hyakkaten* [Tsubasa department store] *Bessatsu komikku bokkusu*, vol. 1 (Tokyo: Fyūjon purodakuto, 1987); and *Seiya ni muchū!* [Mad for Seiya], *Bessatsu komikku bokkusu* 4 (Tokyo: Fyūjon Purodakuto, 1987).

77. Sagawa Toshihiko, "Bungaku to goraku no aida o ittari, kitari" [Going back and forth between literature and amusement], interview by Ishida Minori, in Ishida, *Hisoyaka na kyōiku*, 327.

78. The original *JUNE* ceased publication in 1996. However, the same publisher has subsequently produced various magazines incorporating the *JUNE* name almost continuously since then, including, since 1998 *Komikku JUNE* (Comic *JUNE*). Gender scholar Mori Naoko asserts, however, that, given its distinct editorial focus, *Komikku JUNE* is a "completely different magazine" from the original. See Mori Naoko, *Onna wa poruno o yomu: Josei no seiyoku to feminizumu* [Reading women's porn: Female sexual desire and feminism] (Tokyo: Seikyūsha, 2010), 89n14.

79. Sagawa, "Bungaku to goraku."

80. Ibid., 328.

81. *JUNE* was called *Comic Jun* for the first two issues, with both new and old versions spelled out in capital English/Roman letters on the cover. It was renamed to settle a copyright issue over the name "Jun," which was the name of a clothing company. As the cover for the third issue was already laid out, the producers decided it was simplest just to add an "e" to the name. See *JUNE*, "Editors' Rest Room," no. 4 (April 1979): 180. The name "*JUNE*" is homophonous, and spelled the same in *katakana* script, as the Japanese pronunciation of the surname of infamously homosexual French author Jean Genet. While this is evidently a mere coincidence, links between the writer's name and the magazine name have been made frequently enough to establish an association.

82. Ishida, *Hisoyaka na kyōiku*, 204.

83. The information on the magazine's readership comes from ibid., 222.

84. On the role of *Out* in this sphere, see Nishimura, *Aniparo to yaoi*, 20.

85. See James Welker, "Lilies of the Margin: Beautiful Boys and Queer Female Identities in Japan," in *AsiaPacifiQueer: Rethinking Genders and Sexualities*, ed. Fran Martin, et al. (Urbana: University of Illinois Press, 2008) 50, 61n25.

86. Nanbara Shirō, interview with author, June 2005. In terms of content, *Gekkō* largely lost relevance to this readership by the late 1980s, though it lingered on under different titles until 2006.

87. For details on *Allan's* content and an analysis of the personal ads in "Lily Communications," see Welker, "Lilies of the Margin." For a discussion of female same-sex desire in the context of *shōnen'ai* fandom more generally, see Welker, "Flower Tribes."

88. Hagio, "The Moto Hagio Interview," 161.

89. See Ishida Hitoshi, "Sūji de miru *JUNE* to *Sabu*" [*JUNE* and *Sabu* by the numbers], *Yuriika* 44, no. 15 (December 2012): 170.

90. Comic Market organizers have used "*sōsaku JUNE*" (original *JUNE*) as a genre code to categorize *dōjinshi*, alongside *shōjo*, *shōnen*, and other categories from at least 1987. Only in 2012 did the genre code change to "original *JUNE/BL*." See Komikku maaketto junbikai, *Komikku maaketto 30's fairu*, 384–89, and the lists of genre codes available for recent events in Komiketto, "Komikku maaketto nenpyō" [Comic Market timeline], accessed 18 September 2012, http://www.comiket.co.jp/archives/Chronology.html.

J.Garden first began around 1996 and continues to hold regular spot sales of "original *JUNE*" *dōjinshi*. See Yamamoto Fumiko and BL sapōtaazu, *Yappari, bōizu rabu ga suki: Kanzen BL komikku gaido* [Indeed, we do love BL: A complete guide to BL comics] (Tokyo: Ōta shuppan, 2005), 17; and the event's official website: http://www.jgarden.jp.

91. See *Aran*, "Ninki dōjinshi purezento" [Giveaway of popular *dōjinshi*], October 1980.

92. Yamamoto Fumiko and BL sapōtaazu, *Yappari, bōizu rabu ga suki*, 16.

93. Ibid.

94. The titles of these magazines are a mix of English, Japanese, and other languages, sometimes printed in Roman letters, sometimes in Japanese script. I parenthetically include English translations or Japanese pronunciations of foreign words.

95. Ibid., 15; see also the list of magazines in ibid., 16–17. Yamamoto Fumiko and BL sapōtaazu make a point of noting that this figure does not include BL fiction magazines (ibid., 15). I base my own list above on Yamamoto Fumiko and BL sapōtaazu, as well as on *Pafu*, "Boy's Love Magazine kanzen kōryaku manyuaru" [A complete mastery manual on boy's love magazines], no. 217 (August 1994); the library catalogues of the National Diet Library, and the Yonezawa Yoshihiro Memorial Library of Manga and Subculture; and my own collection of commercial magazines.

96. Matoh Sanami, *Fake*, 7 vols. (Tokyo: Biburosu, 1994–2000).

97. Nishimura dates the appearance of BL sections in bookstores to around 1993. See her *Aniparo to yaoi*, 44.

98. For more on the history of Otome Road, see Patrick W. Galbraith, *Otaku Spaces*, with photographs by Androniki Christodoulou (Seattle: Chin Music Press, 2012), 203–204.

99. See *b-Boy*, "Suki na mono wa suki!!" 3 (1992): 75–77, 79.

100. *Pafu*, "Boy's Love Magazine."

101. Yamamoto and BL sapōtaazu, *Yappari, bōizu rabu ga suki*, 14. This assertion is supported by the compiler(s) of the website *BLlogia junbi shitsu* [BLlogia preparation room] (http://bllogia.files.wordpress.com/), which features a frequently updated and detailed timeline on the history BL. While I have referred back to original materials to confirm specific facts, the *BLlogia* timeline has been quite valuable in helping me map the history of the usage of the term "boys love" in the above paragraphs.

102. *Pafu*, "Boy's Love Magazine," 52. *JUNE*, *Shōsetsu JUNE*, and *Roman JUNE* are also included in beginning of this section, but framed as forebears "without which there would be nothing to talk about" (ibid., 53). The editor of *Image* also stated that she was aiming at something "somewhat different" (*hitoaji chigau*) with the new publication. See *Imaaju*, "Editor's," no. 1 (December 1991): 214.

103. For the descriptions of these magazines, see *Pafu*, "Boy's Love Magazine," 57, 59.

104. For an example of such a distinction between *yaoi* and boys love, see Patrick W. Galbraith, "*Fujoshi*: Fantasy Play and Transgressive Intimacy among 'Rotten Girls' in

Contemporary Japan," *Signs* 37, no. 1 (2011): 212, 218. Galbraith has shared with me (personal correspondence, November 16, 2012) that among his informants in the *dōjinshi* sphere, any semantic distinction between "*yaoi*" and "BL" was far less significant than the distinction between original (*sōsaku*), derivative (*niji sōsaku*), or even twice derivative (*sanji sōsaku*).

105. Yano Research Institute (Yano keizai kenkyūsho), "'Otaku shijō' ni kan suru chōsa kekka 2011: 'Otaku jinkō' no zōka = 'raito na otaku' no zōka to tomo ni shijō kibo wa kakudai" [2011 survey results on the "*otaku* market": Increase in the "*otaku* population" = increase in the number of "light *otaku*" alongside expansion of the scale of the market], press release, October 26, 2011, 3, http://www.yano.co.jp/press/pdf/863.pdf.

106. Dating to the 1960s, "slash fiction" refers primarily to fan-created homoerotic narratives created by pairing characters like Captain Kirk and Spock of the American TV series *Star Trek.* The definitive study on slash fiction is Henry Jenkins, *Textual Poachers: Television Fans and Participatory Culture* (New York: Routledge, 1992).

107. For more on the commercial BL market in the U.S., see Dru Pagliasotti, "GloBLisation and Hybridisation: Publishers' Strategies for Bringing Boys' Love to the United States," *Intersections: Gender and Sexuality in Asia and the Pacific* 20 (2009), http://intersections.anu.edu.au/issue20/pagliassotti.htm.

108. Recent scholarship on this global fandom can be found in Kazumi Nagaike and Katsuhiko Suganuma, eds., "Transnational Boys' Love Fan Studies," special issue, *Transformative Works and Cultures* 12 (2013), http://journal.transformativeworks.org/index .php/twc/issue/view/14 .

THE EVOLUTION OF BL AS "PLAYING WITH GENDER"

Viewing the Genesis and Development of BL from a
Contemporary Perspective

FUJIMOTO YUKARI

TRANSLATED BY JOANNE QUIMBY

Introduction

It was about twenty years ago that I wrote the critical essay "Transgender: Female Hermaphrodites and Male Androgynes," in which I traced the genealogy of gender-bending in *shōjo* manga.[1] The article takes up the subversive use of "girls dressed as boys," "boys dressed as girls," "*shōnen'ai*" (boys love), "lesbians," and "polymorphous perversity" in *shōjo* manga, and goes on to compare the structure of such representation with what appeared in manga for boys and young men. The essay is included in my 1998 book *Where Do I Belong? The Shape of the Heart Reflected in Shōjo Manga* (*Watashi no ibasho wa doko ni aru no? Shōjo manga ga utsusu kokoro no katachi*).[2]

In the intervening twenty years, *yaoi* and "boys love" (*bōizu rabu*), both of which originally developed from *shōnen'ai*, have become increasingly established as genres in their own right and have been gradually taken up as a subject of study by more and more students and researchers. As the number of researchers examining *yaoi* and boys love has grown, so too has the number of references to the portions of my early essay focused on *shōnen'ai*. However, when I encounter such references to my work in Japan, I frequently find myself thinking: "What? Why are they classifying my writing that way?" Or: "There seems to be some kind of misunderstanding." Or: "I'm sure I didn't say anything like that." As I discuss below, while this might be due in part to obvious misunderstandings or bias on the part of authors quoting me, more than anything it is likely due to the fact that in the twenty years that have passed since I first wrote the piece, both the situation surrounding the topic and my own way of thinking about the topic have changed. Furthermore, despite their having emerged at different times in different media and possessing different generic qualities, from the very beginning the four distinct genres of "*shōnen'ai*," "*yaoi*," "BL (boys love)," and "*JUNE*" (explained below) have all been classed together as a single genre depicting "male–male romance." That the four genres have come to be theorized without clearly distinguishing between them has resulted in some confusion and misunderstanding, an issue also addressed by Kazuko Suzuki in this volume.

This chapter demonstrates how *yaoi* and BL developed from *shōnen'ai* and the magazine *JUNE* as an entertaining space in which women can "play with gender," and the constraints of oppressive female gender roles can be removed. To question what motivated the emergence of male–male romance in *shōnen'ai* and *JUNE* or how this plot device directed at women came about is completely different from asking what became possible once male–male romance was established as a device and further developed and conventionalized within the "*yaoi*" or "boys love" genres in terms of *seme–uke* (that is, top–bottom, or dominant–passive) couplings. I believe, therefore, that clearly distinguishing between these four genres—that is, *shōnen'ai*, *JUNE*, *yaoi*, and BL—will be quite useful in characterizing contemporary BL practices.

Two Perspectives: Why Did a Misunderstanding Occur?

The four distinct genres referred to above emerged at different times, in different media, and possess different generic qualities, as James Welker has outlined elsewhere in this volume. *Shōnen'ai* works were published in general *shōjo manga* in the 1970s and early 1980s, while *JUNE*, published from 1978 until 1996, was a commercial magazine specializing in male–male romance.[3] By the middle of the 1980s, the use of the term "*yaoi*" had become established to refer to these narratives both in amateur *dōjinshi* (coterie magazines) that parodied existing *shōnen* manga and *anime*, as well as in original *dōjinshi* depicting male–male romance. Finally, "boys love" (*bōizu rabu*), or BL, generally refers to commercially produced works after around 1992 of original (that is, not parodic) prose fiction and manga. Works dealing with gender necessarily reflect the gender situation of the time, and the author's age (the era in which the author was born) also surely impacts the treatment of gender in her works. Furthermore, the expression of ideas in works appearing in commercial manga magazines and works that, from the beginning, are aimed at an audience of one's peers, also naturally differ.

I will begin my argument with an excerpt from my article, "Transgender: Female Hermaphrodites and Male Androgynes." The passage given below is the main portion of the article in which I discuss *shōnen'ai*.

> ... as I noted ... in the section on cross-dressing young women, for girls sex is first and foremost about "fear," and not desire. Even supposing that there were in a girl some mechanism leading toward "desire," that impulse would be controlled by social sanctions, such as the idea that it is "shameless." As a result there certainly is "a big difference between a girl and a woman," and this is again overshadowed by the fear of sexual maturity. . . . There is no question that this group of *shōnen-ai* works was born out of the "hatred of females" that is shared by all women. However, when these expressions of female-hating come out of the mouths of these fictional beautiful boys, readers hear a dissonant note, and have their attention drawn thereby to the position that women are forced to occupy in society, whether they like it or not. That is, the hatred of females is turned around, the mechanisms by which women cannot help falling into a state of self-hatred are exposed, and a bright light is cast on women's situation. . . .
>
> Moreover, by taking the form of shōnen-ai, shōjo manga were able to enter the domain of "sexuality," which had formerly been taboo. . . . By applying this characteristic to a male body, and by also setting the narrative on a stage completely separated from reality, [highly influential artist] Takemiya [Keiko] has succeeded in depicting this theme in a purified form and in a way that protects the reader from its raw pain. To borrow the words of Ueno Chizuko, male homosexual love "is a safety device that girls use to manage the dangerous weapon of sexuality by separating themselves from their own bodies; it provides wings for girls to fly."
>
> This will become even clearer if we look at the "yaoi" subgenre. . . . These yaoi narratives overflow with sex to an unprecedented degree. . . . Shōnen-ai has made it possible for young women to "play with sex." Here in yaoi, the bitter pain associated with the monuments of shōnen-ai manga has already disappeared, and young women happily squeal, "Oooh, how obscene," while indulging themselves in "dangerous" and "forbidden" liaisons between men.
> . . .
>
> By vicariously taking the form of young male lovers, young women no longer have to see themselves as the only ones suffering pain, even if rape or SM is being portrayed. . . . But the most important thing is that through this means women are freed from the position of always being the one "done to,"

and are able to take on the viewpoint of the "doer," and also the viewpoint of the "looker." This is an extremely significant transformation. For now, *yaoi* has not moved beyond the level of these safe simulations of extreme male–female relations, but it is possible that these depictions of sadomasochistic *shōnen-ai* will cause the emergence of real-life women who assault men.[4]

In the section subsequent to the paragraphs excerpted above, I suggest that a search for "ultimate love" and the desire to pursue a pure relationship provide the background for the emergence of such works. Leaving that argument aside for the time being, here I would like to emphasize two points I made in this article:

1. *Shōnen'ai* first emerged as a mechanism offering an escape from the social realities of gender suppression and the avoidance of sex(uality);
2. Once it had emerged, however, the same mechanism made it possible for girls to "play with sex(uality)" (*sei o asobu*) and opened up possibilities for them to shift their own point of view from passive to active engagement.

The main point I would like to emphasize regarding these two assertions is that the first corresponds to the structure of *shōnen'ai*, while the second corresponds to the development of *yaoi*. Again and again, it has only been my first point above that receives attention, and in extreme cases my argument has been classified together with the so-called "simulation theory" (*shimyureeshon setsu*), which posits that for girls who have yet to experience sex, *shōnen'ai* is nothing more than a dress rehearsal that safely simulates sex before the actual experience. However, I have never offered such an argument. When I wrote that previous article twenty years ago, it was already known even then that some women become interested in *yaoi* after they have married and have children. For this reason, I have never once said (and would never say) that *shōnen'ai* is a safe simulation of physical sexual experience.

To be clear, in the section dealing with my second assertion above, I wrote: "For now, *yaoi* has not moved beyond the level of these safe simulations of extreme male–female relations." In this case, by "extreme male–female relations" I was not referring to ordinary sexual relations but was instead referring to relations involving things such as rape, incest, or hardcore SM that would cause a person to hesitate before becoming physically involved. Use of the word "simulation" seems to have given rise to a misunderstanding. Then, an article published in 1995 classified my work as "simulation theory," which served to reproduce the misunderstanding.[5]

However, it certainly cannot be said that there was no basis for the mis-understanding. I say this because I recall that at the time I wrote that article I was relatively more concerned with the emergence of *shōnen'ai* as an escape from the social realities of gender suppression and the avoidance of sex(uality). At the same time, of course, the tendency toward "playing with sex(uality)" in *yaoi dōjinshi* had also become clear, but I did not have the impression at that time that any impressive, high-caliber *yaoi dōjinshi* had been produced.

More specifically, this was my impression after reading dozens of *yaoi* anthologies published by Comic Box focused on the 1980s and 1990s manga and anime series including *Captain Tsubasa* (*Kyaputen Tsubasa*), *Yoroiden Samurai Troopers* (*Yoroiden samurai torūpaa*), *Legend of Heavenly Sphere Shurato* (*Tenkū senki Shurato*), and *Saint Seiya* (*Seinto Seiya*).[6] Of course, there were some interesting works among these, and some noteworthy authors, but I did not yet think that within this genre a significant number of particularly interesting works would start to appear one after another.[7]

Looking back now, I can appreciate that Kōga Yun's works were exceedingly innovative at that time.[8] However, at the point I learned that she had already debuted in a commercial magazine, I still had not clearly perceived the level of her work. Furthermore, at that time many *yaoi* works still simply inscribed the patterns of dramatic, extreme relationships between men and women onto relationships between men. The anthologies I read presented "selected works" of *yaoi dōjinshi*; as such—as works written by amateurs—most of them tended to repeat the same patterns, which I found to be boring. The works had potential, but their efforts had not yet been perfected; that was my impression at the time. In reality, however, that *yaoi* scene went on to produce many outstanding works and artists, and was ultimately able to significantly shift perspectives and make it possible for girls to "play with sex(uality)."[9] Both *yaoi* and BL, the commercial development of *yaoi*, began to thrive in a way I was not able to foresee at the time.

"Girls Dressed as Boys" and "Boys Dressed as Girls"

In addition to the fact that the development of my second assertion above was still unknown to me, there is another reason why, at that time, I was focused on the motif of "fear of sex(uality)" (*sei e no osore*) and posited that such fear amounted to a "fear of maturity" (*seijuku e no osore*), tantamount to misogyny. The reason for my supposition is that when I began to wonder about taking up the figure of the *shōnen* (boy) rather than the *shōjo* (girl), I realized that it would be necessary to trace the connections back to earlier images of "girls dressed as boys" (*dansō no shōjo*). In other words, I asked why, in standard *shōjo* manga, do girls pose as boys?

In almost all cases, the "girls dressed as boys" in *shōjo* manga do so in order to achieve a social status or take on a social role that would be denied to them as women. In other words, it can be said that the basis for taking on male appearance stems from gender inequality, and that such characters are rather strongly inscribed with an opposition to conventional gender roles. In most cases, however, the heroine abandons her male disguise when she falls in love. That is, such characters do not want to return to being girls in society, but do want to be seen as girls by their love interests. Conversely, it can be said that they want to appear as girls in front of their love interests, but otherwise prefer to remain disguised as men. Another way of saying this would be that the *shōjo* affirms and accepts her own femininity only when she falls in love. In this regard, the *shōjo* considers her male appearance to be a symbol of her denial of sexuality and her reluctance to positively accept her · female gender.

In any case, the figure of the boy (*shōnen*) represents the *shōjo*'s internal refusal of her own female gender. By projecting sexual attributes onto this figure of the boy, which is assumed to be essentially non-sexual, the *shōjo* becomes sexually liberated. At the time I thought: Of course! What an obvious solution. Now, however, I think that I probably should have given more serious thought to the significance of projecting sexual attributes onto the ostensibly non-sexual figure of the boy—that is, the significance of not wanting to have a romantic relationship as a female.

In those days, I thought that it would be a good idea to think about the connections between *shōjo* manga featuring male protagonists in love with other males (otherwise known as "*shōnen'ai*") and authors' motivations to create works with a "girls dressed as boys" motif. Since a "fear of sex(uality)" and a sense of taboo surrounding sex still remained quite strong in Japanese society in general from the 1970s until the late 1980s, as well as in *shōjo* manga as a whole, my writing at that time might have been influenced by this socio-gender situation. While it may sound a bit contradictory, I still believe, somehow, that specific works dealing with serious romantic motifs belong to the genealogy of "girls dressed as boys" in terms of demonstrating an inherent drive to escape from being forced to fit into a defined "female gender."

On the other hand, there is also a genealogy of works featuring "boys dressed as girls" to consider, pioneered by such 1970s works as Kishi Yūko's *Tamasaburō's Love Capriccio* (*Tamasaburō koi no kyōsōkyoku*) and Naka To-moko's *The Beautiful Flower Princess* (*Hana no bijo hime*).[10] Actually, in a

1991 article I suggested that the transition from an earnest and serious style of depicting beautiful homosexuals in *shōnen'ai* toward a type of parody and playfulness was strongly influenced by earlier works featuring "beautiful boys dressed as girls" (*josō suru bishōnen*).[11] At that time it was no more than a hunch, but as I have since studied the development of *yaoi* and BL, and done some fan-based field research, I have become more and more certain that my second point above (regarding the development of *yaoi* and BL) should be considered in terms of the genealogy of "boys dressed as girls."

To summarize, in thinking about the emergence of *shōnen'ai* as detailed in my first point above, the serious works considered to be *shōnen'ai* masterpieces usually come to mind (for example, Takemiya Keiko's *The Song of the Wind and the Trees* [*Kaze to ki no uta*] and Yamagishi Ryōko's *Emperor of the Land of the Rising Sun* [*Hi izuru tokoro no tenshi*]), and the motives behind the creation of such works have frequently been explained (including by myself) in terms of resistance to gender suppression, the desire for equality in relationships, and/or the search for the ultimate couple.[12] These earnest motives were also deeply, though imperfectly, related to the "girls dressed as boys" motif. (Of course, the genre of *shōnen'ai* emerged precisely because there are subjects that cannot be adequately addressed by "girls dressed as boys" works; in particular, the themes "equality in relationships" and "ultimate couple" are especially difficult to implement using "girls dressed as boys.")

Running parallel to the serious *shōnen'ai* works are works sometimes known as "beautiful homosexual works" (*bi-kei homosekushuaru mono*).[13] This subgenre includes many comedic works such as *Eve's Sons* (*Ibu no musukotachi*), by Aoike Yasuko, and *Patalliro!* (*Patariro!*), by male *shōjo* manga artist Maya Mineo.[14] The characteristics of these works clearly indicate that they descended from the genealogy of "boys dressed as girls."[15] In the later evolution of *yaoi* and BL, we can see the increasingly vivid hues of the "boys dressed as girls" lineage.[16] For example, in both *yaoi dōjinshi* and BL, the number of light comedies has been increasing.[17] In addition, it seems that the characteristics of the male heroes in such stories are gradually shifting from representing "a projection of the *shōjo*'s inner self" to "making fun of men" and even "playing with men." This shift seems to indicate that the taste of growing numbers of artists is more in line with "teasing men" than with "identifying with men." Actually, in this regard there is a common thread with the earlier works dealing with "boys dressed as girls."[18]

These days, no matter how I think about it, I get the feeling that many male heroes don't represent the "*shōjo*'s alter ego." (Could it be that they represent the "old man inside of me," as many Japanese women joke between themselves?) I also have the feeling that, putting aside the question of whether such a man really exists or not, in many cases authors choose to model their characters on "real men." (I sense this tendency in works featuring salarymen or middle-aged men as protagonists, or works of *rōjin moe* [feelings of desire toward old men], for example). Of course, there are many works that deal with "the *shōjo*'s inner self," but just as women's observations of men are undoubtedly becoming more astute, the otherness of male protagonists is also becoming more pronounced.

In other words, in the twenty years that have elapsed since I wrote that first article, the "potential" that I first detected (but had yet to be achieved) has taken a slightly different shape than I first imagined, but the resulting development of *yaoi* and BL has exceeded my expectations. Furthermore, while the origin of this development lies in the genealogy of "girls dressed as boys," the present results were achieved more successfully by incorporating the genealogy of "boys dressed as girls" into their works. This is the point which should be emphasized.

A Theory of Yaoi Fiction: A Turning Point and Two Perspectives

Above, I wrote that my first main point corresponds to the structure of *shōnen'ai*, while the second corresponds to the development of *yaoi* and BL. To elaborate on this, it can also be said that each of these points corresponds to the following questions, respectively:

1. Why did a series of works dealing with "love between men" for female readers emerge?
2. What possibilities did this emergence offer?

In fact, the approach suggested by these two questions overlaps perfectly with the shift in emphasis undertaken by Nagakubo Yōko in her groundbreaking 2005 book, *A Theory of Yaoi Fiction* (*Yaoi shōsetsu ron*).[19]

This book is truly outstanding. Based on her doctoral dissertation, her arguments are substantiated by precise statistical analysis. Nagakubo does not ask the same psychological and sociological questions that previous researchers (including myself) have tended to ask—namely, "*Why* do women prefer to read works treating 'love between men?'" Instead, she makes use of detailed analysis and statistics to reveal the structures of the genre, thus shedding light on the question "What possibilities have emerged as a result?" and capturing the very essence of the genre. In other words, her approach represents a complete shift in point of view from my first to my second question, above.

While this might seem like a minor point at first glance, it was, in fact, a remarkable shift in thinking about *yaoi*. In answer to the "why" question, explanations such as "as a result of gender oppression" or "because male homosexuality makes it possible to write differently than in hetero works" tended to produce theories that focused on addressing a negative gap or lack. Such theories cannot adequately address statements frequently heard among the current generation of *yaoi* fans, asserting that they do *not* feel gender oppression and that they enjoy *yaoi* simply because it is "interesting." If we consider the possibility that their enjoyment of *yaoi* might derive from the "boys dressed as girls" genealogy, typical theories based on the "why" questions are even less relevant. Of course, the argument that *yaoi* emerged as a response to gender oppression is not essentially wrong, but the shift in perspective offered by Nagakubo is significant in that it makes possible discussions of *yaoi* and BL in terms other than as a response to gender repression.

In her analysis of the 381 *yaoi* fiction works published in 1996, Nagakubo compared depictions of *seme* (top, dominant) and *uke* (bottom, passive) characters in terms of gender characteristics. She found that while *seme* characters were essentially masculine and *uke* characters were essentially feminine, both *seme* and *uke* characters demonstrated a mixture of masculine and feminine traits. The significance of Nagakubo's findings lies precisely in what she calls the "prescribed mixture of the characteristics of both sexes."

Furthermore, she found that the *seme* and *uke* sexual roles in a same-sex couple are determined by the very contrast between them. That is, the same person can be either a "prince" or a "princess" depending on who their partner is. This, she claims, is why coupling is so important in *yaoi* fiction. In other words, no matter how much a *seme–uke* couple may appear to imitate traditional masculine–feminine gender roles, the differences between them are no more than idiosyncrasies brought about by grouping the two together. The couple is, therefore, free from the oppression of sexual difference. This made it possible, Nagakubo argues, for readers to enjoy—for the first time—"masculinity" and "femininity" free from any sense of oppression. In this regard, Nagakubo says what works of *yaoi* fiction aspire to is the "amusementization of gender" (*jendaa no gorakuka*).

"Playing with Gender"

The "amusementization of gender"! While *yaoi* had previously been described as the "amusementization of sex" (*sei/sekkusu no gorakuka*), it had never before been described as "the amusementization of gender" (*sei-sa/*

jendaa no gorakuka). Indeed, it is the "amusementization of gender" that really is at the heart of the matter. *Seme* and *uke* characters each possess their own sort of gender ambiguity, and true enjoyment comes from the various patterns of *seme–uke* coupling and the "prescribed mixture of the characteristics of both sexes."

In her article "*Yaoi* as Seen from the Perspective of Manga for Boys and Young Men" ("*Seishōnen manga kara miru yaoi*"), Watanabe Yumiko writes:

> The strong and the weak are not determined by a single standard. Each character is measured according to three different scales: society, corporeality, and spirituality. These three factors combine to create a rich system of personal relationships based on subtle power balances. For example, a character with a higher status in society might be spiritually "inferior" to his partner, and therefore depends upon his partner in some way.[20]

Watanabe's assessment is accurate. A wealth of *yaoi* terms have come into being to describe various relationship patterns, such as "*sasoi uke*" (an individual who is mentally *seme* but physically *uke*), "*hetare zeme*" (a loser *seme*), "*jō uke*" (a proud *uke* queen), "*keigo zeme*" (a *seme* who talks to his partner using honorific language), "*yancha uke*" (a naughty *uke*), or "*gekokujō*" (when an *uke* overcomes a *seme*). All of these terms are inherently contradictory, highlighting two different personality traits held by the same character.

When I pointed out that "male–male romance" made a shift in perspective possible, in which "women are freed from the position of always being the one 'done to,' and are able to take on the viewpoint of the 'doer,' and also the viewpoint of the 'looker,'" and wondered if, as a result, "women wouldn't slowly become accustomed to this new acquisition of the active position of the looker," I was still only thinking of a simple reversal in perspective from "passive" to "active."[21] However, the new expressive tools of *yaoi* and BL offer a phenomenon that is already several steps ahead—namely, "the amusementization of gender." The fundamental *seme–uke* rule provides only that a *seme* character and an *uke* character exist. After that, in an all-male world in which no biological sexual difference exists, creators of *yaoi* and BL make couplings by freely combining all sorts of gender factors and power dynamics as they like. Readers, for their part, are able to search for their own preferred couplings among all the possibilities offered. For both readers and creators, this is the pleasure of *yaoi* and BL: a thoroughly gender-blended world.

Yaoi and BL flourish, then, as accumulations of experiments carried out in *shōjo* manga—experiments in transgressing every possible border of sexual difference and in creating worlds of diverse polymorphic perversion, as Rio

Otomo demonstrates in her chapter in this volume. On the other hand, compared with *shōjo* manga, which are frequently set in fantastic or sci-fi situations, *yaoi* and BL works typically take up realistic "daily life" situations. (Of course, love stories featuring unrealistic Middle Eastern millionaires have become quite popular, and there are examples of parody *yaoi* based on original works of science fiction, but in these cases the fundamental approach seems to treat daily life within existing settings, without changing the original setting or world view).

In particular, there is a long tradition of rereading original works through *yaoi* parody. In this regard, the possibility of reinterpreting "daily life" through the same *yaoi* lens opens up before us, as Patrick Galbraith explores in his chapter in this volume. For instance, looking at scenes like two boys walking happily in town, two boys who are physically close to each other, or two boys emotionally attracted to each other, girls'/women's homoerotic fantasies are expanded. Recently, *yaoi* reinterpretations of relationships between middle-aged male politicians have appeared. When I read Sugiura Yumiko's interpretation of influential Liberal Democratic Party figure Ozawa Ichirō as a *sō-uke no hime* (an inveterate *uke* regardless of who he is paired with), I thought, "Ah! Of course!"[22] I have also recently been hearing about people who find themselves to be unintentionally reading accounts in the business and economics newspaper *Nikkei shinbun* of the various dealings and relationships between political and business leaders from a *yaoi* point of view.[23] Headlines that seem to suggest *yaoi* reinterpretations do certainly appear plentiful! While those who engage in such *yaoi*-inspired rereadings may not be aware of it, in the act of reinterpreting what Eve Sedgwick calls homosocial male bonding as homosexuality, it seems to me that a certain parodic point of view emerges.[24] Clearly, such rereadings amount to women looking back at and examining male-dominated society.[25]

At the same time, I am reminded of Kaneda Junko's 2007 article, "Manga *Dōjinshi*: The Politics of Communities' Collective Interpretation."[26] As Kaneda points out, "some *yaoi* theories consider *yaoi* to represent an escape from sex or a hatred of women. However, if we look closely, what *yaoi* avoids or escapes from is not sex or femininity, but the look which sees women simply as sex objects."[27] Women escape from the gaze that sees them only as sex objects, and the gaze they return imbues homosocial male bonding with sexual implications. As Kawahara Kazuko has insightfully observed, "*yaoi* is a re-interpretation of *shōnen* manga from a *shōjo* manga point of view."[28] Thus, as Kaneda points out, as parody, *yaoi* functions as a forum for "communities' collective interpretation" and thus expresses a wide range of critical attitudes toward women. Kaneda's use of the term "communities' collective interpretation" demonstrates an incisive grasp of this aspect of *yaoi*.

As we saw in the case of "girls dressed as boys," a woman who takes on the appearance of a man does so in order to cope with a desperate situation. However, the actions of both *putting* men into women's clothing and rereading male bonding in a sexual way reverse normative power relations in a parodic way. This very act of reversal is simply interesting.

Here again, I would like to reiterate that this kind of women's engagement in male–male relationships originated after the establishment of *yaoi* in the mid-1980s, and developed with the establishment of the generic convention of *uke–seme* and the recognition of "male–male romance" as a means of fostering shared imaginations among specific girls/women. This development, in turn, enhanced the emergence of its successor, BL. It is precisely this development of *yaoi* and BL that answers the second question above—namely, "what possibilities did this emergence (the device of 'male–male romance') offer?"

The flow of the discussion so far can be rephrased as follows. Beginning with the creation of a new form of expression in response to earnest internal motivations, diverse critical responses making use of this new form of expression then developed. Needless to say, there is a difference between the energy of generating something from nothing, and—after certain tools have been established—the energy to use those tools in certain ways. Motivating factors are also different.

It follows, then, that a theoretical analysis of *shōnen'ai* works, for example, and an analysis of *yaoi* or BL works from the mid-1990s or later, will reach different conclusions. In fact, the history of theoretical approaches to *shōnen ai*, *yaoi*, and BL reveals that changes in analyses that define the characteristics of each genre are simply grouped together with changes in the character of the objects of analysis. For instance, studies conducted by young researchers since 2000 frequently emphasize the entertainment factor of male–male romance and criticize earlier studies focused on gender oppression. However, most studies prior to the 1990s were in fact aimed at analyses of *shōnen'ai* or *JUNE*, while the young researchers today are analyzing contemporary *yaoi* or BL.[29] Thus, in most cases the objects of research in the earlier and current studies are different. It goes without saying that an analysis of the earlier *shōnen'ai* or *JUNE* would not be not applicable to the current situation of *yaoi* or BL. Even though all of these genres deal with male–male romance, the young researchers of today should be more aware of the need to state in greater detail which genre their own analyses address.

As an example, in her article "*Yaoi* Fiction as Women's 'Rotten' Dreams: Positive and Negative Attributes of *Yaoi* Fiction," which appeared in the special edition of *Eureka*, "*Fujoshi* Manga Compendium," Nagakubo writes: "For authors of *JUNE* fiction, a scenario of male–male romance is simply chosen as a means of expression, not because they intend to create a concrete manifestation of this [*JUNE*] methodology. Authors of *JUNE* fiction write for themselves, not for like-minded readers they have not yet met." "*Yaoi* fiction, on the other hand," Nagakubo continues, "*are* produced for readers. . . . An author of *yaoi* must try to create a story with a *yaoi* motif that matches both readers' desires and her own as much as possible, and then must give expression to it using her own personality and technique. It is rather close to the realm of craftsmanship."[30]

I found Nagakubo's discussion of this point to be quite interesting. Counter to this, it has also been argued that "all expressions are self-expressions. We can't make such distinctions as '*JUNE* fiction works are self-expressions,' but '*yaoi* fiction works are craftsmanship.'"[31] However, for the reasons I have already stated, I think that it is important to analyze the characteristics of each genre together with a consideration of the publication venue and the year of publication. In addition, it is interesting to note that Nagakubo's attempt to make a distinction between "*JUNE* fiction" and "*yaoi* fiction" seems to overlap with the two points I have been coming back to again and again.

Gender as a Restraining Device: *Yaoi* and BL as "Pressure Point Devices"

In conclusion, I would like to suggest that now more than ever gender oppression has come to function as an invisible restraining device for women. Of course, there are people in every generation who are conscious of being oppressed. Compared with those who grew up in the generations when oppression was easily seen and felt, younger generations are not able to see and feel oppression as easily. However, in *yaoi* and BL the invisible restraints of gender are released. It both feels good and is interesting. Now, oppression is not clearly seen, and can only begin to be felt once the restraints are loosened. What's more, because even the restraints can't clearly be seen, some people aren't even aware that it's when the restraints are loosened that they begin to feel better. In the words of artist Yoshinaga Fumi, it is truly the case that "the pressure points for women differ from person to person."[32] For precisely this reason, each reader's preferred couplings and story patterns differ.

Yaoi and BL offer a space in which the restraints of gender oppression can be removed. Even more than that, like a custom-made tool for relieving pressure points, *yaoi* and BL allow readers to keep certain gender features as they choose, while releasing those stiff points of built-up pressure. This custom-made "pressure point device" allows each reader to enjoy her own preferred arrangement of "the prescribed mixture of the characteristics of both sexes."[33] Thinking about it in this way, we can think of *yaoi* and BL as exploring the question "Which coupling represents your favorite gender blend?" For this reason, female attempts to play with gender in these genres cannot be explained in terms of more general, visible forms of gender oppression. This is because desired gender features, and even self-conscious gender features, differ from person to person. However, we can each choose the combination that makes up our favorite gender blend. That is the pressure point. That is what the device of male–male romance makes possible.

Notes

1. "Transujendaa: Onna no ryōsei guyū otoko no han'inyō" [Transgender: Female hermaphrodites and male androgynes] originally appeared in *Gendai no esupuri*, no. 277 (August 1991) and was reprinted in Fujimoto Yukari, *Watashi no ibasho wa doko ni aru no? Shōjo manga ga utsusu kokoro no katachi* [Where do I belong? The shape of the heart reflected in shōjo manga] (Tokyo: Gakuyō shobō, 1998), 130–76. An English translation was published as "Transgender: Female Hermaphrodites and Male Androgynes," trans. Linda Flores and Kazumi Nagaike, *U.S.–Japan Women's Journal* 27 (2004).

2. Fujimoto, *Watashi no ibasho*; a "*bunko*" paperback version was issued by Asahi shinbun shuppan in 2008.

3. As mentioned above, works published in *JUNE* did not necessarily depict "love between men" (*otoko dōshi no ai*). For the moment, however, I will leave that point aside.

4. Excerpted from Fujimoto, "Transgender," 84–87.

5. See Tanigawa Tamae [Mizuma Midory], "Josei no shōnen ai shikō ni tsuite II: Shikisha no kenkai to, feminizumu ni aru kanōsei" [On women's preference for *shōnen'ai*, part 2: Expert opinions and feminist possibilities], *Joseigaku nenpō* 14 (1995).

6. E.g., *Tsubasa hyakkaten* [Tsubasa department store], *Bessatsu komikku bokkusu*, vol. 1 (Tokyo: Fyūjon purodakuto, 1987); *Torūpaa hana fubuki* [Trooper flower blizzard], *Torūpaa dōjinshi kessaku ansorojii*, vol. 1 (Fyūjon purodakuto, 1989); *Shurato makū gensō* [Shurato enchanted sky fantasy], *Shurato dōjinshi kessaku ansorojii*, vol. 6 (Tokyo: Fyūjon purodakuto, 1990); and *Seiya ni muchū!* [Mad for Seiya!], *Bessatsu komikku bokkusu*, vol. 4 (Tokyo: Fyūjon purodakuto, 1987).

7. To be clear, I did find significant possibility in terms of *yaoi* fiction as a sensual expression. The first time I went to the Comic Market, I was deeply impressed by this possibility, and I purchased a *dōjinshi* magazine by Yamaai Shikiko. She was still unknown at the time, and I didn't even have to wait in line to buy her *dōjinshi*. After that, she became a famous writer in the BL sphere almost overnight.

8. Kōga was extremely popular at *dōjinshi* markets in the late 1980s, and has since become an important presence as a professional manga artist. A number of her works have been published in English translation, such as her series *Loveless*, 12 vols., ongoing, 2001– (Tokyo: Ichijinsha, 2002–), and *Aashian* [Earthian], released as *Kanketsuban Aashian* [The complete version of Earthian], 5 vols. (Tokyo: Sōbisha, 2002–2008); she also designed characters for the anime *Gundam 00* (broadcast 2007–2009).

9. My use of the term *"yaoi"* here is meant to indicate any works published in *dōjinshi*, without distinguishing between original works and parodies.

10. Kishi Yūko, *Tamasaburō koi no kyōsōkyoku* [Tamasaburō's love capriccio], 4 vols. (1972–1979; Tokyo: Shōgakukan, 1976–1978); Naka Tomoko, *Hana no bijo hime* [Beautiful flower princesses], 3 vols. (1974–1976; Tokyo: Furawaa komikkusu, 1977).

11. See Fujimoto Yukari, "Shōjo manga ni okeru 'shōnen'ai' no imi" [The meaning of *"shōnen'ai"* in *shōjo* manga), *Nyū feminizumu rebyū* 2 (1991): 280–284.

12. Takemiya Keiko, *Kaze to ki no uta* [The song of the wind and the trees], 10 vols. (1976–1984; Tokyo: Hakusensha bunko, 1995); Yamagishi Ryōko, *Hi izuru tokoro no tenshi* [Emperor of the land of the rising sun], 11 vols. (1980–1984; Tokyo: Hana to yume komikkusu, 1980–1984).

13. At first, I thought about using the term "comedies of beautiful homosexuals" (*bi-kei homosekushuaru komedi*), but since works such as Kihara Toshie's *Mari to Shingo* [Mari and Shingo], 13 vols. (1977–1984; Tokyo: Hana to yume komikkusu, 1979–1984), can be considered to exist somewhere in between *shōnen'ai* works and "comedies of beautiful homosexuals," I have decided to use the intentionally vague "beautiful homosexual works" here.

14. Aoike Yasuko, *Ibu no musuko-tachi* [Eve's sons], 7 vols. (1975–1979; Tokyo: Purinsesu komikkusu, 1976–1979); Maya Mineo, *Patariro! [Patalliro!]*, 91 vols., ongoing (1978–; Tokyo: Hana to yume komikkusu, 1981–).

15. In the broadest sense, then, it is possible to think of "beautiful homosexual works" as belonging to the *shōnen'ai* genre. In other words, it can also be said that the genre of *shōnen'ai*, broadly conceived, includes both the serious works of the "girls dressed as boys" genealogy as well as the more comedic works of the "boys dressed as girls" genealogy.

16. In fact, in the development of *yaoi* and BL, the "girls dressed as boys" and "boys dressed as girls" lineages were occasionally mixed together in a single work, and the latter gradually came to have a stronger influence.

17. In this regard, there is some overlap between the debate surrounding the genealogy of "boys dressed as girls" and Yamada Tomoko's discussion of "homoerotic comedies" in *"Fujoshi Manga Compendium"* [Fujoshi manga taikei], a 2007 special issue of the literary journal *Eureka [Yuriika]*. Calling works by Kishi Yūko and Naka Tomoko "homo-esque comedies" (*homo-chikku komedi*), Yamada writes, "The roots of BL, in the sense of the 'cheerful *yaoi*' that has become mainstream today, may in fact lie in the confused, glamorous, and beautiful worlds depicted by Kihara, Aoike, Kishi, and Naka—worlds which are not bound by gender or nationality and in which anything can happen, rather than in the balanced, controlled, and bounded worlds depicted by Hagio, Takemiya, and Yamagishi." See Yamada Tomoko, "Pre-'yaoi/BL' to iu shiten kara: 'o-hanabatake' o junbi shita sakkatachi'" [Perspectives on 'pre-*yaoi*/ BL': Artists preparing 'flower gardens' for their descendants], *Yuriika* 39, no. 7 (June 2007): 129.

18. However, when "boys dressed as girls" come to be typically cast as the "protagonist's boyfriend," as in Kawahara Yumiko's *Zenryaku: Miruku hausu* [Dispensing with formalities: Milk house], 10 vols. (Tokyo: Furawaa komikkusu, 1983–1986), even within the same genre of

"boys dressed as girls," a heroine's emotional attachment toward such a "boyfriend" increases, and the viewpoint that this amounts to "playing with the existence of boys/men" is a step backward.

19. Nagakubo Yōko, *Yaoi shōsetsu ron: Josei no tame no erosu hyōgen* [The analysis of *yaoi* fiction: Erotic representations for women] (Tokyo: Senshū daigaku shuppankyoku, 2005).

20. Watanabe Yumiko, "Seishōnen manga kara miru yaoi" [*Yaoi* as seen from the perspective of manga for boys and young men], *Yuriika* 39, no. 7 (June 2007): 72.

21. Fujimoto, "Transgender," 87; Fujimoto, "*Shōjo* manga ni okeru '*shōnen'ai*,'" 284.

22. Sugiura Yumiko, *Otaku joshi kenkyū: Fujoshi shisō taikei* [*Otaku* girls research: A compendium of *fujoshi* thought] (Tokyo: Hara shobō, 2006). This book has been frequently criticized on the grounds that she often misreads details, but I find this section of her work to be exceptionally interesting.

23. The *Nikkei shinbun*, primarily read by businessmen, can be thought of as "Japan's *Wall Street Journal*." Relationships among those in the business and political arenas are frequently the subject of *Nikkei* articles.

24. See Eve Sedgwick, *Between Men: English Literature and Male Homosocial Desire* (New York: Columbia University Press, 1985).

25. In the "*Fujoshi* manga compendium" issue of *Eureka*, Yoshimoto Taimatsu writes that "the existence of BL has shown men that they are the object of 'the returned gaze.' Paradoxically, this has led to an awareness (among men) that women are tightly bound by the male gaze, and that they themselves objectify women in the same way." See Yoshimoto Taimatsu, "Otoko mo sunaru bōizu rabu" [Men also do BL], *Yuriika* 39, no. 7 (June 2007): 110.

26. Kaneda Junko, "Manga dōjinshi: Kaishaku kyōdōtai no poritikusu" [Manga *dōjinshi*: The politics of communities' collective interpretation], in *Bunka no shakai gaku*, ed. Satō Kenji and Yoshimi Shun'ya (Tokyo: Yūhikaku, 2007).

27. Kaneda, "Manga dōjinshi," 177. Kaneda's article itself is exceptionally well-argued and her analysis is superb, but I find it necessary to point out again here that the various works/genres tied together under the heading of the so-called "*yaoi* debate" (*yaoi ronsō*) all have different objects of analysis.

28. Kawahara Kazuko, "Manga to ren'ai/otaku: Make inu to ren'ai" [Manga and love/*otaku*: Losers and love," paper delivered at the July 2005 meeting of *Mangashi kenkyū kai* (The research group on manga history). Kawahara's paper focused on the early stage of *shōnen'ai* and *yaoi*. Similarly, Nakajima Azusa has also written that "from the time the world of the *shōnen* was invaded by *shōjo* fantasies, it had already ceased to be a 'tournament arena' and had been transformed into a space of strange desires and love for love's sake" in her *Tanatosu no kodomotachi: Kajō tekiō no seitaigaku* [The children of Thanatos: The ecology of excessive adaptation] (Tokyo: Chikuma shobō, 1998), 174.

29. For example, most works discussed by Nakajima Azusa in her *Komyunikēshon fuzen shōkōgun* [Communication dysfunction syndrome] (Tokyo: Chikuma shōbō, 1991) are *shōnen'ai* or *JUNE* works, and her subsequent *The Children of Thanatos* uses the word "*yaoi*" but deals with works by creators coming out of the *JUNE* lineage and fiction and manga then newly coming out under the "boys love" label. Furthermore, almost all of the works analyzed by Ueno Chizuko in the chapter "Experimental love in a genderless world" ("Jendaaresu waarudo no ai no jikken") in her *Hatsujō sōchi: Erosu no shinario* [The erotic apparatus: Erotic scenarios] (Tokyo: Chikuma shobō, 1998), 125–54, were published in mainstream *shōjo* manga magazines—in other words, works in the *shonen'ai* genealogy.

30. Nagakubo Yōko, "Josei-tachi no 'kusatta yume' *yaoi* shōsetsu: Yaoi shōsetsu no miryoku to sono mondaisei" [*Yaoi* fiction as women's "rotten" dreams: Positive and negative attributes of *yaoi* fiction], *Yuriika* 39, no. 7 (June 2007): 146.

31. This opinion was expressed at the party celebrating the publication of *Eureka*'s "*Fujoshi* manga compendium."

32. See Miura Shion and Yoshinaga Fumi, "Miura Shion and Yoshinaga Fumi taidan: 'Feminizumu wa yappari kankeinakunai no yo'" [A conversation between Miura Shion and Yoshinaga Fumi: "It is not unrelated to feminism"], in Yoshinaga Fumi, *Yoshinaga Fumi taidanshū: Ano hito to koko dake no oshaberi* (Tokyo: Ōta shuppan, 2007). Yoshinaga's works are discussed in Tomoko Aoyama's chapter in this volume.

33. Nagakubo, *Yaoi shōsetsu ron*, 52.

WHAT CAN WE LEARN FROM JAPANESE PROFESSIONAL BL WRITERS?

A Sociological Analysis of *Yaoi*/BL Terminology and Classifications

KAZUKO SUZUKI

Introduction

In English, "boys love" (abbreviated as "BL") is often explained as a Japanese term for female-oriented fictional media created by female authors that depict male homoerotic desire and romance.[1] Although the genre is called boys love, it deals with relationships involving men who are pubescent or older.[2] In Japan, there is currently also a clear distinction made between female-oriented male–male love fiction written by female authors and gay or queer literature (*gei bungaku*) in terms of their themes, writing styles, narrative structures, and readership.[3] Empirically speaking, Japanese BL does not primarily aim to depict male homosexuals (that is, *dansei dōseiaisha*) or relationships between male homosexuals, despite its focus on romance between two men. The majority of BL protagonists do not identify their sexual orientation as homosexual.[4] Instead, BL in Japan refers to commercialized fiction and fictional media by and for women that focuses on male–male erotic and/or romantic relationships. This genre emerged in the Japanese publishing industry in the 1990s.[5] BL is not restricted to manga and novels (*shōsetsu*). There are also audio dramas called "drama CDs" or "sound dramas" in Japanese, which are voice performances by mainly male voice actors (*seiyū*) based on original BL manga and novels. Anime based on original BL manga/novels and BL games are also popular in Japan.[6] Thus, BL appears in multiple media, with manga and illustrated novels as the most popular and profitable modes in the formal BL industry.[7]

It is important to note, however, that "BL" is not a common term among fans of female-oriented male–male love fiction outside Japan. These works are more popularly known in the Americas and some countries in Europe, Eurasia, and Asia as "*Yaoi*," a Japanese term often used as an umbrella category that can encompass various Japanese subgenres of male–male erotic/romantic fiction by and for women. This tendency to use "*Yaoi*" as an umbrella term also exists in Japan, where the term "BL" is used to describe a specific subgenre within *Yaoi* works. In this chapter, I will use "male–male romance" or "*Yaoi*" interchangeably as a generic term for male–male erotic/romance fiction and fictional media primarily written by and targeted to women. When empirical evidence is to be presented, I will adopt the exact term used by my interviewees and survey respondents: "*Yaoi*" (with a capital "Y") when used as a contemporary umbrella term, in contrast with "*yaoi*" (with a lower-case "y") when used to refer to another specific subgenre within the *Yaoi* or male–male romance umbrella.

As Japanese *Yaoi* works, including commercialized BL, are part of the global circuits of (re)production and consumption—and the *Yaoi* phenomenon and *Yaoi* works have become more acceptable as objects of research—one curious yet fundamental question has emerged among academics in Japan and abroad: Are we talking about the same thing? While this could be an interesting or even amusing discussion topic among *Yaoi* fans, defining one's objects of study is an urgent imperative for academics to further advance *Yaoi*/BL Studies. A failure to distinguish between subgenres can lead to confusion on multiple levels,[8] but also impede development of research that uses subgenres as variables to explain a distinct social phenomenon associated with each. Can *Yaoi*/BL Studies generate operational definitions for constructive dialogue among scholars across national boundaries and disciplines, especially for social scientists who want to incorporate quantitative and systematic cross-national comparative approaches into *Yaoi*/BL Studies? How can Japan/Japanese scholars convey to outsiders the diversity within male–male romance fiction and media by and for women developed in Japan without taking it for granted?[9] In this chapter, I would like to address the importance of making conceptual/analytical distinctions between subgenres/categories of *Yaoi* which have developed in particular socio-historical contexts in Japan. In so doing, I would like to argue that *Yaoi* scholars can achieve more refined historical, cross-national, and comparative analyses encompassing empirical research—both qualitative and quantitative—that can have significance for a broader audience within academia beyond the current position of a niche heavily dependent upon interpretative research in the tradition of the humanities.[10]

Research Design

In order to achieve this goal, I make use of my interviews with Japanese professional BL writers in my ongoing research project. As part of this larger project on Japanese *Yaoi*, I conducted various kinds of interviews in Japan during the winter of 2010 and the summer of 2011. For this chapter, I used primarily nine in-depth interviews with Japanese professional BL novel/manga writers under controlled environments in which they felt comfortable so that they could speak openly. The length of these interviews is about fifty hours in total, with the shortest lasting about two hours and the longest about eleven hours.[11] In these interviews, I used a semi-structured, open-ended questionnaire. Some parts of the interviews were useful for illuminating how these BL authors both consciously and unconsciously perceive subtle nuances among subgenres of male–male romance. I also conducted a short follow-up survey with the same writers to gauge their reactions to concrete images associated with these subgenres held by professional BL writers. This survey was conducted between August and September 2011. All interviews were conducted under the condition that neither authors' real names nor their pen names would be revealed. Therefore, I use pseudonyms throughout this chapter.

Except for one individual who claimed to be a "niche writer," the authors are well-known in the mainstream BL industry with some frequently appearing as "best-selling" in rankings in the broader "book" category. Among the interviews, eight are with novelists, and one is with a manga writer. The latter functions as a sort of a control variable in order to examine whether there is any significant difference between mainstream novelists and a niche manga writer in their understanding of subgenres of male–male romance. The heavy weight of novelists in the number of in-depth interviews is primarily due to my conscious research design. After conducting some informant interviews with BL editors and industry players, I found that the current content and readership of Japanese BL manga have become much more diversified and complex than those of BL novels. As a point of departure to explore differences between BL and other subgenres and to capture the essence of what BL is, I decided to first explore the world of BL novels.

Making Distinctions within Male–Male Romance

Based on the interviews and the follow-up survey, there emerged at least five subgenres or categories within male–male erotic/romantic fiction by and for women (i.e., *Yaoi*) in Japan. These are *shōnen'ai, tanbi, JUNE, yaoi,* and boys love (BL). While these subgenres of *Yaoi* can coexist, BL is the most dominant subgenre in the contemporary *Yaoi* market in Japan. Putting the term "*tanbi*" aside, these terms were each adopted in Japan, in this order historically, to refer to an emerging genre of male–male love fiction.[12] Japanese professional BL writers consciously and unconsciously distinguish BL from other subgenres of male–male romance with a sense of professionalism as *BL writers* in their creation of commercial BL, in particular by keeping to the principles of BL writing. This tendency might be even stronger when they are involved in other genres (e.g., "light novels") as professional writers.

Another important finding in this study is that Japanese professional BL writers, as creators, might sometimes want to cross boundaries of subgenres or even genres for various kinds of experiments. However, this creative desire may be suppressed due to their sense of professionalism. As professional BL writers, they have to provide what BL readers want to read by adhering to the principles of BL; they also have to make constant sales by publishing on a regular basis. As a result, their desire to be more experimental in male–male romance found an outlet of non-commercial self-publication in the form of *dōjinshi* where they can conduct writing experiments that serve a more specific group of readers who might share the same taste with them, without being concerned with sales. I will demonstrate below how these professional BL writers distinguish BL from other *Yaoi* subgenres by presenting some concrete images associated with each subgenre based on the responses to the survey.

Perceptions of "shōnen'ai"

For Japanese professional BL writers, *shōnen'ai* is most closely associated with *shōjo* manga, in particular the works of the pioneering writers in the Year 24 Group (*nijūyo'nen-gumi*, also called the "Forty-Niners").[13] Among representative works, my respondents most frequently mentioned *The Song of the Wind and the Trees* by Takemiya Keiko.[14] Works by Hagio Moto, such as *The Heart of Thomas* (*Tōma no shinzō*) and *The Poe Clan* (*Pō no ichizoku*), are also mentioned but with less frequency (Figures 5.1 and 5.2).[15] *Mari and Shingo* (*Mari to Shingo*), a *shōjo* manga written by Kihara Toshie—who is often included as a member of the Year 24 Group—is also referred to.[16] The term "boarding school," or "*kyūsei kōkō*," has a close association with their image of *shōnen'ai*. One of the main settings of this long serial *shōjo* manga by Kihara is an old-style Japanese boarding high school exclusively for boys where romantic relationships could take place among the students. Boarding

Figure 5.1 Cover of *The Heart of Thomas.*

schools are used as settings in the works by Takemiya and Hagio. Professional BL writers tend to associate the term "*shōnen'ai*" specifically with the medium of *shōjo* manga, as opposed to prose fiction. This understanding of *shōnen'ai* is quite similar to that of mainstream Japanese academia. However, if the term is defined broadly, literary works like Thomas Mann's *Death in Venice*, in which an older man, Gustav von Aschenbach, is obsessed with a beautiful young Polish boy, Tadzio, could also be classified as belonging to this category.[17]

Furthermore, what is noteworthy in this survey is the mention by the writers of Inagaki Taruho, especially his work entitled *The Aesthetics of Boy Loving* (*Shōnen'ai no bigaku*), while there is no mention of works by well-known writers Mishima Yukio or Shibusawa Tatsuhiko, who showed interest in male–male relations in their own works and praised Inagaki's book.[18] The image of *shōnen'ai* as platonic love or love beyond the confinement of

Figure 5.2 Cover of *The Poe Clan*.

the body has much more affinity with works by Inagaki than with those by Mishima and Shibusawa, whose work was inclined more toward the direction of carnal gay desire or gender/sex perversity.[19] One important thing that we can learn from the representative works of *shōnen'ai* manga mentioned by the writers is that, unlike the term's ordinary meaning of pederasty, the genre called *shōnen'ai* is not limited to relationships between an adult man and an adolescent boy. While this kind of intimate relationship (in which a boy is loved by a man) is occasionally depicted, the main theme of *shōnen'ai* in the context of *Yaoi* and *shōjo* manga is that the boy is an agent who actively loves the other, rather than simply being loved passively. For example, *The Song of the Wind and the Trees* depicts the relationship between two boys, Gilbert Cocteau and Serge Battour, in the face of various adversities surrounding them, including an abusive relationship between Gilbert and Auguste Beau, who is the real father of Gilbert. In *Mari and Shingo*, the main theme is the strong spiritual bonding between Takatō Mari and In'nami Shingo, despite some sexual relationships between Mari and older men. Thus, within the different types of *Yaoi*, and especially within *shōjo* manga, *shōnen'ai* for them typically refers to works with themes focused on love and desire between boys, rather than love between an adult man and an adolescent boy. Overall, they agree that the tone of stories is often melancholic and pensive.

Perceptions of "tanbi"

Japanese dictionaries define *tanbi* similarly—for instance, "the pursuit of and fascination with beauty, giving beauty the supreme value."[20] The word is also linked to *tanbi shugi* (aestheticism), which is also called *yuibi shugi* in Japanese. Aestheticism, having some overlap with decadence, was an art movement around the end of the nineteenth century in France and England, emphasizing aesthetic values in literature and other arts. In Japan, aestheticism is frequently represented by figures such as Charles Baudelaire, Walter Pater, Oscar Wilde, and Edgar Allan Poe. This movement was introduced to Japan around the end of the Meiji period by writers such as Mori Ōgai and Ueda Bin and continued in later literary works by Tanizaki Jun'ichirō and Nagai Kafū. Some *tanbi* works—such as *The Dancing Girl* (*Maihime*), by Mori, and *A Portrait of Shunkin* (*Shunkinshō*), by Tanizaki—are regarded as canonical literature in Japan and appear in state-endorsed Japanese textbooks for secondary education.[21] At the same time, Pre-Raphaelite fine arts, which aimed at *l'art pour l'art* or "art for art's sake" and made "beauty" a main theme, are very popular among Japanese girls and women.

Japanese professional BL authors, when they were readers of male–male romance prior to becoming writers themselves, often turned to *tanbi* literature, which might have hints of boy–boy/male–male love, when *yaoi* or BL did not exist. However, as my respondent Hana, a seasoned BL writer, correctly pointed out, *tanbi* literature itself does not necessarily depict male–male relationships. Even for professional BL authors, *tanbi* means mostly pure literature that aims to appreciate beauty. Therefore, famed novelists such as Oscar Wilde, Izumi Kyōka, and Tanizaki Jun'ichirō are closely linked as representative figures of the *tanbi* genre. Hana, Yukari, and Miki specifically emphasized the place held by the *tanbi* genre in the domain of high culture, particularly *jun bungaku* (pure literature), as opposed to BL which falls under entertainment or mass culture. Here, we can clearly see the influence of Japanese formal education on how they perceive *tanbi* as a mainstream subgenre of pure literature that emphasizes beauty. More casually, *tanbi* can mean "a gorgeous yet decadent atmosphere" and "embellished texts." Even

花闇
はなやみ
皆川博子

中公文庫

Figure 5.3 Cover of
Blooming Darkness.

among BL authors, the term "*tanbi*" comes to have a connotation of male–
male romance only when it is contexualized in *Yaoi.* In the *Yaoi* context,
works by Mori Mari were frequently mentioned as "*tanbi.*" Another respondent, Yukari, mentioned that "Some Japanese *Yaoi* fans consider Yamaai Shikiko as a *tanbi* writer, but from my point of view, she is a *JUNE* writer," since
Yukari draws a boundary between *bungaku* (literature) and *entaateimento*
(entertainment).²²

Drawing a boundary between high and low/mass cultures has long been
controversial in modern art and literature. Generally speaking, high culture
is often defined as the forms of art and literature that are produced for artistic or non-commercial reasons, whereas low or mass culture is openly commercial and is not judged or valued in the same way as artistic work. However, the division between high and low cultures is not firm. Nevertheless,
in discussing male–male romance for women, comparing cover illustrations

Figure 5.4 Cover of
Alexandrite.

of subgenres is particularly insightful to capture the nuanced differences described by these authors. Figure 5.3 is the cover of Blooming Darkness (*Hanayami*), by Minagawa Hiroko, whose works are often described as "*tanbi* and decadent."²³ *Hanayami* is a story of the gloriously tragic life of *oyama/ onnagata* (female-role) kabuki actor, Sawamura Tanosuke (1845–1878), in which homosexual relationships are depicted. The cover illustration is the work of Tachibana Sayume entitled "Sawamura Tanosuke." Tachibana's paintings and illustrations are known for capturing diabolically erotic desires hidden inside women (and men). He is the illustrator of the first edition of Tanizaki's representative *tanbi* work, *The Tattooer* (*Shisei*). Figure 5.4 is a cover of *Alexandrite* (*Arekisandoraito*), by Yamaai Shikiko, a work with a strong flavor of *JUNE*.²⁴ The title symbolizes the changing color of the eyes of the main protagonist, St. General Sheryl Eleonore; his emerald-colored eyes, like real alexandrite, turn violet whenever he feels aroused. Violet-colored

Figure 5.5 Cover of
Nemesis.

eyes combined with fair blond hair are a frequently used motif in aesthetic
male–male romance tales including works in the *JUNE* genre. In this story,
when the secret of his body as a hermaphrodite was revealed, he became prey
to two men who mercilessly and repeatedly raped him. It is a story of the
revenge sought by Maximilian (one of the men who rape him), in which
a sexually abusive relationship with hatred eventually became sublimated
into love when the misunderstanding between them was resolved. Yamaai
also writes BL works. Figure 5.5 is a cover illustration of *Nemesis* (*Nemesisu*),
volume 5 of her serialized BL work in which the setting is future Japan after
the abolition of the death penalty.[25] These three cover illustrations not only
reflect the content of each work but also mirror the essence of each genre.

Figure 5.6 is a cover illustration of *Deadlock*, one of the best-selling BL
novels by Aida Saki.[26] Just like the cover illustration of *Nemesis*, it is quite
clear which person is the *seme*, the penetrator in the sexual relationship

Figure 5.6 Cover of
Deadlock.

(Dick: Anglo-Saxon, blond hair and taller, with broader shoulders and bold blood vessels on both hands, with a "beautiful face," yet more masculine than his *uke* partner) and the *uke*, the penetrated (Yūto: Japanese American, black hair and shorter with a head-canting pose which, according to Erving Goffman, is a posture frequently attributed to the "feminine").[27] The setting is a contemporary American prison, which is rather unusual among BL works. When we compare these illustrations, one can easily sense the importance of coupling in BL works (figures 5.5 and 5.6), and an aesthetic yet melancholic atmosphere of the work, which could be labeled as *JUNE* or *tanbi* in a narrower sense.

In short, for Japanese professional BL writers: 1) *tanbi* is a regular Japanese word that is used more generally outside the context of *Yaoi* and it is a domain of high culture; 2) when it is used specifically in the context of male–male love, *tanbi* works typically hold more literary value than other works in the *yaoi* and BL genres; and 3) the protagonists should be beautiful, and stories ought to emit an atmosphere of decadence and melancholy bereft of obviously happy outcomes.

Perceptions of "JUNE"

If mainstream canonical *tanbi* works are considered in the domain of high culture and do not specifically refer to male–male romance, an important question still remains: When and how did the term "*tanbi*" enter into the *Yaoi* lexicon or even become a subgenre of male–male romance? Moreover, how is the term "*JUNE*" perceived among Japanese professional BL writers? Not surprisingly, the latter term is most closely associated with the magazine *JUNE*. According to its founding editor, Sagawa Toshihiko, *JUNE*, which was issued from a pornography publisher, is a magazine "that goes between literature and pornography" for "girls who were awakened to eros by *shōnen'ai* manga" by the Year 24 Group.[28] This style was distinctive in its fusion of the more highbrow concept of "*tanbi*" with an entertainment-driven element. It also consciously strengthened the association of the "*tanbi*" style with the format of male–male love stories created by and for women, as the original style was not specifically tied to this theme. The first issue of *JUNE* has the catch copy "aesthetic magazine for gals" in English on the cover. Nakajima Azusa, who had been deeply involved in the magazine *JUNE*, has stated "We, fans of *JUN[E]* literature, should not lower our criterion to the level that mere depictions of it are satisfying. We insist that only works with literary quality and aesthetic refinement are to be acknowledged as *JUN[E]* literature."[29] According to Hana, the word "*JUNE*" evokes the image of forbidden and immoral love in which the suffering stemming from socially unacceptable relationships is its main theme. Therefore, *JUNE* stories usually end with unhappy or tragic outcomes. The view of *JUNE* stories (or the *JUNE* genre) as tragedies seems widely shared by other BL writers and the older generation of *Yaoi* fans. Yukari, who is relatively young among the writers I interviewed, positions the *JUNE* genre as "an older version of BL" in the sense that the goal of both *JUNE* and BL is to serve readers. Miki, a professional BL manga writer, also perceives *JUNE* as "the foundation of contemporary BL."

 This kind of perception among BL writers stands in stark contrast to what the Year 24 Group have achieved through the creation of *shōnen'ai* manga and, subsequently, the inception of *JUNE*. One of the pioneer writers of *shōnen'ai* manga, Takemiya, puts it this way: "In the field of contemporary BL, I cannot convey what I want. *JUNE* was staged to convey what I wanted to say, in my favorite culture, my favorite words, and my favorite truth. I think that most BL works are lovers' games: a service [for readers] rather than an assertion of something [by the author]."[30] Existing literature written in Japanese tends to draw a boundary between *shōnen'ai*/*JUNE* categories and *yaoi*/BL categories by emphasizing the latter's distinctive, rigid formality in its narrative structure. But the way of linking *JUNE* to BL among the younger-generation professional BL writers is interesting, since it shows us one similarity between *JUNE* and BL: as a terrain where the role of readers is critically important for their very existence.[31] Haruka, reflecting on her best-selling BL serial, states, "I was defeated by my readers in my own creative activity. The couple I wanted to write about most was not the most favored couple by my readers. I was allowed to write about the couple I like the best, because of the overall sales led by the popular couple among my readers."

While Japanese researchers and *Yaoi*-related guidebooks started making a distinction between before and after the invention of strict narrative structures, depending solely upon the formality in writing is risky when defining the nature of *JUNE* as a subgenre.[32] My respondents found some affinities between *JUNE* and BL. First, both *JUNE* and BL are produced mainly for the entertainment of readers. Second, the distance between writers and readers is very close. As Naomi put it, "A woman that I met yesterday as a fan could appear in front of me as a professional BL writer tomorrow. There is no clear boundary between professional writers and readers in the BL industry." Interestingly, younger BL fans and those who are not familiar with *JUNE* perceive old *JUNE*-type works as something new that breaks the stereotype and rigid formality of BL. From a historical point of view, this is a misunderstanding of the development of male–male romance narratives in Japan. These kinds of comments can be heard especially when old works, which were once out-of-print, are published anew under explicit BL labels with new illustrations by BL illustrators or comic writers. As discussed above, *JUNE* is not an easy category to operationalize in empirical research, especially when it is used as an explanatory variable to illuminate a specific phenomenon. More thorough analyses should be done on this old-yet-new-again genre.

Perceptions of "yaoi"

Professional BL writers closely associate *yaoi* with parody or *niji sōsaku* (derivative work) in *dōjinshi* (self-published work) activity. The term "*yaoi*" was originally adopted by amateur writers of *dōjinshi* around the end of the 1970s to sarcastically refer to their own works on male–male love that were characterized by the poor quality of plot structure but contained many sexually explicit scenes. Since *yaoi dōjinshi* works often extrapolated settings and characters from conventional anime, manga, and novels, developing them into spoofs of the original, the term *"yaoi"* has also sometimes been conflated with parody or *niji sōsaku* (secondary/derivative works).[33] Even after the latter half of the 1980s, when more serious stories were developed in *yaoi dōjinshi*, the term "parody" (*parodi*) remained. Thus, according to my interviewees, currently *yaoi* parody does not necessarily imply comedy.

It is important for the purpose of enhancing classification to recognize three aspects of the development of *yaoi*. First, like other *dōjinshi*, *yaoi dōjinshi* is a venue for self-expression without the intervention of various social restrictions placed on other mass media such as TV and commercial works. Second, *yaoi dōjinshi* played a significant role in the dissemination of male–male love fiction by and for women in Japan. Third, *yaoi* distinguished itself through a specific narrative structure through its pairing of men who are not in male homosexual relationships in the original anime and manga in accordance with a convention called *"kappuringu"* (coupling).[34] In this coupling, the sexual positioning of the pair is divided into two roles: *seme* and *uke*. As suggested above, *seme* refers to a protagonist who takes a position as the penetrator in sexual intercourse, whereas *uke* refers to a protagonist who takes the position as the penetrated. Again, existing studies show that one way to make a distinction within the genre of male–male romance fiction by and for women is to pay attention to stylistic aspects and draw a boundary between the *shōnen'ai/JUNE* categories and the *yaoi/*BL categories, that is, before and after the invention of the *yaoi* narrative structure and method. What separates these subgenres into the two groups is whether the rigid formality in narrative structure, in particular the *seme–uke* framework, is adopted or not. This rigidity of the sexual positioning is not conspicuous in any of the early subgenres of male–male romance.

Perceptions of "BL"

There are some distinctive features of BL from the perspective of professional writers and editors. First, BL denotes commercially based publications mostly made for entertainment. Many professional writers make *dōjinshi*, but their *dōjinshi* works are not labeled as BL at various events called *"sokubaikai"* (spot sale events), where their fans can obtain side stories of their commercial BL. For instance, at the Comic Market, the largest *sokubaikai*, their *dōjinshi* is usually classified into a category called *sōsaku JUNE*, which might be translated as "original *yaoi dōjinshi*." When extrapolations from original manga or anime are sold by the professional BL writers at the site, they are inclined to use the term "parody" even if the stories are not comedic.[35] This seems to distinguish them from their original works and side stories of their commercial BL works. Second, in contrast to the tragedies commonly seen in the *JUNE* genre, there is an expectation among readers that BL must end happily and no main protagonists must die. Finally, BL has inherited the *seme–uke* framework of *yaoi*. However, unlike *yaoi*, there are many rules that BL writers have to follow such as the principle of *"ichibō ikketsu"* (one stick, one hole), meaning that the couple needs to be monogamous. Naomi is a popular professional BL writer who also publishes various kinds of *dōjinshi* including side stories of her commercial BL. She writes stories that cannot be published in BL in *dōjinshi* due to their violation of basic principles of BL. Others also state that they turn to *dōjinshi* when their editors reject their plots and tell them, "Please write the story in your *dōjinshi*." On the one hand, the rigid formality of BL may constrain authors' creativity; on the other hand, it helps to tighten a feeling of belonging and a sense of community with its acceptance of the form. As Yukari put it:

> There is a worldview shared among us. Anything can be classified as *uke* and *seme* in a specific relationship. For instance, [by pointing out a tea cup and teapot in front of her] the tea cup is *uke* while the teapot is *seme*. [Then, taking the cover off from the teapot and putting it back] . . . the cover of the tea pot is *seme*, while the teapot is *uke*.
>
> [Interviewer: Why is the tea pot cover *seme* in this case?]
>
> Because it covers. Implying an inserter.

Yukari also mentioned another benefit of BL's formality: "Initially, I wanted to write mysteries. But I couldn't. Then, I tried BL. I was able to write. So, I became a BL writer." Yukari is a very skillful writer, but what she implies here is that the ready-made template of BL sets the threshold for becoming a professional lower so that many people who aspire to be writers can at least attempt professional writing. This, of course, makes the distance between professional writers and readers closer. In the following sections, I will delve further into my interviews with professional BL writers to back up my discussion thus far. These interviews are helpful in showing how they make distinctions among various subgenres of male–male romance and how the nuanced distinctions of subgenres affect their creative activity as professional BL writers.

Principles of BL

Naomi is an extremely productive BL writer who has published more than
100 books. Some of her works were turned into drama CDs, and she has
some popular serials. In answering my questions about when and how she
got interested in male–male love fiction or the *Yaoi* genre, she said:

> I read *The Heart of Thomas* when I was in the third grade of elementary school.
> That was my first experience of reading boy–boy love (*otoko no ko dōshi no
> ren'ai*). The work itself was far from carnal desire. I thought I liked this kind.
> This triggered my interests in *shōjo* manga with boy protagonists in relation-
> ships with a hint of love more than friendship. When I was a second-year
> student in middle school, a magazine called *JUNE* was published. I thought,
> "Wow, there is such a world!" Since then, my interest has not been limited to
> the *JUNE* kind. I obtained a list of books on male–male love, and I went to
> libraries to read them. By this time, I was deep in the world of male–male love.
>
> A few years after I started working for a Japanese company, I did not have
> time to read manga and books. That was the time when I was away from
> *JUNE*. Around 2000, I came to have more free time and my sister gave me a
> computer, so I started writing my own original male–male love stories on my
> homepage. At that time, I even didn't know that the trend had shifted from
> *JUNE* to Boys Love. I felt it was strange because I did not know about BL.
> On my homepage, I posted my original male–male love stories with unhappy
> outcomes. Then, I started receiving a lot of complaints from readers, saying,
> "It is annoying. You must indicate 'unhappy ending' when the stories end with
> unhappy outcomes!" I was shocked. I have a friend who did not like *JUNE*
> when I loved *JUNE*. Later, she suddenly fell in love with BL, and began buy-
> ing a lot of books, especially from the Ruby imprint. She told me that the
> mainstream had shifted to BL, and BL stories must end with happy outcomes.
> Also, she told me that BL must have one couple *a priori*, in particular, with
> a one-on-one relationship between the *seme* and *uke* protagonists. I knew
> the world of *yaoi* parody by that time. But in *yaoi* parody, generally speaking,
> the *uke* is often *sō-uke*. [In other words,] the *uke* may have relationships with
> other men as long as his sexual position is *uke*. In BL, this is unacceptable.
> Moreover, it is a taboo in BL that an *uke* is raped by anyone aside from his
> *seme*. I did not know these BL rules at all and thought, "OK, now the world
> of male–male love fiction has changed and become like that." It was hard for
> me to learn these new rules of BL since they are different from what I used to
> read in *JUNE*.

Here Naomi clearly distinguishes boy–boy love (later she used the term *"shōnen'ai"* in this interview), depicted in *The Heart of Thomas* and *JUNE*, from BL, which is premised on happy outcomes. Also notable is the mention of the rigid one-on-one relationship between *uke* and *seme* in BL. As Naomi mentioned, the *yaoi* subgenre established the rigid *seme–uke* format in male–male love fiction by and for women, not seen in the earlier subgenres such as *shonen'ai* and *JUNE*. BL inherited this and added another characteristic rule that is called "the principle of one stick, one hole." In other words, in Japanese BL it is totally acceptable if an *uke* is raped by his *seme* partner, but it is a taboo for an *uke* to have sexual relationships with multiple *seme* characters. The crisis of the *uke* almost being raped by others must be averted by his one and only *seme* partner, which is usually one of the highlights of the storyline of many BL to show how cool and masculine the *seme* protagonist is. This point was repeatedly emphasized in my interviews with other BL writers—with the exception of the niche comic writer used as a control in the research design. In *yaoi*, or to be more specific *yaoi* as parody in *dōjinshi*, there is no principle like "one stick, one hole." While the *uke* and *seme* positioning in sexual intercourse is expected to be fixed for each character, an *uke* can be assaulted or raped by other *seme* characters who are not his real *seme* partner. The bottom line is that BL readers do not want to see an *uke* protagonist have sexual relations with others who are not his *seme* partner.[36] Some writers confessed that while they occasionally attempted to get out of these principles in their story-making, their editors usually advised them to stick to the classic rules, based on the assumption that Japanese BL readers expect and even favor this highly rigid, stylized pattern in male–male romance.[37]

Throughout the interview, Naomi also used *"Yaoi"* as a term to generally refer to male–male love fiction for women, because she could not think of any other appropriate term to encompass other subgenres. This usage of *"Yaoi"* as an umbrella for female-oriented male–male romance by women is, again, very common throughout my interviews. One reason for this is that, despite recognizing subtle distinctions between subgenres, there is no appropriate and convenient Japanese shorthand term to embrace all subgenres of male–male love fiction by and for women. Mizuma Midory, who wrote a book about women's love of reading *shōnen'ai* from a psychoanalytic viewpoint, states that

In mass media, after the appearance of the *yaoi* style, all work under the category of *shōnen'ai* has tended to be called *"Yaoi."* For instance, *shōnen'ai* works in *dōjinshi*, "*tanbi*" works commercially circulated before the rise of *dōjinshi*—these are aggregated and labeled *Yaoi* culture. Currently, since most professional writers have prior writing experience in *dōjinshi*, it may not be so inconvenient to use "*Yaoi*" as an umbrella term.[38]

Tanbi as High Culture and BL as Entertainment

Haruka, who is in her late forties, has a unique career as a professional BL writer since she did not have any prior experience of posting her work on the web or making *dōjinshi*. She states:

> When I was a child, there was no such thing as BL. I liked ordinary *shōjo* manga. I do not remember how, but I had a chance to read *The Heart of Thomas* in *tankōbon* [paperback] form when I was in the fourth grade of elementary school. So I guess I was about ten years old. When I read it, my heart trembled beyond control. This was so different from other *shōjo* manga that I had read before, which was usually something enjoyable and for fun. I was utterly moved by *The Heart of Thomas*. I did not know what to do. I was still a child and didn't know exactly what was written there, so I just recommended it to my friends and classmates. That's how I encountered *shōnen'ai* works. However, at that time, even *shōnen'ai* was not yet established as a mainstream genre. It was regarded as one of the minor genres within *shōjo* manga. So there were not many works with *shōnen'ai* themes. That's why I was starving for something that had even a hint of *shōnen'ai*. I was never deeply moved by works depicting romance between a man and a woman. Perhaps what attracted me so much to *shōnen'ai* was a feeling of there being a taboo.
>
> I wasn't so crazy about either *The Song of the Wind and the Trees* and *The Poe Clan*. Both are *shōnen'ai* works, and I remember I enjoyed *Poe*. Perhaps because I don't like *tanbi*. When I was a middle school student, I encountered *JUNE* in a small store. It was the first issue, so it was called *JUN*, not *JUNE*. I could not believe there was such a thing in the world! It was 750 yen at the time, which was more than a month's pocket money for a middle school student then. But I eventually bought it. . . . I was naïve and still a babe. When I read *The Heart of Thomas*, my heart pounded even just for a kissing scene. You can easily imagine that I didn't understand what was going on in *JUNE*. So I brought it to school and asked my classmates who had older sisters. They knew more about these things through their older sisters. They taught me that was that! I was so shocked that my *chakra* opened at that very moment!! Before, it wasn't clear to me, but I clearly got to know what I liked. . . . But

there weren't so many things with *shōnen'ai* themes. So I had to look into the *tanbi* literature to find [more examples of] male–male love.

Nearly all of the professional BL writers whom I interviewed mentioned direct or indirect influence by Takemiya or Hagio as 1) some sort of entrance to or encounter with *shōnen'ai*, and 2) a point of departure for their curiosity about male–male love fiction in general. What is noteworthy in Haruka's case was the fact that she did not like the *tanbi* aspect of *shōnen'ai*, although she clearly noticed that she loved reading romance between boys. *Shōnen'ai*-themed works pioneered by *shōjo* manga writers of the Year 24 Group had a close affinity with *tanbi* components. Haruka later confirmed that she preferred male–male love without *tanbi* components. What this case and other interviews show is that not all BL writers possess a strong taste for *shōnen'ai* or *tanbi* categories. Haruka read the *tanbi* literature as an alternative or substitute, because *yaoi* or BL did not exist yet at that time. Her appreciation for male–male love without a *tanbi* component is well reflected in her BL oeuvre as pure entertainment for women, in which the setting is usually in contemporary Japan and good-looking, capable Japanese men with stylish occupations and executive positions are the protagonists. Contrary to the dilettante style and decadence in *tanbi* male–male love and early *shōnen'ai* genres that are marginalized in contemporary Japanese BL, Haruka's BL works are often favorably labeled as *ōdō* (literally "royal road"), meaning the mainstream, in the BL industry—a result, perhaps, of her having created a series in the 2000s that was a smash hit both in manga and novel formats.

BL as the Japanese Version of Harlequin Romance

Mai, who is also well known as an *ōdō* BL writer, is very popular not only in Japan but also in other parts of Asia. She expressed her dislike for *JUNE* in my interview.

> It was when I was a high school student. Someone showed me *JUNE*. Vivid [violent and pornographic] scenes and also *yakuza* (gangster) type characters were portrayed. I thought, "Don't show me such things!" [Her tone of voice expressed disgust.] Later, I read works by Mori Mari. It was very different from what I saw in *JUNE*.

Mai told me that Mori Mari was a point of departure for her exploration of male–male romance fiction for women: "When I first read novels by Mori Mari, I was shocked; but I was not quite sure what was described in her works. What I adored was the gorgeous atmosphere floating in the Mori world." In fact, Mai's BL works are a catalogue of rich, good-looking, and sophisticated *seme* protagonists (often Europeans, which is relatively unusual in contemporary Japanese BL, but acceptable since their *uke* partners are usually Japanese or Northeast Asians) who are well-suited for gorgeous settings and the atmosphere of high society. Mai boldly states that BL's primary goal is to serve readers rather than to show off the authors' creativity or to be a venue of self-expression. In the highly stylized format of the Japanese BL, including the *seme–uke* coupling pattern and the premise of happy outcomes of male–male romance, what is demanded of BL authors, according to Mai, is to provide readers with high quality entertainment by adding the authors' own tastes onto what readers favor and find amusing. Occasionally, her BL works are criticized as being "like Harlequin romances," but she thinks that the premises of Harlequin novels are important and indispensable aspects of contemporary BL. She even states that she would be willing to write about heterosexual romance if there were an established Japanese equivalent to Harlequin romances. According to Mai, Japanese women are not fully satisfied with either translated Harlequin romances with unfamiliar foreign settings and characters or with "ladies comics" (*rediisu komikkusu*), which tend to focus on pornographic aspects of relationships rather than romance. Objectively speaking, however, her BL works have a very distinctive feature relative to typical Harlequin romances. Almost all of her BL stories are written in a unique narrative structure in which the exact same scene is depicted from the first-person narrative mode of the *uke* and the *seme*, by turns. In this way, her readers can enjoy the same scene both from the *uke* and *seme* viewpoints. For her, BL is a ready-made genre that is available to her and meets the needs of readers who want Japanese versions of Harlequin, despite the twist of the focus being on male–male relationships. Thus, in many of her works, unlike early *shonen'ai* manga and *tanbi* literature, a sense of "taboo" or "immorality" is rendered as a mere plot device or a worldview wherein male–male love does not seem unusual. With the fixed narrative development and the promise of a happy outcome, the idealistic, gorgeous romances created by Mai entertain many women beyond Japan. According to Mai, her female readers enjoy her BL world even in reality by going on trips and visiting the locations used in her works to share in the same atmosphere experienced by her BL protagonists.

As we can see from these comments by Mai and other Japanese professional BL writers, there is diversity even within the female-oriented male–male love fiction by women. In my interviews with them, these authors used various terms for male–male relationships such as *shōnen'ai, JUNE, tanbi, yaoi* parody, and BL. They consciously and unconsciously use these terms in order to distinguish their BL works from other subgenres.

Conclusion: Toward Operational Definitions

The purpose of this chapter is to encourage each researcher to explore operational definitions of subgenres of male–male desire/romantic fiction by and for women useful for empirical research and fine-tune comparative/cross-national analyses in future *Yaoi/*BL studies. Based on semi-structured, in-depth interviews with Japanese professional BL writers and a follow-up survey, this chapter identified five subgenres: *shōnen'ai, tanbi, JUNE, yaoi,* and boys love. After I identified the subgenres most commonly used in Japan, I presented images associated of each genre held by professional BL writers. The distinction is consistent with other parts of my research that adopts informant interviews with BL industry players, including editors of BL novels, although some editors expressed a difficulty in defining the scope of current BL manga due to the nebulousness of favored tastes of contemporary BL manga consumers.

What we find in this study is not only that there is diversity within the *Yaoi* genre but also that professional BL writers consciously and unconsciously distinguish BL from both its predecessors and coexisting subgenres of male–male romance. A highly formalized narrative structure, in particular, as well as the centrality of coupling and the *seme–uke* framework, was an invention of *yaoi* and was inherited by BL, which has added further rigidity via additional formal rules. This kind of framework and formality (that is, the *yaoi* narrative structure and various methods for manipulating gender display beyond binary gender codes) cannot be observed in the *shōnen'ai, tanbi,* and *JUNE* genres. Thus, we need to think about what was rendered possible or impossible by the invention and adoption of the *yaoi* narrative structure and method in the development of male–male romance in Japan. This chapter underscores the perception among professional writers of BL as entertainment as opposed to *tanbi,* defined as high culture. How do we interpret this finding in order to better understand contemporary *Yaoi*-related phenomena, such as *dōjinshi* activities which include both original stories like *sōsaku JUNE* and derivative creations such as *yaoi* parody, as well as both professional and amateur writers in a single event? What are the contributing factors of changing motivations that led *shōnen'ai* manga to aspire to the quality of literature and contemporary BL to pure entertainment? In the study of sociology of knowledge and culture, what is important is not classification itself, but the ways in which things are categorized and how meanings are imposed on certain categories in specific times and spaces. Hence, we should also explore how different local understandings of the subgenres emerged. These are a few examples of future agendas for *Yaoi*/BL studies.

By making analytical distinctions between subgenres and clearly presenting operational definitions in one's research, *Yaoi*/BL research will be able to encompass the fact-based, empirical research of the social sciences, which incorporates subgenres as explanatory variables for various phenomena, as well as conventional interpretative research in humanities, including one that focuses on historical evaluation of male–male romance. In so doing, this area will develop further into an established research area that can foster its own theories. Studies of male–male romance are at the intersections of gender, sexuality, culture, and media, which are often in dialogue with contemporary developments in adjacent areas of research, including feminist theory, queer studies, cultural studies, and communication studies. While analyses of "diversity within" have become a vantage point in these areas, scholars of *Yaoi*/BL must turn their eyes more consciously to the "diversity within" their field in order to avoid becoming peripheral to other academic disciplines.

Acknowledgments

This chapter uses data obtained from an ongoing project funded by the Program to Enhance Scholarly and Creative Activities of the College of Liberal Arts, the College of Liberal Arts Faculty Seed Grant Program, the Melbern G. Glasscock Center for Humanities Research, the Institute for Pacific Asia, and the Department of Sociology at Texas A&M University. The author acknowledges the assistance of Ryan Redmond in data entry for this project.

Notes

All translations in this chapter are mine aside from the translations of certain books and other media titles that have been altered for the sake of uniformity across chapters in this volume.

1. The term is also written "Boys' Love"; it is pronounced *bōizurabu* in Japanese.

2. In my ongoing research examining 779 Japanese BL novels that are popular and high selling on Amazon.co.jp from 2007 to the present (as of August 6, 2012) based on a particular sampling method, the majority of the protagonists are in their twenties and thirties. In the

early stages of BL, there were more young protagonists (such as high-school and college students), but as the readers and authors grew older, so did the protagonists in BL novels.

3. In my semi-structured, in-depth, and informant interviews with professional Japanese BL writers and BL editors conducted between 2010 and 2011, I confirmed that the overwhelming majority of BL readers are women. While writers and editors acknowledge that there might be a very small percentage of male BL readers, they are clear on the point that current BL is produced and marketed for female readers. The distinction between male–male romance by and for women and other literary works that depict homosexual relations seems to have developed gradually in Japan in the process whereby the former have become valued commodities in the capitalist market. See, for instance, the classification of various works in Kakinuma Eiko and Chiyo Kurihara, eds., *Tanbi shōsetsu/gei bungaku bukkugaido* [Guidebook to aesthete fiction and gay literature] (Tokyo: Byakuya shobō, 1993), which called these kinds of works "perverted literature" (*hentai bungaku*) in the preface and aimed to map the works in the context of "queer" literature. Note that *tanbi*, *yaoi*, and BL works are all aggregated into the category of "*tanbi* literature," and there is no appearance of the term "BL" in this guidebook.

4. In the research mentioned above, the crude descriptive statistics show that only less than one-third of both *seme* and *uke* protagonists possess a predilection for "same-sex love" (*dōseiai*). Stories in which both *seme* and *uke* protagonists have male homosexual orientations are even more rare in BL novels. Fujimoto Sumiko offers one statistic on sexual orientation in BL novels. Focusing on BL novels published from the Kadokawa Ruby imprint, she states that gay characters *seem* to be increasing and that the result is inconclusive. The sample size (100 or fewer) in three time periods is too small to obtain any statistically significant result. However, this kind of analysis is important since fact-based empirical research is currently scant in this field. See Fujimoto Sumiko, "Kankeisei kara miru BL no genzai" [The current status of BL from a relational viewpoint], *Yuriika* 39, no. 16 (2007): 89–95.

5. As one example of the public visibility of BL in Japan, when you go to the homepage of Amazon.co.jp, you can find "boys love" as one of the categories of "books."

6. It is usually manga or novels that are turned into anime or drama CDs once they become popular. However, there are some reverse cases in which popular BL games are later remade into manga or novels. The audience of BL media does not necessarily overlap; rather, it seems to vary depending on the medium. The readers of BL novels might read BL manga, but we cannot equate BL manga readers and BL novel readers. Demographic analyses of BL media are underdeveloped and thus much needed in *Yaoi*/BL studies.

7. According to Sugiura Yumiko, the main target of the Japanese BL market is women with high disposable incomes who are around thirty years old. As of 2005, there existed approximately a $120 million BL annual market in Japan. See Sugiura Yumiko, *Fujoshika suru sekai: Higashi Ikebukuro no otaku joshitachi* [Fujoshi-izing world: The *otaku* girls of East Ikebukuro] (Tokyo: Chūō kōron shinsha, 2006), 27. This, of course, excludes transactions of primarily "non-commercial" works such as *dōjinshi*. It is not easy to estimate the scale of the *dōjinshi* market associated with BL. In my informant interviews, I heard that the sales amount of *dōjinshi* could be an important part of annual income even among some professional BL writers. A cross tabulation (gender and annual income from *dōjinshi* sales) by Sugiyama Akashi and his associates on manga *dōjinshi* at the Comic Market is also insightful. See Sugiyama Akashi, Research outcome report on "Komikku dōjinshi sokubaikai 'Komikku Maaketto' no bunka-shakaigakuteki kenkyū" [A sociocultural study on comic

dōjinshi sokubaikai, 'Comic Market'], Grants-in-Aid for Scientific Research, no. 16330100 (Japan Society for the Promotion of Science, 2008), 239.

8. See Fujimoto's chapter in this volume.

9. This does not mean that non-Japan/non-Japanese scholars ignore the diversity within male–male romance by and for women. For instance, Pagliassotti seems aware of differences in subgenres of *Yaoi* and notes, "The terms boys' love, *yaoi*, *shōnen-ai*, June, and the like have slightly different meanings; this article will use 'boys' love' to encompass all of these terms." See Dru Pagliassotti, "GloBLisation and Hybridisation: Publishers' Strategies for Bringing Boys' Love to the United States," *Intersections* 20 (April 2009), http://intersections.anu.edu.au/issue20/pagliassotti.htm, n15. The recently published book on BL manga by Levi, McHarry, and Pagliassotti has a glossary relevant to *Yaoi*-related manga and other media, which might be useful for "Western" readers. See Antonia Levi, Mark McHarry, and Dru Pagliassotti, eds., *Boys' Love Manga: Essays on the Sexual Ambiguity and Cross-Cultural Fandom of the Genre* (Jefferson, NC: McFarland, 2010), 257–63. However, this glossary is confusing for those who are accustomed to Japanese ways of understanding the terms. An interesting topic of research could be how we perceive the same Japanese terms differently in the *Yaoi* globalization process. What I would like to assert in this chapter is that trivializing differences in subgenres of male–male romance limits our academic potential.

10. By this, I do not wish to suggest any hierarchy between humanities and social sciences. Rather, I mean the lack of rigorous cross-disciplinary and interdisciplinary dialogue in current *Yaoi*/BL Studies in Japan and abroad.

11. I did not expect that most of my interviewees would be very generous with their time to the degree that they were, considering the overall skepticism and unpleasant feelings that they had toward existing BL research that dealt with their works. They were mostly very cooperative. One reason for this is that I used a snowball sampling method in recruiting my interviewees. You can find other interviews with them in commercial magazines, but according to them, in these "interviews," questions were often given to them in advance, and conversations were edited through fax/email correspondence.

12. Kazuko Suzuki, "Pornography or Therapy? Japanese Girls Creating the Yaoi Phenomenon," in *Millennium Girls: Today's Girls Around the World*, edited by Sherrie A. Inness (Lanham, MD: Roman and Littlefield, 1998); Akiko Mizoguchi, "Male–Male Romance by and for Women in Japan: A History and the Subgenres of *Yaoi* Fictions," *U.S.–Japan Women's Journal* 25 (2003).

13. For more on the Year 24 Group, see Welker's chapter in this volume.

14. Takemiya Keiko, *Kaze to ki no uta* [The song of the wind and the trees], 10 vols. (1976–1984; Tokyo: Hakusensha bunko, 1995).

15. Hagio Moto, *Tōma no shinzō* [The heart of Thomas] (1974; Tokyo: Shōgakukan bunko, 1995); Hagio Moto, *Pō no ichizoku* [The Poe clan], 3 vols. (1972–1976; Tokyo: Shōgakukan bunko, 1998).

16. Kihara Toshie, *Mari to Shingo* [Mari and Shingo], 13 vols. (1977–1984; Tokyo: Hana to yume komikkusu, 1979–1984).

17. Thomas Mann, *Venisu ni shisu* (*Death in Venice*), translated by Saneyoshi Hayao, rev. ed. (Tokyo: Iwanami bunko, 2000).

18. Inagaki Taruho, *Shōnen'ai no bigaku* [The Aesthetics of boy loving] (Tokyo: Tokuma shoten, 1968).

19. While different conceptualizations of male homosexuality between Inagaki and writers such as Mishima are intriguing, especially from queer and gender-studies viewpoints, this is beyond the scope of this chapter. For further analysis of conceptual differences between *shōnen'ai* and work by Mishima and Inagaki, refer to Ishida Minori, *Hisoyaka na kyōiku: "Yaoi/bōizu rabu"* zenshi [A secret education: The prehistory of *yaoi*/boys love] (Kyoto: Rakuhoku shuppan, 2008), 99–102, 106–108.

20. *Sūpaa Daijirin* [Super daijirin], 2nd ed., s.v. *"tanbi."*

21. Mori Ōgai, *Maihime* [*The Dancing Girl*] (1890; Tokyo: Shūeisha, 1991); Tanizaki Jun'ichirō, *Shunkinshō* [A portrait of Shunkin] (1933; Tokyo: Shinchōsha, 1951).

22. For the characteristics of the *JUNE* genre of *Yaoi* derived from the magazine of the same name, see Fujimoto in this volume.

23. Minagawa Hiroko, *Hanayami* [Blooming darkness] (Tokyo: Chukō bunko, 1992).

24. Yamaai Shikiko, *Arekisandoraito* [Alexandrite] (1992; Tokyo: Kadokawa bunko, 2006).

25. Yamaai Shikiko, *Nemeshisu* [Nemesis] (Tokyo: Daria bunko, 2010).

26. Aida Saki, *Deadlock* (Tokyo: Tokuma shoten, 2006).

27. Refer to Erving Goffman, *Gender Advertisements* (Cambridge, MA: Harvard University Press, 1979).

28. Ishida's interview with Sagawa, cited in Ishida, *Hisoyaka na kyōiku*, 206–11, 326–28.

29. Nakajima, cited in Ishida, *Hisoyaka na kyōiku*, 231.

30. Cited in Ishida, *Hisoyaka na kyōiku*, 290–91.

31. Frederik Schodt describes *JUNE* as "a kind of 'readers' magazine, created by and for the readers." See Frederik L. Schodt, *Dreamland Japan: Writings on Modern Manga* (Berkeley, CA: Stone Bridge Press, 1996), 120–23.

32. For examples of such distinctions being made, see Asupekuto, *Raito BL e yōkoso* [Welcome to light BL] (Tokyo: Ōunsha, 2012); Fujimoto Yukari, "Shōnen'ai/*yaoi*, BL: 2007-nen genzai no shiten kara" [Shōnen'ai, *yaoi*, and BL: from the perspective of 2007], *Yuriika* 39, no. 16 (2007): 36–47; Ishida Minori, *Hisoyaka na kyōiku*; Nagakubo Yōko. *Yaoi shōsetsu ron: Josei no tame no erosu hyōgen* [Theorizing *yaoi* fiction: Erotic representation for women] (Tokyo: Senshū daigaku shuppankyoku, 2005); Yamamoto Fumiko and BL sapōtaazu, *Yappari bōizu rabu ga suki: Kanzen BL komikku gaido* [Indeed, we do love BL: A complete guide to BL comics] (Tokyo: Ōta shuppan, 2005); *Yuriika*, special issue, "Fujoshi manga taikei," [Fujoshi manga compendium] 39, no. 7, 2007; *Yuriika*, special issue, "BL (bōizurabu) sutadiizu," [BL (boys love) studies] 39, no. 16, 2007; *Yuriika*, special issue, "BL on za ran!" [BL on the run!], 44, no. 15, 2012.

33. When *yaoi dōjinshi* works are purely the creation of (amateur) writers, they are classified as *"sōsaku JUNE"* (literally, "creative *JUNE*"), which might be described in English as "original *yaoi dōjinshi."* *Saint Seiya* (*Seinto Seiya*) and *Captain Tsubasa* (*Kyaputen Tsubasa*) are two of the critically important original manga adopted by many *yaoi* writers when *yaoi* emerged as a social phenomenon in Japan. They appeared in manga form as Kurumada Masami, *Seinto Seiya* [Saint Seiya], 28 vols. (Tokyo: Shūeisha, 1986–1991); and Takahashi Yōichi, *Kyaputen Tsubasa* [Captain Tsubasa], 37 vols. (Tokyo: Shūeisha, 1982–1989).

34. Suzuki, "Pornography or Therapy?"

35. Ibid.

36. One interviewee calls herself a "niche writer," or is regarded in this way by others, because she likes "bitch" *uke* protagonists who sleep with more than one *seme* character.

According to her, only a small group of fans like this type of *uke*, and her works characterized by this type of *uke* are not in the mainstream of Japanese BL.

37. According to some BL writers, what is acceptable and taboo has become slightly different between contemporary Japanese BL novels and manga. They state that BL novels are expected to be "more rigid in terms of formality."

38. Mizuma Midory, *In'yu toshite no shōnen'ai: Josei no shōnen'ai shikō to iu genshō* [*Shōnen'ai* as metaphor: The phenomenon of women's taste for *shōnen'ai*] (Osaka: Sōgensha, 2005), 29.

WHAT IS JAPANESE "BL STUDIES?"

A Historical and Analytical Overview

KAZUMI NAGAIKE AND TOMOKO AOYAMA

Introduction

The term "BL" (boys love) has been widely used since the mid-1990s to indicate prose and graphic novels and associated genres such as games, animated works, and films that deal with male–male romance, often including sexually explicit material and usually produced by women for female audiences. The theme of male homosexuality in women's literary texts, however, has a much longer history. The novelist Mori Mari (1903–1987) is regarded as the pioneer of this innovative theme with her novellas published in the early 1960s. Even though at the time Mori was treated as an eccentric writer with unique aestheticism, her work inspired many younger women writers, artists, readers, and critics who were to develop the theme of *shōnen'ai* (love of boys, love between boys) in the 1970s in the genre of *shōjo* manga (girls' comics) and in the 1980s in both manga and prose fiction. Associated terms such as *tanbi* (aestheticism, as in the European fin-de-siècle and early twentieth-century Japanese art and literature movements) and *yaoi* have also been used mainly in relation to amateur writing.[1]

In the 1970s and 1980s, *shōnen'ai* and *yaoi* attracted only limited critical and scholarly attention, but only recently has BL been acknowledged more widely, by Japanese and non-Japanese scholars alike, as a significant component of Japanese popular culture. However, "BL" might not always be the most appropriate term with which to analyze narratives expressing female fantasies of male homosexuality. Fujimoto Yukari and Kazuko Suzuki in this volume categorize genres such as *shōnen'ai, yaoi,* and BL based on their narrative themes and patterns, and this approach does deserve academic recognition. For instance, Fujimoto asserts that her discussion concerning the relationship between the female escapist impulse and female fantasies of male homosexuality should only apply to *shōnen'ai,* but not to *yaoi* or BL. However, our analysis avoids drawing clear borderlines among these categories for several important reasons. Firstly, many BL researchers use "BL" or, less frequently, "*yaoi*" as umbrella terms, without clearly delineating these subgenres. Secondly, as Fujimoto herself points out, clear definitions of these terms have never been fixed. And finally, even though for analytical purposes these subcategories may be loosely characterized as separate entities, they remain thematically intertwined.

Not only has the number of researchers engaged in BL studies remarkably increased, but the thematic issues explored in these studies have also become increasingly diverse. In general, it may be said that Japanese BL became a significant cultural force around the beginning of the 1990s, when several publishers (including large publishing houses) launched new BL magazines and began publishing BL manga and novels on a regular basis. These social phenomena gradually began to attract media attention and stimulated academic research. As critics such as Fujimoto (mentioned above) and Kaneda Junko point out, Nakajima Azusa's *Communication Dysfunction Syndrome* (*Komyunikēshon fuzen shōkōgun*), published in 1991, has been recognized as the first full-fledged critical analysis of Japanese BL—which, we would argue—marks the beginning of BL studies as a field.[2] Nakajima Azusa/Kurimoto Kaoru (1953–2009) was an established novelist who published a large amount of fiction depicting male homosexuality as Kurimoto and cultural criticism as Nakajima, as well as a publically acknowledged intellectual who frequently appeared in the Japanese media.[3] Nakajima's self-reflexive analysis evokes a number of important questions, including that of why significant numbers of Japanese women crave male homosexual narratives.

More than twenty years have passed since the advent of Japanese BL studies, and these studies have developed to include diverse thematic and stylistic issues. It is therefore an appropriate time to trace the historical development of the discourse surrounding Japanese BL studies and to analyze some of the key issues voiced by researchers. This historical and analytical overview will also investigate new paths yet to be developed in future Japanese BL studies.

Psychoanalytic Approaches and Beyond

Academic discussion of BL narratives initially focused on the motivations
that led a number of Japanese women to write/read supposedly "perverse"
narratives concerning male homosexuality. The approach taken at this initial
stage of analysis was essentially psychoanalytic.[4] During this period, critics
generally read BL as exclusively female-oriented narratives that reflected the
subconscious female desire to escape socially established norms of femininity, and thus, as a perversion of (or deviance from) such idealized norms—
the essence of BL narratives was seen as their ability to at least temporarily
sate this desire.

For example, Nakajima argues that women who are consistently exposed
to a normative masculine gaze in the context of a patriarchal society attempt
to elide their female bodies (and such socially imposed paradigms as female
beauty, motherhood, and the reproductive function of sex) by taking refuge
in the idealized sphere of male homosexual fantasies.[5] Similarly, in the 1990s,
Fujimoto argued that, in BL works, the problematic aspects of female sexuality unquestionably involve an impulse to escape the pain associated with being passive in sexual acts.[6] Fujimoto's point is reinforced by Midori Matsui's
analysis of the character of Gilbert, in Takemiya Keiko's *The Song of the Wind
and the Trees* (*Kaze to ki no uta*, 1976–1984), who is repeatedly raped. Matsui
argues that the fact that Gilbert is the victim of rape—a form of victimiza-
tion generally associated with being female—enables the female reader to
identify with him by experiencing a vicarious fear that reflects her own vulnerability as a past or potential rape victim.[7] Kazuko Suzuki also points out
that BL fantasies allow female readers to escape the hegemonic patriarchal
discourse that limits female sexuality to the function of childbearing.[8] According to Suzuki, the "abandonment of the female body via the depiction
of male homosexual relations emerges as the result of disappointment with a
society characterized by sexual oppression."[9]

Through an analysis of the sociocultural context that results in a female
sense of guilt and shame when accessing erotic materials, Kazumi Nagaike
argues that female psychological attitudes toward the consumption of BL
as pornography are essentially ambivalent.[10] She demonstrates that the psychological complexities of projective identification and scoptophilic dissociation are necessary, so that women BL readers can enjoy pornographic
materials while sublimating their inevitable feelings of guilt and shame.
Nagaike asserts that, by projecting repressed aspects of female sexuality (especially its pornographic aspects) onto the male characters in BL, female
readers attempt to evade having to deal with their own sexual repression. In

this way, the sexual repression involved in "enjoying" pornographic sex can be entirely projected onto the male homosexual characters in BL, as female readers identify with these male characters, who are now signified as erotic. Paradoxically, however, dissociation from male BL protagonists (due to female readers' scoptophilic orientation) enables these readers to engage in a safe (and emotionally comfortable) involvement with the pornographic. The theoretical perspective of these BL critics has thus assumed that female sexuality is essentially passive. This assumption is demonstrated in their consistent use of ideas such as pain, fear, abandonment, and shame. This negative attitude toward female sexuality completely dominates their consideration of sexuality within the BL context.

Since 2000, however, this widespread psychoanalytic approach has been questioned by some scholars of Japanese BL, who argue that reading BL as reflecting a female impulse to escape the negative aspects of femininity is incomplete. Instead, these scholars approach BL narratives as being essentially "pleasure-oriented." For instance, Kaneda criticizes Nakajima for "pathologizing" BL readers and writers and re-inscribing the myth that Japanese women are psychologically vulnerable.[11] Kaneda wishes to turn the focus of Japanese BL studies in a different direction, in particular the ways in which female readers are entertained through their interactions with BL texts.[12] In this context, Patrick Galbraith's analysis of *moe* communication demonstrates the significance of "pleasure-oriented" female BL activities.[13] According to Galbraith, *moe*, a desire or a particular attachment for certain fantasy representations, is manifested in BL women's autonomous desire to create and play with BL fantasies. In actively seeking out *moe* materials, female creators and consumers of BL share what Galbraith calls a "rotten filter," through which *fujoshi*—or "rotten girls"—view the world.[14]

In a different vein, what Nagakubo Yōko calls "*jendaa no gorakuka*"—the amusementization of gender—parallels Derrida's "endless play of the signifier."[15] Nagakubo quantitatively analyzes the character traits depicted in 381 BL novels, finding that BL's entertaining elements are closely associated with an endless variation on the *seme–uke* theme, in which BL characters may perform either the *seme* (top) or *uke* (bottom) role according to the personality traits of their potential partners. Nagakubo concludes that the binary distinction between *seme* and *uke*, which seemingly re-inscribes the heterosexual paradigm, actually functions as a parody of it by revealing the possibilities inherent in gender performativity. Mori Naoko similarly suggests potentially liberatory readings of BL as autoerotic female pornography.[16] Rio Otomo's chapter in this volume also discusses the pornographic aspects of BL. However, Otomo's analysis emphasizes the problematic, self-referential aspects of female critics' readings of BL as pornography for women. Taking a different tack, by comparing pornographic scenes in manga for men with the sexual scenes depicted in BL, Mori discovers that the latter do not merely reproduce porn directed at men; instead, they are constituted by an autonomous female pleasure-seeking impulse. For instance, while in men's pornographic manga a woman experiencing sexual pleasure is solely depicted in close-up (and the male penetrator's body disappears, except for his sexual organ), in BL manga the sexual pleasures of both lovers are clearly depicted. Thus, in BL erotic or pornographic stimuli are inseparable from the depiction of mutual romantic attachment between the characters portrayed. Ōtsuka Eiji's *A Theory of Narrative Consumption* (*Monogatari shōhi ron*) also refers to the entertaining aspects of BL (especially BL *dōjin*, that is, "amateur" activities) in similar terms.[17] Ōtsuka argues that, within the dominant context of capitalist consumer society, consumers are not limited merely to the consumption of products; they also consume narratives and are, at the same time, interested in producing (or deconstructing) narratives. According to Ōtsuka, BL *dōjinshi* (amateur manga and fiction) typically manifest this concept of narrative by emphasizing the consumer's active involvement in narrative creation.

While such scholars and theorists contribute significantly to our understanding of BL production and consumption, we certainly do not wish to invalidate the psychoanalytic approach to Japanese BL studies that some of them are writing against. For one thing, this approach has given us the insight that BL represents a kind of "*écriture féminine*" (women's writing) and has thus served to uncover problematic (as well as subversive) issues concerning female subjectivity and femininity in the Japanese sociocultural context. Nonetheless, previous BL research which has taken this approach needs to be incorporated into the developing analysis of the ways in which female readers actually interact with BL texts and activities. A psychoanalytic approach addressing such questions as why people read BL may still potentially provide a thematic space in which to analyze, *inter alia*, heterosexual male BL consumers' motivations and reading practices, the advent of live-action BL films, and the epistemology of *fujoshi*.

Representation of Minorities

Another important aspect of Japanese BL studies involves the representation of sexual minorities. This issue demonstrates that the focus of critical attention in relation to BL cannot be limited to female BL participants.

Vocal criticism of BL by some Japanese gay male activists started in the 1990s. Some gay readers have harshly censured this female-oriented genre due to the limited, stereotypical images of gay characters portrayed in it. For example, Satō Masaki, a gay activist and ringleader of the so-called *yaoi ronsō* (*yaoi* debate) over the representations of gay characters in BL, condemns female BL writers/readers for entertaining themselves through the commodification and consumption of artificial images of gay male characters.[18] A more recent article by Ishida Hitoshi (an extended version of which is included in this volume) helped to reignite a second phase of the *yaoi ronsō* by raising issues surrounding subconscious female homophobia and women's "plundering" of gay men's images.[19] According to Ishida, self-identified gay characters in BL are generally portrayed in terms of the deviant, pathological other. He notes how gay characters are never depicted as protagonists since it is the self-identified heterosexual male characters (who accidentally fall in love with other men and have sexual intercourse with them) who always assume this narrative role. Ishida also points to numerous strongly homophobic statements appearing in BL narratives. Ishida's argument clearly parallels Mizoguchi Akiko's critical stance, which categorizes BL as a homophobic genre.[20] According to Mizoguchi, BL narratives clearly reflect female readers' sense that they do not want to identify with "real" gay men, even in fantasy.

Several female critics counter that the vital force of the fantasy elements in BL derives from the fact that BL has nothing to do with the actual social situation of "real" gay men. Hori Akiko's analysis reveals the dilemma which female BL participants face. When Hori concludes, however, that "*yaoi* is never directed at gay men, since *yaoi* does not tell stories about gay men but rather about love between heterosexual men," her argument points to the paradox that gay men are essentially excluded from BL discourse.[21] Nobi Nobita, a BL artist and critic, also asserts that gay men are necessarily absent from BL narratives:

> While the male characters in *yaoi* fantasies are depicted as male, they are different from men in reality because these characters are constructed as artifacts which correspond to female images of men. . . . Thus, gay men do not need to be distressed by these female fantasies of male homosexuality. Gay men are not *tōjisha* (directly involved parties) in female *yaoi* fantasies.[22]

By contrast, responding to feminist readings of BL, such as those by Nobi and Hori, noted above, Keith Vincent strikes a cautionary note, stating, "If there is a subversive cross-gender identification taking place here or a possibility for gay identification, it comes at the price of the total effacement of the realities of misogyny and homophobic oppression."[23] Vincent rightly cautions that some feminist readings of BL may risk silencing gay men's voices in the BL context.

Wim Lunsing points out that taking an identity-politics stance in relation to the analysis of BL works limits one's critical perspective: "If *yaoi* manga are criticized for giving false presentations of gay men, how come gay manga [created by gay men] are not?"[24] We would note in response to Lunsing's question that, in their influential articles, Satō and Ishida never call into question gay narratives created by and for gay authors, nor do they even mention them. The overall tone of Satō's and Ishida's critiques reflect the assumption that *tōjisha* (in this context, self-identified gays) have the right to judge—and to create—gay images, so they are not critical of gay narratives directed at gay men. Mark McLelland discusses the problems which arise from over-investment in *tōjisha* speaking positions in current debates about the rights of sexual minorities in Japan, arguing that emphasizing the sexual orientation of the critic necessarily limits the field of debate.[25] In the 1990s, during the final stage of the *yaoi* debate, some female critics ended up arguing that women can only be involved in BL activities if they recognize their shame and guilt as plunderers of gay images.[26] In opposition to this view, we argue that such criticisms fail to deal with the unresolved disconnect between reality and representation which BL manifests. For us, the representations are what matters, not the sexual identities of the creators and critics of those representations.

The complex issues of representation raised by BL are not limited to the representation of sexual minorities. For example, Nagaike's analysis demonstrates that the specific signs associated with the non-Japanese characters represented in BL manga (for instance, the high social status of Caucasians and the wealth and eroticism of petrodollar Arabs) enable female BL readers to find imaginative satisfaction through their identification with such ostensibly superior signs.[27] Moreover, the almost complete absence of certain types of foreign others, such as other Asian or black characters, in BL manga may be theoretically associated with Robert Albright's concept of the "invisible minority."[28] The fact that a specific race is not represented in a specific context does not signify the liberation of that race, but rather its invisibility; the negative connotations attached to specific races are thus merely repressed, not eliminated.

In light of such counterexamples, minority discourse in relation to BL thus arguably needs to eschew complicity with *tōjisha* discourse. Previously, both female BL critics and some of their gay male counterparts have limited their analysis to responding to the *tōjisha* argument, as Nobi has defined the term. Here, we would like to use issues of identity politics, using Homi Bhabha's postcolonial discourse as a springboard. According to Bhabha, postcolonial discourse needs to shift from recognizing certain images as positive or negative in relation to the identity politics to analyzing the process through which such images are made.[29] Taking a theoretical perspective similar to that of Bhabha, we would suggest that further research is required concerning minority representations in Japanese BL, in order to reveal the processes through which these stereotypical images are produced within a specific sociocultural context. Such an approach would also involve a comparative analysis of the stereotypes depicted in gay narratives directed at gay men with those in narratives primarily directed at female BL readers.[30] Another possible aspect of this approach would involve an inquiry into the meaning of BL to gay men on both the social-identity and individual levels; for example, does BL entertain or have the potential to liberate gay men?[31] This approach might introduce a different, more productive phase in the hitherto antagonistic relationship between certain female BL writers/readers and gay critics.

Media Discourse

In contrast to the aforementioned critics, McLelland analyzes BL in terms of a specific media discourse, focusing on the image of gay men projected by the 1990s Japanese media, which sought to depict them as idealized partners for Japanese women.[32] As McLelland writes, during the 1990s a so-called *"gei būmu"* (gay boom) occurred throughout the Japanese media and was primarily reflected in popular materials directed at women, such as women's magazines. Gay men's seeming refusal to engage in "masculine" behavior renders them less intimidating to women, who are thus provided with some degree of "healing" in relation to stereotyped gender norms. Relating such media images of gay men to the idealized male homosexual characters in BL fantasies, McLelland shows that BL, which has sometimes been labeled antisocial, actually reflects certain Japanese social-cultural realities. However, Ishida Hitoshi's approach to such representations of gay men during this period reveals the problematic aspects of the idealization of gay men which was promoted by Japanese media at that time. According to Ishida, this idealization entailed segregating gay men from the category of "men" and effectively silencing their voices. The "absence of gay men" from this supposed *gei būmu* was obviously not beneficial to sexual minority discourse.[33]

In terms of media analysis of Japanese BL, Nishihara Mari demonstrates that an historical transition in Japanese newspapers and magazines occurred during the period from 1975 to 1997. During the late 1970s and the early 1980s, in the rare instances when they discussed it, Japanese media presented BL as a specific subgenre of male-oriented *gei bungaku* (gay literature) and thus treated it as part of a subversive movement challenging heteronormative gender formations. However, as BL gradually became recognized as a female-oriented cultural phenomenon, the media began to focus specifically on the characteristics of the "young female consumers" of these male homosexual narratives. The popular media (especially magazines directed at men) depicted the female fans of BL fantasies as socially/sexually immature, escapist, and essentially antisocial.[34] A consideration of McLelland's and Nishihara's respective analyses concerning media portrayals of female consumers of gay narratives shows that the social impact of the reality–fantasy binary distinction requires further discussion. It is noteworthy that, during the same period when unmarried women's lives with gay partners were idealized by the media, women's BL fantasies were denigrated in what virtually became a small-scale moral panic. It may be argued that these media narratives serve to legitimize the negative attributes of manga and anime *otaku* images which coalesced in the popular imagination as a result of media coverage of the Miyazaki Tsutomu "*otaku*" murder case in the late 1980s.[35]

The cybercultural aspects of BL have also been examined in terms of media discourse studies, a focus which extends the examination of Japanese BL beyond the confines of Japan. A limited amount of research has been done on the impact of the Internet on the dissemination of Japanese BL outside Japan, partly due to the marketing success in Japan of printed BL media. However, transnational recognition of Japanese BL undoubtedly correlates with the development of global communication via the Internet. McLelland's early research on Japanese BL in cyberspace opened BL studies to new theoretical viewpoints concerning both the globalization and localization of various BL cultures.[36] McLelland argues that, while in cyberspace BL is seemingly becoming globalized, this process is accompanied by a simultaneous localization of BL. For example, McLelland points out that in the early 2000s websites featuring BL and other fan-based homosexual narratives in North America engaged with more politically sensitive issues, such as controversies over the definition of pornography, than did similar Japanese websites. McLelland also points out that BL-related sites in Western countries are very anxious about the issue of child pornography, although as he notes in his contribution to this volume, anxieties about fictional minors in sexual contexts are increasingly apparent in Japan, too.[37]

Although previous research on Japanese BL from the perspective of media studies has been rather limited, this approach may be expected to become quite fruitful. As McLelland shows in his recent study of censorship issues in relation to Japanese BL, an analysis in terms of media discourse may contribute to a better understanding of the current sociocultural context in which Japanese BL is situated both in Japan and internationally.[38] Research concerning censorship issues in relation to BL may also be explored cross-culturally, by discussing, for example, the official persecution of Chinese female BL writers (whose online sites were banned in 2010, when thirty-two young women in their twenties who participated in these sites were also arrested) and the harsh criticism which BL writers have received from the state-controlled media.[39] In addition, since the marketing of Japanese BL has now broadened to include games, live-action films, animated works, and other media, the sociocultural effects of BL, both in Japan and abroad, may be expected to become increasingly apparent as one aspect of Japan's soft power.

Queer(er) Readings: Lesbianism and *Fudanshi*

While BL and related discourse can have the effect of marginalizing—even silencing—sexual minorities, as some of the scholars discussed above have shown, BL is arguably queer in its unsettling of heteronormativity, and BL reading practices have the potential to render it queerer. Indeed, in the next phase of development of BL studies, some critics attempted to open new interpretive possibilities by showing how BL narratives might be further queered.

One potential queer reading of BL derives from discourse on lesbianism. For example, Mizoguchi suggests that lesbians such as herself may project their sexuality and sexual pleasures onto male BL characters by reading them as women in drag.[40] Since previous critical analyses of BL had primarily explored it in relation to the presumed heterosexual orientation and desires of Japanese women, Mizoguchi's attempt to read BL as lesbian fantasy is significant. According to Mizoguchi's analysis, while BL characters are biologically "male," feminine characteristics are definitely attributed to them, and this renders their representations essentially androgynous. In this context, James Welker provides ethnographic research concerning lesbian readers of BL (or a lesbian continuum in relation to it) by analyzing the readers' comments that appeared in early BL magazines.[41] Welker discovers that a significant number of these female contributors identified themselves as in some way "queer," frequently using the label *"yuri"* (lily, a flower associated with female same-sex love in this context) and occasionally *rezubian* in reference to themselves and other girls and young women; some of them wrote that they were looking for a female *"yuri"* friend or partner. At an early stage, then, BL magazines apparently provided a communal space for women readers to explore a range of sexual identities, including bisexual, transgender, and lesbian.

As Mizoguchi points out, BL may be explored in terms of lesbian discourse as a subversive space in which monolithic heterosexual categories can be deconstructed. In the BL context, lesbianism does not necessarily refer to "real" lesbian sexuality, but instead functions as a metaphor enabling "heterosexual" female BL participants to become more conscious of monolithically constructed conceptions of heterosexuality or heteronormativity. As Mizoguchi remarks of these female BL participants: "They are not generally considered lesbians nor do they identify themselves as lesbians. . . . [but] is it still accurate to refer to them as completely heterosexual?"[42] Thus, the lesbianism in BL may be considered more strategically as belonging to what Adrienne Rich calls the "lesbian continuum."[43]

Further extending the discourse of the queer potential of this genre, some recent research on BL examines heterosexual male readings in terms of the discursive queerness reflected in BL narratives. The specific label *fudanshi* ("rotten boy") refers to self-identified heterosexual male readers of BL, as well as gay and bisexual male readers. Critics such as Yoshimoto Taimatsu and Nagaike (in this volume) have attempted to unveil the specific motifs, narratives, and aesthetic elements which attract some heterosexual male readers to BL and enable them to consume these narratives. Yoshimoto, a pioneer researcher on this topic, points out that, in the last several years, a substantial number of heterosexual male viewers/readers have emerged who are not afraid to declare an interest in the BL genre.[44] In critical discussions concerning the motivations of these *fudanshi*, Yoshimoto and Nagaike both discern a curious return to earlier explanations of women's interest in the genre, in the sense that the escapist potential of these texts is often emphasized. In the case of male BL consumers, however, this is seen as involving an escape from the bounds of conventional masculine identity. As Yoshimoto shows, what many male readers find enjoyable in BL characters is their freedom to express their vulnerability and passivity. The beautiful boys of the BL world frequently "fail" to perform in accordance with the tough image demanded by conventional masculine norms. Hence, it is not so much the sexual orientation of the BL characters that is of interest to *fudanshi*, but rather these characters' embodiment of qualities that have traditionally been gendered as feminine and thus stigmatized when expressed by males.

Research concerning the heterosexual male readers of BL might be enhanced further by focusing on the diversity of their motivations (beyond an escapist impulse). Such an analysis would ideally mediate between heterosexual male desires and other forms of desire (for instance, female, lesbian, gay, transgender, and so forth). In short, critical discussion of heterosexual male readers' desire for BL cannot merely offer a converse male version of previous simplistic arguments regarding female BL readers. For instance, male BL consumers might "play" with BL (or the representations of gender in BL) in order to entertain themselves or search for an autonomous subjectivity in a non-patriarchal genre, just as female BL participants do. Accordingly, many queer readings of BL may be proposed, since in this context "queer" may be viewed as an umbrella term which functions to disorient heteronormative mainstream discourse.

Community and Collectivity in BL *Dōjinshi*

It can be argued that, in the development of BL studies, the most important debate has been over the recognition of female BL *dōjinshi* (amateur manga and fiction). The overall critical discussion of BL *dōjinshi* so far may be broadly epitomized in terms of the enhancement of the autonomy of female self-expression and the attempt to construct an independent female-oriented BL community. Natō Takako's analysis of female *dōjinshi* activities/communities should be mentioned in this context.[45] Through her analysis of the data which she collected by means of interviews and questionnaires, Natō demonstrates that the female desire for subjective autonomy may be seen, for example, in female *dōjinshi* authors' freedom in playing with (and parodying) the original texts of published stories. Natō remarks that *dōjinshi* "create their stories as they like, even reviving favorite characters who died in the original story. . . . If they find elements of the original story (such as plot development) unsatisfying, they alter it as they like."[46] Sharalyn Orbaugh's analysis of Harry Potter *dōjinshi* also demonstrates how, through the act of eroticizing the original stories, these female writers express their own subjectivity.[47] As Orbaugh argues, one of the thematic issues in BL *dōjinshi* writings is female eroticism, and she thus focuses on BL *dōjinshi* authors' attempts to insert sexual content into the "canonic original universe" of the stories which they parody. In this way, the authors of *dōjinshi* self-reflexively place these original stories into their own fantasized sexual context.

Somewhat in contrast to Orbaugh, Azuma Sonoko's approach to *dōjinshi* writings defines their meanings and effects in terms of autonomous female interpretations of homosociality.[48] Azuma agrees with Eve Sedgwick's theory that the male–male bond needs to be based on a socially acknowledged form of spiritual, non-corporeal interaction, in order to conceal male homosexual desire. However, Azuma demonstrates that Sedgwick's male homosocial principle, in which subconsciously acknowledged homosexual desire precedes homosociality, is not exactly reflected in BL *dōjinshi*. Azuma instead defines the construction of homosexuality in BL as a medium which subtly conceals the female temptation to re-inscribe male homosocial ideology in female terms. Examining the characters in BL *dōjinshi* in relation to *kankeisei* (ways of match-making) issues, Azuma defines BL as narratives of homosociality rather than homosexuality. Homosexuality has merely been (accidentally) chosen as a narrative device that serves to naturalize a homosocial framework.

All of these BL *dōjinshi* scholars point out that, in order to understand the discursive contexts of female BL *dōjinshi*, the processes through which these texts are constructed and the formation of *dōjinshi* communities must be explored and contextualized. Natō argues that, because these female-oriented BL *dōjinshi* communities create specific jargon and activities that can only be shared among group members, this serves to enhance the solidarity of these communities. Kaneda's analysis of BL *dōjinshi* also relies on a community-based approach which she frames as the "communities' collective interpretation" (*kaishaku kyōdōtai*).[49] This framework refers to a phantasmic arena which only members of specific BL *dōjinshi* communities can access and in which their identities as community members are reinforced. The importance of this community-based arena in BL *dōjinshi* activities reflects what Orbaugh calls the "hive mind." However, Orbaugh's analysis of BL *dōjinshi* asserts that members of such communities also share an intense attachment to particular texts—a "canonic original universe"—and this further serves to enhance the solidarity of BL *dōjinshi* communities. Her analysis resonates with Ishikawa Yui's narratological studies regarding BL *dōjinshi*, which we will discuss below.[50] Another primary element in Orbaugh's analysis of Harry Potter *dōjinshi* involves the subversive aspects of *dōjinshi*, insofar as these texts function to denaturalize the essentially authoritarian common understandings of "author" and "original." She demonstrates the ways in which *dōjinshi* activities dissolve the dichotomies of production and consumption, and professional and amateur, as well as "traditional notions of what constitutes an Author, a Reader, and a Text."[51] She goes on to consider how this process of deconstruction of established writing/reading tradition has been accelerated by rapid advances in Internet technology. According to Orbaugh, the Internet has also facilitated the creation of BL *dōjinshi* communities.

Ishikawa's outstanding Ph.D. dissertation discusses the application of diverse narratological theories to BL *dōjinshi*. She attempts to integrate narratology and theories of manga expression (*manga hyōgen ron*) on the basis of Gerald Genette's concept of hypertexuality (that is, the interrelations among various texts). Ishikawa demonstrates how the "derivative writings" of BL *dōjinshi* appropriate elements of original texts. In particular, she examines which elements in specific texts are maintained in BL *dōjinshi* and which are altered. As she says, "previous research done on *yaoi* (BL *dōjinshi*) overemphasizes the sociological impact of BL *dōjinshi*, failing to discuss the intertextuality of *dōjinshi* and the original stories."[52] For instance, in analyzing *dōjinshi* based on the wildly popular *One Piece* series in terms of characterization, Ishikawa demonstrates how a "character" is constructed as a combination of "images" (*zūzo*), "symbols" (*imi*), and "interior" (*naimen*).[53] Thus, as long as *dōjinshi* maintain some degree of fidelity to these character attributes in the original text, that text can be endlessly modified. For example, in *One Piece*, Luffy's straw hat is an "image," while his constant refrain, "I'll become a kind of patriot," functions as an "symbol" of his sincere ambition; this "image" and "symbol" can then be playfully signified in any number of ways. In terms of Kaneda's concept of collective interpretation, *dōjinshi* authors and readers share the same canonical universe as the original text, while others who lack such BL literacy are excluded from it.

As we have seen, the primary analytical issues dealt with in previous BL *dōjinshi* research have included female-oriented communities and narrativity. Further analysis of male involvement in BL *dōjinshi* activities is required in order to provide further insight into this subgenre as it is important not to define BL *dōjinshi* communities as exclusively "female." Kaneda makes the controversial assertion that male BL participants should be considered as *fujoshi* (not as *fudanshi*). Her assertion derives primarily from the fact that *fudanshi* are psychologically attached to a "community's collective interpretation" of BL as constructed by and for women, and this idea definitely deserves further consideration.[54] Overemphasizing the process of "collective interpretation" in BL *dōjinshi* runs the risk, however, of producing a totalitarian concept of BL discourse and narrow discussion regarding individual readings of BL.

A significant body of BL *dōjinshi* research focuses on print publications and face-to-face communications among participants at *dōjinshi* events (such as the Comic Market, or *Komike*).[55] Further research on amateur BL writings should also include cybercultural activities, since a large number of amateur BL writers now upload their work on the net, which provides a space in which their friends/readers can establish virtual BL communities.

This research should also consider issues concerning the growing transnationality of *dōjinshi*, since a wide variety of amateur BL texts can be easily accessed online, by both overseas and domestic fans. In this way, Japanese BL research will begin to respond to this broader transnational context.

Literariness Reviewed

The growing interests in intertextuality, mentioned above, is, in a sense, a sign of liberation from the hierarchical positioning of (men's) literature over (girls') "subculture." In fact, BL and its earlier forms have always been closely linked to literary texts. Mori Mari, who, as mentioned at the outset of this chapter, is regarded as the pioneer of what is now called BL, saw herself as a writer of literature (*bungakusha*) rather than a woman writer (*joryū sakka*) and had her work published in major literary magazines and by leading literary presses. Nakajima recounts in her earliest collection of essays, *An Introduction to Beautiful Boy Studies* (*Bishōnen-gaku nyūmon*), the captivating impact Mori's 1961 novella *The Bed of Fallen Leaves* (*Kareha no nedoko*) had on her when she finally found a secondhand copy in the early 1970s.[56] Scholars such as Aoyama, Vincent, Nagaike, and Otomo attempt to read the BL tradition within the specific genealogy of Japanese literature (*Nihon bungaku*), or analyze BL texts in comparison to literary works which deal with male homosexuality/homoeroticism.[57] Concluding that Mori's male homosexual works are failed gay narratives created by an overly imaginative female author who refuses to grow up, Vincent exhorts Mori's female "descendants" (contemporary female BL writers/readers) to deal sensitively with issues of male homosexuality, even in fantasy narratives. Nagaike's book *Fantasies of Cross-Dressing: Japanese Women Write Male–Male Erotica* attempts to bridge the evident gap between literary works on male homosexuality/homoeroticism produced by female authors (Mori Mari, Okamoto Kanoko, Kōno Taeko, and Matsuura Rieko) and BL works. Nagaike employs the Freudian theory exemplified in the essay "A Child is Being Beaten," wherein Freud defines the formation of the sexual fantasy in which women "watch" male–male eroticism. Otomo's chapter in this volume discusses the female reader of BL who can only attain pleasure when she successfully discards her own agency, comparing this reader to the established and self-reflective subject represented in Mishima Yukio's confessional novels.

As pointed out by a number of scholars in the field of *shōjo* (girl/girl-hood) studies, including Honda Masuko, Kawasaki Kenko, and Takahara Eiri, the act of reading plays a vital role in *shōjo* culture. It is important not to dismiss reading as a passive act or mere consumption as it is a basis for critical and creative acts and communication among those who share the same texts.[58] Ishida Minori remarks in her comprehensive "pre-history" of *yaoi*/BL that the very genre *shōnen'ai*, which she regards as one of the major achievements of 1970s *shōjo* manga, was itself generated by mixing the literature of Herman Hesse, who was at the center of the mainstream culture, with the concepts/metaphysics (*kannen*) of Inagaki Taruho, who was outside orthodox Japanese literary history. Furthermore, Ishida argues that this *shōnen'ai* "was a device for women to love 'the manner in which the *shōnen* [boy] loves.'"[59]

Ishida's comments significantly differ from the kind of naïve amazement that was found in earlier comments on the literariness (*bungakusei*) of *shōjo* manga. For decades a number of critics have praised the literary quality of the genre. However, a lingering hint of condescension is evident in their recognition of *shōjo* manga (including *shōnen'ai* manga) aspiring for and then superseding literature as serious high art in its literariness.[60] As Ishida notes, Hesse was a touchstone in the liberal arts tradition in Japan, whereas Taruho was given a peripheral position in modern Japanese literature. However, Ishida does not suggest any hierarchical order among Hesse, Taruho, and *shōjo* manga. Nor is it simply the tracing of "influence" from European and Japanese source texts. Rather, the focus of the discussion is placed on the innovative choice and transformation of preceding texts. The focus on intertextuality opens up the understanding of "literariness" in manga from the predominant view that identifies the depiction of a psychological "interior" (*naimen byōsha*)[61] as that which opens literature to a much wider range of issues such as forms and structure, irony, and comic subversion, none of which can be explained in terms of psychology.

Another important change in recent studies of "literariness" of BL and *shōjo* manga in general is the increasing dominance of women critics and scholars with expert knowledge in related genres such as *shōjo* fiction, classical literature, and German and other literatures, as well as feminist and/or queer studies approaches.[62] Many of these scholars take a sympathetic view toward *shōjo* culture, combining their own interpretations not only of primary texts but also of critical and theoretical works produced by earlier scholars such as Honda. As comparative literature scholar Saeki Junko summarizes, detailed textual analysis continues to enrich our discussions of "femininity" in Japanese literature, while at the same time it is important to pay attention to the reception of women's texts. As she points out,

> Women as senders of messages and women as recipients of messages try to
> relativize or change conventional gender positioning, [while] they may also

conspire with each other in taking part in reproduction and reinforcement of oppressive gender norms.[63]

In this context, further research is needed concerning the intertextuality of BL and related literary works (including male homosexual/homoerotic works written by male Japanese authors), in order to recognize the significance of the intertexual issues inscribed in BL texts.

Conclusion

The above analysis represents a critical attempt to examine the historic and thematic issues surrounding Japanese BL studies. As we have seen, although previous analyses of BL fantasies are diverse, further research still needs to be done. In order to fully explore the circumstances of Japanese BL studies, we need to investigate the worldwide influence of the BL tradition. Even though BL has become increasingly popular, not only in Asian countries but also in North America and Europe, little research has been done by Japanese scholars writing in Japanese in relation to the globalization and localization (glocalization) of BL overseas. Regrettably, it seems to us that Japanese BL scholars writing in Japanese appear indifferent to the developing BL tradition in other countries and their frame of reference is usually limited to Japan.[64] Nevertheless, Japanese BL continues to spread globally through the publication of legitimate and pirated translations/scanlations of manga, BL Internet sites, BL-themed conventions, and so forth. This transnational development of BL has also transformed local BL contexts, both abroad and in Japan. BL conventions are now held in numerous countries overseas, and local manga artists produce and publish BL stories influenced by Japanese BL. In order to develop further, Japanese BL studies will need to incorporate the changes brought about by globalization and localization. Whatever path future BL studies may take, scholars will have to open their eyes to the transnational reality of contemporary BL forms, practices, and community.

Notes

1. See James Welker's chapter in this volume for a historical overview of the various genres.

2. Nakajima Azusa, *Komyunikēshon fuzen shōkōgun* [Communication deficiency syndrome] (Tokyo: Chikuma shobō, 1991). See Fujimoto Yukari's chapter in this volume; and Kaneda Junko, "Manga dōjinshi: Kaishaku kyōdōtai no poritikusu" [Manga *dōjinshi*: The politics of communities' collective interpretation], in *Bunka no shakaigaku*, ed. Satō Kenji and Yoshimi Shun'ya (Tokyo: Yūhikaku, 2007). There are critical essays and studies on BL

which precede Nakajima's *Komyunikēshon fuzen shōkōgun*, including her previous essays compiled in *Bishōnen-gaku nyūmon* [Introduction to the study of beautiful boys] (Tokyo: Shūeisha, 1984); and Ueno Chizuko's essays published in *Hatsujō sōchi: Erosu no shinario* [The erotic apparatus: Erotic scenarios] (Tokyo: Chikuma shobō, 1998). Tomoko Aoyama's "Male Homosexuality as Treated by Japanese Women Writers," in *The Japanese Trajectory: Modernization and Beyond*, ed. Gavan McCormack and Yoshio Sugimoto (Cambridge: Cambridge University Press, 1988) is the earliest study in English. However, because Nakajima's *Komyunikēshon fuzen shōkōgun* achieved much public attention and had a significant impact on the early development of BL studies, this work is generally considered the first full-fledged critical analysis of Japanese BL.

3. It should be noted that several prominent analyses of Japanese BL have been written by BL creators themselves, including the aforementioned works by Nakajima, as well as, e.g., Sakakibara Shihomi, *Yaoi genron: "Yaoi" kara mieta mono* [Phantasmic discourse on *yaoi*: Things seen from a "*yaoi*" perspective] (Tokyo: Natsume shobō, 1998); and Nobi Nobita, *Otona wa wakatte kurenai: Nobi Nobita hihyō shūsei* [Adults won't understand us: The critical essays of Nobi Nobita] (Tokyo: Nihon hyōron sha, 2003).

4. See, for instance, Nakajima, *Komyunikēshon fuzen shōkōgun*; Midori Matsui, "Little Girls Were Little Boys: Displaced Femininity in the Presentation of Homosexuality in Japanese Girls' Comics," in *Feminism and the Politics of Difference*, ed. Sneja Gunew and Anna Yeatman (Halifax, NS: Fernwood Publishing, 1993); Tanigawa Tamae, "Josei no shōnen ai shōkō ni tsuite II: Shikisha no kenkai to feminizumu ni aru kanōsei" [On women's preference for *shōnen'ai*, part 2: Expert opinions and feminist possibilities], *Joseigaku nenpō* 134 (1993); and Sakakibara, *Yaoi genron*.

5. See Nakajima, *Komyunikēshon fuzen shōkōgun*.

6. See Fujimoto Yukari, *Watashi no ibasho wa doko ni aru no? Shōjo manga ga utsusu kokoro no katachi* [Where do I belong?: The shape of the heart reflected in *shōjo* manga] (Tokyo: Gakuyō shobō, 1998); cf. her chapter in this volume.

7. See Matsui, "Little Girls Were Little Boys"

8. See Kazuko Suzuki, "Pornography or Therapy? Japanese Girls Creating the Yaoi Phenomenon," in *Millennium Girls: Today's Girls Around the World*, ed. Sherrie I. Inness (Lanham, MD: Rowman and Littlefield, 1998).

9. Suzuki, "Pornography or Therapy?," 250.

10. See Kazumi Nagaike, "Perverse Sexualities, Perversive Desires: Representations of Female Fantasies and *Yaoi Manga* as Pornography Directed at Women," *U.S.–Japan Women's Journal* 25 (2003).

11. Kaneda Junko, "'Seme X uke' no mekuru meku sekai: Dansei shintai no miryoku o motomete" [The world surrounding "*seme* X *uke*": Searching for the attractiveness of male bodies], *Yuriika* 39, no. 16 (December 2007), 13–14.

12. See Kaneda, "Manga dōjinshi."

13. See Patrick W. Galbraith, "*Moe*: Exploring Virtual Potential in Post-Millennial Japan," *Electronic Journal of Contemporary Japanese Studies* (October 2009), http://www.japane-sestudies.org.uk/articles/2009/Galbraith.html.

14. See Patrick W. Galbraith, "*Fujoshi*: Fantasy Play and Transgressive Intimacy among 'Rotten Girls' in Contemporary Japan," *Signs* 37, no. 1 (2011). "*Fujoshi*" is a play on the Japanese homophone for "girls and women" that can also be written with characters meaning "rotten girls."

15. See Nagakubo Yōko, *Yaoi shōsetsu ron: Josei no tame no erosu hyōgen* [Theorizing *yaoi* fiction: Erotic representations for women] (Tokyo: Senshū daigaku shuppankyoku, 2005).

16. See Mori Naoko, *Onna wa poruno o yomu: Josei no seiyoku to feminizumu* [Women read porn: Female sexual desires and feminism] (Tokyo: Seikyūsha, 2010).

17. See Ōtsuka Eiji, *Teihon monogatari shōhi ron* [A theory of narrative consumption] (Tokyo: Kadokawa shoten, 2001).

18. Satō Masaki, "Shōjo manga to homofobia" [*Shōjo* manga and homophobia], in *Kuia sutadiizu '96*, ed. Kuia sutadiizu henshū iinkai (Tokyo: Nanatsumori shokan, 1996).

19. See Ishida Hitoshi, "'Hottoite kudasai' to iu hyōmei o megutte: Yaoi/BL no jiritsusei to hyōshō no ōdatsu" [On the declaration "Please leave me alone": The autonomy of *yaoi*/BL and the appropriation of representation], *Yuriika* 39, no. 16 (December 2007).

20. See Mizoguchi Akiko, "Homofobikku na homo, ai yue no reipu, soshite kuia na rezubian: Saikin no yaoi tekisuto o bunseki suru" [Homophobic homos, rapes of love, and queer lesbians: An analysis of recent *yaoi* texts], *Kuia Japan* 2 (2000).

21. Hori Akiko, "Yaoi wa gei sabetsu ka?: Manga hyōgen to tashaka" [Does *yaoi* discriminate against gay men?: Manga portrayals and the creation of "others"], in *Sabetsu to haijo no ima 6: Sekushuariti no tayōsei to haijo*, ed. Yoshii Hiroaki (Tokyo: Akashi shoten, 2010), 45.

22. Nobi, *Otona wa wakatte kurenai*, 240–41.

23. Keith Vincent, "A Japanese Electra and Her Queer Progeny," *Mechademia* 2 (2007), 75.

24. Wim Lunsing, "*Yaoi Ronsō*: Discussing Depictions of Male Homosexuality in Japanese Girls' Comics, Gay Comics and Gay Pornography," *Intersections: Gender, History and Culture in the Asian Context* 12 (2006), http://intersections.anu.edu.au/issue12/lunsing.html.

25. See Mark McLelland, "The Role of the '*Tōjisha*' in Current Debates about Sexual Minority Rights in Japan," *Japanese Studies* 29, no. 2 (2009).

26. See Tanigawa Tamae, "Josei no shōnen'ai shikō ni tsuite III: 'Yaoi ronsō' kara" [On women's preference for *shōnen'ai* Part 3: From the "*yaoi* debate"], *Joseigaku nenpō* 16 (1995), for more details of these arguments. Tanigawa argues that several female participants in the *yaoi* debate conclude by accusing themselves of being psychological assaulters of gay men.

27. See Kazumi Nagaike, "Elegant Caucasians, Amorous Arabs, and Invisible Others: Signs and Images of Foreigners in Japanese BL Manga," *Intersections: Gender and Sexuality in Asia and the Pacific* 20 (2009), http://intersections.anu.edu.au/issue20/nagaike.htm.

28. Robert Albright, ex-president of Johnson C. Smith University uses this term in a roundtable talk attended by John G. Russell and others. The transcript of this talk is included in Russell's *Nihonjin no kokujin kan: Mondai wa "chibi kuro Sambo" dake dewa nai* [Japanese attitudes toward black people: The problem is not just "little black Sambo"] (Tokyo: Shinhyōron, 1991).

29. See Homi Bhabha, *The Location of Culture* (London: Routledge, 1994).

30. In his *Male Homosexuality in Modern Japan: Cultural Myths and Social Realities* (Richmond, England: Curzon, 2000), McLelland argues that the *seme–uke* pattern in BL is more or less equivalent to the *sempai* (senior)–*kōhai* (junior) pattern in Japanese gay male porn, pointing out that the latter is much more hierarchical and power-oriented.

31. There has been a limited amount of previous research on how BL influences Japanese gay men's identity-creating process. See, for instance, Yajima Masami, *Dansei dōseiaisha no raifu hisutorii* [Life histories of homosexual men] (Tokyo: Gakubunsha, 1997).

32. See Mark McLelland, "Gay Men as Women's Ideal Partners in Japanese Popular Culture: Are Gay Men Really a Girl's Best Friends?" *U.S.–Japan Women's Journal* 17 (1999).

33. See Ishida Hitoshi, "Gei ni kyōkan suru joseitachi" [Women who identify with gay men], *Yuriika* 39, no. 7 (June 2007).

34. See Nishihara Mari, "Masu media ga utsushidasu *yaoi* no sugata: Gensetsu bunseki ni yoru" [A discourse analysis approach to the depiction of *yaoi* in the mass media], *Ronsō kuiaa* 3 (2010).

35. See Mark McLelland's chapter in this volume for a discussion of the effects of this incident on manga regulation.

36. See Mark McLelland, "Local Meanings in Global Space: A Case Study of Women's 'Boy Love' Web Sites in Japanese and English," *Mots Pluriels* 19 (2001), http://motspluriels.arts .uwa.edu.au/MP1901mcl.html.

37. See Mark McLelland, "Australia's Proposed Internet Filtering System: Its Implications for Animation, Comic and Gaming (ACG) and Slash Fan Communities," *Media International Australia* 134 (2010).

38. See McLelland's "Thought Policing or the Protection of Youth? Debate in Japan over the 'Non-Existent Youth Bill,'" *International Journal of Comic Art (IJOCA)* 13, no. 1 (2011), for details concerning the Tokyo Metropolitan Government's attempt to use zoning regulations to censor sexually explicit materials (including BL) which depict "seemingly" underage characters. See also McLelland's chapter in this volume.

39. See Tina Liu's "Conflicting Discourses on Boys' Love and Subcultural Tactics in Mainland China and Hong Kong," *Intersections: Gender and Sexuality in Asia and the Pacific* 20 (2009), http://intersections.anu.edu.au/issue20/liu.htm, which discusses BL as a female-oriented resistance against collective authority in mainland China and Hong Kong; and Erika Junhui Yi's "Reflection on Chinese Boys' Love Fans: An Insider's View," *Transformative Works and Cultures* 12 (2013), http://journal.transformativeworks.org/index.php/twc/article/ view/424.

40. See Mizoguchi Akiko's "Homofobikku na homo"; "Male–Male Romance by and for Women in Japan: A History and the Subgenres of *Yaoi* Fictions," *U.S.–Japan Women's Journal* 25 (2003); and "Reading and Living Yaoi: Male–Male Fantasy Narratives as Women's Sexual Subculture in Japan" (Ph.D. diss., University of Rochester, 2008). Jennifer Robertson points out that individual female fans of the Takarazuka Revue, a form of all-female musical theater, project their conscious/subconscious lesbian (or lesbian-like) desires onto female Takarazuka Revue performers who play gender-bending romantic male leads. Her book, *Takarazuka: Sexual Politics and Popular Culture in Modern Japan* (Berkeley: University of California Press, 1998), discusses the ways in which gender-bending influences the non-heteronormative psychology of female Takarazuka fans in contemporary Japan.

41. See James Welker, "Lilies of the Margin: Beautiful Boys and Queer Female Identities in Japan," in *AsiaPacifiQueer: Rethinking Genders and Sexualities*, ed. Fran Martin et al. (Urbana: University of Illinois Press, 2008).

42. Akiko Mizoguchi, "Theorizing Comics/Manga Genre as a Productive Forum: Yaoi and Beyond," in *Comics Worlds and the World of Comics: Towards Scholarship on a Global Scale*, ed. Jaqueline Berndt (Kyoto: International Manga Research Center, 2010), 157, http://imrc.jp/ images/upload/lecture/data/143-168chap10Mizoguchi20101224.pdf.

43. Adrienne Rich, "Compulsory Heterosexuality and Lesbian Existence," *Signs* 5, no. 4 (1980).

44. See Yoshimoto Taimatsu, *Fudanshi ni kiku* [Interviewing *fudanshi*] (Japan: Self-published, 2008); and *Fudanshi ni kiku 2* [Interviewing *fudanshi* 2] (Japan: Self-published, 2010).

45. See Natō Takako, "'Niji sōsaku' katsudō to sono nettowaaku ni tsuite" ["Derivative writings" and their networks], in *Sore zore no fan kenkyū: I am a fan* (Tokyo: Fūjinsha, 2007).

46. Natō, "'Niji sōsaku' katsudō," 82.

47. See Sharalyn Orbaugh, "Girls Reading Harry Potter, Girls Writing Desire: Amateur Manga and *Shōjo* Reading Practices," in *Girl Reading Girl in Japan*, ed. Tomoko Aoyama and Barbara Hartley (London: Routledge, 2010).

48. See Azuma Sonoko, "Onna no homosōsharu na yokubō no yukue: Niji sōsaku 'yaoi' ni tsuite no ichi kōsatsu" [In search of the female desire for homosociality: Thoughts on *yaoi* and derivative writings], in *Bunka no shakaigaku: Kioku, media, shintai*, ed. Ōno Michikuni and Ogawa Nobuhiko (Tokyo: Bunrikaku, 2009).

49. See Kaneda, "Manga dōjinshi."

50. See Ishikawa Yū, "Monogatari tekusuto no saiseisei no rikigaku: Yaoi no monogatari ron teki bunseki o chūshin to shite" [The dynamics of reproducing narratives: A narratological analysis of *yaoi*] (Ph.D. diss., Osaka Municipal University, 2012).

51. Orbaugh, "Girls Reading Harry Potter," 178.

52. Ishikawa, *Monogatari tekusuto*, 130.

53. Oda Ei'ichirō, *One Piece*, 71 vols., ongoing (Tokyo: Shūeisha, 1997–).

54. See Kaneda, "Manga dōjinshi."

55. The role of the Comic Market is discussed in Welker in this volume.

56. See Nakajima, *Bishōnen-gaku nyūmon.*

57. See Tomoko Aoyama, "Male Homosexuality as Treated by Japanese Women Writers"; Vincent, "A Japanese Electra and her Queer Progeny"; Kazumi Nagaike, *Fantasies of Cross-Dressing: Japanese Women Writes Male–Male Erotica* (Leiden: Brill), 2012; and Rio Otomo's chapter in this volume

58. See Tomoko Aoyama "Transgendering *Shōjo Shōsetsu*: Girls' Inter-text/sex-uality," in *Genders, Transgenders and Sexualities in Japan*, ed. Mark McLelland and Romit Dasgupta (London: Routledge, 2005); and Aoyama and Hartley, *Girl Reading Girl in Japan.*

59. Ishida Minori, *Hisoyaka na kyōiku: "Yaoi/bōizu rabu" zenshi* [A secret education: The prehistory of "yaoi/boys love"] (Kyoto: Rakuhoku shuppan, 2008), 102. For a discussion of the modernist writer Inagaki Taruho (1900–1977) in this context, see Tomoko Aoyama, "Eureka Discovers Culture Girls, Fujoshi, and BL: Essay Review of Three Issues of the Japanese Literary Magazine, *Yuriika* (Eureka)," *Intersections: Gender and Sexuality in Asia and the Pacific* 20 (April 2009); and Jeffrey Angles, *Writing the Love of Boys: Origins of Bishōnen Culture in Modernist Japanese Literature* (Minneapolis: University of Minnesota Press, 2011).

60. See, for example, Suzuki Takayuki, ed., *Bungaku wa naze manga ni maketa ka!?* [Why did literature lose to manga!?] (Kyoto: Kyoto seika daigaku jōhōkan, 1986). See also Ōtsuka Eiji's essay entitled "Manga wa ika ni shite bungaku de arō to shi, bungaku wa ika ni shite manga tari enakatta ka," [How manga tried to become literature and how literature could never become manga] in the literary journal *Bungakukai*, included in his *Sabukaruchaa bungaku ron* [A theory of subculture literature] (Tokyo: Asahi shinbunsha, 2004), 88–123. The main example discussed in this essay, however, was Nakagami Kenji's "failed" attempt, in Ōtsuka's view, to use stereotype flat characters without entertainment devices (ibid., 122).

61. Ishida, *Hisoyaka na kyōiku*, 59, citing Ōtsuka Eiji's "Manga wa ika ni shite bungaku de arō," in his *Sabukaruchaa bungaku ron*, 110. Ōtsuka, in turn, attributes the term "*naimen byōsha*" as identifying an essence of literature that manga tried to imitate to a comment by manga scholar Natsume Fusanosuke on eminent manga artist Tezuka Osamu (ibid., 101).

62. Recent examples in addition to those mentioned above include Masuda Yumiko and Saeki Junko, eds. *Nihon bungaku no "joseisei"* [The "femininity" in Japanese literature] (Tokyo: Nishōgakusha daigaku gakujutsu sōsho, 2011); and Kan Satoko, Dollase Tsuchiya Hiromi, and Takeuchi Kayo, eds. *"Shōjo manga" wandaarando* ["Girls' manga" wonderland] (Tokyo: Meiji shoin, 2012). See also the special issue of *U.S.-Japan Women's Journal* 38 (2010) on *shōjo* manga.

63. Masuda and Saeki, *Nihon bungaku no "joseisei,"* 219.

64. A very limited number of works in Japanese deal with overseas BL phenomena. For example, Shiina Yukari's "Amerika de no BL manga ninki" [The popularity of BL manga in America], *Yuriika* 39, no. 16 (December 2007), analyzes the acceptance (and rejection) of BL manga in American society; and Nagaike Kazumi's "Gurōbaruka suru BL kenkyū: Nihon BL kenkyū kara toransunashonaru BL kenkyū e" [The globalization of BL studies: The transition from Japanese BL studies to transnational BL studies], in *Josei to manga* [Women and manga], ed. Ōgi Fusami (Tokyo, Seikyūsha, forthcoming), summarizes diverse analyses of contemporary transnational BL studies written in English.

POLITICS OF UTOPIA

Fantasy, Pornography, and Boys Love

RIO OTOMO

Introduction

Photographic artworks by Robert Mapplethorpe (1946–1989) caused controversy in the United States in the late 1980s. Religious-right activists, calling for censorship, claimed that the explicit homosexuality and nudity presented in the photographs were offensive. They also argued that public funding for the exhibition of such works should be withdrawn. These activists who believed in traditionalist values generally disagreed with feminists on issues such as gender and sexuality. On this occasion, however, they buttressed their own campaign with feminist critiques of the pornographic representation of women, in particular by Andrea Dworkin and Catherine A. MacKinnon. This turn of events exposed a political vulnerability in second-wave feminism based on identity politics, in which "woman" is a clearly demarcated and unified category. For a feminist scholar like Judith Butler, the Mapplethorpe case was a point of departure in her shift towards queer politics, in which gender identity is changeable, and sexuality is not viewed as a set of fixed categories.[1]

Mark McLelland's account of the Sakai Library incident (in this volume) and the library's initial decision to withdraw from purchasing and displaying Boys Love, or BL, material demonstrates a parallel to the Mapplethorpe case.[2] As McLelland and Ishida Hitoshi (also in this volume) point out, the anti-BL camp includes not only traditionalists, but also male gay activists who argue against the misrepresentation of gay men in BL, which is comparable to the feminist criticism of pornography. It is evident that representation is the key idea to which the discussion keeps returning. In the queer (and also postmodern) view of the world, however, terms like "identity" and "representation" are inapplicable. To represent, or to misrepresent for that matter, there must first and foremost exist something to represent, such as gay men, or women, as an identifiable category. When the boundaries of each category blur, therefore, a different approach is called for.

In this chapter, I aim to present an approach that could be more effective in discussing expressions of sexual desires. Sexual desires are expressed not just by creating narratives and images, but also by reading; my focus here is on the act of reading, which is a self-expression and performance. The most prominent name given to expressions of sexual fantasy is pornography. If attention is given to the fact that women can also be consumers of sexual fantasy, opportunities exist to transform "pornography" into a more inclusive term, perhaps a vehicle to express multitudes of sexual fantasy. And in this positive sense I consider BL to be an example of pornography, one which counteracts the misogyny historically attached to the genre.[3]

My approach draws on works by post-Lacanian Judith Butler, French feminist Luce Irigaray, and Michel Foucault. I am also indebted to works by feminist writer Angela Carter and Japanese women's liberation activist Tanaka Mitsu. I aim to establish a consensus among the BL discussants that identity is a tentative (and even tenuous) property in fantasy, and that the nature of reading practices in BL demonstrates that it is so. Fantastic narratives and images do not seek to "represent" real people, and readers of fantastic narratives do not find real people in them either. For that reason, the place of the "I" in reading fantastic narratives is a critical issue in this discussion. Drawing on Foucault's critiques of the modernist ideology of the unique subject, I discuss Mishima Yukio's canonical text *Confessions of a Mask* (*Kamen no kokuhaku*) with the aim to highlight the self-effacing nature of BL in comparison.[4] In the latter part, I hark back to 1970s feminist writings to arrive at the theme of this essay, that expressions of sexual desire and fantasy are a politics of utopia that enables us to visualize a liberated form of the world to live in.

Butler's View of Fantasy

I begin with Butler, who elaborates on the relationship between fantasy and the real. In psychoanalytic terms, fantasy is a psychic reality, which is not outside the real but one dimension of it. Butler turns to "Fantasy and the Origin of Sexuality," an essay by J. Laplanche and J. B. Pontalis which re-examines

Freud's shifted positions on unconscious fantasy and daydreams.[5] She argues that fantasy uses "unauthorized" language to pose as the real in our psyches, which in effect problematizes the (semantic) ambiguity of the real itself.[6] Fantasy exposes reality's unstable nature, and it does so knowingly and willfully by simulating the powerful linguistic effect of the real. To put it another way, as an individual, my fantasy—which is a personal, changeable narrative construct—has a built-in function to make me question its ontological claims. By contrast, in the domain of the real I accept the authority of a singular narrative and am already prepared to trust what I perceive as the real.

Butler goes on to argue that fantasy should not be conceived as entirely outside the real, but rather it emerges from within it. She also points out that fantasy remains in a suspended time, meaning that fantasy ignores chronology and instead floats in non-historical time. And because of this nature, once we bring temporality into view, it is possible for us to conceive fantasy as a moratorium, a "not-yet" and "yet-to-come" reality that resides within the same field of vision of the world as the real.[7] The notion of fantasy being a possible future, a realizable utopia, is a decisive aspect which draws Butler away from feminism, since the expression of the phantasmatic—the workings of the imagination—is naturally a vehicle not only for gender politics but for minority activism at large.

One consequence of this view is a refutation of the idea that the consumption of pornography produces a sexually perverse reader. Fantasy is a tongue-in-cheek expression of the real; fantasy simulates the power of the real, but it does so with built-in self-mockery, casting doubt on its own claim to be real. This aspect of fantasy provides me with a distance from my own corporeality, or from the sense of my being in the world. The distance I maintain prevents me from acting out in the real world the pleasure I find while reading fantasy. Because of this, pornography, as fantasy, in fact *cannot* itself produce a sexually perverse reader.

Carter's View of Pornography

One of Angela Carter's literary achievements is a rewriting of fairy tales from feminist viewpoints. In the same line she wrote *The Sadeian Woman: An Exercise in Cultural History*, a rewriting of Marquis de Sade's novels *Justine* and *Juliette*. While Carter draws our attention to the fact that sexual relations depicted in pornography are all about power relations, she also points out the irony that pornographic texts perform only within readers' libidinous fantasy:

> Pornographic writing retains this in common with all literature—that it turns the flesh into word. This is the real transformation the text performs upon libidinous fantasy. . . . We know we are not dealing with real flesh, or anything like it, but with a cunningly articulated *verbal simulacrum* which has the power to arouse, but not in itself, to assuage desire.[8] (emphasis mine)

There first exists an agreement between the writer and the reader that what is presented on the pornographic text is a "verbal simulacrum," a "cunningly articulated" phantasmatic story. Pornography has a mission to arouse the reader as often as it can and as intensely as it can, while, importantly, mocking its own mission. To reiterate, this function of self-mockery stipulates a distance from the very beginning between the text and the reader. Pornography thus belongs primarily to the genre of irony, and it is, therefore, possible to conceive it as a creative vehicle with a potential quality to liberate us from a self-justifying monological view of the world.

I will not here argue further in favor of Butler or Carter's positions. Rather, they are my starting points for the following discussion of BL. Carter is, I think, right in saying that pornography does not have the power in itself to satisfy readers' desire, and so is Butler, who contends that pornography, or erotic fantasy, does not produce a sexually perverse reader. Importantly, this relates to the falsity of popular assumption that participating writers and readers of BL are *fujoshi*, the "rotten girls," who are sexually deprived in real life.[9] Readers and writers are in fact spread widely across the social stratum and sexual orientations.

What Is a Reader?

Viewed as irony, a seemingly monological pornographic text turns into a dialogical space, in which, as a reader, I extract, through a negotiation of distance, a pleasure of my own. This act of reading is an expression of my personal sexual fantasy, and I perform it in my own private space. Although it is my private practice, it is not a simple reflection of my private desire. I purchase the material to read, participating in public consumption, and at the same time my choice is to a large extent formed by the selection available to me in the market. Thus, what I believe to be *my* taste may not be truly mine, or rather, I may have been directed to prefer one thing to another by the socially constructed notions of what is desirable. Indeed, it can be said that the way I dress, the way I walk, and the way I speak, all are my *learned* choices, and that my desire itself is largely what I learned to want. And yet, once I am aware that I embody and act out socially constructed desire through my reading, I can choose to be a critical and creative participant. A reader is, in this context, a public performer. In the following sections I look into different modes of reading in attempt to clarify particularities of BL reading.

The Autoerotic Reader in Mishima

One of the canonical texts widely taught in literary studies as a Modern Confessional text, is Mishima Yukio's *Confessions of a Mask*.[10] While all such texts involve hidden sexual desires, Mishima's is at once a *Bildungsroman*— that is, a coming-of-age story—and a coming-out story. The narrator discovers eroticism in the male body, which includes his own, when he accidentally encounters an image of Christian martyr St. Sebastian, who is tied to a tree and pierced by arrows. The young narrator then goes further to write his own story of St. Sebastian. This act of rewriting aims to recreate the original pleasure that he felt at the first sighting and to possess it exclusively by reading it by himself. The same desire is at work in BL, except that the latter is communal. Sharing the pleasure with others instead of aiming to possess it is, therefore, a key difference to note here.

The confessional mode of writing like Mishima's is a narrative strategy in which the narrator speaks to the confessor (the reader) endlessly to postpone his necessary transformation. If one truly wishes to transform oneself, an encounter with the Other is a necessary passage. One could even say that the modernist confessional texts are a demonstration of psychological resistance to that encounter.[11] The confessional narrative in general is structured like a closed circuit, which results in the confessant being unable to recognize the existence of the Other that resides beyond his self-surveillance. The only person the Mishima's narrator encounters through his confessional narrative is himself. He desires the sameness; he is in love with himself talking about himself.[12] He is in essence autoerotic. While BL narratives share this desire for the sameness, shutting down the possibility of meeting with the Other, their autoeroticism does not aim to construct a unique and unified subject, as Mishima's does.

In the first half of *Confessions of a Mask*, ten childhood memories are listed as evidence of the narrator's homosexuality, and in each case he wants to be the object he desires. He wants to turn into St. Sebastian and simultaneously wants to be the arrow that pierces his body. Throughout the novel, the narrator is *reading* homosexual desires in his memories, and along with it, narrativizing, or more precisely, *constructing* a desiring subject who discovers his "true Self." Discovery of the truth is, as we know, all the more seductive when it is prohibited.[13] Mishima frequently capitalizes that mechanism of prohibition in his novels. In contrast, prohibition, and hence a sense of guilt, are absent in, for example, the beautiful boy (*bishōnen*) novels by Mori Mari (1903–1987), which, in my view, substantially reduces the intricacy of their narratives. With or without a sense of guilt, however, readers of fantastic narratives are not concerned with the concept of a "true Self." In this respect, both BL texts and readers are outside the paradigm of modernity.

Confessions of a Mask was certainly a modernist project of making a case for the existence of a Japanese (male) subject who *knows himself*.[14] It is because being homosexual risks a downgrading of one's social power that "knowing oneself" in this novel gains more gravity than otherwise. The narrator realizes he *is* homosexual, disregarding the other strands of his sexuality such as sadomasochism, cannibalism, and autoeroticism, all of which are also described in minute detail as the narrator's sexual fantasies. The novel exemplifies the Foucauldian thesis that homosexuality alone among other sexual orientations becomes the privileged identity category in the modernist discourse. The fact that the reimagining of a Japanese male subject, who is equipped with psychological depth and articulation, is accomplished through homosexuality does not necessarily prove the idiosyncrasy of the author, but it does demonstrate the ways in which the forces of modernity take hold of people's minds.

The Autoerotic Reader in BL

BL critic Ishida Minori juxtaposes Mishima with the Fabulous Forty-Niners (*Hana no nijūyo'nen-gumi*), the vanguard women manga artists of the BL genre, describing the different directions they took after their respective first trips to Europe.[15] Ishida argues that Mishima discovers in Europe the significance of the body-in-presence (and exclusively the male one) over the linguistic effect of the body (his texts), a discovery which leads him to his own physical body-sculpting regime at the age of thirty.

The women manga artists, Ishida continues, are determined to capture the details of European cities, buildings, fashion, smells, colors, and historical facts, information which they later utilize to provide depth for their fantasy, love stories between beautiful boys. This includes manga artists Takemiya Keiko, Hagio Moto, and writer Masuyama Norie, who formed the backbone of the group of women who created this new trend in *shōjo* manga in the 1970s. Their European experience culminates in works like *The Heart of Thomas* (*Tōma no shinzō*, 1974), by Hagio, and *The Song of the Wind and the Trees* (*Kaze to ki no uta*, 1976–1984), by Takemiya, which subsequently gained critical acclaim from outside the sphere of *shōjo* manga enthusiasts.[16] While Mishima was prolific in the 1960s when the body became a cultural spectacle and a political agenda—such as at the Tokyo Olympic Games, the *angura* (underground) theater movement, Butoh dancing, and the students' New Left movement—the Fabulous Forty-Niners had their own revolution in the 1970s. They integrated the human body into the scenery, as if it was a transcendental, non-organic carrier of emotions. Through the phantasmatic images of beautiful boys they expressed their own desire, which could not be expressed within normative heterosexual romance. While Mishima's fetish was the three-dimensional Greek sculpture, the women artists developed a two-dimensional code of desire.[17] Despite the usual assumption that the images of beautiful boys are the fetish objects of BL, these manga artists started their project by rejecting the presence of the body and a desire to possess it.

When I read BL texts, I first identify different bodies, which are codes for different positions in the networks of human relations.[18] The recognition of their differences provokes desire in multiple directions. I then re-enact the difference playing multiple roles in my single body—and, thus, reading (and writing) BL I am able to play with gender itself—a point also discussed by Fujimoto Yukari in her chapter in this volume. I am, thus, autoerotic, but my (female) body is erased in this process. Fantasy in its broad sense tells me a story in which I am everywhere. In BL texts, I am simultaneously the character's downcast eyes; the texture of the velvet couch he lounges on; the windows that fling open; and the wind that blows his curly locks. When his lover enters the room, I am also that lover who looks at him with heated desire. In reading like this, no single identification takes place, since the "I" is multiplied to govern each detail of the scene. The subject "I" as the unified center no longer exists in this activity. Unlike Mishima's narrator, I do not consolidate the subject "I" but instead lose sight of it in the landscape.

The distance that I thought existed between fantasy and myself does not seem reliable any more because I am now becoming my fantasy, writing the script, acting the roles, and capturing the scenes. I am efficient in creating pictures and narratives since my focus is on acquiring the utmost pleasure through the fantasy I am making. In the process, however, the "I" who is making disappears, a consequence that Mishima's narrator could not afford despite the happiness he knew it was offering. The disappearance of the "I" is the ultimate goal of fantasy making; I forget where I am and what I am. I do not remember whether I have even existed, when I am in a phantasmatic space. At that very moment of happiness I do not care how I appear to others; I am back in my childlike innocence. I have forgotten my gendered body.[19] The reading subject is not born there, but disappears, as my auto-erotic pleasure peculiarly excludes myself along with my body.

Politics of Utopia—Feminism and Queerism

To say the reader disappears in BL may sound negative. But forgetting one's gendered body, or floating away from a fixed identity, is essentially a liberating concept and, for that reason, it is the core idea of queer theory. This issue takes us back to a continuing debate within feminism in which some argue that identity politics remains as a necessary standpoint for the promotion of equality and freedom. Though it may sound liberating, the concept of a "gender-free" society is problematic. It can preempt action by ignoring the existing power balance between men and women, heterosexual and homosexual, and nullify the struggle of those whose self-identification is a mismatch to the socially given identification. Queer theory is, therefore, not calling for "gender-free," but on the contrary it actively seeks to change the existing power balance by focusing on gender inequality. Taking the role of fantasy seriously is precisely a strategy for that aim. Fantasy contributes to social transformation by creating a vision of utopia in people's psyche, thereby quietly but steadily spurring political action.

In 1977, Luce Irigaray put forward a vision of a feminist utopia by creating the image of an autoerotic woman's body, in which two lips of a vulva can meet whenever and wherever to produce *jouissance*—an excessive, endless bodily pleasure—without phallic mediation.[20] It is noteworthy that, according to Irigaray, the erogenous zone is not confined to sexual organs, but spread all over the woman's body. At the time, this was a powerfully subversive message against the myth of woman's sexuality, which was the image of an empty hole waiting to be filled. It undermined the predominant assumption in misogynic pornography, which has always relied on that myth to tailor its product for the masculine libidinal economy.

Introducing the woman's body into the critique of phallogocentrism was not confined to French feminism. In 1970, the same year that the Fabulous Forty-Niners began exchanging their ideas at the Ōizumi Salon, as they called the apartment they shared in Tokyo, Japanese women's liberationist Tanaka Mitsu wrote an influential leaflet entitled "Liberation from the Toilet" (*Benjo kara no kaihō*). She condemned the social attitude to designate a woman either as *mother* (a comfort-giver for men) or *toilet* (a waste-disposal for men), neither of which granted a woman the status of an individual social being.[21] Tanaka also pointed out that this discourse revealed the social consciousness of sex as unclean. Like Irigaray, Tanaka envisages a feminist utopia, in which a woman can live as she is, without reflecting on this other image of ideal womanhood that patriarchy projects on her. Tanaka uses the expression "me who is here as I am" (*ima koko ni iru kono mama no watashi*) and envisages a new social relationship, in which a woman is perceived as a whole package, equipped with her own sexual desire that exists outside the patriarchal imagination of feminine sexuality.

Forty years on, there are many women who enjoy writing and reading BL stories, which are a different sort of pornography than that tailored for heterosexual male enjoyment, in the sense that they do not confine eroticism to sexual organs, and that, through them, a woman can express her desire without reflecting on the image of that phantom woman, the ghost of patriarchy. These aspects are BL's most significant political contributions. In the mid-1990s, Nakajima Azusa made her feminist position clear, describing what she calls the "world of *JUNE*":

> The standing position for these girls has already been removed from the world they create . . . there is no "opposite" sex as the object of love. Turning themselves into shadow, the girls can play to their hearts content with materials unfamiliar to them, connecting one person to another, or making someone fall in love with another, without fear of being made to enter the "ring" where she is on display to be purchased by men.[22]

JUNE magazine (1978–1979, 1981–1996), a popular BL-focused periodical, was during its time the hub for BL enthusiasts.[23] While autoerotic Mishima always turns to his own body as his fetish, the interpersonal relationship, or "connecting one person to another," is arguably the most seductive element for BL readers. I have mentioned that BL readers' autoeroticism is devoid of an actual body. That does not mean that the space is unpopulated. Rather, the act of reading in BL involves vigorous mental exercise in social relations.[24] Power relations, and in particular, the plasticity of those relations, fascinates the reader. Of course, this reader may not necessarily be a woman, but instead a man who has a *desire* to transform existing social relations, and, hence is searching for a new utopian vision.[25]

The difference between Mishima and BL is perhaps now clearer. The object of desire is by nature a metonymic sign, which is endlessly replaceable and without a meaning of its own.[26] Mishima understood this mechanism and in one sense managed to valorize the name *Mishima* and the texts, which were attached to that name, by deliberately leaving his scandalous body for a global audience to see.[27] There is no hint of obsession with the body of that nature in the BL phenomenon; the reader is not necessarily aroused by the image of a beautiful boy in the text, but more so by the relationship he has with another person. She does not wish to own the beautiful boy, but to simulate his metamorphoses, such as the powerless boy who becomes powerful when he has come to embody the pleasure he was first forced to learn.

A network of relationships is an important part of a utopian blueprint, feminist or non-feminist, because human beings are social mammals whose happiness depends on others. While BL writers and readers are not generally deprived of actual sexual relationships, as Patrick Galbraith and Jeffry Hester in this volume discuss, they certainly do express unfulfilled desires. It is a basic desire to be in a society that will allow a person to be a whole *package* equipped with his or her own pleasure, and to relate to others as what Tanaka calls "me who is here as I am."

I have argued that Mishima's narrator constructed a solid, unchangeable subject, and made sure his voice was heard; while the BL reader pursues the moment of her own disappearance as a subject. The self that is expressed through reading pornography, including BL stories, is a far cry from the self that is determined by the notion of identity. There is no urgent need of her "coming out" as a BL reader in order to feel that she is "truly" understood by her family or her colleagues. Being a "*fujoshi*" is not an identity category; it merely indicates an individual's preference or taste, which is in no way unique to her, but a shared taste among many. Perhaps, *fujoshi* has now been transformed from a derogative to an ironical, intelligent self-naming, just as has been done with the term "queer" in mainstream discourse. "Queer" is best seen not as an identity category, but as a celebration of heterogeneity, a way of living and a *utopian* worldview. The relationships between beautiful male characters in the BL enjoyed by *fujoshi* today have become very formulaic and clichéd, and in that sense, are not very "queer." I end this article with an open question, whether it is possible for BL narratives to present new, more liberal relationships in the place of the formalized, clichéd patterns they have used as a most effective love machine.

Notes

1. Judith Butler, "The Forces of Fantasy: Feminism, Mapplethorpe, and Discursive Excess," in *Feminism and Pornography*, ed. Drucilla Cornell (Oxford: Oxford University Press, 2007).

2. "Boys Love" or "Boy's Love" (abbreviated as BL) is a term used along with *yaoi* (both in *hiragana* and *katakana* scripts) and *shonen'ai* to address women's novels and manga that depict sexual relationships between men. For the definitions of these terms, see the introduction to this volume, as well as discussions in chapters by James Welker, Fujimoto Yukari,

and Kazuko Suzuki; see also Mizuma Midory's *In'yu toshite no shonen'ai: Josei no shōnen'ai shikō to iu genshō* [*Shōnen'ai* as metaphor: The phenomenon of women's inclination for *shōnen'ai*] (Osaka: Sōgensha, 2005) and Ishida Minori's attempt to provide a socio-historical background of BL in *Hisoyaka na kyōiku: "Yaoi/bōizu rabu" zenshi* [A secret education: The prehistory of yaoi/boys love] (Kyoto: Rakuhoku shuppan, 2008).

3. While it is a "positive model" on the one hand, it often mimics conventional heterosexual power relations between same-sex lovers on the other. I discuss this in the chapter.

4. Mishima Yukio, *Kamen no kokuhaku* [*Confessions of a Mask*] (Tokyo: Kawade shobō, 1949).

5. Jean Laplanche and J. B. Pontalis, "Fantasy and the Origin of Sexuality," in *Unconscious Phantasy*, ed. Riccardo Steiner (London: H. Karnac, 2003). Note that Butler uses three terms—"the phantasmatic," "fantasy," and "psychic reality"—interchangeably.

6. Judith Butler, "The Forces of Fantasy: Feminism, Mapplethorpe, and Discursive Excess," in *Feminism and Pornography*, ed. Drucilla Cornell (Oxford: Oxford University Press, 2007), 490.

7. Butler, "The Forces of Fantasy," 488. José Esteban Muñoz also explains the concept of "not-yet" reality: a potentiality is a certain mode of nonbeing that is eminent, a thing that is present but not actually existing in the present tense, in *Cruising Utopia: The Then and There of Queer Futurity* (New York: New York University Press, 2009).

Nakajima Azusa, one of the key writer-critics of BL novels, critiques male *otaku* culture (with a narrower definition than now used), girls' anorexia and bulimia, and finds in all of them the desire to remain in a moratorium. See *Komyunikēshon fuzen shōkōgun* [Communication deficiency syndrome] (Tokyo: Chikuma shobō, 1995). The link between fantasy making, youths, and their desire to remain in a moratorium is an important issue in the discussion of BL, albeit beyond the scope of this chapter.

8. Angela Carter, "Polemical Preface: Pornography in the Service of Women," in *The Sadeian Woman: An Exercise in Cultural History* (London: Virago Press, 2006), 15. Carter is here discussing novels, but I would extend her argument to other visual pornographic materials.

9. See Sugiura Yumiko, *Fujoshika suru sekai: Higashi Ikebukuro no otaku joshitachi* [*Fujoshi*-izing world: The *otaku* girls of East Ikebukuro] (Tokyo: Chūō kōron shinsha, 2006), 40; Mori Naoko, *Onna wa poruno o yomu: Onna no seiyoku to feminizumu* [Women read porn: Female sexual desire and feminism] (Tokyo: Seikyūsha, 2010), 101; and Ishida, *Hisoyaka na kyōiku*, 340. See also Mizuma, who critically analyzes existing discourses used in public discussions of *shōnen'ai* cultures and the damaging effect such an approach will have on young women.

10. Others include Jean-Jacques Rousseau's *The Confessions* (Oxford: Oxford University Press, 2000); and Fyodor Dostoevsky's *Notes from the Underground* (Harmondsworth, England: Penguin, 1989).

11. In both Dostoevsky's and Mishima's texts, a woman approaches the narrator, eager to communicate, but ends up being in vain, which demonstrates the woman-as-the-Other formula repeated beyond cultural borders.

12. I am using the masculine pronoun here, as it relates to the narrator of Mishima's text.

13. The narrator had stealthily entered his father's study and found the painting of St. Sebastian. In Mishima's later work, *The Temple of Dawn* (*Akatsuki no tera*, 1970), the protagonist creates a peephole in a wall full of German law books, inherited from his father,

only to find the object of his desire, a young Thai princess, in the next room engaged in sex with another woman. Instead of admitting her otherness, he sees only what he wants to see: a mark on her body that she is the reincarnation of his first love, a beautiful young man who died at the age of twenty.

14. See Michel Foucault, *History of Sexuality*, vol. 3, *The Care of the Self* (Harmondsworth, England: Penguin, 1986).

15. Ishida discusses this in *Hisoyaka na kyōiku*, 109–54. It is noteworthy that her discussion includes their different approaches to Luchino Visconti's costume drama films, such as *The Damned* (1969), *Death in Venice* (1971), and *Ludwig* (1972).

16. Hagio Moto, *Tōma no shinzō* [*The Heart of Thomas*] (1974; Tokyo: Shōgakukan bunko, 1995); Takemiya Keiko, *Kaze to ki no uta* [The song of the wind and the trees], 10 vols. (1976–1984; Tokyo: Hakusensha bunko, 1995).

17. Ishida, *Hisoyaka na kyōiku*, 112, 150.

18. See also Kazumi Nagaike, *Fantasies of Cross-Dressing: Japanese Women Write Male-Male Erotica* (Leiden: Brill, 2012) on BL readers' taking multiple identifications in their reading.

19. That the BL readers escape from their own gendered body is well explored in the debates documented in Keith Vincent, "A Japanese Electra and Her Queer Progeny," *Mechademia 2* (2007).

20. Luce Irigaray, *This Sex Which is Not One* (New York: Cornell University Press, 1985).

21. See Tanaka Mitsu, *Inochi no onna tachi e: Torimidashi ūman ribu* [To the women of life: Tearing my hair out women's liberation] (Tokyo: Kawade shobō shinsha, 1992), 18, and also Mori, *Onna wa poruno o yomu*, 12. On 1970 as the originary year of the *shōnen'ai* genre, see Welker's chapter in this volume.

22. Nakajima, *Komyunikēshon fuzen shōkōgun*, 232–33.

23. *JUNE* is discussed extensively in Fujimoto's chapter in this volume.

24. My discussion here is focused on individual readers and differs from the relationships among reader-creators discussed by Patrick Galbraith in this volume.

25. On male fandom of BL and its relationship to dissatisfaction with the current gender and sexual order, see Kazumi Nagaike's chapter in this volume.

26. For a clear explanation of the Lacanian concepts of metonymy, desire and fetishism, I recommend Dylan Evans, *An Introductory Dictionary of Lacanian Psychoanalysis* (London: Routledge, 2001).

27. Mishima had notified journalists before his final action including the foreign press. See Henry Scott-Stokes, *The Life and Death of Yukio Mishima* (New York: Ballantine Books, 1985). The postscript to this book reveals a tabloid interest in the homosexuality that Mishima's body may have, or may not have, given "proof" to by autopsy.

MOE TALK

Affective Communication among Female Fans of *Yaoi* in Japan

PATRICK W. GALBRAITH

"They say that the compulsion to consume certain kinds of manga is a sickness (*byōki*). But we all have our sicknesses. The question is what is your sickness? And what sickness can we live together with?"
—SAGAWA TOSHIHIKO, FOUNDER OF *JUNE*[1]

Introduction

In the growing body of literature on boys love (BL) manga in Japan, more attention is paid to texts than readers. Where discussions of BL readers do appear, they tend to be autobiographical or abstract.[2] This has led to much speculation about the identifications and orientations of BL readers—they are straight women, lesbians, men in women's bodies, gay men, straight men[3]—which is fascinating in its own right. However, at a time when erotic manga face public criticism for their possible deleterious effects,[4] despite academic writing on the complexity of engagement with fiction,[5] there is an urgent need for grounded discussion of what readers do with BL manga and with one another. This chapter explores how female fans of BL in Japan talk to one another about relationships between fictional male characters, which is not only pleasurable, but also productive of new ways of interacting with the world of everyday reality.[6]

Drawing on fieldwork conducted in Tokyo from 2006 to 2007,[7] I focus primarily on three female university students and friends named Hachi, Megumi, and Tomo, who started reading BL in middle school and later became producers and consumers of *yaoi*. Distinct from BL, a genre of

153

commercial manga, *yaoi* is a form of fan-fiction and art that depicts romantic and/or sexual relationships between straight male characters from manga, anime, games, and other popular media, as well as media personalities and public figures. BL is a formula—a couple comprised of two male characters, where one is the top (*seme*) and the other is the bottom (*uke*)—and *yaoi* is reading this formula in unexpected places.[8] One imagines that a relationship between men might be romantic or sexual, in other words a character "coupling" (*kappuringu*).[9] At the time of our encounters, Hachi, Megumi, and Tomo no longer read BL manga because the relationship between the two original male characters was already apparent, so the space for imagining and producing the relationship was closed down. While BL manga (and its historical antecedent, *shōnen'ai*) can be serious in tone, *yaoi* fan-fiction and art tends to be playful and parodic. Indeed, the term "*yaoi*" is an acronym for "no climax, no punch line, no meaning" (*yama nashi, ochi nashi, imi nashi*). If, as BL scholars have noted, relationships between male characters that neither look like men nor identify as homosexual opens up the possibility of "perverse readings,"[10] then this is amplified in *yaoi*, which is not burdened by expectations of "meaning" and "reality." In *yaoi* fan-fiction and art, women can "play sexuality."[11]

The bulk of this chapter is devoted to unpacking what Hachi, Megumi, and Tomo called "*moe* talk" (*moe-banashi*), where they discussed affective relationships between not only fictional male characters, but also animate and inanimate objects. The goal is to show how *yaoi* fans use their imagination to interact differently with media, one another, and the world around them. I conclude that fans understand and negotiate their own relations far better than outside observers can, which should discourage hasty intervention by "authorities." Indeed, the true authorities are not lawyers and researchers, but rather the fans themselves. I certainly learned from Hachi, Megumi, and Tomo, who graciously included me in sessions of *moe* talk. This chapter is an attempt to work through and convey, however imperfectly, the experience of hanging out with three *yaoi* fans in Japan, which changed my perspective on things.

Fujoshi: The Imagination of "Rotten Girls"

Many *yaoi* fans that I encountered, including Hachi, Megumi, and Tomo, self-identified as "*fujoshi*," literally meaning "rotten girls."[12] When I asked informants what makes *fujoshi* "rotten," three explanations were recurrent. One, *fujoshi* are in relationships with fictional men rather than actual members of the opposite sex. Two, *fujoshi* prefer male–male romance to male–female romance. This is taken to be abnormal, a perception reinforced by sometimes extreme depictions of sex in *yaoi* fan-fiction and art. Three, *fujoshi* have deviated from the social roles and responsibilities that define women. In homosocial and imaginary relations, *yaoi* fans do not have to face reality and grow up (they are "girls") and fail to achieve reproductive maturity (they are "rotten"). Symbolically, the term "*fujoshi*" is a pun that transforms the Japanese term "women and girls" into a homonym meaning "rotten girls."[13]

While obviously an example of labeling and negative identity politics, we should not forget that the word "*fujoshi*" is used among *yaoi* fans themselves. This can be a form of self-deprecating humor, but also something more. Some women embrace being "rotten girls," announcing themselves as *fujoshi* and performing this identification when among friends and fellow fans. Being a *fujoshi*—up to and including having "abnormal" fantasies—can be a source of pride. *Fujoshi* consider themselves to be different from "normals" (*ippanjin*), and even "normal" fans of manga, anime, and games (so-called *otaku*). Megumi made a distinction between normals, who are satisfied with things as they are, and *fujoshi*, who seek alternatives. From Megumi's perspective, normals have no dreams and no imagination. In contrast, Hachi said that *fujoshi* have "abundant imagination" (*mōsōryoku yutaka*). They can "fantasize about anything" (*nan ni demo mōsō suru*). Hachi, Megumi, and Tomo all agreed that what makes a *fujoshi* different from others is her appreciation of *moe*, or an affective response to fictional characters. In pursuit of *moe*, the *fujoshi* interacts with fiction, other people, and the world differently.

Moe: Affective Response and Communication

The *moe* response is triggered first and foremost by personal interactions with a fictional character or characters interacting with one another. A character can be a written description or drawn image, an actual person reduced to a character (or one that is a "character" or known personality), or anthropomorphized animals, plants, machines, objects, concepts, and so on. The material that triggers a *moe* response can come from anywhere, if one is able to read for the signs of a BL relationship. As Megumi explained, "*Fujoshi* see *moe* in anything. [Fantasizing about *yaoi* narratives] changes one's way of seeing things and imagining relationships between things." In general, only fiction or what is associated with fiction can be *moe*; a physical object such as a figurine or a person in costume can be *moe*, but only to the extent that they are associated with a character or its world. The trigger of *moe* is made distinct from reality. Fans of *yaoi*, for example, refer to relationships between male characters as "pure fantasy" (*junsui na fantajii*).[14] Even though they are aware of the realities of relations between men and women, the fantasy is made pure by deliberately separating it from everyday life. In this way, Hachi argued that drawings of beautiful boys have nothing to do with "real gays" (*riaru gei*).[15] Hachi described herself to me as a lesbian, with no interest in men, gay or straight, but she was attracted to the fictional characters of manga, anime, and games. Further, she explained, if a man is gay in reality, then it is not fun to imagine that he is—hence the separation of fictional characters from "real gays." Similarly, Megumi imagined her boyfriend, who she later married, in romantic and sexual relationships with other men. Megumi's partner was not homosexual, and she did not exactly want him to be. Rather, Megumi told me that she enjoyed playing with his "character" (*kyara*), which she knew was surely a submissive bottom just waiting to be taken by the right man. Just as Hachi made drawings of beautiful boys distinct from real gay men, Megumi made her partner's character distinct from him, which allowed her to interact with him in different ways.

Following Saitō Tamaki, one might say that *fujoshi* are attracted to "fictional contexts" (*kyokō no kontekusuto*),[16] specifically patterned relationships between men called "boys love." *Fujoshi* enjoy "layering," as Saitō puts it, contexts one upon the other, and playfully putting fiction into relation with reality. In the specific case of Megumi, she layered a fictional context onto reality—BL character relations on top of actual male relations—which allowed her to be "multiply oriented" to her partner.[17] To recap, Megumi was imaginatively producing *yaoi* fan-fiction using her partner's character. Because the fictional character was "real" (embodied) and the real person was "fictional" (her partner as character), Megumi could interact with fiction and reality in different ways. Megumi was particularly attuned to this kind of layer play. For example, when watching anime, she would comment on an imagined relationship between an actor and the male character that he voiced. Saitō would explain this behavior not as confusion about what is real, but rather the pleasure of straddling layered contexts and crossing boundaries.

When an imagined character coupling proves affective, *fujoshi* call it "*moe*," a term used widely among diverse fandoms of manga, anime, and games in Japan. Hachi, Megumi, and Tomo all insisted that what one does and does not find *moe* differs from person to person. Because they had grown up together reading and sharing BL and *yaoi*, the three women felt that they had developed into friends who could talk about *moe*, or "*moe* friends" (*moe tomo*).[18] The pursuit of *moe*, shared among *fujoshi*, is key to understanding

Figure 8.1 Selling fanzines at the Comic Market. Photo by Androniki Christodoulou.

the sociality of *fujoshi*. For example, *yaoi* fan-fiction and art is intended to convey what one responds to as *moe*. Fans are highlighting precisely what it is about the character, design, scene, interaction, or series that excites, and do this with the intention of sharing that affection. *Yaoi* has been called "pornography" and "masturbation fantasy,"[19] but its pleasures are nevertheless meant to be shared. The exchange can be direct. At events to buy and sell *yaoi* fanzines (*dōjinshi*), *fujoshi* interact face to face. Hachi was a relatively well-known producer of fanzines, and I observed her at several events. As Hachi described it, sitting behind a table laden with fanzines is like advertising one's fantasy. When someone stops at a table, picks up a fanzine, and flips through it, there is palpable tension; the creator waits in nervous anticipation of a response. Only if the prospective reader decides to buy the fanzine do the two women begin to engage in conversation, first confirming what the work is about and then discussing their shared interest. As a rule at many events, the personal website of the author/artist is printed inside her fanzine, so readers can connect with them online.[20]

There are a variety of interactions that occur on the personal websites of *fujoshi*, but, due to issues of space, I will limit myself to an account of two types. The first is *echa* ("picture chat"), where participants gather on a designated website at a designated time to draw, upload and discuss images. If the fanzine is an expression of what one responds to as *moe*, then the *echa* is an intimate association of imagination, where one is open to being affected by others in a real-time exchange of images and ideas. In one example, Hachi hosted an *echa* dedicated to generating *moe* for *Pokémon* creatures, which she and her friends anthropomorphized and put into character couplings. The drawings and discussion evolved collectively, as participants were excited and inspired by what others suggested as sexy interpretations of *Pokémon* creatures and relationships between them. Another example of online interaction among *fujoshi* is *naricha* ("become a character to chat"), where participants role-play *yaoi* narratives, which can include virtual sex between characters. The *naricha* might be seen as an example of what Uli Meyer calls "creative transvestism," or a transgression of sexuality and gender that carries over from fiction into reality, "enabling its readers/creators to identify or feel with the male characters on a physical level."[21] Note, however, that not all of the *fujoshi* I spoke with who participated in *naricha* (and, by extension, virtual sex with one another) considered themselves to be lesbians. Even Hachi, who did identify this way, explained to me that *naricha* was a relationship between fictional male characters, a form of *yaoi* fan-fiction that has nothing to do with the producer's sexual orientation. After all, *yaoi* is supposed to be meaningless. If the *naricha* is a form of fan-fiction, then participants "characterize" themselves to (role-)play sexuality in *yaoi*, much as Megumi "characterized" her male partner and played out relations between him and other men.

When together on- or offline, *fujoshi* friends engage in what Hachi, Megumi, and Tomo called "*moe* talk" (*moe-banashi*).[22] As the name implies, *moe* talk entails talking about what one responds to as *moe*, which is usually a particular character coupling. Even as one gets carried away in the moment of *moe* talk, "enthusiasm is tempered by a kind of self-awareness that gives it a performed quality."[23] Morikawa Ka'ichirō notes that describing certain characters, relationships, or situations as *moe* is an intimate expression of taste,[24] but at the same time talking about *moe* relationships with and between fictional characters allows for distance. For example, Sugiura Yumiko observes that *fujoshi* talk about sex as if evaluating food or handbags,[25] because they are not talking about themselves or real people but rather the *moe* points of sex between fictional characters. Though Morikawa and Sugiura's points may seem at odds, *moe* talk is both talking about personal taste and talking about things outside the self. The object of conversation is both distant and intensely personal. Take for example the single most common debate among *fujoshi* who recognize the same character coupling: Who is the top (*seme*) and who is the bottom (*uke*)? Just as there are cues that make certain relationships between men more likely to be reinterpreted as romantic or sexual, there are elements of character that *fujoshi* pick up on to make the distinction between top and bottom, but there are also disagreements. As Hachi, Megumi, and Tomo said, though *moe* is a response to things outside the self and can seem like detached observations, it differs from person to person, and hence talking (or arguing) about *moe* can get personal in a hurry. As Daisuke Okabe and Kimi Ishida note, "How fujoshi [*sic*] choose to categorize characters from the original work can energize or ruin their communication with one another."[26] Though fans do come together in more general ways, belonging to an abstract and homogenous community only lasts until one is confronted with internal difference.[27] *Moe* talk is a concrete, joyful encounter, an intense form of communication among fans with similar tastes.

Though the moment of affective response to the fictional character has passed, *moe* talk affects in its own way. Not only are fictional characters summoned and relations with them enlivened by *moe* talk, but also one's understanding of characters and relations expands. Hachi referred to *moe* talk as "sharing one big brain," where she could gain access to a collective consciousness or shared imaginary concerning character coupling. (Recall the *echa* here.) The evolving relationship with and between characters can take an unexpected turn based on input from other *fujoshi* who participate in *moe* talk. For her part, Hachi sought out *moe* friends who had close enough interests to understand the character coupling, but also enough imagination to say something new and interesting that would inspire conversation. Moments of being taken by surprise were among the most intense in *moe* talk. Shrieks and squeals, shouting, thrashing arms, gnashing teeth, clapping hands—I observed all of these in *moe* talk among *fujoshi*.[28]

The pursuit of *moe* and the interactions that it engenders with media, objects and others, both fictional and real, approaches what Gilles Deleuze and Félix Guattari call a "plateau," or a continuous "region of intensities whose development avoids any orientation toward a culmination point or external end."[29] *Yaoi* is a plateau, in that relations with and between characters are open-ended and ongoing. (There is "no climax.") For example, when I met Hachi's friend Kei in 2006, she was still actively producing *yaoi* fan-fiction about a character coupling from an anime series that aired on Japanese TV in the 1990s. She also gravitated toward new character couplings that reflect elements of this older one. Kei's pursuit of *moe* is an example of what Dominic Pettman calls a "love vector," where "distributed qualities [are] splashed across a multitude of people, characters, images and avatars,"[30] and this vector is not oriented toward a point of culmination. The love vector also allows us to see what Megumi was talking about when she said that *fujoshi* imagine relationships between things in the world around them: a distribution of affective qualities and relations across a multitude of animate and inanimate objects. Brian Massumi notes of the plateau that "the heightening of energies is sustained long enough to leave a kind of afterimage of its dynamism that can be reactivated or injected into other activities, creating a fabric of intensive states between which any number of connecting routes could exist."[31] In the case of *fujoshi*, the intensity of interactions with and between fictional characters does not immediately dissipate in a climax and is instead injected into interactions among *fujoshi*. If, as Deleuze and Guattari suggest, the intensive stabilization of the plateau can occur in "sexual games, and even quarrels," then *moe* talk is certainly one example.[32]

Examples of *Moe* Talk

In this section, I offer some examples of *moe* talk from my fieldwork. To begin, Hachi, Megumi, and Tomo are all fans of *Angelique*, a series of games in which the player takes the role of a queen and simulates romance with a bevy of beautiful boy characters. As *fujoshi*, however, the three women preferred

Figure 8.2 The characters of *Angelique*.

to imagine relationships between male characters. One evening, Hachi and Tomo came to visit Megumi, who lived in an apartment in central Tokyo while attending university and working part-time. Because Megumi lived on her own, she could have friends over without imposing on her family. This is a luxury in Tokyo, and Megumi's apartment was the group's unofficial spot to hang out. Sitting together in the living room, the three friends recalled their shared experiences playing *Angelique*, which inevitably led to a discussion of character coupling. Tomo asked, "How would you couple Randy?" All three took for granted that Randy was the bottom, and instead focused on who the top should be. Megumi responded bluntly, "He's too damn sweet. It's impossible." Hachi chimed in, "Juliuos and Randy, like as big brother, little brother?" Not convinced, Megumi interjected, "Randy needs a firm hand, like a teacher, so it has to be Sei-Lan. He may be mean, but imagine him spoiling cute little Randy while bullying everyone else." Megumi's character coupling—older and younger, teacher and student, cruel and kind—struck a chord with Tomo, who blurted out, "*Moe!*" The discussion gained momentum as the three friends began to imagine romantic and sexual relations between the characters. Someone suggested that if Sei-Lan was mean to Randy most of the time, then the affect would be amplified when he was finally nice to him (a relational pattern called *tsundere*). A "hurt/comfort" scenario[33] was suggested with Sei-Lan violently raping Randy then caring for him afterward; Randy's vulnerability, even when caused by Sei-Lan's abuse, was said to make him cuter. Though this may sound extreme, there are comparable scenarios in global fan-fiction and even canonical Japanese literature.[34] The relationship between Randy and Sei-Lan referred to intertextual codes of fiction, not the reality of human relationships, where assault and battery is not "hot." It is important to remember that Hachi, Megumi, and Tomo were talking about character couplings, which do not necessarily reflect their desires for what they called "real life." Rather than trying to read possible identifications in the fantasy of male–male character relations, I instead would simply draw attention to how sharing the fantasy is productive of human relations among *fujoshi*.

One of the pleasures of *moe* talk is encountering unanticipated ideas that throw participants into upheaval. For example, Hachi and Tomo came to visit Megumi and, during a lull in the conversation, used her computer to surf the Internet. Sitting in front of the same screen, Hachi and Tomo viewed and read together, at times even verbalizing text and responding to it aloud. They settled on a particular webpage and began reading *yaoi* fan-fiction posted there. Hachi clicked on a link embedded in the text and she and Tomo were suddenly exposed to a digitization of one of Hokusai's woodblock prints, *The Great Wave at Kanagawa*. The image is iconic—a wave about to crash over a tiny boat with Mount Fuji in the background—and seemed terribly out of place. Both Hachi and Tomo dived into the accompanying text, giggling as they questioned the poster's strange maneuver. Hachi read aloud: "The strong and confident boatman went too far and was caught up in the pounding surf." After a moment of silence, the connection was made: wave as top and boatman as bottom. As in the *yaoi* fan-fiction they were reading, the top was a quiet and reserved man who was pushed too far by the bottom, and so responded with overwhelming force and power. *The Great Wave at Kanagawa* was a visualization of the concept of "assaulting bottom" (*osoi uke*), where the bottom attacks and provokes the top, instigating a sexual encounter. Hachi and Tomo started laughing uncontrollably. Hachi said, "This is so great! I'd have never thought of such a thing." Tomo commented that the poster, like the boatman, had "gone too far" (*yarisugi*), but this was a positive assessment. Tomo said that she might "die from *moe*" (*moe shinu*). Play is often about getting out of hand and pushing limits, a phenomenon noted of *fujoshi*,[35] who spend much of their time hiding interests from normals,[36] but among friends and fellow fans relish losing control. (The intensity of *moe* talk, which includes loud voices and animated gestures, comes to mind.) Many *fujoshi* I met recounted stories of friends who "go wild" (*araburu*) or "go on a rampage" (*bōsō suru*). Again, this was not a bad thing. On the contrary, these people were some of the most fun to be around. Sharing wild fantasies and behavior bonds *fujoshi* together and encourages others to participate and go beyond limits. In the wave and boatman example, Hachi and Tomo were exposed to the thoughts of the poster, whose creativity shattered inhibitions and opened channels of creative expression.

In another example, Hachi, Megumi, and Tomo were walking home after buying *yaoi* fanzines at an event. Inspired by what they had seen, the three friends started debating whether or not a bottom acting in a self-destructive way out of love for a top might be *moe*. Tomo was at first skeptical. Hachi impulsively decided to use her surroundings as an illustration of the coupling: "Is this road *moe*? See, it's virgin, freshly paved, but is doing its best with the cars on top. What if he was trying so hard to please his lover?" (figure 8.3). Despite the sudden turn in the *moe* talk, Megumi did not miss a beat: "The road is a loser bottom (*hetare uke*) in love with one particular car, who is an insensitive pleasure seeker (*kichiku seme*). In order to win his love, the road agreed to be his sex slave and is now being broken in by the top's clients [that is, random cars pounding it on a daily basis]." Tomo joined Megumi and Hachi in laughter and a chorus of "*moe, moe, moe*." In this communicative

Figure 8.3 *Moe* relationships can even be read into an ordinary road in Tokyo. Photo by the author.

event, the interpretive game of *yaoi* effectively re-enchanted the world, making the very ground under the women's feet part of a fantasy capable of affecting them.[37] Inspired, the three friends discussed character couplings between other complementary objects such as knife and spoon, and shampoo and conditioner.[38] It occurred to me that this is what Megumi meant by the pursuit of *moe* leading to a different way of seeing things and "imagining relationships between things." Among *fujoshi*, the only limit to what could be included in imagined character couplings was the limit negotiated by friends. Among the right people, anything seemed possible, which was an exciting prospect indeed.

Concluding Remarks

Scholars have noted that BL manga allows readers to safely explore sex outside of themselves,[39] and Hachi, Megumi, and Tomo, long-time BL readers, have internalized patterns of character coupling, which they utilize to imaginatively produce *yaoi* fan-fiction about the world around them. In other words, Hachi, Megumi, and Tomo use their imaginations to interact differently with media, one another, and the world around them. They share a space of imagination set apart from "meaning" and "reality," allowing them to play sexuality. Spaces of shared imagination are an example of what Anita Harris calls "safe spaces" where women can express their desires in relative freedom and without fear of censure.[40] Harris highlights the importance of these spaces at a time of mass surveillance, reactionary politics, and the inflation of norms. Amid struggles to delimit the "possible imaginary,"[41] fanzines and websites allow women "to engage in unregulated dialogue and debate with one another" and "generate their own meanings and terminologies around sexual desire."[42] This is certainly on display among *fujoshi*, who generate their own meanings and terms around sexual desire in relation to imagined character couplings and engage in *moe* talk with one another.

Based on extended social contact with *fujoshi*, it is my position that the safe spaces of fan interaction and imagination are beneficial, and should not be legislated and policed due to fear of unknown possible risks of exposure to erotic manga such as BL.[43] It is true that Hachi, Megumi, and Tomo were long-time BL readers, which changed their way of seeing things and relations between things, but this enhanced rather than detracted from their ability to interact with others. It is also true that these three women, who self-identified as *fujoshi* or "rotten girls," embraced fantasies that they described as abnormal, but we must allow for safe spaces to desire outside of socially acceptable forms.[44] Mark McLelland argues that *yaoi* is deliberately transgressive, and that fans organize into counterpublics supportive of critical stances toward the mainstream.[45] Such dissent must be allowed even if, or precisely because, it challenges norms. Further, in interaction with one another, fans negotiate their own community standards and values. They regulate themselves far more effectively than outside authorities can. I observed in my fieldwork that *fujoshi* follow their own "ethics of *moe*" (*moe no rinri*),[46] whereby they pursue affective responses to fictional characters, but also set limits to avoid harming real people. The ethics of *moe* resonates with what Michael Warner calls the ethics of alternative life.[47] Channeling Warner alongside Hachi, Megumi, and Tomo, one might say that the trouble with normals is that they do not have the imagination to understand and participate in the alternative social world of *fujoshi*.

Notes

1. Kakinuma Eiko and Sagawa Toshihiko, *"Eien no rokugatsu (JUNE)"* [Eternal June/ JUNE], talk given at the Yoshihiro Yonezawa Memorial Library of Manga and Subcultures, June 26, 2011. I chose this quote as the epigraph for this chapter not only because Sagawa

Toshihiko is a voice for tolerance and free imagination, but also because he anticipates the alternative ways of relating to others that I observed in my fieldwork.

2. For a review, see Kaneda Junko, "Yaoi-ron, asu no tame ni, sono 2" [*Yaoi* studies for tomorrow, part 2], *Eureka* 39, no. 16 (2007). Some exceptions to the rule of abstraction are provided by Sugiura Yumiko, Matthew Thorn, and Daisuke Okabe and Kimi Ishida, who observe, interact with, and interview BL readers. See Sugiura Yumiko, *Otaku joshi kenkyū: Fujoshi shisō taikei* [*Otaku* girls research: A compendium of *fujoshi* thought] (Tokyo: Hara shobō, 2006); Sugiura Yumiko, *Fujoshika suru sekai: Higashi Ikebukuro no otaku joshita-chi* [*Fujoshi*-izing world: The *otaku* girls of East Ikebukuro] (Tokyo: Chūō kōron shinsha, 2006); Matthew Thorn, "Girls and Women Getting Out of Hand: The Pleasure and Politics of Japan's Amateur Comics Community," in *Fanning the Flames: Fans and Consumer Culture in Contemporary Japan*, ed. William Kelly (Albany: State University of New York Press, 2004); and Daisuke Okabe and Kimi Ishida, "Making *Fujoshi* Identity Visible and Invisible," in *Fandom Unbound: Otaku Culture in a Connected World*, ed. Mizuko Ito, Daisuke Okabe, and Izumi Tsuji (New Haven, CT: Yale University Press, 2012).

3. Straight female BL readers are discussed in Fujimoto Yukari, *Watashi no ibasho wa doko ni aru no? Shōjo manga ga utsusu kokoro no katachi* [Where do I belong? The shape of the heart reflected in *shōjo* manga] (Tokyo: Gakuyō shobō, 1998). Homosexual female BL readers are discussed in James Welker, "Flower Tribes and Female Desire: Complicating Early Female Consumption of Male Homosexuality in *Shōjo* Manga," *Mechademia* 6 (2011). Transgendered BL readers are discussed in Sakakibara Shihomi, *Yaoi genron: "Yaoi" kara mieta mono* [Phantasmic discourse on *yaoi*: Things seen from a "*yaoi*" perspective] (Tokyo: Natsume shobō, 1998). Male BL readers are discussed in Yoshimoto Taimatsu, *Fudanshi ni kiku* [Interviewing *fudanshi*] (Japan: Self-published, 2008).

4. Mark McLelland, "Australia's 'Child-Abuse Material' Legislation, Internet Regulation and the Juridification of the Imagination," *International Journal of Cultural Studies* 15, no. 5 (2012); see also McLelland, this volume.

5. Setsu Shigematsu, "Dimensions of Desire: Sex, Fantasy, and Fetish in Japanese Comics," in *Themes in Asian Cartooning: Cute, Cheap, Mad, and Sexy*, ed. John A. Lent (Bowling Green, OH: Bowling Green State University Popular Press, 1999).

6. I am inspired here by Constance Penley, who asks "what women *do* with popular culture, how it gives them pleasure, and how it can be consciously and unconsciously re-worked to give them *more* pleasure, at both a social and psychical level." See Constance Penley, "Feminism, Psychoanalysis, and the Study of Popular Culture," in *Cultural Studies*, ed. Lawrence Grossberg, Cary Nelson, and Paula A. Treichler (London: Routledge, 1992), 488.

7. I conducted participant observation and ethnographic interviews with twenty Japanese women between the ages of eighteen and twenty-five encountered in Tokyo between April 2006 and March 2007. Informants were recruited using the snowballing technique, which al-lowed me to focus on overlapping networks of friends. Most were from middle-class families and were students at a prestigious women's university (name withheld for issues of privacy). Living at home, they had money and time to indulge in hobbies. Most identified as hetero-sexual, and some had boyfriends. Interviews were conducted in Japanese; all translations of these women's comments are my own. All informants were aware of my status as a researcher, and gave permission for me to include their words and stories in this write-up of my field-work. All their names are pseudonyms.

8. Sagawa Toshihiko speculates that the separation of male characters into top (*seme*) and bottom (*uke*) was not intentional in the *shōnen'ai* manga that was commercially published in the 1970s. Rather, he recalls that fans read this dynamic into the works, and then read for it elsewhere in relationships between male characters in manga, anime, and so on. Kakinuma and Sagawa, "Eien no rokugatsu."

9. For a discussion of *yaoi* fans reading signs of intimacy, see Azuma Sonoko, "Mōsō no kyōdōtai: 'Yaoi' komyuniti ni okeru ren'ai kōdo no kinō" [Fantasy community: The function of the love code in the '*yaoi*' community], in *Shisō chizu, vol. 5: Shakai no hihyō*, ed. Azuma Hiroki and Kitada Akihiro (Tokyo: NHK shuppan, 2010), 258.

10. Andrea Wood, "'Straight' Women, Queer Texts: Boy-Love Manga and the Rise of a Global Counterpublic," *Women's Studies Quarterly* 34, nos. 1–2 (2006): 399–400; see also Penley, "Feminism," 488–89, and Sharalyn Orbaugh, "Girls Reading Harry Potter, Girls Writing Desire: Amateur Manga and *Shōjo* Reading Practices," in *Girl Reading Girl in Japan*, ed. Tomoko Aoyama and Barbara Hartley (London: Routledge, 2010), 181.

11. Tomoko Aoyama, "*Eureka* Discovers *Culture Girls, Fujoshi*, and *BL*: Essay Review of Three Issues of the Japanese Literary Magazine, *Yuriika* (Eureka)," *Intersections: Gender and Sexuality in Asia and the Pacific* 20 (2009); see also Thorn, "Girls and Women Getting Out of Hand," 176.

12. The fact that my informants identified as *fujoshi* is perhaps overdetermined, because our encounters in 2006 and 2007 coincided with a media boom concerning BL and *yaoi* fans, who were at times called *fujoshi*. See Hester, this volume.

13. In Japanese, *fujoshi* can mean both women and girls (婦女子) and rotten girls (腐女子), depending on which Chinese character or *kanji* is used to express "*fu*."

14. Pure fantasy also indicates a fantasy about purity. The relationship between male characters in BL manga and *yaoi* fan-fiction is imagined to be about "pure love" (*jun'ai*). There are several reasons for this: one, the relationship is between individuals who love one another as individuals rather than members of a particular sex; two, the relationship is not oriented toward the goal of biological reproduction but rather the pleasure of the lovers; and three, the relationship endures in spite of numerous obstacles. For a complementary discussion of the pure relationship, see Anthony Giddens, *The Transformation of Intimacy: Sexuality, Love and Eroticism in Modern Societies* (Cambridge: Polity Press, 1992), 190.

15. While female readers of manga featuring male–male romance have in the past also been attracted to actual gay men—see Welker, "Flower Tribes," and Welker, in this volume—debates in the 1990s about BL fans appropriating and abusing the image of gay men encouraged separation of fantasy and reality. Hachi, who started reading BL in middle school in the 1990s and went on to produce her own *yaoi* fanzines, told me that she consciously approached characters as "fantasy," which she clearly distinguished from reality so as not to harm actual gay men. Some might call this separation of fiction and reality reactionary, if not also call into question the mantra of no harm to gay men (see Ishida, this volume), but my project does not include interrogating the truth of Hachi's claims.

16. Saitō Tamaki, "*Otaku* Sexuality," translated by Christopher Bolton, in *Robot Ghosts and Wired Dreams: Japanese Science Fiction from Origins to Anime*, ed. Christopher Bolton, Stan Csiscery-Ronay, Jr., and Tatsumi Takayuki (Minneapolis: University of Minnesota Press, 2007), 227.

17. Saitō, "*Otaku* Sexuality," 227.

18. Hachi used the phrase "*moe* friends," but some informants referred to other *fujoshi* with whom they were close as "friends" (*furendo*), where the first syllable—the *fu*—of the Japanese pronunciation of the English word friend is replaced with the Chinese character or *kanji* meaning "rotten." As used by *fujoshi*, one might translate "friends" as "rotten friends."

19. Sugiura, *Otaku joshi*, 144.

20. Not everyone I met was attracted to the prospect of opening up this way. For example, Hikaru, one of my youngest informants at eighteen years old, was adamant about not wanting to share her drawings. In her mind, they were simply too personal, and she was disturbed by the thought of others seeing them. In another example, Hachi was extremely upset when a man at a convention bought her fanzine, which was dedicated to a character coupling from the popular videogame franchise *Dragon Quest*. Hachi assumed, perhaps unfairly, that the man had bought the fanzine on a whim, would not understand the content, and would use the link printed inside the fanzine to visit her website, effectively destroying the in-group atmosphere. In fact, Hachi's friend Kei entirely avoided large conventions so as not to draw unwanted attention to her work. Kei preferred to limit her activity to the Internet because she could screen others in chats before inviting them to her personal website, which was made unreachable by standard web searches through clever coding, hidden links and intentional misspellings. This is a common practice among *fujoshi* called "avoiding search engines" (*kensaku yoke*).

21. Uli Meyer, "Hidden in Straight Sight: Trans*gressing Gender and Sexuality via BL," in *Boys' Love Manga: Essays on the Sexual Ambiguity and Cross-Cultural Fandom of the Genre*, ed. Antonia Levi, Mark McHarry, and Dru Pagliassotti (Jefferson, NC: McFarland, 2010), 233.

22. Another Japanese term with the same meaning is *moe-gatari*. See Okabe and Ishida, "Making *Fujoshi* Identity Visible and Invisible," 213.

23. Saitō, "*Otaku* Sexuality," 230.

24. Morikawa Ka'ichirō, *Shuto no tanjō: Moeru toshi Akihabara* [Learning from Akihabara: The birth of a personapolis] (Tokyo: Gentōsha, 2003), 28–29.

25. Sugiura, *Otaku joshi*, 156–57; see also Saitō Tamaki, "Moe no honshitsu to sono seisei ni tsuite" [The essence of *moe* and its genesis], *Kokubungaku* 53, no. 16 (2008): 12.

26. Okabe and Ishida, "Making *Fujoshi* Identity Visible and Invisible," 215. Much like Morikawa and myself, Okabe and Ishida note that genres and couplings (i.e., what one responds to as *moe*) "allow fujoshi [*sic*] to express their inclinations and interests to one another."

27. Aida Miho, "Komikku maaketto no genzai: Sabukaruchaa ni kan suru kōsatsu" [The contemporary Comic Market: A consideration of Japanese subculture], *Hiroshima shūdai ronshū, jinbun-hen* 45, no. 2 (2005).

28. This resonates with what Alan Williams calls "minds and bodies in communication." See Alan Williams, "Raping Apollo: Sexual Difference and the *Yaoi* Phenomenon," in Levi, McHarry, and Pagliassotti, 227.

29. Gilles Deleuze and Félix Guattari, *A Thousand Plateaus: Capitalism and Schizophrenia*, translated by Brian Massumi (Minneapolis: University of Minnesota Press, 1987), 22.

30. Dominic Pettman, "Love in the Time of Tamagotchi," *Theory, Culture and Society* 26, nos. 2–3 (2009): 201.

31. Brian Massumi, "Translator's Foreword: Pleasures of Philosophy," in Deleuze and Guattari, *A Thousand Plateaus*, xiv.

32. Deleuze and Guattari, *A Thousand Plateaus*, 22.

33. Orbaugh, "Girls Reading," 180.

34. Orbaugh, "Girls Reading," 179–83; Margaret H. Childs, "The Value of Vulnerability: Sexual Coercion and the Nature of Love in Japanese Court Literature," *Journal of Asian Studies* 58, no. 4 (1999): 1065–67.

35. Thorn, "Getting Out of Hand."

36. Okabe and Ishida, "Making *Fujoshi* Identity Visible and Invisible."

37. In her early writing on *fujoshi*, Sugiura also suggests this aspect of BL culture. On the cover of *Otaku joshi kenkyū*, she writes, "Tell tales of the world in terms of *moe* and top/bottom relations" (*uke seme moe de sekai o katare*).

38. This resonates with Marni Stanley, who notes BL authors/artists encouraging readers to see couplings in objects around them. See Marni Stanley, "101 Uses for Boys: Communing with the Reader in *Yaoi* and Slash," in Levi, McHarry, and Pagliassotti, 101–103.

39. Ueno Chizuko, *Hatsujō sōchi: Erosu no shinario* [The erotic apparatus: Erotic scenarios] (Tokyo: Chikuma shobō, 1998), 131; Kimberly S. Gregson, "What if the Lead Character Looks Like Me? Girl Fans of *Shoujo Anime* and Their Web Sites," in *Girl Wide Web: Girls, the Internet, and the Negotiation of Identity*, ed. Sharon R. Mazzarella (New York: Peter Lang, 2005), 127; James Welker, "Beautiful, Borrowed, and Bent: 'Boys' Love' as Girls' Love in *Shōjo Manga*," *Signs: Journal of Women in Culture and Society* 31, no. 3 (2006): 866.

40. Anita Harris, "Discourses of Desire as Governmentality: Young Women, Sexuality and the Significance of Safe Spaces," *Feminism and Psychology* 15, no. 1 (2005): 41.

41. Shigematsu, "Dimensions of Desire," 127; David Graeber, *Fragments of an Anarchist Anthropology* (Chicago: Prickly Paradigm Press, 2004), 102.

42. Harris, "Discourses of Desire," 42.

43. McLelland, "Australia's 'Child-Abuse Material' Legislation," 479.

44. It seems to me that the fictional male character in BL and *yaoi* offers a way out of "woman," which in Japan is related to the "body politic centered by the reproduction of family." See Anne Allison, *Permitted and Prohibited Desires: Mothers, Comics, and Censorship in Japan* (Berkeley: University of California Press, 2000), 173. In embracing "rotten" fantasies and rejecting "normal" reality, *fujoshi* are redefining what it means to be a "woman," as in the word "*fujoshi*" itself, which twists "women and girls" into the homonymous "rotten girl." See also Welker, "Beautiful, Borrowed, and Bent."

45. Mark McLelland, "The World of Yaoi: The Internet, Censorship and the Global 'Boys' Love' Fandom." *Australian Feminist Law Journal* 23 (2005): 75; see also Wood, "'Straight' Women, Queer Texts."

46. Harata Shin'ichirō, "Vaacharu 'jidō poruno' kisei no ronri to 'moe' no rinri" [The logic of regulating "virtual child pornography" and the ethics of "*moe*"], *Shakaijōhōgaku kenkyū* 11, no. 1 (2006): 115.

47. Michael Warner, *The Trouble with Normal: Sex, Politics, and the Ethics of Queer Life* (New York: The Free Press, 1999).

FUJOSHI EMERGENT

Shifting Popular Representations of *Yaoi*/BL Fandom in Japan

Introduction

The neologism *fujoshi* is playfully derived from a homophone in Japanese referring politely to "women" or "women and girls." By a wry replacement of the Sino-Japanese character for "woman" with one used in compounds for "putrid," "corrupt," or "decayed," this self-mocking appellation for "a rotten or depraved girl(s)" has been created as an inclusive term for the female fandom of *yaoi*/BL. The term is generally regarded as having arisen from the *yaoi*/BL community itself. It refers both to producers and consumers of amateur manga (*dōjinshi*) in which the characters are predominantly males poached from mainstream genres of commercial boys' manga, anime, or the entertainment world, and placed in homoerotic situations, as well as to fans of a wide range of commercial "boys love" (BL) genres of manga, novels, games, and other narrative and graphic forms. Alongside the real girls and women who engage in a variety of consumptive and productive practices centering on images and narratives of male–male romantic and erotic relationships, the *fujoshi* as a gender-specific social type socially constructed through a variety of media representations has recently emerged as a new model of "bad girl" in the landscape of the Japanese social imaginary.[1] It is *fujoshi* as an emergent, constructed social type with which this chapter is concerned.

There is no question that a fandom related to what is represented by the term "*fujoshi*" has been emerging, growing, and shifting now for some three decades, a fandom both self-aware and subject to scholarly, critical, and fan-based discursive representation. From around the middle of the first decade of the 2000s, however, something of a "*fujoshi* boom"—a small explosion of representations—has both sharpened the profile of this fandom and exposed it more widely to popular awareness and scrutiny. *Fujoshi*, therefore, represent a newly emergent fandom in terms of representations targeted at, or made accessible to, a more "mainstream" audience.

Fandoms, broadly defined as self-selected, ephemeral networks of individuals sharing investments of time, emotion, and identity in a particular genre, narrative, media(ted) personality, et cetera, are fluid and complexly positioned social collectivities.[2] The social position of fans is shaped by their relations with the objects of their enthusiasm, with an imagined community of those who share their pleasures and practices, and with "others" who form a constitutive outside that helps define felt boundaries of affiliation.[3] The subjectivity of fans is constructed through interactions with these objects, communities, and broader discourses—discourses that are increasingly transnational and digitally mediated—that position fans within the larger society.

In a succinct description of the construction of "fans" as social representations, popular culture scholar Koichi Iwabuchi suggests that

> the "fan" is a discursively constructed taxonomy of those who are assumed to share certain cultural attributes. To follow Raymond Williams, we could say: "There are in fact no fans. There are only ways of seeing people as fans." A fundamental feature of the fan might be defined as a passionate devotion to a particular media text or icon, but the term is often used to objectify those people and their activities with an element of judgment, be it negative or positive.[4]

The topic of contestation over constructions of "the fan" and fandoms holds a venerable place in discussions of the cultural politics of popular media consumption. In this chapter, I aim to contribute to the investigation of mass media representations of the *fujoshi* fandom in Japan. *Fujoshi* have taken their place within a discursively constructed taxonomy, as suggested by Iwabuchi, defined by their devotion to a range of perspectives, practices, and products centered on the consumption and production of male–male romantic and erotic relationships most often represented in the images and narratives of *yaoi*/BL. This almost-exclusively female fandom that had received relatively little attention for most of its existence suddenly became fodder for a host of narratives, ushering the fandom out of the shadows and into the light of journalistic accounts, manga renditions, television appearances (including at least one TV series), and feature-length films. The fandom has been rendered "luminous," as Angela McRobbie suggests of young women in another context, "so that they become visible in a certain kind of way."[5] It is the precise manner of how they have become visible that concerns me here. In their newly found luminosity, *fujoshi* haven't simply been discovered, but have come to be constructed in the process of exposure.

In examining emerging representations in mass media of the fan-type known as "*fujoshi*," I offer an outline of shifts in characterizations, briefly introduce three of the most popular texts, namely *Fantasizing Girl, Otaku-Style* (*Mōsō shōjo otaku-kei*), *My Neighbor Yaoi-chan* (*Tonari no 801-chan*), and *Fujoshi Girlfriend* (*Fujoshi kanojo*), involved in disseminating the image, and undertake a closer reading of the last of these.[6] It must be noted that the texts discussed here are only a subset of the popular narratives through which *fujoshi* have been represented, and that these depictions hardly exhaust the ways in which the *fujoshi* social character has been brought into narrative form and socially positioned. Yet their mass-market targeting and relative commercial success suggest the texts' importance for discerning the shifting position of the *fujoshi* character in the popular imagination. My goal here is to explore how these representations depict fan practice within the larger social contexts that these narratives present, particularly in terms of gender relations in contemporary Japan and the meaning attributed to the potentially transgressive reading practices of *fujoshi*.

Emerging Media Representations

In her suggestive analysis, Nishihara Mari has traced the representation of "*yaoi*"—broadly defined in her investigation to include amateur and commercially distributed works—and its audiences in the mass media over the period from 1975 through 1997.[7] Nishihara divides her analysis into two periods. The first begins in 1975 with what may be the initial appearance of a report in the mass media of women's interest in male homoerotic genres. The second begins in 1991, with the appearance of the "boys love" label used in marketing commercial works, and runs to 1997, ending prior to the first use in early 1998 of the term "boys love" within mass media reporting or commentary.[8] Using a keyword search of Japan's major national newspapers, general interest magazines and popular weeklies, Nishihara has located 111 articles in mass circulation newspapers and magazines discussing some aspect of *yaoi* over the period. Among her findings, what interests me most here are the shifts in the discursive boundaries of fandom, that is, what changing mass media constructions of genre and audience suggest about the emergence of the *fujoshi* as an increasingly coherent social character visible in popular culture.

For the period before the market boom for commercial BL from the early 1990s, Nishihara suggests two notable tendencies worth highlighting. First, the genre centered on male homosexual themes that emerged commercially out of the work of the so-called "Year 24 Group" of female manga artists from the early to mid-1970s, was treated, until the early 1990s, within the same framework as gay male literature.[9] Secondly, the mass media discussed such commercial genres and their consumers separately from amateur *yaoi dōjinshi* works and their producers and consumers.[10] The commercial work finally "comes to be conveyed as autonomous women's culture" only following the advent of "boys love" in the early 1990s.[11] The world of *yaoi dōjinshi*, on the other hand, received less attention overall during this period, and, when it was noticed, was rather differently positioned.[12]

The historical shift in nomenclature from the 1970s *"shōnen'ai"* (boys love) genre of male–male romance in commercial *shōjo* manga (girls' comics) to "boys love" in the early 1990s occurred alongside, and is a constitutive element of, what has come to be called the "gay boom." The term designates both mass-media attention to gay worlds—foreign and domestic, real and imaginary—offered up for women's consumption, as well as that burst of consumption itself.[13] Nishihara interestingly notes the different media positionings of the general female consumers of the "gay boom," and the producer/consumers of *yaoi dōjinshi*. The former were understood as "today's young women" consuming as a "fashion"—even if to the discomfort of some commentators. The latter, the *"yaoi-zoku"* (*yaoi* tribe) producing/consuming *yaoi dōjinshi*, were criticized for their predilection for what was described as "extreme," "radical," or "superfluous" sexual depictions and characterized as immature "Peter Pans" who "didn't understand men's bodies" and resisted marriage.[14] It is worth remembering here that, along with the commercial *shōnen'ai* component carried into the 1990s from the previous decade, the "gay boom" unfolded in mainstream fashion/lifestyle magazines, on television, and in domestic and imported cinema.[15] *Yaoi dōjinshi*, however, came to media attention through its association with the increasingly visible Comic Market, a colossal gathering of female and male enthusiasts of manga and anime. Such attention was intensified in the wake of the so-called "*otaku* murders" between 1988 and 1989, the gruesome murders of four little girls for which Miyazaki Tsutomu was tried and convicted. Miyazaki came to be labeled by the media the *"otaku* murderer" because of the large collection of manga and anime found in his residence. The media coverage of the incident helped to bring the term *"otaku"* as a label for extreme fans into broader public discourse, while also bringing to public prominence the male *otaku* figure, in a most negative way. It further resulted in greater scrutiny of the activities of Comic Market, including those of its numerous female participants.[16]

I take Nishihara's analysis to serve as something of an archaeology of the contemporary social character of the *fujoshi*. It suggests the contingency of the present configuration of the *fujoshi* as well as some of the complex streams of elements that have intersected in its construction. While there has long been recognition of a consumer subject position centered on male–male romantic/erotic coupling, more widespread popular recognition of the social character of the *fujoshi* constructed around this position would not appear until nearly a decade after the point at which Nishihara concludes her analysis.

More (and Less) Than Female *Otaku*

Fujoshi are generally understood as a kind of *otaku*. From my own participant-observation research, interviews, as well as casual interactions with *fujoshi*, I would suggest that women and girls who identify as devoted consumers of male–male erotic narratives are more likely to refer to themselves as *otaku* than as *fujoshi*.[17] The *fujoshi*, however, is endowed in the popular imagination with a gender specificity that gives her a quite distinctive niche within the taxonomy of fandoms to which Iwabuchi refers.

Amongst the diverse social characters that have been introduced through media and marketing in Japan in the postwar era, the *otaku* has been one of the most enduring, even if subject to diverse interpretations. The *otaku*'s endurance and indeed its spread and localization far beyond Japanese borders is noteworthy in an environment in which such social categories can be ephemeral.[18] The term "*otaku*" itself is polysemous, lexically ambiguous, and socially complex. *Fujoshi* are understood in mainstream discourse as simultaneously representing a kind of female *otaku*, as well as standing in gender-specific contrast to the highly male-marked *otaku*. If there is a unifying core in the concept of the *otaku* in its present-day, most neutral (or even positive) usage, it is the aspect of devotion to a leisure activity, genre, popular icon, et cetera. And in this it is a gender-neutral concept. However, amidst all of the concept's accumulations and transformations over the past quarter century, it has become packed with other connotations, most of them reflecting a strongly male bias. These accreted associations range from the moral panic aroused by the case of the "*otaku* murderer," to the gender-specific challenges

and opportunities facing the eponymous *Train Man* (*Densha otoko*) protagonist, a sensitive and harmless *otaku* made famous by the narrative of his
rescue and then courting of a "damsel in distress," to the specific content that
is commonly understood as most typical of (male) *otaku* consumption.[19]
This dominant, sedimented rendering of *otaku*, with all its implied criticism,
I would suggest, is very much a critique of an array of transgressions of morally proper masculine adulthood. The dominant image of the *otaku* in the
mass media was constructed in the context of arguments about how adult
men should spend their time, engage their minds, and apply their labor and
talents in the world. So in one dominant folk usage, "*otaku*" does not simply
refer to a person's activities, but includes ascriptions, largely negative, of personality characteristics, habits of personal hygiene, and social capabilities, as
well as evaluations of degree of conformity to normative male social aspirations. In short, the *otaku* has been rendered in the popular imaginary as a
specific kind of person, one strongly male inflected.

In contrast, the "female *otaku*" has been a derivative and misty presence.
In its unequivocal gender specificity, however, the *fujoshi* character emerges
in bold relief, out from the shadow of the (male) *otaku*.[20] In addition to its
differently gendered social character, in contrast to the omnivorous consumption practices often associated with the variety of *otaku*, *fujoshi* have
a quite distinctive thematic focus for their enthusiasms: male romantic and
homoerotic relationships.

Fujoshi Made Visible

The mass media popularization of the *fujoshi* social character can be traced to
the period 2004–2005. If the *otaku* was initially made luminous as a kind of
social monster in popular consciousness in the late 1980s through a social labeling process at the intersection of the popular press and the police blotter,
the *fujoshi* has been made visible and brought into popular culture narrative
as a commodity, in the form of popular media products. This occurred more
or less contemporaneously with the so-called "*otaku* boom" centered on the
cross-media property *Train Man*, mentioned above, launched in 2004.

The term "*fujoshi*" itself seems to have been in use for a while, circulating
through chatty comments of various authors of *dōjinshi*, on blogs, through
interchanges on the popular Internet bulletin board *2-channel*, and other real
and virtual sites where *fujoshi* gather. But through a number of media products and attendant journalistic coverage, the *fujoshi* character came to be
narrativized—given a face, a personality, and relationships in mass-mediated

オタク女子研究

腐女子思想大系

杉浦由美子

Figure 9.1 A journalist reports
on the *fujoshi* world: Sugiura
Yumiko's *Otaku Girls Research: A
Compendium of Fujoshi Thought*
(*Otaku joshi kenkyū: Fujoshi shisō
taikei*, 2006).

form. In short, the *fujoshi* was given a solid and accessible social presence
without precedent.[21]

One of the earliest journalistic accounts was a feature article by Sugiura Yumiko published in the June 20, 2005, issue of the prominent current
events weekly magazine *Aera*. Entitled "*Moeru onna otaku*," or "Excited
Women *Otaku*," the article offers a brief overview of the practices and pleasures of *fujoshi*, and introduces readers to many of the elements of the *fujoshi*
image that would come to be elaborated in other works.[22] Sugiura herself has
written several books since this first article dealing with various aspects of
women's lifestyle and popular culture consumption, most prominently the
lifestyle and consumption practices of *fujoshi* (figure 9.1).[23]

Alongside such journalistic accounts, the diverse media products that
contribute to the discourse on *fujoshi* include fictional or fact-based narratives spanning blogs, novels, manga, films, audio drama CDs, and so on.
There are also essays, including those in manga form, that present an authori-
al *fujoshi* voice, as well as a variety of guidebooks, including "field guides" to

the *fujoshi* character, *fujoshi* lexicons, guides to the Tokyo *fujoshi* hotspots of Nakano and Higashi Ikebukuro, and other "*moe* spots" that spur *fujoshi* excitement.[24] In the aggregate, these serve to disseminate a complex discourse on the *fujoshi* character and to further define *fujoshi* within a fan taxonomy linked to elements of lifestyle, language, and urban space.

The Fujoshi Character Mobilized in Narrative

Three major properties centered on the *fujoshi* theme are the cross-media narrative works *Fantasizing Girl, Otaku-Style*, *My Neighbor Yaoi-chan*, and *Fujoshi Girlfriend*, all launched between 2004 and 2006.[25] The first of these to appear was the manga *Fantasizing Girl, Otaku-Style*, penned by Konjoh Natsumi, a woman who herself apparently has experience participating in circles and publishing *dōjinshi* targeting heterosexual adult men.[26] *Fantasizing Girl, Otaku-Style* is a comedy following the interactions of the *fujoshi* Rumi and her friends in the familiar setting of a high school. The central device of the manga is the love confusion arising from the fact that male student Abe is interested in Rumi, while Rumi is convinced that Abe and his best friend, the handsome hunk Chiba, are romantically involved and that they are made for each other. The manga was made into a feature film released at the end of 2007, and two drama CDs have also been issued.

My Neighbor Yaoi-chan began life on the Internet as a blogged manga-with-commentary by male author Kojima Ajiko in March 2006, and was then revised and released in book form at the end of that year.[27] Since the release of the original book, a further four volumes plus a "special selections" volume of *My Neighbor Yaoi-chan* have been released.[28] A live-action film was released directly to DVD in September 2007, followed by two drama CDs in 2008. In addition, three volumes of manga inspired by Kojima's work relating "*fujoshi* high school life," originally serialized in the *shōjo* manga magazine *Bessatsu furendo* (Friend extra) from January 2008, have been released, along with a single-volume spinoff relating a year in the life of a junior high school student *fujoshi*.[29]

Kojima's work is formatted as a series of four-panel manga. It unfolds as a first-person account—presented as based in reality—of the relationship of the author, an *otaku* and company employee known as Chibe-kun, and his girlfriend, Yaoi. The central marketing device of the story is the monstrous furry green version of his girlfriend, "801-chan" (pronounced Yaoi-chan), who appears out of a zipper along Yaoi's back with an abundance of barely contained energy and excitement whenever she is overcome by feelings of

小島アジコ

となりの801ちゃん

OHZORA SHUPPAN

Figure 9.2 Yaoi embraces her "inner *moe*" on the cover of *My Neighbor Yaoi-chan*.

moe (burning excitement) instigated by fantasies of male–male romance (figure 9.2). The central dramatic interest is located in the author's account of Yaoi's *fujoshi* lifestyle and perspectives, which he often finds quite overwhelming, though also charming. In this and several other aspects, *My Neighbor Yaoi-chan* has much in common with Pentabu's *Fujoshi Girlfriend*.

The light novel series *Fujoshi Girlfriend*, like Kojima's *My Neighbor Yaoi-chan* manga, began life as an Internet blog. The first entry is dated November 8, 2005, and the first of the two book volumes ends with the entry of October 1, 2006, and was released on December 20, 2006. The second volume contains blog posts from December 7, 2006, to the end of July 2007.[30] The narrative was subsequently adapted as a manga, serialized in the magazine *B's Log* (*Biizu rogu*), and later released in comic book form.[31] A feature film of *Fujoshi Girlfriend* was released in Japan in 2009 (figure 9.3). As the prose book, manga, and film versions diverge in important respects, I will here be discussing the book version authored by Pentabu, based on the original blog.[32]

Figure 9.3 *Fujoshi* hit the big screen in this adaptation of Pentabu's blog, *Fujoshi Girlfriend.* The tagline (printed vertically between the two characters), in the male voice, reads, "I love you whatever you are."

The protagonists of the story are a male and a female character, in the book respectively designated as the male first-person pronoun "*boku*," or "I" and the female, "Y-ko." Claiming to report real events among real people, like its generic and thematic predecessor *Train Man*, their names are not given, presumably to protect the individuals whose lives are being described.[33]

The narrative voice is that of "*boku*." The story unfolds through a combination of direct quotes from the two main protagonists as well as from a handful of other characters—Y-ko's friends, a couple that they know, one of the narrator's schoolmates, and both sets of parents—all of whom appear infrequently. This is combined with *boku*'s commentary on the reported conversations, which appears as asides to the reader. Thus, we know the narrator's interior world, and we learn about his girlfriend (*kanojo*) through the conversations and incidents that he chooses to report and through his framing commentary on those conversations and incidents. In short, it is fundamentally *his* story of *her*. And it's a love story, the love story of a "normal person," or "*ippanjin*," and a *fujoshi*.³⁴ It is her ardent interest in producing and consuming narratives of male–male coupling that provides the central dramatic tension in the story. This tension might simply be described by the question, "Can a normal guy find love with a *fujoshi*?" But there's a bit more to it than this, to which I return below.

Their respective social positions provide important context for the relationship that unfolds. She is an office worker, respected at work, with a full-time position. He is a student, some two years her junior, and a part-time worker at her company, where they first meet. Throughout the book, he speaks to her in polite language (using her personal name with honorific, as "Y-ko-san," and generally using the polite -*desu*/-*masu* forms), which she, senior in age and status at the workplace, does not reciprocate. This element of ranking in their relationship is maintained in their private moments, which comprises the great bulk of the story.

The story proceeds episodically, without real dramatic decision points or transformative crises. Instead, the reader is treated to a series of interactions between the two in their daily lives together that, for the most part, follow a similar pattern. Y-ko, in pursuing her *yaoi* enthusiasms, challenges the narrator's common-sense understandings, with the dramatic tension residing in his response to these challenges. One important element should be made clear here: The question is not simply whether he will tolerate her *fujoshi* activities, as if they were simply a hobby she pursued on her own. Her challenge to him is greater, as she insists on incorporating him fairly comprehensively into her activities, which comprise more of a lifestyle or a worldview than a hobby.

An example or two may help illustrate this dynamic. Y-ko has taken to calling the narrator "Sebasu," a pet name taken from a favorite butler character, Sebastian. He does, in fact, take on a domestic role resembling a servant, as he cooks for her (as her salaried position gives her less time for such tasks), and makes her tea when she asks. While he seems to have rationalized his service to her, he objects to the name, and her incorporation of him as an *uke*—that is, the passive, often feminized, role in the *fujoshi*'s *seme–uke* code of the active and passive partners in male homoerotic relations.³⁵ One day, she insists he accompany her to "Otome Road"—Maiden Road—an area in Tokyo's Ikebukuro district where shops targeting *fujoshi* are concentrated. He is "pressed into service," he says, as she has him carry the shopping basket that she fills to capacity with BL books. He describes the experience in the shop as being in "enemy territory," something akin to being a salaryman, or male white-collar worker, stuck inside the women-only car on the subway.³⁶ On another occasion, while they are at her place, she takes out her high school uniform and suggests they "cosplay" (role-play in costume). To do this, she pushes him to get his old high school uniform out of mothballs in order that they can do it together properly.[37] In yet another incident, she invites her *fujoshi* friends to visit his place, with no advance warning, during the winter Comic Market *dōjinshi* event, which he describes as "an invasion." During their stay, her friends confirm Y-ko's framing of the narrator as an *uke* and express their appreciation for his fitness in the role.[38] Again, in her behavior and in expressed intent, Y-ko insists that the narrator become familiar with the codes that define her pleasure, and that he join in, in order that they can share. They thus have a very companionate model of relationship, indeed, but mostly on her terms.

Her terms are defined by *fujoshi* practices, for instance, participation in female-dominated spaces and enacting solidarity with other members of the interpretive community of *fujoshi*, as well as what can more specifically be called "*yaoi* play." This latter refers to the symbolic codes, transformative procedures and processes of communication by which *fujoshi* reinterpret as homoerotic male relationships not originally presented as such and recirculate these rereadings in images, text, and talk among like-minded practitioners.[39] As some of the examples here illustrate, this play can target the real world as well as media texts.

The narrator's reactions to these incidents are expressed in his running commentary—ranging from incredulity to outrage, exasperation, and, occasionally, bemused wonderment. But it is all a part of *yaoi* play, and therefore within the codes she masters. His protests and exasperation are not feigned, but nor is there ever a suggestion that he might reject her over her behavior. He seems to be able to withstand her willfulness indefinitely, and not without pleasure, as he seems to accept, if sometimes begrudgingly, her framing of their interactions within this code of play.

Discussion and Conclusions

Much academic and popular commentary on women's consumption and production of *yaoi*/BL works has ascribed girls' and women's attraction to these male homoerotic narratives to the mental space they give to consumers to explore sexual possibilities relatively free from the gendered hierarchies of heteronormative relationships.[40] Readers are allowed to imagine pure, ideal relationships without interference from real-life gendered power relations and role constraints.[41] This mental space, in turn, has been posited as the basis for a subversive potential in *yaoi*/BL consumption insofar as it opens up possibilities for the creation of alternative subjectivities and identities through "creative feminine fantasy."[42] A less strongly developed but nevertheless present theme in the discourse on *fujoshi* lies in the recognition that these mental spaces can be *shared* and offer "narrative safe havens" from the demands of dominant heteronormative structures, where readers can "develop the strength necessary to find others like themselves and a sense of belonging."[43] Andrea Wood refers to the contribution such texts make to the creation of a "discursive space . . . among an intimate network of strangers," a "counter-public resistant to blithely consuming idealized heteronormative media."[44]

How do these characterizations of the potential for *yaoi*/BL consumption practices to subvert heteronormative structures and promote shared identifications stand up against mainstream media depictions of *fujoshi*? What happens when women's practices of *yaoi* production and consumption are made to intersect with the sexual scripts of heterosexual romance, as they do in all three major media narratives discussed above?

Two of the dominant narratives of *fujoshi* I have discussed here, namely *My Neighbor Yaoi-chan* and *Fujoshi Girlfriend*, were written by men and are anchored in more or less gender- and sexually normative masculine perspectives, revolving around the implications for heterosexual men of women's practices of *yaoi* consumption and production. More generally, I believe all three of these narratives reflect changes both in the image and in the reality of gender(ed) relations in Japan—changes that are located at the intersection of women's increasing power as consumers on the one hand, and the growing commodification of romance and preeminence of a companionate model of heterosexual coupling on the other.[45] There is a double move in these narratives, by which women's power is acknowledged, but then recaptured within more-or-less conventional trajectories of heterosexual romance.

Women's power is acknowledged, for instance, in the increasing presence of female-dominated spaces—Otome Road, *yaoi dōjinshi* shops, "butler cafés," and *yaoi dōjinshi* conventions—where heterosexual men, including the narrator of *Fujoshi Girlfriend*, are excluded or rendered uncomfortable or irrelevant.[46] Girl culture here is no longer confined to the bedroom.[47] Women's subjectivity and desires, in a particular construal, are thus acknowledged. Through the production and consumption of male homoerotic images and narratives as practices of pleasure—activities central to the distinction of *fujoshi*—women escape the female worlds to which they had been largely confined and enter a special kind of heterosocial space where they are able to impose their version of a pleasurable and playful reality.[48] Rumi, Y-ko-san, and Yaoi-chan each bend the will of the men in their lives to suit their own developed *fujoshi* tastes, whether it is Rumi's manipulation of Abe into a pose with cat ears, Y-ko-san's demand that the narrator cosplay in his mothballed high school uniform, or Yaoi-chan's request that Chibe-kun wear a suit, the men are made to recognize and accommodate the women's dynamic pursuit of pleasure. Women's desires are rendered public, and in the narratives, the women are endowed with the agency to see that these desires are satisfied.[49] Furthermore, the conventional female maneuvering for male approval that takes place in dominant heteronormative scripts is also compromised in these narratives through the unbending devotion the *fujoshi* main characters display toward their *yaoi* play—their love interests' incomprehension or disapproval be damned.

On the other hand, the "queer" aspects of the *fujoshi's yaoi* practices and of the texts themselves operate in the narratives only quite narrowly in terms of their effect on heteronormative assumptions. The *fujoshi's* consuming enthusiasms for *yaoi*/BL and the associated practices and pleasures come to represent a core of gender difference, a world that heterosexual men may come to understand, to some degree, indulge, or accommodate, but can never call their own. While the male love interests in these stories come to

Figure 9.4 From junior high through working life, at each transition in *My Neighbor Yaoi-chan*, Yaoi considers exiting the *otaku* world. Now facing marriage, "looks like it's impossible." *Fujoshi* devotion can be an irresistible force.

appreciate their partner's devotion to *yaoi*/BL, they can never enter and be fully comfortable in the *fujoshi* world as subjects of the interpretive codes and practices in which their *fujoshi* partners are so fluent and from which they derive so much pleasure. To the contrary, the men are more likely to be rendered into objects of those interpretive codes.

The *fujoshi*'s enthusiasms for male homoerotic coupling, in fact, work to structure the central dramatic tension in the narratives: Can heterosexual men succeed in romance with women who see male homoerotic relationships most everywhere they look? Ironically, this dramatic thematization of "can love overcome?" repeats the common *yaoi*/BL theme of overcoming difficulty (in this case, located in social hostility to same-sex love) to find pure love (the difficulty willingly confronted serving as evidence of its purity), but is written back into a boy–girl hetero-narrative. For instance, in *Fujoshi Girlfriend*, Y-ko-san insists to the end that she will always be a *fujoshi* (a common theme in *fujoshi* narratives, see figure 9.4), and playfully suggests at the conclusion of the story that her greatest dream is to have a room overflowing with BL books. The narrator insists that this is not a dream he shares. Yet they both insist on their enduring love. So we are left with gender-inflected positions that remain in tension, yet can somehow be successfully accommodated within a conventional heteronormative script.

Fujoshi Girlfriend ends with Y-ko accepting the narrator's proposal of marriage. In *Fantasizing Girl, Otaku-Style*, Rumi finally comprehends the difference between "*moe*" and "love," accepts Abe's professions of a long-standing love, and walks with him, hand-in-hand, into the cold, dark night, silhouetted in the glow of the *dōjinshi* convention they are departing (figure 9.5). And we learn in volume 3 of *My Neighbor Yaoi-chan* that the couple, who were already two years into a relationship at the opening of the narrative, has, tied the knot.

The narratives I have discussed here, I would suggest, perform a double move. On the one hand, they present some of the challenges and discomforts that *fujoshi* practices pose to a heteronormative habitus—the taken-for-granted assumptions regarding the gendered organization of romantic desire as exhibited by the male partners of these *fujoshi*. On the other, they simultaneously demonstrate that these practices can be assimilated to, and accommodated within, a heteronormative romantic script. The women are strong in their commitment to, and command of, the world of *yaoi* play. But they are also successful in forging satisfying romantic relationships with the men they love. At the level of the text, I would suggest that this is a case of institutional practices working to contain and reorient, and thereby help normalize, the more gender-troubling or destabilizing aspects of *fujoshi*

Figure 9.5 "Let's remember this night . . . and use it as material for the next *dōjinshi*." Rumi finds happiness with Abe at the conclusion of *Fantasizing Girl, Otaku-Style*. But will she give him up as an object of her homoerotic coupling fantasies?

practice. Transgression is contained within the framework of play, while *yaoi* play and heterosexual desires are reconciled in accommodative happy endings all around.[50]

The image of *fujoshi* presented in the works discussed here, albeit but one dimension of the diversity of representations of *fujoshi* in Japan, reveals shifts from earlier images of *yaoi*/BL fans. While perhaps eccentric in their tastes (at least from the point of view of the male characters who become involved with them), they are neither deviant nor radical. Rather, they are exemplary consumers—savvy, creative, and resourceful—of images of men in relationships reimagined for their own pleasure. These reimaginings do not displace the heterosexual longings the *fujoshi* characters express and pursue. The anxiety their practices cause their partners does not preclude continued, devoted attraction. *Fujoshi* practices need not deprive the practitioners of access to normative routes to happiness. Love can indeed triumph—perhaps all the more pure for the troubles it has overcome.

Notes

I would like to express my gratitude to the editors of this volume for constructive comments and suggestions throughout the drafting of this chapter, as well as to the organizers and participants of the Workshop on Glocal Polemics of "Boys Love" (BL), University of Oita, Oita, Japan (January 2011), where an early version of the chapter was presented.

1. On the notion of "bad girls," see Laura Miller and Jan Bardsley, eds., *Bad Girls of Japan* (New York: Palgrave Macmillan, 2005).

2. John Fiske, "The Cultural Economy of Fandom," in *The Adoring Audience*, ed. Linda A. Lewis (New York: Routledge, 1992), 30.

3. Benedict Anderson, *Imagined Communities: Reflections on the Origins and Spread of Nationalism*, new ed. (London: Verso, 2006).

4. Koichi Iwabuchi, "Undoing Inter-National Fandom in the Age of Brand Nationalism," *Mechademia* 5 (2010): 87.

5. Angela McRobbie, *The Aftermath of Feminism: Gender, Culture and Social Change* (London: Sage Publications, 2009), 55. McRobbie cites Gilbert Deleuze, *Foucault*, trans. Seán Hand (Minneapolis: University of Minnesota Press, 1988) as her source for the concept of luminosity.

6. Konjoh Natsumi, *Mōsō shōjo otaku-kei* [Fantasizing girl, *otaku*-style], 7 vols. (Tokyo: Futabasha, 2006–2010); Kojima Ajiko, *Tonari no 801-chan* [My neighbor Yaoi-chan], 5 vols. (Tokyo: Ohzora shuppan, 2006–2010); Pentabu, *Fujoshi kanojo* [Fujoshi girlfriend], 2 vols. (Tokyo: Enterbrain, 2006–2007). A licensed English translation of the first three volumes of *Mōsō shōjo otaku-kei* has been published in paperback under the title *Fujoshi Rumi* (New York: Media Blasters, 2008–2009). The entire seven volumes were available as digital comics on the now defunct *Jmanga* website under the title, *Otaku-Type Delusion Girl*. The two prose volumes of *Fujoshi kanojo* have been issued in a licensed English version as *My Girlfriend's a Geek* (New York: Yen Press, 2010–2011).

7. Nishihara Mari, "Masu media ga utsushidasu 'yaoi' no sugata: Gensetsu bunseki ni yoru" [A discourse analysis approach to the depiction of *yaoi* in the mass media], *Ronsō kuia* 3 (2010). While Nishihara limits her analysis to mass media and therefore doesn't track discourse in less dominant media outlets, for present purposes her approach is most useful.

8. A history of the use of BL-related terminology among fans may be found in James Welker's chapter in this volume.

9. The Year 24 Group (*24-nen gumi*) refers to a cohort of young female manga artists born around the year 24 of the Showa era (1949) who are said to have brought revolutionary innovations in theme, graphic style, and psychological depth to girls' manga. For further details, see Welker in this volume. On their treatment within the same framework as gay literature, see Nishihara, "Masu media," 73–75.

10. Ibid., 73–74.

11. Ibid., 75.

12. Ibid., 73.

13. See the chapters by Welker and Yukari Fujimoto in this volume as well as Mark McLelland, "Why Are Japanese Girls' Comics full of Boys Bonking?," *Refractory* 10 (2006),

http://refractory.unimelb.edu.au/2006/12/04/why-are-japanese-girls'-comics-full-of-boys
-bonking1-mark-mclelland/.

14. Nishihara, "Masu media," 73–74.

15. Ibid., 73.

16. Ibid., 82.

17. Of course, most *fujoshi* are, in the first instance, enthusiastic fans of (often male-targeted) mainstream manga and anime, toward which their *fujoshi* practices are a form of fan labor, allowing self-identity as *otaku*. Then there are self-identified female *otaku* who are devoted consumers of such mainstream media but do not take up *fujoshi* practices. Then again, there are more casual fans of BL who may neither exhibit the devotion generally assumed of *otaku*, nor possess particular enthusiasm for other manga or anime genres.

My understandings here are informed primarily by interviews with women who self-identify as *fujoshi* or female *otaku*. In addition, I have attended Comic City *dōjinshi* events (among others), since the early 2000s; interviewed *dōjinshi* event organizers; participated in the organization of an "only" event (see Welker, this volume); and attended *fujoshi* social activities. I also regularly encounter identity discourse by and about *fujoshi* and *otaku* in the course of my teaching activities.

18. See, e.g., Matt Hills, "Transcultural *Otaku*: Japanese Representations of Fandom and Representations of Japan in Anime/Manga Fan Cultures," paper presented at Media in Transition 2, Cambridge, MA: Massachusetts Institute of Technology, 2002; Lawrence Eng, "Strategies of Engagement: Discovering, Defining, and Describing Otaku Culture in the United States," in *Fandom Unbound: Otaku Culture in a Connected World*, ed. Mizuko Ito, Daisuke Okabe, and Izumi Tsuji (New Haven, CT: Yale University Press, 2012).

19. Nakano Hitori, *Densha otoko* [Train man] (Tokyo: Shinchōsha, 2004). On the "Train Man" phenomenon, see Alisa Freedman, "*Train Man* and the Gender Politics of Japanese 'Otaku' Culture: The Rise of New Media, Nerd Heroes and Consumer Communities," *Intersections: Gender and Sexuality in Asia and the Pacific* 20 (April 2009), http://intersec tions.anu.edu.au/issue20/freedman.htm.

20. The *fudanshi* or "rotten man," generally understood as a male interested in *yaoi*/BL narratives, presents intriguing complications to the feminized subject position of *fujoshi*, but has drawn attention, I would suggest, precisely because it is anomalous. See Kazumi Nagaike's chapter in this volume for a discussion.

21. For a consideration of the important question of audience, see Aida Miho, "Fujoshi no sekushuariti wa kyokō ka? Media ni okeru gensetsu o tsūjite" [Is *fujoshi* sexuality a fiction? An examination through media discourse], paper presented at the first meeting of the Japanese Association for Queer Studies, Hiroshima Shudo University, Hiroshima, November 8–9, 2008. In her treatment of some of the same works I discuss here, Aida raises the important question of audience. Texts are usually produced with particular audiences in mind, and readings may well shift with different interpretative communities. Aida puts weight in her analysis on the functions of the recent *fujoshi* narratives for male *otaku* in allowing them access to positions within hegemonic masculinity through fantasy and identification with the male protagonists and their social success in having girlfriends. Aida also draws attention to an article reporting that the some 70 percent of the readers of *Tonari no 801-chan* were women ("'Fujoshi' manga ga bureeku chū," *Asahi shinbun*, February 3, 2007, http://www .asahi.com/culture/news_culture/TKY200702030159.html). The article cites an editor who suggests that both *fujoshi* and a more general female audience were considered as targets.

22. Sugiura Yumiko, "Moeru onna otaku" [Excited women *otaku*], *Aera*, June 20, 2005.

23. These include Sugiura Yumiko, *Otaku joshi kenkyū: Fujoshi shisō taikei* [*Otaku* girls research: An compendium of *fujoshi* thought] (Tokyo: Hara shobō, 2006); Sugiura Yumiko, *Fujoshika suru sekai: Higashi Ikebukuro no otaku joshitachi* [*Fujoshi*-izing world: The *otaku* girls of East Ikebukuro] (Tokyo: Chūō kōron shinsha, 2006); Sugiura Yumiko, *Kakure otaku 9-wari: Hotondo no joshi ga otaku ni natta* [90 percent hidden *otaku*: Almost all girls have become *otaku*] (Tokyo: PHP kenkyūsho, 2008); and Sugiura Yumiko, *101-nin no fujoshi to ikemen ōji: Fujoshi "ren'ai kan" kenkyū* [101 *fujoshi* and handsome princes: Research on the perspectives on love of *fujoshi*] (Tokyo: Hara shobō, 2009).

24. On the *moe* affect, see Patrick Galbraith's chapter in this volume.

25. *Mōsō shōjo otaku-kei* (2006–2010) is one of the longest-running manga to date devoted to a *fujoshi* theme. The *obi*, or promotional sash, on a recent printing of *Tonari no 801-chan* states total sales of over 300,000, making it a "great hit." Likewise, the *obi* on a recent printing of *Fujoshi kanojo* states total sales of over 320,000 between the two prose volumes.

26. Some of her pornographic works targeting heterosexual men are catalogued in *The Doujinshi & Manga Lexicon*, at http://www.doujinshi.org/browse/author/5196/Konjou-Natsumi/.

27. The blog was still up and running, at http://indigosong.net/ as of October 2013, though entries had become less frequent.

28. Kojima, *Tonari no yaoi-chan*, 2006–2010; Kojima Ajiko, *Yorinuki tonari no 801-chan* [Selections from my neighbor Yaoi-chan] (Tokyo: Ohzora shuppan, 2010).

29. Jin and Kojima Ajiko, *Tonari no 801-chan: Fujoshi-teki kōkō seikatsu* [My Neighbor Yaoi-chan: *Fujoshi*-esque high school life], 3 vols. (Tokyo: Kodansha, 2008–2009); Minamikata Sunao, *801-shiki chūgakusei nikki* [Yaoi-style junior high school student diary] (Tokyo: Ohzora shuppan, 2009).

30. Pentabu, *Fujoshi kanojo*, 2006, 2007. The author's blog, with new material and entries on the earlier work, is available at http://pentabutabu.blog35.fc2.com/.

31. Shinba Rize, *Fujoshi kanojo* [Fujoshi girlfriend], 5 vols. (Tokyo: Enterbrain/B's Log Comics, 2007–2010); released in English as *My Girlfriend's a Geek* (New York: Yen Press, 2010–2011).

32. The following discussion is based on the Japanese edition. All translations are my own.

33. It is not unusual for blogs to be authored anonymously or under pseudonyms in Japan.

34. On distinctions between *otaku* and *ippanjin*, see Mizuko Ito, "Introduction," in: Ito, Okabe, and Tsuji, *Fandom Unbound*, xvii–xviii.

35. Pentabu, *Fujoshi kanojo*, vol. 1, 88–91. For further discussion of *seme–uke* pairing, see the chapters by Galbraith, Fujimoto, and Kazuko Suzuki in this volume.

36. Pentabu, *Fujoshi kanojo*, vol. 1, 69–78.

37. Ibid., 233–53.

38. Ibid., 138–46.

39. See Galbraith, this volume, on "*moe* talk" (*moe-banashi*), a crucial part of *yaoi* play.

40. Kazumi Nagaike, "Perverse Sexualities, Pervasive Desires: Representations of Female Fantasies and *Yaoi Manga* as Pornography Directed at Women," *U.S.-Japan Women's Journal* 25 (2003); see also chapters by Fujimoto, and by Kazumi Nagaike and Tomoko Aoyama in this volume.

41. Kazuko Suzuki, "Pornography or Therapy? Japanese Girls Creating the *Yaoi* Phenomenon," in *Millennium Girls: Today's Girls around the World*, ed. Sherrie A. Inness (Lanham, MD: Rowman and Littlefield, 1998).

42. Midori Matsui, "Little Girls Were Little Boys: Displaced Femininity in the Representation of Homosexuality in Japanese Girls' Comics," in *Feminism and the Politics of Difference*, ed. Sneja Gunew and Anna Yeatman (Halifax: Fernwood Publishing, 1993), 193; Sharalyn Orbaugh, "Creativity and Constraint in Amateur Manga Production," *U.S.–Japan Women's Journal* 25 (2003); James Welker, "Beautiful, Borrowed, and Bent: 'Boys' Love' as Girls' Love in *Shōjo* Manga," *Signs: Journal of Women in Culture and Society* 31, no. 3 (2006).

43. Welker, "Beautiful, Borrowed, and Bent," 866. On the sharing of narratives, see Galbraith in this volume.

44. Andrea Wood, "'Straight' Women, Queer Texts: Boy-Love Manga and the Rise of a Global Counterpublic," *Women's Studies Quarterly* 34, nos. 1–2 (2006): 396, 404.

45. Akiko Takeyama, "Commodified Romance in a Tokyo Host Club," in *Genders, Transgenders and Sexualities in Japan*, ed. Mark McLelland and Romit Dasgupta (New York: Routledge, 2005); Akiko Takeyama, "The Art of Seduction and Affect Economy: Neoliberal Class Struggle and Gender Politics in a Tokyo Host Club" (Ph.D. diss., University of Illinois at Urbana-Champaign, 2008).

46. Among these, *Fujoshi Girlfriend* most forcefully plays with conventions of heteronormative gender power, beginning with its very setup. Y-ko is older, with a career, and is a wage earner. He (*boku*) has yet to achieve adult social status, is domestic, and acknowledges her age and occupational superiority in language. She is demanding and assertive; he is reactive, indulgent, and serves her.

Butler cafés are designed to appeal to young women patrons by featuring handsome waiters in "butler" roles offering solicitous service in an elegant setting. They are counterparts for the female customer to the "maid cafés" marketed primarily to male *otaku*.

47. See, for instance, a classic discussion of girls' consumption of British popular culture in Angela McRobbie, "Girls and Subcultures," in *Resistance through Rituals: Youth Subcultures in Post-war Britain*, ed. Stuart Hall and Tony Jefferson, 2nd ed. (1976; London: Routledge, 2006).

48. See chapters by Rio Otomo and Galbraith in this volume, for a discussion of the relationship between the real and fantasy and the public aspects of what is felt as private tastes and desires.

49. A notable aspect of these narratives that deserves further analysis is the decentering of the text in the *yaoi* fan practice of the characters. While texts (*dōjinshi*, BL manga books, BL games, et cetera.) appear in abundance, there is great weight placed on rereading through *yaoi* codes the "actual social world" as given in these narratives. As such, *yaoi* practice becomes less a devotion to a broad narrative genre than a way of perceiving and re-encoding the social world more broadly. See Galbraith in this volume.

50. Back in the real world, the transgressions of *fujoshi* practice may be more consequential. See Mark McLelland's chapter in this volume for a discussion of the increasingly intense policing of *yaoi*/BL works, through legislation and enforcement practice, by the Japanese authorities.

DO HETEROSEXUAL MEN DREAM OF HOMOSEXUAL MEN?

BL *Fudanshi* and Discourse on Male Feminization

KAZUMI NAGAIKE

Introduction

The contemporary understanding in Japan of BL (boys love) media as a female-oriented product is epitomized by the word *"fujoshi,"* or "rotten girl(s)."[1] These BL media—namely, media focused on male–male romance narratives—have recently received a significant increase in public attention. This is in no small part due to the popularization in the mainstream media of the idea that there actually are in Japanese society *fujoshi*—adolescent girls and adult women—who indulge in these female-oriented fantasies concerning male–male romantic and erotic relationships. Because of the association of such women with BL, research to date on BL has often concluded or been premised on the idea that BL works are predominantly produced by and for women.[2] It is undeniable that BL studies and BL criticism have generally assumed that the BL genre represents an exclusively female-oriented romantic sphere which, in effect, bars all uninvited male participation. Thus, the BL genre may be viewed as part of an unbroken continuum with what Alice Jardine calls "gynesis"—that is, an exclusively female narrative space.[3]

However, this does not necessarily mean that actual male voices have been totally absent from BL throughout the genre's history. In 1978, the magazine *JUNE* first emerged as the pioneering commercial venue for female fantasies about male homosexuality. The first chief editor of *JUNE* was a man, Sagawa Toshihiko, whose contribution to the development of the BL genre is undeniable. There have also been several subsequent male editors-in-chief of the

189

magazine. Furthermore, a dialectical relationship vis-à-vis BL between women and gay men can be seen as early as 1992 in the so-called *"yaoi* debate" (*yaoi ronsō*). In this controversy, some gay men harshly criticized the genre, broadly defined, on the basis of its limited and stereotypical images of the supposedly gay characters. These men claimed that, on a subconscious level, female BL writers/readers are themselves homophobic, and that this genre thus "plunders" images of gay men.[4] Regardless of the veracity of that assertion, an analysis of the *yaoi* debate shows that the debate itself constructed and reinforced a simplistic opposition between women and "gay" men.[5]

Heterosexual men, on the other hand, have essentially remained invisible in both BL production and consumption, as well as in the critical discourse surrounding BL. Just over a decade ago, however, the term *"fudanshi,"* a play on the term *"fujoshi,"* and meaning "rotten boy(s)," emerged in popular media. According to the pseudonymous Budōuri Kusuko, a male fan of BL, in 2002 a self-identified male fan of BL suggested the term on the notorious Japanese Internet forum *2-channel*, and soon after it began to gain currency within and beyond the sphere of BL fandom, domestically and abroad.[6] In 2008, another male fan and critic of BL, Yoshimoto Taimatsu, self-published a study, *Interviewing Fudanshi* (*Fudanshi ni kiku*) in an initial attempt, by means of an innovative analysis of heterosexual male readings of BL, to make heterosexual male readers of BL (i.e., *fudanshi* or "rotten boys") visible for the first time.[7] *Fudanshi* in Yoshimoto's survey is used as a generic term to refer to all (biologically and socially acknowledged) male readers of BL, no matter what sexual orientation they may have (or are believed to have), including homo, hetero, bi, and other. (Indeed, the respondents in Yoshimoto's research also include many self-identified gay and bisexual men). However, in this chapter, using Yoshimoto's study as a springboard, I specifically examine the heterosexual male readership of BL in Japan. I attempt to extend his analysis of the discursive queerness reflected in heterosexual male readings of male homosexual narratives such as BL. To pursue the thematic goal of this research, in later sections I generally use *"fudanshi"* to refer to heterosexual male readers of BL.

Here, the analytical focus on *fudanshi* demonstrates the existence of a (subconscious) psychological male desire for self-feminization through male readers' identification with those images of seemingly gay men that were originally designed by and for women. This aligns with a temptation felt by many men to negate the socially imposed construction of a strong, "masculine" ego. Thus, as I discuss in the following sections, the concept of "male-feminization" reflects subversive elements relating to active male involvement in (easily accessed) female-oriented subcultural activities, and it presents an ideological challenge to—or a negation of—socially constructed archetypes of strong "masculinity." Since this analysis is one of a very few preliminary attempts to systematize heterosexual male readings of these male homosexual narratives, I tentatively introduce hypotheses concerning the possible psychological orientations of heterosexual male BL readers by outlining a number of relevant issues, including the romance narrative, the concept of masculinity, the desire for androgyny, Freud's beating-fantasy theory, and the epistemology of the *shōnen* (boy) within the context of Japanese modernism. In this way, how and why self-identified heterosexual men enthusiastically consume BL narratives will be analyzed as a means to take BL studies beyond previous gynesis-oriented research approaches.

Interviewing Fudanshi (Fudanshi ni kiku): Yoshimoto Taimatsu's *Fudanshi* Study

In 2008, Yoshimoto carried out an Internet-based survey of male BL readers, and subsequently presented his analysis in the form of a *dōjinshi* (coterie magazine), entitled *Interviewing Fudanshi (Fudanshi ni kiku)*. Yoshimoto recruited his respondents from the Internet community using *mixi* (a social networking website). One of the prerequisites for taking part in this questionnaire was that respondents should be self-identified *fudanshi*, and a total of ninety-nine individuals completed the survey. As Yoshimoto himself points out, the validity of any Internet-based survey in terms of accuracy of self-reporting can be challenged in a number of ways. However, Yoshimoto backs up his analysis by directly interviewing some of the *fudanshi* who filled out the questionnaire.

One of the questions included in Yoshimoto's questionnaire concerns respondents' sexual orientation. Thirty of the ninety-nine identified themselves as "gay," twenty-seven as "bisexual, preferring men," twenty-one as "bisexual, preferring women," and fifteen as "straight," while six indicated that they "do not feel sexual desire toward others." Yoshimoto carried out a similar Internet survey two years later, in 2010, that showed a similar range of sexual orientations. Out of a total of 111 respondents, twenty-one indicated that they are attracted "only to men," thirty-five indicated that they "like both men and women, but prefer men," thirty indicated that they "like both men and women, but prefer women," twenty indicated that they are attracted "only to women," and five indicated that they were not sexually attracted to others. Both surveys clearly show that a certain proportion of heterosexual men identify themselves as *fudanshi*.

腐男子にきく。
改訂版

表紙：依田沙江美

編：吉本たいまつ

Figure 10.1 Cover of
Interviewing Fudanshi
(*Fudanshi ni kiku*).

Yoshimoto acknowledges that his analysis of these surveys relies on the respondents' self-reports, and this poses some ideological questions in relation to the socially imposed disavowal of gay identity itself, as well-known gay manga artist Tagame Gengoroh remarks:

> The question is, which puts less pressure on men, coming out as gay or as a *fudanshi* who loves BL? Perhaps self-identifying as a *fudanshi* creates less pressure. Those who would have identified themselves as gay in relation to ordinary gender categories may now be inclined to say something like: "No, I'm not gay, but a *fudanshi*." It would be problematic if the deep-rooted homophobia attached to gay sexuality per se could be easily evaded (or covered-up) by the word *fudanshi*.[8]

The emergence of *fudanshi* as a popular term may thus be double-edged, precisely because it could render gay sexuality invisible, reflecting ongoing discriminatory attitudes toward gay men, as Tagame pessimistically hypothesizes. However, at the same time, the concept of *fudanshi* can also provide a queer space in which established Japanese attitudes toward gender formation can be challenged, as I will subsequently discuss in more detail.

"You Are the Only Love in My Life!": *Fudanshi* Desire for Romantic Narratives

Of those who have conducted research on men's studies (*danseigaku*) in Japan, Itō Kimio most clearly illuminates the sociocultural phenomena that enforce compulsory expressions of masculinity on Japanese men. For example, Itō demonstrates in detail how both formal and informal education teach Japanese boys to behave in a stereotypically "manly" fashion, encouraging them to take pride in being aggressive, authoritative, and dominant.[9] In contrast, I believe that BL texts prompt *fudanshi* to reevaluate socially established gender paradigms and thereby enable them to develop a postmodern reading of maleness and masculinity by acknowledging a male desire to access a female-oriented sphere—a desire/process/act which I call "self-feminization." I suggest that the voices of other *fudanshi* are, therefore, persuasive in helping individual *fudanshi* to overcome the dilemmas they confront in relation to the perceived necessity to "perform" a socially imposed male role when they, in fact, do not wish to or feel unable to (naturally) perform this role. In this regard, one *fudanshi* interviewed by Yoshimoto states: "I somehow feel myself freed from [established] gender consciousness [through reading BL]. I'm not at all skilled at expressing masculinity in a particularly appropriate way."[10] Other *fudanshi* also express their understanding of BL as texts that subvert mainstream masculinity:

"BL was salvation for me. And I think that it would be the same for a lot of men in contemporary Japan."[11]

"BL/*yaoi* was a tool that my generation (I was born in 1970) could use to liberate ourselves from the pretense that we were tough guys."[12]

"A competitive principle such as 'men have to win' affects men's psyches quite effectively. I felt so burdened by such ideas. I was really saved by [the magazine] *JUNE* and by *yaoi*, which offered me a new perspective on accepting [myself] being a passive man."[13]

"I started getting the idea that men can enjoy specific texts, like *yaoi*, that were originally made by and for women, in order to live with less stress and psychological pressure."[14]

In reviewing *fudanshi* readings of BL in terms of the concept of male feminization (and the partial negation of masculinity), it is important to stress that BL originated as a romantic narrative genre produced by and for women. BL narratives thus definitely retain their female orientation, that is, their orientation toward female readers. This does not exclude male readers from the BL genre, but acknowledges the fact that BL continues to represent a combination of romantic and aesthetic elements and plots designed by female artists to impress and attract female readers. Both BL's popularity among women and its public recognition as a female-oriented genre demonstrate that BL provides specific narratives which attract female readers and "allow" these women to consume such narratives enthusiastically.

Just as critic and BL novelist Nakajima Azusa considers *yaoi* (or BL) to be the "ultimate love fantasy" and the "harlequin romance of male homosexuality," so too may BL be characterized as a form of romantic narrative which highlights dramatic and erotic tension between beautiful male characters.[15] In sum, the thematic energy of BL narratives remains associated with the romantic idea that "you are the only love in my life," while what may be termed BL's artistic and thematic value is generally expressed through the dramatic tension between two male characters who are portrayed as being "meant for each other" and who thus embody the romantic force of an idealized monogamous relationship. Yūya's *King of the Earth* (*Chikyū no ōsama*) represents one example of this pattern. In this narrative, King William (who rules an imaginary kingdom in an unnamed land) even attempts to rewrite his kingdom's constitution so that he can officially "marry" his Japanese male lover.[16] Similarly, in Kajimoto Jun's *It May Be Fate But He Is the Worst Teacher* (*Unmei na no ni saiaku na kyōshi*), the narrative concludes, "Our meeting was destiny. I finally met the only love of my life."[17] The following romantic lines appear in Shimizu Yuki's *Yes!* (*Ze*): "Shōi, please give me that ring again. This time, I'll pledge to you that my love for you will never change, so that even after I die, and I'll be with you in the next life forever."[18] An idealized romantic love becomes quite visible and intelligible here, expressed through a specific medium—romance narratives—from which women are socially "allowed" to derive pleasure—albeit, as noted in the opening of this chapter, when they depict male–male relationships, the social acceptability of romance narratives is called into question.

I had the opportunity to interview five editors of commercial BL manga magazines and ask their opinions about how and why some self-identified heterosexual men are drawn to BL narratives.[19] Most mentioned the fact that BL narratives express a supreme form of love, and that this differentiates BL from other popular forms of narrative produced for girls/women. *Fudanshi* themselves also manifest a strong attraction to the romanticized love stories found in BL, as one respondent of Yoshimoto's interview survey indicates: "BL presents pure love stories which are epitomized by the phrase, 'We are deeply in love and meant for each other.' BL negates the idea of an instinctual sexual drive or any standard form of love which is compulsorily imposed by society."[20] Further, as another respondent remarks, "I should say that, in contemporary Japan, BL is the only manga medium which provides the reader with genuine love stories. BL makes me feel most romantically excited."[21] In *Interviewing Fudanshi* and *Interviewing Fudanshi 2*, Yoshimoto lists his subjects' favorite BL manga artists. As Yoshimoto indicates in his summaries of *fudanshi* surveys, *fudanshi* read a variety of BL works.[22] However, one of the characteristics of the BL manga artists listed as *fudanshi* favorites—including artists such as Kojima Natsuki, Kyōyama Atsuki and Kuraō Taishi—is that they are primarily known for romantic stories featuring cute-looking characters, and they seldom draw sexually explicit scenes. In contrast, other popular BL manga artists, such as Nitta Youka and Shimizu Yuki, whose works contain hard-core sex scenes, are generally not well-liked by *fudanshi* readers.[23]

Japanese patriarchal assumptions—in contrast with the clear desire for romance narratives expressed by these *fudanshi*—consider masculinity as strictly opposed to such romanticism: men are psychologically conditioned not to show enthusiasm for such (supposedly) trite romance narratives directed at women. The dialectical opposition between male-oriented narratives (such as *shōnen*/boys' manga) and female-oriented narratives (such as *shōjo*/girls' manga) has been analyzed by several other scholars.[24] While *shōjo* manga often highlights the romantic "boy meets girl" motif, through its depiction of competition and fighting, *shōnen* manga generally epitomizes the necessity for boy/male readers to construct a socially acceptable masculine identity. However, unlike the traditional and stereotypical image of Japanese men as distancing themselves from female-oriented romantic narratives, *fudanshi* seem eagerly to consume these narratives, and do not hesitate to immerse themselves in this supposedly female-oriented sphere. In this respect, BL seems to respond to a subconscious desire among *fudanshi* to access a specifically female-oriented cultural form, in which norms of masculinity are less apparent than in comparable patriarchal forms.

Fudanshi's Strong Attachment to BL *Uke* Characters and the Subconscious Desire for Androgyny

In order to better understand *fudanshi's* desire for self-feminization, the fact that many *fudanshi* report an inclination to identify with the *uke*—or sexually passive—characters should be addressed in particular. The issue of the stylized depiction of the male couples in BL has considerable significance in that the conventions governing their depiction generally reinforce the binary oppositional relationship between penetrating *seme* (literally "attacker," connoting the male sexual role) characters and penetrated *uke* (literally "receiver," connoting the female sexual role) characters in ways that parallel heterosexual couplings. One of the questions that Yoshimoto's 2010 Internet survey asked concerns *fudanshi's* psychological sympathy toward and identification with BL characters. Of the 111 *fudanshi* who answered the question, "Suppose you had fallen in love with a BL character, would you prefer to play the role of a *seme* or an *uke*?" roughly 41 percent of informants chose *uke*, while roughly 19 percent chose the role of *seme*. This survey also shows *fudanshi's* essentially playful attitude toward established gender concepts in that the majority of *fudanshi*—40 percent—expressed a desire to play a "reversible" role. This question was answered by twenty-one *fudanshi* who self-identified as heterosexual. Nine of these heterosexual *fudanshi* chose to be an *uke*, while five chose a *seme*, and seven indicated they would rather play a reversible role—a character type that is, in fact, rather rare in BL.

Another question asks, "When you are enjoying BL works, which type of character do you emotionally identify with more, the *seme* or the *uke*? Or do you like to take an objective, third-person perspective?" This question inquires more directly about *fudanshi's* identification with BL characters. A total of 54 percent of the *fudanshi* respondents chose to take an objective, third-person perspective. However, when only the *seme* and the *uke* are compared with each other, it is obvious that *fudanshi* predominantly identify with *uke* characters (36 percent), rather than with *seme* characters (10 percent). I certainly understand some of the problematic aspects of this question, which seems to narrow down the act of identification to a simple binary choice. As I have discussed elsewhere, readers' potentially divergent impulses of identification in relation to BL characters should not be minimized.[25] The format of this Internet survey (multiple choice) does not allow us to discuss the complicated process of male BL readers' psychological identification with multiple characters in any detail. In addition, *fudanshi's* inclination to identify with *uke* characters might be encouraged by the typical narrative pattern of BL works, which are mostly told from the perspective of the *uke* character, as Nagakubo Yōko's quantitative analysis of BL novels shows.[26] Nonetheless, this survey of *fudanshi*'s identification with BL characters clearly demonstrates subconscious desires for feminization among a group of heterosexual males.

Discourse on androgyny in the context of Japan may be employed here to make sense of the formation processes of *fudanshi*'s desire for self-feminization. However, existing theoretical and ideological understandings and analyses regarding androgyny are so complex and divergent that some of these critical approaches are too distant from each other to be compatible. Jennifer Robertson, a scholar of the Takarazuka Revue, an all-female musical theater troupe, discusses androgyny within the Japanese sociocultural context, providing an historically contextualized analysis of such terms as *ryōsei* (ambiguously indicating bisexuality or hermaphroditism) and *chūsei* (broadly, androgyny).[27] In attempting to disclose the systematized formation of androgyny which is (subconsciously) desired by *fudanshi*, here I use the general term "androgyny" to refer to any combination of masculine and feminine characteristics and view it as a means by which *fudanshi*'s conflicted sense of masculinity may be interpreted. Thus defined, androgyny must be considered to underlie *fudanshi*'s desire to consume BL narratives, in which most of the male characters are depicted as feminized—in other words, androgynous.[28]

Most of the male characters depicted in the BL genre as a whole are feminized—that is, androgynous—in terms of both their physical and psychological characteristics. However, biologically they can clearly be defined as "male" in that readers can see (or sometimes imagine) their naked bodies and genitals. And yet the way in which male genitals are typically portrayed in BL enables us to understand its potential for androgynous seductiveness. The genitals of these BL characters are usually portrayed abstractly or ambiguously: the penis is not shown clearly, but only in outline, or whited out, or otherwise obscured. We know (or imagine) that these characters possess penises, but paradoxically we are not allowed to "see" them clearly, and this serves to mystify these characters' sexualized bodies just as their same–sex desire mystifies their sexual identities. In terms of biological characteristics, these characters are "male." However, the ways in which they are drawn represents these characters (including *seme* characters) as feminine; they are drawn as *bishōnen* (beautiful boys), with beautiful faces similar to the girl characters in *shōjo* manga.

As suggested above, the thematic energy of BL narratives arguably originate in their embodiment of the erotic and seductive power of androgyny. On this basis, it may be argued that *fudanshi*'s attraction to BL narratives is itself rooted in androgyny, that is, a desire for (narratives about) feminized men/androgynous characters. I have already asserted that *fudanshi's* readings of BL exemplify a subconscious male desire for self-feminization. It is therefore also arguable that, while the maleness (masculinity) of BL characters is initially defined by their biological sex, their recognizably male characteristics are displaced by the more feminine context—that is, the discursive field of BL itself—in which these characters are portrayed, as well as the many ways (noted above) in which BL characters are narratively feminized. I would like to emphasize here that this androgynous context, centered on the physical masculinity of BL characters but also thus flavored by femininity, constitutes the basis for *fudanshi's* attraction to the BL genre, which reverberates with their desire for self-feminization, while enabling them to maintain their masculinity to a greater or lesser degree through identifying with physically male characters.[29]

The male-oriented androgyny inherent in *fudanshi's* reading of BL must be explained in relation to the features which distinguish BL from other female-oriented romantic genres, such as the heterosexual romance genre of *shōjo* manga as well as *yuri* (female same-sex romance) manga targeting *shōjo* readers.[30] These popular forms of female-oriented romantic stories might also seem to offer specific narrative spaces that could potentially enable male readers to accommodate their inclinations toward feminization. However, it is BL, rather than these genres, that has engendered the *fudanshi* readership. Revealing the difficulties involved in determining exactly which elements of BL attract *fudanshi*, Yoshimoto's heterosexual *fudanshi* respondents express their own puzzlement concerning why they are exclusively attracted to BL works.

However, despite the seemingly patriarchal construction of androgyny in this genre, the power of androgyny in BL narratives cannot be completely limited to mechanisms which reinforce normative concepts of masculine identity. Instead, one could argue that the potentially subversive influence of BL androgyny on *fudanshi* is based on the fact that the "male" archetypes in the BL genre combine textual elements originally imagined or fantasized about by women. Robertson argues that the androgyny manifested in the gender-bending performances of the Takarazuka Revue actually reflects a patriarchal ideology that privileges masculinity over femininity. She concludes that specific male-oriented archetypes are essentially constructed by men (even in the case of an all-female art form such as Takarazuka), in order to guide gender-bending performers to perform in accordance with this ideology.[31] Robertson's analysis of androgyny in Takarazuka leads us to rethink the idea that broadly androgynous archetypes must essentially be originated and produced by men, and that therefore these archetypes reinforce the subordination of the female. This concept is contradicted by the fact that the androgynous archetypes in BL which attract *fudanshi* are definitely originated and produced by women. The point I would like to stress here is that the male inclination to identify with androgynous archetypes created by women enables the inherently subversive nature of BL androgyny to have its full effect on *fudanshi* readers.

The Negation of the Strong Ego and Self-Love in BL *Shota* Narratives: Freud and Modern Japanese Literature

Yoshimoto suggests that the concept of "*shota*"—which may indicate pre- or barely adolescent *shōnen* (boy) characters, an attraction to such characters, or works that feature them—represents one of the key elements in understanding *fudanshi* psychology.[32] Strong female appreciation for *shōnen* can also be seen in Japanese popular culture. The term "*shota*" derives from the name of the boy hero Shōtaro of the long-running 1950s–1960s Japanese manga and TV anime series *Tetsujin 28-gō* (Steel man no. 28; released in the U.S. as *Gigantor*). Among women, Shōtaro, who has a cute face and wears short pants, is considered the epitome of the prepubescent, innocent *shōnen* figure—cute perhaps, but not beautiful like *bishōnen* (beautiful boy) characters in *shōjo* manga. Women who are attracted by such young *shōnen* are sometimes described as having *shotakon*, a "Shōtaro complex." One BL *manga* subgenre, called *shota-mono*, specifically deals with the sexuality of such prepubescent boys. Nagayama Kaoru, a critic who has studied the *shota* genre, demonstrates that *shota* developed as a specific subgenre of BL; he concludes that, by the mid-1990s, *shota* had become a manga genre directed primarily at men. According to Nagayama, the second phase of the *shota* boom for men began in the early 2000s, when a number of *shota* anthologies were published.[33] The typical couplings represented in *shota* works (both in the "BL" version targeting female readers and the works targeting men) are either two boys (*shōnen*) or a young man and a boy (*seinen* and *shōnen*). While the *seme–uke* relationship is generally not apparent with two boys, when a young man and a boy are represented, the boy is seldom depicted in the *seme* role.

In his 2008 Internet survey, Yoshimoto asks his *fudanshi* respondents, "What brought you to BL?" Fourteen percent selected an answer indicating they are "*shota*," that is, a fan of *shota* characters/works, or that they like "*otoko no ko*" (a term meaning boys, but written with the character for girl/

daughter). Indeed, as can be seen below, his respondents do not hesitate to disclose their emotional attachment to *shota*:

> INFORMANT B: Yes, I'm attracted to *shota* [characters/works]. I sense differences between *shōnen–shōnen* eroticism and heterosexual relationships.
>
> YOSHIMOTO: So, do you feel, ultimately, that your favorite scenario involves *shōnen–shōnen* relationships?
>
> INFORMANT B: I've always been attracted to the close bond between *shōnen*. Sexual contact is possibly inserted into the *shōnen–shōnen* narrative in order to express this bond.[34]

> YOSHIMOTO: Do you think that the *shota* element guided you to the world of BL?
>
> INFORMANT C: Yes, it did. I discovered that *shota* stories were included in *manga* comic books with *rorikon* themes [themes that eroticize prepubescent or barely pubescent girls for adult male readers/viewers]. Reading these *shota* stories got me interested in *shōnen–shōnen* relationships.[35]

In addition, in Yoshimoto's 2010 Internet survey, one question asks *fudanshi*, "Are there any other cultural genres that you enjoy, apart from BL?" The second most chosen answer was "*shota* works aimed at men." Here, as Yoshimoto indicates, *fudanshi*'s desire for *shota* seems to reflect a rather masculine orientation, involving petting small, cute creatures in a domineering way. However, *fudanshi*'s love of *shota* adds an element of complexity to their psychological orientation, including their hidden desire for self-feminization. This is expressed in their serious consideration of the wish to become pure and innocent boys themselves, and thus to be loved unconditionally. In this context, Nagayama's analysis of *shota* reveals the very essence of the desire of *fudanshi* to identify themselves with *shota* characters. Nagayama analyzes men's desire for *shota* as their subconscious desire to "becom[e] cute boys themselves."[36]

However, Nagayama's discussion of *shota* takes a different perspective from mine in that he defines men's *shota* desire as "auto-eroticism" rather than a desire to be loved by the stronger partner in the *shota* relationship. Nagayama concludes that male *shota* desire is primarily stimulated by reading stories concerning *shota–shota* relationships, an act of reading which allows men to play both the *seme* (*shota*) and *uke* (*shota*) roles, without having to choose one or the other. His analysis thus suggests that the *shota* genre for men represents a narrative involving "having sex with myself" (*watashi to watashi no sekkusu*), signifying that this desire is essentially "auto-erotic."

Figure 10.2 Image of *shota* in Kotobushi Tarako's *The Neighbor's Lawn* (*Tonari no shibafu*).

Moreover, the potential capacity of men to identify with *shota* characters may be discussed in terms of previous research on the consumption by adult men of *rorikon* manga (and other media) that portray "underage" female characters in sexual contexts. Patrick Galbraith's argument that adult male *rorikon* obtain pleasure by identifying with the sexually submissive girl (*rori*) characters depicted, rather than by taking the perspective of the male characters in *rori* works, is certainly persuasive. This act of self-feminization has some similarity to adult men's identification with *shota* characters, in that both processes broaden the terms of male gender/sexual identity.[37]

This framework involving *fudanshi*'s (subconscious) desire to become a boy (one aspect of self-feminization) parallels Sigmund Freud's analysis of "beating fantasies" in terms of male fantasies of homoeroticism/homosexuality.[38] In his famous article entitled "A Child is Being Beaten," Freud discusses the complicated structure of female and male fantasies, along with concomitant sexual arousal, in relation to the degree and type of subjectivity and identification which such fantasies involve. Freud considers the male beating fantasy to be a reflection of men's subconsciously repressed homosexual and masochistic desires. Male beating fantasies can be discussed in terms of the three-stage Freudian structure:

1. "I am loved by my father": This phase clearly indicates the boy's feminine (that is, passive) attitude toward his father. This first phase does not include any sadistic impulses, in contrast with the first phase of female beating fantasies.
2. "I am being beaten by my father": This phase is equivalent to the second phase of female beating fantasies. While the girl represents her incestuous desires toward her father at this stage, the second stage of the male version of beating fantasies indicates the boy's repressed (homosexual and incestuous) desires toward his father.
3. "I am being beaten by my mother": Even though here the subject performing the beating has changed from the individual's father to his mother, the beater still manifests masculine (that is, dominant) qualities. Thus, this third stage can also be discussed in terms of the boy's (homosexual) desires toward his father, precisely because here the "mother" represents a disguised "father."[39]

I would like to suggest that the male beating fantasy represents a (subconscious) male desire to become a small boy (self-feminization) and thus be loved unconditionally by a strong, masculine Other—in this case, the Symbolic Father. Thus, this psychological frame definitely has homoerotic, or rather homosexual, connotations. As Freud says: "The original phantasy, 'I am being beaten by my father,' corresponds, in the case of the boy, to a feminine attitude, and is therefore an expression of that part of his disposition which belongs to the opposite sex."[40] *Fudanshi* can be discussed in relation to Freud's theory of the male beating fantasy in a similar way. A *fudanshi* fantasizes himself as a boy who is "beaten" (that is, loved) by the Father and thereby feminizes himself. Saitō Tamaki, a Japanese psychoanalyst and critic of popular culture, takes a similar stance to Freud's concerning male desire for *shota*. Saitō concludes that this *shota* desire constitutes a specific form of *otaku* (extreme fan) sexuality that is "deliberately separated from everyday life."[41] He argues that the fictionality (fantasy existence) of *shota* is realized by means of its absolute distance from realistic everyday life, and he then proceeds to explore the similarities between the discourse of male *shota*

desire and the "space of perfect fictionality" of superflat art.[42] A deeper exploration of Saitō's concept of *shota* reveals that the imaginative nature of *shota*
provides a proxy for an ultimate fictionality through which men can express
their repressed desire to be a boy (or something which is not a "man").

In order to reorient the analysis back to male feminization (or masoch-
ism), the unquestionable passivity (both linguistic and emotional) of the
male "I" in this beating fantasy should be noted. This powerlessness, this
constant placing of the self in a passive and dominated role, which such
male beating fantasies consistently express may stimulate a persistent desire
for other masochistic pleasures, as Kaja Silverman indicates.[43] However, this
male desire for masochistic pleasures cannot be satisfied except in relation to
a strong, masculine Other (Symbolic Father) and within a scenario of psychological feminization.

Now, I would like to examine the strong attraction of *fudanshi* to BL shota more closely in relation to the fundamental epistemological significance of
shōnen identity as a means of self-actualization that contradicts established
understandings of Japanese modernization, in particular vis-à-vis the establishment of modern masculinity and the masculinization of the Japanese
nation-state. As philosopher and literary critic Karatani Kōjin points out,
Japanese modernization (and the establishment of modern Japanese literature) has been accompanied by the discovery of a strong *"jiko"* (self or
subject), which was introduced under the influence of the supposedly more
advanced, modernized West.[44]

Literary critic Takahara Eiri, however, suggests a different approach to
the problematic process of constructing a modernized Japan.[45] Analyzing the
works of several male authors who were active during the period of Japanese
modernization from the late nineteenth through the mid-twentieth centuries—including Orikuchi Shinobu (1887–1953), Edogawa Ranpo (1894–
1965), Inagaki Taruho (1900–1977), and Mishima Yukio (1925–1970)—
Takahara demonstrates how they all represent *shōnen* as perfect objects for
adult men's sexual desire. In this role, *shōnen* are consistently idealized in these
authors' writings as never attempting to establish the modern idea of strong
ego; for this reason, they can be loved by adult males. As Takahara writes:

> Refusal to fight for the establishment of a strong self and longing to be loved
> without projecting a strong self are the essential qualities in these *shōnen* im-
> ages. Such a longing [to negate the necessity of developing a strong ego] is a
> quality commonly shared [among specific Japanese people], and its existence
> provokes [male authors] to create works that project self-love in the form of
> appreciating *shōnen'ai* [love of *shōnen*].[46]

Takahara also analyzes the images of *shōnen* prevalent in modern literary works created by male authors, concluding that these *shōnen* figures are all furnished with a concept of *jikoai* (self-love, or narcissism). While *shōnen* are typically described as weak, unstable, and fragile, without a strong sense of self, these *shōnen* characters themselves are inclined to cherish their own passivity.

Thus, my analysis of *fudanshi*'s attraction to *shota* overlaps to some extent with Takahara's analysis of the idealized images of *shōnen* that appear in modern Japanese literary expressions of male homosexuality. According to Takahara, *shōnen* identity is dramatized and idealized in such works, precisely because it never becomes an established (Western-oriented) self. This kind of endless self-objectification is fully acknowledged and accepted by the *shōnen* characters themselves, and can be epitomized as self-love for a passive, weak self. Similarly, *fudanshi*'s attraction to *shota* is stimulated by *shota* characters' stubborn refusal to relinquish the objectified, androgynous self by establishing any form of strong subjectivity or behaving according to socially imposed gender norms. *Shota* is constructed as a fantasy of perfect existence, which is able to embrace the nullification of a strong ego, in the same way that, in the context of modern Japanese literature, *shōnen* are also portrayed in terms of self-objectification. The *shota* characters, too, apparently escape complicity with the aims of modernization, which have as their corollary the development of a strong male ego and a comparably masculinized nation. In this regard, having previously been overwhelmed by the power of this nationalist myth of masculinity, *fudanshi* project *shōnen* attributes onto *shota* as a potential means to escape this myth. *Fudanshi* themselves wish to be unconditionally loved, as if they were *shōnen*, with none of the gender responsibilities that Japanese society has otherwise assigned them.

As Takahara shows, the (homosexual or homoeroticized) *shōnen* characters created by modern Japanese male authors represent a means by which they can challenge, undermine and reject the fanatical nationalist ideological construct of an egocentric male identity, which only serves to replicate the strong gender and class privileges pertaining in the West. In a similar vein, *fudanshi* may use BL *shota* to express their opposition to the contemporary Japanese social situation, in which a man is only valued if he behaves like a perfect, self-established man. It would therefore seem that *shota* provides a specific subversive space in which *fudanshi* can review traditional Japanese images of masculinity and learn to acknowledge, accept, and ultimately love such elements of maleness as weakness, fragility, and passivity, which do not necessarily accord with socially imposed gender roles. In this sense, BL *shota* paradoxically provide *fudanshi* with a means of loving themselves (*jikoai*).

Conclusion

A consideration of heterosexual male readings of BL narratives raises a number of complex and controversial questions with regard to gender formation, fantasy formation, and the sociocultural criteria on which these are based. An overview of male heterosexual readings of BL demonstrates that these readers can sublimate the dilemmas involved in being a man within a patriarchal context by identifying with feminized male/androgynous characters originally produced by and for women. The romantic narratives expressed in BL represent a kind of salvation for them, precisely because this genre provides a specifically queer space (via androgynous adolescent and adult male characters and significantly younger *shota* characters) in which the established paradigms of masculinity in Japan can be deconstructed. This analysis of *fudanshi* definitely needs to be expanded via an exploration of such issues as the theoretical utility and conceptual hazards involved in using the popular term *fudanshi*, the subcultural phenomenon of men's appreciation for *shota* outside the field of BL culture, the controversies surrounding Japanese men's studies, and so forth. In this way, it may become possible to discern a broader range of gender possibilities and begin to reach an understanding of their significance in transforming gender roles and sexualities in Japanese society.

Notes

1. As some scholars have pointed out, the category "BL" may ultimately need to be differentiated from other related terms (see the chapters by Fujimoto Yukari and Kazuko Suzuki in this volume). However, I use the term "BL" more generically to designate the entire range of popular narratives written by and for women, which include fantasies about male–male eroticism.

I would like to point out here that some of the editors of BL publications whom I interviewed in September 2010 are reluctant to use the word "*fujoshi*," saying, for example, that they would never label consumers with such a derogatory term as "rotten"; others, in contrast, seem to positively promote the word "*fujoshi*," evidently as part of a specific marketing strategy, and publish works with the word "*fujoshi*" placed prominently in their titles.

2. See, for instance, Nakajima Azusa, *Komyunikēshon fuzen shōkōgun* [Communication deficiency syndrome] (Tokyo: Chikuma shobō, 1991); Midori Matsui, "Little Girls Were Little Boys: Displaced Femininity in the Representation of Homosexuality in Japanese Girls' Comics," in *Feminism and the Politics of Difference*, ed. Sneja Gunew and Anna Yeatman (Halifax, NS: Fernwood Publishing, 1993); Tanigawa Tamae, "Josei no shōnen ai shikō ni tsuite II: Shikisha no kenkai to feminizumu ni aru kanōsei" [On women's preference for *shōnen'ai*, part 2: Expert opinions and feminist possibilities], *Joseigaku nenpō* 134 (1993); and

Sakakibara Shihomi, *Yaoi genron: "Yaoi" kara mieta mono* [Phantasmic discourse on *yaoi*: Things seen from a *"yaoi"* perspective] (Tokyo: Natsume shobō, 1998).

3. Alice Jardine, in her *Gynesis: Configurations of Woman and Modernity* (Ithaca, NY: Cornell University Press, 1985), discusses the problematic nature of discourses that are coded as "feminine"—abstract discourses defined in terms that have little to do with actual women but that are necessary for the construction and maintenance of modernity. She coined the term "gynesis"—suggesting a specifically female (gyn-) form of poiesis (creation)—to designate an epistemological space that transcends (or is separate from) the constructed contexts of modernity. That is, gynesis points to an alternative, female narrative space.

4. Ishida Hitoshi's article, "'Hottoite kudasai' to iu hyōmei o megutte: Yaoi/BL no jiritsusei to hyōshō no ōdatsu" [On the declaration "Please leave us alone": The autonomy of *yaoi/BL* and the appropriation of representation], *Yuriika* 39, no. 16 (December 2007), helped to reignite the debate over the representations of gay characters in BL. One of his central theses here is based on the fact that, in the past, a certain number of female BL creators/fans have themselves expressed disdain concerning the lack of seriousness of BL as a genre. Moreover, they have shown a strong aversion to any serious criticism/analysis of BL (or its creators and readers).

5. See Wim Lunsing, "*Yaoi Ronsō*: Discussing Depictions of Male Homosexuality in Japanese Girls' Comics, Gay Comics and Gay Pornography," *Intersections: Gender, History and Culture in the Asian Context* 12 (2006); and Keith Vincent, "A Japanese Electra and Her Queer Progeny," *Mechademia* 2 (2007).

6. See Budōuri Kusuko, "Fudanshi fukei jishō nenpyō: Hosokuban for fudanshi nau" [A chronological table of *fudanshi* and *fukei* (rotten older brothers): Supplemental version for contemporary *fudanshi*] (Japan: Self-published PDF), http://p.booklog.jp/book/54367. The term "*fudanshi*" frequently appears on BL-related sites, both in Japan and abroad. Moreover, when I interviewed approximately twenty female BL fans in Hong Kong (October 2012) and the Philippines (December 2012), all of them were aware of the existence of heterosexual male readers of BL in Japan.

7. See Yoshimoto Taimatsu, *Fudanshi ni kiku* [Interviewing *fudanshi*] (Japan: Self-published, 2008.)

8. Cited in Yoshimoto, *Fudanshi ni kiku 2* [Interviewing *fudanshi* 2] (Japan: Self-published, 2010), 60.

9. See Itō Kimio, *Danseigaku nyūmon* [An introduction to men's studies] (Tokyo: Sakuhinsha, 1996), 95–108. As Tanaka Toshiyuki, *Danseigaku no shintenkai* [New developments in men's studies] (Tokyo: Seikyūsha, 2009), points out, the cumulative results of men's studies in Japan somehow leave the privileged position of maleness/masculinity untouched, and this limits the analytical focus to the ways in which society pressures men. Men's studies in Japan include a range of phenomena that need to be discussed in more detail, though this is beyond the scope of this chapter.

10. Yoshimoto, *Fudanshi ni kiku*, 30.

11. Ibid.

12. Ibid., 60.

13. Yoshimoto, *Fudanshi ni kiku 2*, 41.

14. Ibid., 41–42.

15. Nakajima Azusa, *Tanatosu no kodomotachi: Kajō tekiō no seitaigaku* [The children of Thanatos: The ecology of excessive adaptation] (Tokyo: Chikuma shobō, 1998), 23.

16. Yūya, *Chikyū no ōsama* [The king of the earth] (Tokyo: Ōkura shuppan, 2008).

17. Kajimoto Jun, *Unmei na no ni saiaku na kyōshi* [It may be fate but he is the worst teacher] (Tokyo: Kaiōsha, 2011), 258.

18. Shimizu Yuki, *Ze* [Yes!], vol. 9 (Tokyo: Shinshokan, 2010), 40.

19. Four of my interviewees are female and the fifth is male. They are editors of the BL magazines *Gush* (Kaiōsha), *Magazine Be-Boy* (Libre shuppan), *Karen* (Nihon bungei sha), and *JUNE* (Magajin magajin). All interviews were conducted in September 2012.

20. Yoshimoto, *Fudanshi ni kiku* 2, 10.

21. Yoshimoto, *Fudanshi ni kiku*, 37.

22. See Yoshimoto, *Fudanshi ni kiku*, 17, and *Fudanshi ni kiku* 2, 10.

23. Both of these BL manga artists are highly popular, to such an extent that their works have been translated into English. Further, Nitta's representative BL work, *Haru o daiteita* (Embracing spring), has been made into animated works which are available both in Japanese and English.

24. This use of the term "*shōjo* manga" as a separate category from BL manga is shared by critics such as Oshiyama Michiko, *Shōjo manga jendaa hyōshōron: "Dansō no shōjo" no zōkei to aidentiti* [On gender representation in *shōjo* manga: The shape of "girls dressed as boys" and identity] (Tokyo: Sairyūsha, 2007), who defines *shōjo* manga as the origin of BL manga, which both derived from and expanded upon it. On the distinctions between *shōnen* and *shōjo* manga, see, for instance, Frederik L. Schodt, *Manga! Manga!: The World of Japanese Comics* (New York: Kodansha America, 1983).

25. See Kazumi Nagaike, "Perverse Sexualities, Perversive Desires: Representations of Female Fantasies and *Yaoi Manga* as Pornography Directed at Women," *U.S.–Japan Women's Journal* 25 (2003).

26. See Nagakubo Yōko, *Yaoi shōsetsu ron: Josei no tame no erosu hyōgen* [Theorizing yaoi fiction: Erotic representations for women] (Tokyo: Senshū daigaku shuppankyoku, 2005).

27. See Jennifer Robertson, *Takarazuka: Sexual Politics and Popular Culture in Modern Japan* (Berkeley: University of California Press, 1998).

28. The androgyny of BL characters—that is, their openness to being read as either male or female—is supported by the views of scholars such as Akiko Mizoguchi and James Welker, who discuss the potential lesbian paradigms that may be read in BL narratives. Mizoguchi, for example, suggests that some lesbians (like herself) may possibly project their sexuality and imagined sexual pleasures onto BL male characters, reading them as women in drag. See Akiko Mizoguchi, "Male–Male Romance by and for Women in Japan: A History and the Subgenres of *Yaoi* Fictions," *U.S.–Japan Women's Journal* 25 (2003); and James Welker, "Beautiful, Borrowed, and Bent: 'Boys' Love' as Girls' Love in Shōjo Manga," *Signs* 31, no. 3 (2006).

29. My own stance regarding androgyny in BL is that the reasons the androgynous context projected by BL attracts *fujoshi* (i.e., female readers) differ markedly from those of *fudanshi*. For women, BL may be considered as a medium of resistance against socially imposed, monolithic, and subordinate concepts of femininity. For more details concerning the female psychological orientation, which conditions androgynous (or bisexual) fantasies, see Nagaike, "Perverse Sexualities, Perversive Desires."

30. "*Yuri*" (lily) is used to label narratives depicting female–female romantic relationships; *yuri* plots are found in *shōjo* manga and anime, as well as in text targeting other readerships, such as adult males. A history of *yuri* manga can be found in James Welker, "Drawing

Out Lesbians: Blurred Representations of Lesbian Desire in *Shōjo* Manga," in *Lesbian Voices: Canada and the World; Theory, Literature, Cinema*, ed. Subhash Chandra (New Delhi: Allied Publishers, 2006).

31. See Robertson, *Takarazuka*, 150. The Takarazuka Revue was founded in 1914 by a man, Kobayashi Ichizō. Since then, it has been organized according to strongly patriarchal ideas concerning gender roles. See Robertson's *Takarazuka* for details on the rigid heteronormativity prevailing in the revue.

32. In this chapter, the term "*shota*" refers to both the genre and the characters portrayed. In contrast with the usage of the term "*rorikon*," which basically signifies the genre (with the characters described as "*rori*"), *shota* also refers to the characters themselves.

On the significance of *shota* to understanding *fudanshi*, see Yoshimoto, *Fudanshi ni kiku*, 25. We should be clear that *shota* should not be discussed in the same discursive frame as pedophilia. The analytical features of *shota* and pedophilia in the Western context need to be explored separately. As I will discuss in later sections, *shota* involves fantasy narratives which contain idealized images of boys, rather than expressing any overt sexual desire toward actually existing boys. See Saitō Tamaki, "Otaku Sexuality," in *Robot Ghosts and Wired Dreams: Japanese Science Fiction from Origins to Anime*, ed. Christopher Bolton, Istvan Csicsery-Ronay, Jr., and Takayuki Tatsumi (Minneapolis: University of Minnesota Press, 2007), for a detailed discussion of the lack of commensurability between pedophilia and *shota*.

33. Nagayama Kaoru, *Ero manga sutadiizu: "Kairaku sōchi" toshite no manga nyūmon* [Erotic manga studies: Introduction to manga as a "pleasure device"] (Tokyo: Iisuto puresu, 2006), 238.

34. Yoshimoto, *Fudanshi ni kiku*, 29–30.

35. Ibid., 35.

36. Nagayama, *Ero manga*, 241.

37. Patrick W. Galbraith, "*Lolicon*: The Reality of 'Virtual Child Pornography' in Japan," *Image and Narrative* 12, no. 1 (2011): 103, http://www.imageandnarrative.be/index.php/imagenarrative/article/view/127.

38. See Nagaike, "Perverse Sexualities, Perversive Desires" for a detailed analysis of female beating fantasies, which can also be discussed in terms of the three-stage Freudian structure. Freud emphasizes the differences between male beating fantasies and female beating fantasies, although he focuses more on the psychological orientation underlying female beating fantasies in this famous article.

39. See Sigmund Freud, "'A Child is Being Beaten': A Contribution to the Study of the Origin of Sexual Perversions," in *The Standard Edition of the Complete Psychological Works of Sigmund Freud*, vol. 17, ed. and trans. James Strachey (London: The Hogarth Press, 1955).

40. Freud, "'A Child is Being Beaten,'" 202.

41. See Saitō, "Otaku Sexuality," 245. "*Otaku*" was originally a derogatory term that referred to an obsessive and narcissistic fan of something (particularly of manga and anime).

42. "Superflat" is a postmodern artistic style, founded by the artist Murakami Takashi. Japanese manga and anime have had a discernible influence on the development of superflat art, which is based on the premise that "absence" of reality (flatness) itself can be conceived of as the "presence" of postmodern reality.

43. See Kaja Silverman, *Male Subjectivity at the Margins* (New York: Routledge, 1992).

44. See Karatani Kōjin, *Nihon kindai bungaku no kigen* [*Origins of Modern Japanese Literature*] (Tokyo: Kōdansha, 1980).

45. See Takahashi Eiri, *Muku no chikara: Shōnen hyōshō bungaku ron* [The power of innocence: Literary studies on the representations of boys] (Tokyo: Kōdansha, 2003).

46. Takahashi, *Muku no chikara*, 230.

REPRESENTATIONAL APPROPRIATION AND THE AUTONOMY OF DESIRE IN *YAOI*/BL

ISHIDA HITOSHI

TRANSLATED BY KATSUHIKO SUGANUMA

Apologetic Gestures and Shielding

"I am sorry, but leave us alone . . ."

How are we to comprehend *yaoi* and BL? *Yaoi* and BL, in essence, represent a range of practices through which intimacies between men can be redrawn and redefined. How shall we interpret the meanings of love, romance, sex, marriage, and childbearing carried out by male couples? The debate over whether the relationships described in *yaoi* and BL represent either the subversion or reinforcement of gender norms is a familiar one in discourse about *yaoi*/BL. No definitive answer currently exists. Some argue that there is no point in generalizing about the genre, as each work of *yaoi* or BL needs to be dealt with individually. That is all well and good, but is it sufficient?

It seems to me that a number of critical insights and considerations are left unaddressed by each individual critique. In this chapter, I examine the patterns emerging in discussions among some "rotten girls," or *fujoshi*, which I term acts of "apology" as well as of "shielding." This is an important perspective which it seems has not received sufficient attention thus far.

There is a famous line spoken by the female character Ōno Kanako in the well-known manga series *Genshiken*: "There isn't a single girl who hates gay men!!" (figure 11.1).[1] Due to the line's strong impact, it has been quoted in various places, including fan fairs promoting BL products, as well as in *My Neighbor Yaoi-chan* (*Tonari no 801-chan*) (figure 11.2), a major meta *yaoi*/BL text.[2] In the book entitled *Indeed, We Do Love BL: A Complete Guide to BL Comics* (*Yappari bōizu rabu ga suki: Kanzen BL komikku gaido*), Yamamoto

ホモが嫌いな女子なんかいません!!!!

Figure 11.1 Ōno proclaims, "There isn't a single girl who hates gay men!!" in the manga *Genshiken*.

Fumiko praises the line as a "wise statement."[3] As these instances might show, at first glance it would seem that *yaoi*/BL demonstrates a generous attitude toward "homosexuals."

However, we can also discern in some "meta *yaoi*/BL" an ambivalent feeling that cannot be contained by this generosity.[4] Take for instance an introductory book on BL cultures called *Love-tan: Basic Knowledge for* Fujoshi (*Rabu-tan: Fujoshi no tame no kiso chishiki*).[5] A line that appeared on the *obi* (promotional sash) on the book cover reads, "Please excuse us for being too rotten!!" This might be construed as a gesture of apology on the part of *fujoshi*. At the same time, we also find in the book a pattern of resentment against critiques from outsiders. The resentment often takes the form of protecting what is perceived to be their own *yaoi*/BL subcultural territory. This is evident in the phrase, "we would appreciate no entering into or messing with our territory from the outside. . . ."[6] We encounter a similar case in the second volume of *My Neighbor Yaoi-chan*. In response to mockery for being a

Figure 11.2 Yaoi-chan declares, "There isn't a single girl who hates gay men!!" in *Tonari no 801-chan*.

fujoshi, the protagonist, Yaoi-chan, gestures for a moment towards defending herself by stating that "mine is different . . . mine is just a fantasy . . ." only to make a humble apology in the end, conceding that her existence could indeed be unpleasant to some.[7]

This way of apologizing constitutes, according to Kaneda Junko, a form of defensive communication. For instance, in response to accusations about assigning homoerotic meanings to any male–male relationship, some *fujoshi* justify their behavior by insisting that "we know what we are doing is no good. We figure that much."[8] On the other hand, Saitō Mitsu provides an alternative interpretation of the word "rotten." Relationships between men have long been a main inspiration for BL novels, and now they are overused.

Saitō applies the metaphor of "being rotten" to describe this topical rut which BL culture in general has fallen into. Things go "rotten" or become stagnant when they are enclosed in one place for too long, just as food goes bad in similar conditions. Saitō's interpretation of the word "rotten" in relation to *fujoshi* dissociates it from the implication of being dirty or foul-minded.[9] However, these self-reflective interpretations are far from common.

There is another tendency that has become prominent in recent years— that is, a tendency to deny the connection between what *fujoshi* imagine in *yaoi*/BL materials and gay men in real life. This claim about a lack of a connection between them is often made when *yaoi*/BL are accused of containing homophobic discourse, or criticized for appropriating the representation of male homosexuals. According to Mizuma Midory, canonical BL writers such as Mori Mari and modern contemporaries alike have declared that male homosexuality in reality is in no way identical to the representations that they, as writers, create in their imaginations. And there has been no sign that this sentiment has diminished. Furthermore, recent BL writers go so far as to craft stories in which some main characters defensively dissociate their romance—and even make it distinct—from male homosexuality in realty.[10]

Objectives

Before we turn to concrete discussions, I wish to address the objectives of this chapter in more academic as well as social terms. In the age of globalization, any studies that do not take into account the conditions of postcoloniality are considered suspect. Needless to say, analyses of appropriations of representations constitute one of the main objectives in those disciplines of the humanities and social sciences that maintain a close correlation with postcolonial conditions. However, it seems that critical insights into issues of representational appropriation are not altogether shared among fans or by critics of *yaoi*/BL. Even if some critical voices appear, they are often overlooked in the end.

For instance, although there is a humble recognition of the tremendous terror and violence born from nationalism and war, many fans of *yaoi* and BL are enthusiastic about *Hetalia*, a gag comic which anthropomorphizes the nations of the Axis powers, and puts those nations' characters into homoerotic relations. Some go so far, in some online forums, as to render the relationship between airplanes and tower buildings in a somewhat homoerotic and sexual way, through anthropomorphizing those objects. Needless to say, this is inspired by the terrorist attacks of 9/11, even though the writers well know the number of causalities and the grief caused by the attacks.

Further still, the popularity of one recent BL genre called *Arabu-mono*, meaning "things Arabic," is on the rise, although those fans can be assumed to be aware of the harsh conditions facing people with homosexual orientations in many Islamic countries. To be fair, it is true that there exists a gesture of apology for all this in meta *yaoi*/BL discourse. However, it seems to me that this apology is always just a formality without any sincerity. Worse still, some even appear to be adopting a "so-what" attitude when making apologies. I am not offended by the attitude; I am rather intrigued. I am most intrigued by the fact that their apologies are always accompanied by a discourse of shielding and self-protection.

In this chapter, I focus on the ways in which critical issues of representational appropriation are belittled by way of both apologetic gesture and shielding. This chapter's analysis is twofold. While critiquing the separation between fantasy and reality—"they do not represent gay men in reality"—my aim is not to merely attack the genre of *yaoi* and BL, but rather to critically reflect upon this perspective in order to better understand the elements intrinsic to the genre.

Reality Versus Fantasy

As previously mentioned, the discourse arguing that male homosexuality depicted in *yaoi*/BL needs to be distinguished from that in reality is now a familiar one. And yet this discourse perhaps requires further contextualization. Historically speaking, this particular separatist discourse became prevalent only after what is now called the *"yaoi ronsō"* (*yaoi* debate) that took place between 1992 and 1996. It finds its origin in an essay by Satō Masaki, published in the feminist coterie magazine *Choisir* in 1992. In the essay, Satō, a self-proclaimed gay man, expressed his indignation against female readers of *yaoi*, describing them dismissively as "those disgusting women who . . . have a perverse interest in sexual intercourse between men. . . . I wish them all dead."[11] Satō's initial essay provoked responses from two women. In her response, Takamatsu Hisako stated that "as expected, the day when we finally receive this type of criticism from gay men has come."[12] Yanagida Ryōko likewise confessed that "this is exactly the kind of criticism we imagined we'd receive from others, even if not from gay men."[13] As is evident in these quotes, some female readers were well aware of the possibility of *yaoi* being linked to discrimination against gay men.

One of the most frequently cited essays in the *yaoi* debate was written by Yanagida, and from her essay onwards, it has often been assumed that the *yaoi* debate has fallen into a polarization between *yaoi* women and Satō, a gay man. She writes that

> what was most unexpected was the fact that you [Satō] considered *yaoi* to be something that had something to do with you. . . . Gay people might feel their own turf being intruded upon when they have once read a *yaoi* book. But we also feel the same way when *yaoi* books are read and commented on by gay men (and others who may not appreciate *yaoi* in general).[14]

Another vocal participant in this debate was Kurihara Tomoyo, who was the co-editor of the *Guidebook to Aesthete Fiction and Gay Literature* (*Tanbi shōsetsu, gei bungaku bukkugaido*), and was serving as a book review editor of the magazine *JUNE*.[15] Kurihara states:

> Imagine some American author dashes off some absurd adventure-romance novels about Japan like [James Clavell's] *Shogun*, and yet assumes a defiant attitude by insisting that what is described in his/her works is not representative of Japanese reality but simply his/her ideas and fantasies. How is it possible to come to terms with such nonchalance?[16]

Despite the complexity of each critic's opinion, there was a unified view within the *yaoi* debate that *yaoi* representations do entail elements which can be discriminatory to gay men. Irokawa Nao, the editor of *Choisir*, confirms this when she states that to insist on the idea that "*yaoi* representations are no more than simply imaginary works, whereby no discrimination against gay men is intended" is nothing but "mere vindication and self-protection."[17] Given the zine *Choisir* was a "private magazine," as claimed by Irokawa, in which all editorial decisions on which articles to be included and so forth were single-handedly made by her, it is more precise to argue that the possibility that *yaoi* could damage the image of gay men was clearly recognized, at least within the discursive sphere of *Choisir*.[18]

The discussion took a new turn shortly after the *yaoi* debate in *Choisir*, when a discourse arguing that the men appearing in *yaoi*/BL have nothing to do with gay men in reality became prominent in many meta *yaoi*/BL materials. There are several examples, and the first comes from Kotani Mari, a critic of SF fantasy novels. In her book, published in 1994, she makes the following point in reference to slash novels based on the American *Star Trek* series:

> For one thing, they invited criticism from the gay community. In the US, a [slash] rewriting of the liaison between captain Kirk and Spock by women

was dismissed as "disrespectful of and discriminatory against homosexuality," no matter how subversive their relationship claims itself to be in terms of re-thinking gender norms. . . . However, many critics who studied this phenom-enon, both those in Japan and the US, support the idea that fictitious male characters cannot represent men in reality. . . .[19]

Kotani goes on to describe the criticisms of *yaoi* by gay men as a "peculiar incident" which was tagged onto *yaoi* culture, and dismissed them as an "at-tack" and a "denunciation."[20] Similar counterarguments were put forth by Fujimoto Yukari, a critic of *shōjo* manga (girls' comics), and Natsume Nariko (aka Nobi Nobita). In her book, published in 1998, Fujimoto insists that the boys in *yaoi* are not a reflection of men in reality. She writes:

> In recent years, criticism against these [*yaoi*] girl readers has been raised by gay men. However, it can be said that the boys in question are alter egos of those girls rather than representing men in reality. This is obvious in part by realizing how identical those characters' lines and story settings are with those in girls comics.[21]

In her book, Nobi similarly pointed out that there exists confusion between reality and fantasy among both the women who read and write *yaoi*, and the gay men who disapprove of them:

> . . . there is also the problem of confusion between fantasy and reality among both constituents. It is perfectly clear that *yaoi* representations are fantasy cre-ations shared among women, and thus there is no connection between these imaginary characters and gay men in reality. . . . [Having noted this] women who enjoy *yaoi* had better not impose their fantasies upon gay relationships in life, and there is, in return, no need for gay men to be offended by these female fantasies.[22]

Reviewing these responses, we can see a pattern here. While acknowledg-ing *yaoi*'s potential to be offensive to gay men, the acknowledgment only comes with an excuse saying that no confusion between imagination and reality is intended. This line of rhetoric still persists in more recent con-texts.[23] In a 2007 special issue of the literary magazine *Eureka* (*Yuriika*), featuring articles on BL studies, Kotani recalls the past debate over con-nections between *yaoi* representations and gay men. She maintains her past stance on this subject, which is to deny any implied link between them, and subsequently argues that it is nonsensical to simply apply "notions of justice and ethics" into the polemics over creative materials.[24]

But the question still remains: is it truly the case that *yaoi*/BL representations and gay men in reality are all that different? In the next section, we tackle this question by examining actual instances, such as lines and scripts provided for characters, in *yaoi*/BL materials.

"I know that you are not . . ."/"disgusting"

Let us consider the following examples:

"Don't play the homo-game on me!"
"No way! Keep your mouth shut! I don't want to know about my old friend being homo, gay, and *Sabu*!"[25]

"Are you a homo by any chance?"
"No kidding! You know that's not possible. . . ."
"Thank goodness, I know you cannot be a homo."
" . . ."[26]

The first quote is taken from a scene in which one of the characters was overwhelmed by a sudden fear when his longtime friend showed uncommon affection for him. It is interesting to note that in the line quoted above, the term "*Sabu*," the title of a major gay magazine in Japan, is deployed as a signifier for being gay and "homo." In the second quote, an exchange ends with one character left speechless, perplexed by a situation in which he does not have the means to express his affection for another character. In both situations, a sense of fear and confusion over the possibility of being gay in the male characters' minds is obvious. But how could these scenes be intelligible if there were no connections between *yaoi*/BL characters and gay men in reality? What is there to be afraid of if *yaoi*/BL has no clear reference to social reality?

One of the prevalent expressions seen in *yaoi*/BL texts is "*kimochi warui*," meaning "disgusting." Take the two following instances:

"This is how grownups would do it."
"Hey man . . . Two men together?! How disgusting. . . ."[27]

"I have feelings for someone . . . actually they are for Hamaya . . . I know two men together is . . . but . . ." (silence).

"I am leaving."
"Oh hey, wait! . . ."
"That's disgusting."[28]

Normally there are two patterns in which the word "*kimochi warui*" is deployed in *yaoi*/BL. One is a pattern seen in the first case above. Similar to the examples given in the previous paragraph, *kimochi warui* functions as a means to express a sense of fear and confusion. The third dialogue takes place in a scene where character A, unable to control his feelings, forces sex on B. Overwhelmed by the superior physique and strength of A, B can only utter "*kimochi warui*" in desperation to show his disapproval of the act forced upon him. What B is most disapproving of in this context is the idea of homosexuality rather than the act of sexual aggression itself.

The second pattern is the use of "*kimochi warui*" as an expression of jealousy, represented in the fourth dialogue. In this pattern, the dialogue often begins with reference to a third character, C, who is physically absent in the scene. Character A admits to B that he has feelings for C. However, B is unsettled by A's confession since B is secretly fond of A. With no better word to describe his feelings, B helplessly utters "*kimochi warui*" to describe A's feelings for C. This popular plot line often comes to an end when A, at first disturbed by B's reaction, later realizes that it was jealousy, and not just a disgust about homosexuality itself, that B was struggling to come to terms with.

All in all, it seems evident that the term "*kimochi warui*" is deployed as a sign of ambivalence about homosexuality. While the first and second dialogues represent ambivalence about the idea of homosexuality itself, in the third case "*kimochi warui*" refers to a homoerotic act, and in the final case it indicates disappointment about homosexual romance. What is of utmost interest here, however, is why these dialogues can be interpreted as being about ambivalence. Put differently, would the feeling *kimochi warui* itself still function as an indication of confusion if the word "homo" in the first two cases was replaced by "hetero" or if "two men together" in the latter two examples was changed to "man and woman together"? If these changes were made, the revised dialogues would not be as intelligible as the originals.

As is obvious by now, the sense of confusion surrounding *yaoi*/BL characters indeed references and reflects the actual social conditions that homosexuality and gay men face. A certain set of common-sense ideas and social norms that tend to deny and discredit homosexuality make this particular use of *kimochi warui* in *yaoi*/BL all the more possible. In short, it can be said that "homosexual" characters in *yaoi*/BL are always already rendered intelligible with reference to gay men in reality, and, by extension, it is rather disingenuous to argue otherwise by emphasizing the fictitious nature of *yaoi*/BL works.

On Allocation

"Hetero that counts"

In the manga *Happy Fujoshi* (*Happii fujoshi*), there is a scene in which Chi-chan, a *fujoshi*, was asked by Haru, her gay online-chat friend, to teach him how to put on proper makeup. Chi-chan says to Haru in an unfriendly manner that he should "go on browsing on the Internet and find out by yourself. I cannot be bothered!" Standing by and observing the interaction was Chi-chan's boyfriend, who remarked that he was rather surprised by her indifference to her gay friend's concern. In response, Chi-chan replied, "It's hetero (men) that really count, and real gay men don't do it for me" (figure 11.3).[29] It is a common practice in *yaoi*/BL for gay characters to be invoked in the plot only to be dismissed in the end. In this case, the figure of the gay friend appears as a representative of gay men with feminine qualities (who, for instance, want to apply makeup), but is soon disposed of. This exemplifies the familiar process of representational appropriation.

Some might counter that representational appropriation is common to all creative works, and thus is far from particular to *yaoi*/BL. In fact, signs and symbols are infinitely open to interpretation. Therein lies the possibility of representation. Some might go so far as to claim that creative works are, in essence, grounded in appropriation and borrowing from preexisting contexts.

Another opposing view takes the notion of "freedom of speech" as its basis. When I presented an earlier version of this chapter at one particular workshop, it met with criticism which assumed that my own sort of critique of *yaoi*/BL could lead to the censoring of expression, or pose a threat to the foundations of freedom of speech. Further still, some commentators attempted to discredit my argument by pointing out that biases in expression seen in manga and fiction are simply part of many other representational features, such as dramatization and characterization, all of which are fundamental to the genre.

These types of counterarguments seem to me to miss a fundamental point of this rebuke of *yaoi*/BL. If we concede that the arts in general afford infinite opportunities for expression and interpretation, then why in *yaoi*/BL do

Figure 11.3 Chi-chan replies to her boyfriend with a cold attitude in *Happy Fujoshi*.

we only see some particular patterns of representation incessantly repeated, whereby they are reproduced and reinforced. This is a question which merits thorough examination.

Asymmetrical binary positioning

In Japanese animation hero series for children, there is a prevalent pattern in which characters with regional dialects, such as that of the Kansai region (surrounding Osaka), normally assume supporting roles. According to this pattern, characters with Kansai dialects often represent someone with stranger-like qualities, such as villains or mysterious figures. Even if they are portrayed as friends, they still remain outcasts.[30] The same can be applied to characters who use "*okama kotoba*," a camp style of speech. It is almost customary in such series that characters with campy speech make frequent appearances, and assume similar roles to those with dialects. This asymmetrical binary, positioning those with standard Japanese as normal and those with either dialects or campy speech as abnormal, functions as a means through which the boundary between what constitutes the cultural as well as linguistic center and the periphery is marked.

In the context of *yaoi*/BL, most of the male protagonists represent persons of an innocent disposition who believe in pure love romance to such an extent that it is customary to say, without hesitation, words such as "I am not a homo! It's not the case that I love men in general! I just love you!"[31] Meanwhile, a number of gay characters appear in supporting roles (often as friends) and act as agents who violate the chastity of the allegedly "straight" protagonists. In such situations, as Mizoguchi Akiko points out, these gay characters are deemed "monstrous," and exist only as scapegoats to make the pure romance plot lines concerning the main "straight" protagonists even more sacred and spectacular.[32] Emerging from this familiar pattern is the juxtaposition of "straights who are under threat" and "homos who threaten."

In *yaoi*/BL the reverse never happens. Heterosexual supporting characters, who violently come on to gay protagonists, saying things like, "He is my type, so I will get him," never appear. It is invariably the case that only the main male characters—in denial of their homosexual proclivities—are allowed to speak of "love." This is not an option for the supporting gay characters, who can only speak, instead, of their "type."

A new tendency

In recent years, critics have started to acknowledge that fewer and fewer characters in *yaoi*/BL make explicit homophobic remarks. Even more, Mizoguchi states that "increasing numbers of characters who self-identify either as gay or bisexual have started to appear."[33] Fujimoto Sumiko also confirms this tendency from her quantitative research.[34]

Here are several instances of this new tendency. Printed on the *obi* (promotional sash) of Awaji Nae's 2009 comic book, *Kiss Me Chocolate*, is a strip in which two men can be seen kissing with the dialogue, "Are we alright?" and "No way. Two men together ain't right."[35] The incongruence between their acts and words does not go unnoticed, and it even casts doubt on the genuineness of the main character's dismissive tone towards male homoerotic acts. Since the latter half of the last decade, this once dominant *yaoi*/BL grammar, which includes a denial of homosexual identity among characters, has started to be modified and restructured, however.

Figure 11.4 A male character is confessing his feeling towards another male character in tears in *Prince of Happiness.*

Take, for instance, Mizushiro Setona's *Rats Dream of Cheese* (*Nezumi wa chiizu no yume o miru*), published in 2006. In this work, there is a scene in which the gay protagonist comes on to a heterosexual character with the lines, "Why do you apologize? I am the one who should since I know we gays should leave you [straight men] alone."[36] This is exemplary of referring back to, while simultaneously recomposing, *yaoi*/BL grammar. In this particular example, the common grammar in *yaoi*/BL—gays should not get involved in straight men's business—is referenced not to follow it, but rather to color scenarios that actually deviate from it.

Tanaka Suzuki's *Prince of Happiness* (*Kōfuku no ōji*), published in 2005, does this debunking of the original *yaoi*/BL grammar in a most radical way. Right at the beginning of the story, one boy confesses to another in desperation, declaring, "To tell the truth, I . . . I'm a . . . homosexual." Tickled pink, the recipient of this news, on the other hand, felt a sense of joy, saying to himself, "Wait a minute, shouldn't I be pretending not to be pleased?" (see figure 11.4).[37] Tanaka's debunking of *yaoi*/BL's common grammar, which took off from the first page, set a new trend and was welcomed by amused readers.

This is not to suggest that the negative social sentiment attached to homosexuality has been dispelled altogether. Even in these alternative works, the idea of homosexuality still remains socially deviant. This is necessary so long as *yaoi*/BL continue to represent pure romance between men who dare to pursue their relations against struggle and hardship. In the *yaoi* debate, Nobi stated that the "stigma attached to homosexuality becomes irrelevant if all characters were non-human, such as aliens or ghostly apparitions."[38] I question Nobi's contention, however. Even if a story is set in such a way that the stigma attached to homosexuality is overlooked, the very process of over-looking in turn necessarily recognizes the stigma as something in need of forgetting, hence the recognition of the stigma itself cannot be evaded. As a result, the stigma attached to homosexuality remains, and even incites the desire to recognize the very thing that is prohibited. For instance, Hoshino Lily is an acclaimed *yaoi*/BL writer whose work is known for its high sense of fantasy. In her 2006 *Love Quest* (*Rabu kue*), the following interaction takes place:

"I am not so sure if it is good to get used to kissing a man too much. I (for instance) no longer feel excited about kissing a man, you know. . . ."
". . . ."[39]

It is possible to interpret this silence—represented by the ellipses—between the two male characters as an unresolved sense of shame on acknowledging their desire for homoerotic romance, which still remains seductive, despite their claim to the contrary.

In Despair

Critiques from lesbian and gay studies

The problem of *yaoi*/BL lies in the process of reproducing the hierarchical relation between center and periphery, and almost always relegating repre-sentations of homosexuality to the realm of the latter. Such criticism has so far derived from lesbian and gay studies perspectives. For instance, Ogura Tō, who once worked for the Japanese gay magazine *Badi*, accused *yaoi* of forcing women's fantasies upon gay men.[40] Keith Vincent, who co-authored a key Japanese gay studies text, *Gay Studies*, with Kazama Takashi and Kawa-guchi Kazuya, remarked that "gay men appearing in *yaoi* works are not real people, but rather represent unicorn-like figures," and those representations bother many gay men.[41] We have already looked at Satō's similar criticism made in *Choisir*. Satō repeats himself in *Queer Studies '96* by insisting that *yaoi* representations of gay men leads not only to commodification but also to stylization of gay men's sexualities in such a way that heterosexism pre-vails.[42] Mizoguchi finds that the frequent deployment of rape scenes in *yaoi* is attributable to the fact that most of the male characters are forced to em-body "normal," hence aggressively masculine, personalities.[43]

Feign ignorance, or break her writing brush

How can one cope with issues of representational appropriation within *yaoi*/ BL? Some might elect to feign ignorance, while others apologize to the gay men who claim to be affected. Some *yaoi*/BL writers might even decide not to write anymore. This is reminiscent of what Kurihara Chiyo demanded in the early stages of the *yaoi* debate:

> I am not insisting that everyone [*yaoi*/BL readers] should quit reading "ro-mantic stories between men." I am simply asking them to make their choices. One thing they could do is to quit reading if they feel guilty. If they, instead, elect to cling on, then live your life with the shame of being a wrongdoer and beg no mercy from anyone. If you do not concede either position, then justify your actions to the world.[44]

Towards the end of the *yaoi* debate, Kurihara even demanded that *yaoi* read-ers choose from the three options of "dissent," "explanation," and "justifica-tion of their actions."[45]

Many women who got involved in the *yaoi* debate in *Choisir* became the targets of severe critique. What made it so complex was that they were aware that a *pro forma* apology was not a solution for many vocal critics of *yaoi*, including Satō. *Yaoi* writers such as Takamatsu Hisako and Nomura Fumiko (aka Nakamura Fuyumi) were psychologically affected by the debate to such an extent that the latter broke her writing brush, professing "no more boys love for me."[46]

"Mine is different"

While I wish to understand and respect the decisions that each participant of the debate made, there still remain concerns to be addressed. I would like to return to an example from *My Neighbor Yaoi-chan*. In response to accusa-tions of *fujoshi* being perverse, Yaoi-chan, the leading character, apologizes but goes on to defend herself, stating, "mine is different . . . mine is just a fan-tasy . . . " (figure 11.5).[47] The phrase "mine is different . . . mine is just a fantasy . . ." (*ore no wa chigau . . . ore no wa fantajii na no ni . . .*) is easily recognized

[俺のはファンタジー]…「ジョジョの奇妙な冒険」(集英社)第7部の登場人物、スティーブン・スティールの台詞。ちなみにみんなそう言う。

Figure 11.5 Yaoi-chan recoils from criticism of *fujoshi* in *My Neighbor Yaoi-chan*.

by many comics fans as a homage to a signature line from Araki Hirohiko's well-known *shōnen* manga (boys' comics) series *The Bizarre Adventure of Jo Jo* (*Jo Jo no kimyō na bōken*—hereafter *Jo Jo*).[48] However, I am more interested in what is claimed to be the leading character's specific desire, which is emphasized by the repetitive use of the saying, "mine is" (*ore no wa*). In this comparison, what is the perverse object from which "mine is" claims to be different? Some might simply settle on the idea that after all it is homosexuality itself which is perverse, and it is this which Yaoi-chan, and by extension all *fujoshi*, distance themselves from. However, this would inevitably make *fujoshi* appear homophobic, and would predispose them to become objects of critique.

It is possible that things could be much more complex and contextualized than the explanations above. It is possible to interpret the emphasis placed on "mine is," which is already a parody of an original (*Jo Jo*), as an attempt to camouflage the actual contour or original identity of *fujoshi*.[49] Through this camouflaging effect, it makes it possible for Yaoi-chan—and other *fujoshi*—to willfully efface and shift their subject position thereby enabling them to circumvent criticism directed at their assumed singular/original subject position. For instance, in the face of being accused of homophobia,

Yaoi-chan—and *fujoshi* in general—could possibly counterargue that it is *fujoshi* themselves, not homosexuals, who are perverse and rotten. They could use this counterargument as the grounds on which to claim that they are not discriminating against homosexuals. Even if they have conceded the idea that *fujoshi* are perverse and rotten, it could still leave room for 801-chan to yet again distance herself from perversity itself through the demarcating effect of "mine is different. . . ." Of particular interest, however, is that all these different ways of representing their subject positions come down to one aim. The aim is to evade criticism directed at *fujoshi*, and in turn legitimize their claim of non-involvement—"leave us alone, because after all we are not that guilty."

Anarchist writer Hakim Bey coined the term "temporary autonomous zone" (TAZ) to refer to a temporal space through which to elude attacks and control from outside.[50] In a peculiar way, we may see the deployment of a TAZ in Yaoi-chan's use of "mine is." That is because Yaoi-chan's use of "mine is" affords her a subjective elusiveness that is capable of relocating and effacing itself in such a way that criticism from outside never reaches in. In this way, a *fujoshi*'s desire forever retains its own territory. I call this *fujoshi* practice the "autonomy of desire."

Earnest Desire

Integrating the divided

It is often pointed out that in pornography for heterosexual men women are portrayed as figures torn into two: the Madonna and the whore. In the context of *yaoi*/BL, ways of portraying gay men are not a simple inversion of those in heterosexual pornography. While there are two characters whose personalities are divided, *yaoi*/BL always requires them to integrate with each other through sexual acts.

It has been argued that readers of *yaoi*/BL possess eccentric ways of constituting sexual desire. Arimitsu Mamiko insists that sources of libidinal sensation for readers stem from relationality itself rather than visual components.[51] According to Nobi, it is a trilogy of desire that matters in *yaoi*/BL. First, it is a desire to be loved as an *uke* (passive partner). Second, there is also a desire to love as a *seme* (active partner). Third, there arises a genuine attraction to the romantic idea of loving each other.[52] In this *yaoi*/BL grammar, the relationship between two men is torn through being forced to assume "straight" roles, only to heighten the significance of pure romance when the two eventually embrace after many trials and errors. The more dramatic and complex the manner in which this plot of reconciliation is orchestrated, the more like "gay doll play" for girls *yaoi*/BL might appear to be.[53] As a consequence, *fujoshi* become the target of critique from the perspective of representational appropriation.

Are the activities of *yaoi*/BL readers all that indecent? Some argue otherwise by insisting that the male characters appearing in *yaoi*/BL are in fact avatars of the female readers themselves, and thus have no associations with men in reality. As mentioned earlier, Kotani reasons that what is embodied in the male characters are the readers themselves:

> However, many critics who studied this phenomenon both in Japan and the US support the idea that fictitious male characters cannot represent men in reality, and instead embody women's ideals. . . . Therefore, I cannot be certain that those [*yaoi*/BL] representations necessarily lead to discrimination against or "commodification" of gay men's sexuality. . . . Worthy of attention is the "potential" arising from slippages between what is assumed as problematic in terms of representation and what is actually drawn in the works.[54]

The claim that both *seme* and *uke* in *yaoi*/BL are a "reflection of girls' self images," is nothing new, but rather shared among critics from the onset of *yaoi*/BL polemics.[55] According to Nakano Fuyumi, many women invested in *yaoi* "see themselves both in a controlling male character and an oppressed boy character appearing in *yaoi*."[56] Fujimoto Yukari, too, perceives those male characters as female readers' "alter egos."[57] Fujimoto also points out that in contrast to *shōnen* manga, the theme of "multiple personality" has never developed in *shōjo* manga. On the other hand, an alter ego as another self, most often symbolically represented by stories about twins or gender transgression, is a major theme in girls comics. The theme of split and discord between the ideal self that others expect of you and the ordinary self has been explored.[58] Rather than "multiple selves," what has been repetitively depicted is a story about two "I"s who are divided, and then reunited. According to science fiction writer Noa Azusa, the art of *yaoi* is "a means through which to express girls' subconscious experience of repression," and therefore in order to make the experiences surface, "there is a necessity of the art's [*yaoi* stories] repeating and imitating."[59] Murota Naoko states:

> Equipped with *yaoi*, girls can at last establish their selves both by turning themselves into a *seme*, "a woman who obtains a penis," and by simultaneously becoming a *uke*, "a man who has lost his penis." It has been a real long journey to even come this far.[60]

Nobi further elaborates on the complex processes of simultaneously embodying *seme* and *uke*. In her short essay, "Anatomy of *yaoi* girls," Nobi, relying on her own experience, points out that both *seme* and *uke* have dual meanings, which constitute the essence of *yaoi*. According to Nobi, *uke* represent men who have been ostracized by female *yaoi* readers, and who have been transformed from subjects of desire to objects. On the other hand, *seme* embody those women who have taken and applied men's penises, and turned themselves into subjects of desire. Simultaneously while the *uke* also signifies her ideal self—not as socially constructed "woman"—who wishes to be blindly loved by someone, the *seme* appears as a prince charming who fulfills her unsatisfied desire. Moreover, women's desire to be in a mutual relationship with men always remains unfulfilled as they are painfully aware that their bodies are incomplete, unlike those of men. It is this complex circuit of desire and disappointment through which *yaoi* culture is made possible.[61] This is how Nobi herself became a *yaoi* girl.

It is easy to dismiss Nobi's psychoanalytic explanation as too anecdotal and abstract. What is important, however, is to understand what kinds of *yaoi*/BL discourse this self-conscious line of explanation for autonomous female desire makes intelligible or unintelligible.

Concluding Remarks

To realize the autonomy of female desire among the practices and discourses of *yaoi*/BL inevitably leads to a "sympathetic" evaluation of gender constructions portrayed in this subculture. Nobi points out that "it is indeed pleasurable for one to take control of one's love and desire. While this is often taken for granted for men, it appears to be a wholly new, joyous experience for many women."[62] Fujimoto once argued that *yaoi*/BL made it possible for female readers to obtain the "gaze of someone who rapes and looks" rather than "one who is raped."[63] She even wholeheartedly praises more recent situations in which many women go so far as to craft "a world of thorough gender blending in which . . . combinations of any possible gender and power dynamics one can imagine are skillfully made, utilizing a space with no biological gender division—'a world of two men.'"[64]

Commentaries and analyses put forth by several critics, such as Nobi, Fujimoto, and Kotani, all discussed above, have contributed to discursive shifts concerning the practices of *yaoi*/BL. Once perceived as a means for "escapism, misogyny, or retaliation," their practices are now seen as ways of "overturning heterosexist norms, or obtaining pleasure specific to women."[65]

However, we need to ask the question, what makes this discursive change possible? As I have consistently argued in this chapter, in order to maintain a positive evaluation of *yaoi*/BL practices, it needs to be repeatedly emphasized that the men appearing in *yaoi*/BL have nothing to do with men in reality. In other words, for the autonomy of women's pleasure to be materialized, they need to legitimize their behaviors by claiming innocence regarding representational appropriation—i.e., shielding, while at the same time to an extent acknowledging the problems for gay men that their desire may cause; i.e., apologetic gesture. This is evident in Kotani's claim that it is an "invariable principle" that one should not "let anyone invade one's own territory of pleasure" for the purpose of "serving as the autonomous pleasure of women" and of "immersing oneself in the world of no oppression and struggle."[66]

I still question this line of reasoning. Is this the only possible way to decipher the logic of *yaoi*/BL narratives? For us to carry out more productive discussions about *yaoi*/BL, there is a need to rethink things. One way to do this is not to keep repeating the discourse assuming that "*yaoi*/BL representations contain no discrimination against gay men, because those 'boys' are actually women themselves." Instead, we first need to accept that those "boys" are indeed gay and males *on top of* being female readers themselves.

In sum, my argument is simple. That is, the argument that both representational appropriation and self-projection (autonomy of desire) are indispensable elements of *yaoi*/BL. The two are mutually constitutive in the genre. It can be said that *yaoi*/BL is a reflection of these two elements. Any analyses that do not take the commingling of the two into consideration need to be considered suspect. Understanding the intersection of representational appropriation and self-projection will help us see why *yaoi*/BL endlessly demands the reinsertion of gender power dynamics via the roles of *uke* and *seme* to a world where the gender binary is deconstructed through featuring two characters of the same sex.[67]

Notes

1. Kio Shimoku, *Genshiken*, vol. 4 (Tokyo: Kōdansha, 2004), 154.

2. Kojima Ajiko, *Tonari no 801-chan* [My neighbor Yaoi-chan], vol. 1 (Tokyo: Ohzora shuppan, 2006), 4. The title of this work might also be translated "My darling, Yaoi-chan."

3. Yamamoto Fumiko and BL Supporters, *Yappari bōizu rabu ga suki: Kanzen BL komikku gaido* [Indeed, we do love BL: A complete guide to BL comics] (Tokyo: Ota shuppan, 2005), 204.

4. In this chapter, I use the term "meta *yaoi*/BL" to refer to discourse about the lives of *fujoshi* and their practices.

5. Rabu-tan seisaku iinkai, *Rabu-tan: Fujoshi no tame no kiso chishiki* [Love-tan: Basic knowledge for *fujoshi*] (Tokyo: Sandeesha, 2006).

6. Ibid., 60.

7. Kojima Ajiko, *Tonari no 801-chan* [My neighbor Yaoi-chan], vol. 2 (Tokyo: Ohzora shuppan, 2007), 28.

8. Miura Shion, Kaneda Junko, Saitō Mitsu, and Yamamoto Fumiko, "2007-nen no BL kai o megutte: Soshite 'fujoshi' to wa dare ka" [About a BL circle in 2007: Who are "*fujoshi*"], *Yuriika* 39, no. 16 (December 2007): 23.

9. Ibid., 24.

10. Mizuma Midory, *In'yu toshite no shōnen'ai: Josei no shōnen'ai shikō to iu genshō* [*Shōnen'ai* as metaphor: The phenomenon of women's inclination for *shōnen'ai*] (Osaka: Sōgensha, 2005), 18.

11. Satō Masaki, "Yaoi nante shinde shimaeba ii" [I wish all *yaoi* dead], in *Choisir yaoi ronsō gappon I*, ed. Irokawa Nao (Japan: Self-published, 1994), 1.

12. Takamatsu Hisako, "'Teki mikata' ron no kanata e: Miyou to suru koto, mietekuru koto" [Thinking through a perspective of friend or foe: Things that we attempt to see and that come into view], in *Choisir yaoi ronsō gappon I*, ed. Irokawa Nao (Japan: Self-published, 1994), 3.

13. Yanagida Ryōko, "Satō-san e no tegami" [A letter to Satō-san], in Irokawa, *Choisir yaoi ronsō gappon I*, 13.

14. Ibid., 14.

15. Kakinuma Eiko and Kurihara Chiyo, eds., *Tanbi shōsetsu, gei bungaku bukkugaido* [Guidebook to aesthete fiction and gay literature] (Tokyo: Byakuya shobō, 1993).

16. Kurihara Chiyo, "Shikarubeki hanron no tame no hanron" [A refutation for proper refutation], in *Choisir yaoi ronsō gappon II*, ed. Irokawa Nao (Japan: Self-published, 1994), 24.

17. Irokawa Nao, "Byōki o idaki tsuzuketai onna ni 'kagaisei' wa jikaku dekinai" [Women who wish to maintain their propensity are incapable of realizing their "malicious intents"], in Irokawa, *Choisir yaoi ronsō gappon II*, 30.

18. Irokawa Nao, "Tadai na konwaku no ato no awai teinen" [A faint sense of resignation after great confusion], in *Choisir yaoi ronsō gappon V*, ed. Irokawa Nao (Japan: Self-published, 1996), 48.

19. Kotani Mari, *Joseijō muishiki: Tekunogaineeshisu, josei SF-ron josetsu* [Techno-gynesis: The political unconscious in feminist science fiction] (Tokyo: Keisō shobō, 1994), 249–50.

20. Ibid., 249.

21. Fujimoto Yukari, *Watashi no ibasho wa doko ni aru no?: Shōjo manga ga utsusu kokoro no katachi* [Where do I belong? The shape of the heart reflected in shōjo manga] (Tokyo: Gakuyō shobō, 1998), 143.

22. Nobi Nobita, *Otona wa wakatte kurenai: Nobi Nobita hihyō shūsei* [Adults won't understand us: The critical essays of Nobi Nobita] (Tokyo: Nihon hyōron sha, 2003), 240.

23. The term "*homo*" in the Japanese *hiragana* script is often used to refer to male–male intimacy described in *yaoi*/BL, which may reflect an attempt on the part of *yaoi*/BL fans to dissociate this kind of intimacy from that described by "*homo*" written in the *katakana* script—more commonly recognized as a discriminatory term against male homosexuals.

24. Kotani Mari, "Fujoshi dōshi no kizuna: C-bungaku to yaoi-teki na yokubō" [Bonding among *Fujoshi*: C-literature and *yaoi*-like desire], *Yuriika* 39, no. 16 (December 2007): 35.

25. Shimada Masako, *Dorakira* [Dracula Kira] (Tokyo: Biburosu 2004), 85.

26. Tojitsuki Hajime, *Shironeko* [White cat] (Tokyo: Kaiōsha 2005), 111–12.

27. Matsumoto Temari and Hodaka Parugo, *Paradaisu e oideyo!* [Come to paradise!] (Tokyo: Kadokawa shoten 2003), 34.

28. Tsukumogō, *Saigo no sangatsu* [The last March] (Tokyo: Shōbunkan 2008), 148–49.

29. *Happii fujoshi* [Happy *fujoshi*] (Tokyo: Hobii Japan 2007), 139.

30. Kuroda Isamu, "Uchi naru tasha 'Osaka' o yomu" [Reading "Osaka" as an internal other], in *Media bunka no kenryoku sayō*, ed. Itō Mamoru (Tokyo: Serika shobō 2002), 206–207.

31. Miura Shion and Kaneda Junko, "'Seme X uke' no mekuru meku sekai: Dansei shintai no miryoku o motomete" [The world surrounding "*seme X uke*": Searching for the attractiveness of male bodies], *Yuriika* 39, no. 7 (June 2007): 17.

32. Mizoguchi Akiko, "Homofobikku na homo, ai yue no reipu, soshite kuia na rezubian: Saikin no yaoi tekisuto o bunseki suru" [Homophobic homos, rapes of love, and queer lesbians: An analysis of recent *yaoi* texts], *Kuia Japan* 2 (2000): 197.

33. Mizoguchi Akiko, "Sore wa, dare no, donna, 'riaru'? Yaoi no gensetsu kūkan o seiri suru kokoromi" [That is whose and what kind of 'real'? An attempt at sorting out the discursive space of *yaoi*], *Image and Gender* 4 (2003): 45.

34. Fujimoto Sumiko, "Kankeisei kara miru BL no genzai" [Examining contemporary BL works through the concept of matchmaking], *Yuriika* 39, no. 16 (December 2007): 91–92.

35. Awaji Nae, *Kisu mii chokoreeto* [Kiss me chocolate] (Tokyo: Libre 2009). In the actual manga, the line, "No way … Two men together ain't right," is a monologue, rather than part of a dialogue. Moreover, the line is read before the two male characters actually kiss each other.

36. Mizushiro Setona, *Nezumi wa chiizu no yume o miru* [Rats dreams of cheese] (Tokyo: Shōgakukan kurieitibu 2006), 136.

37. Tanaka Suzuki, *Kōfuku no ōji* [Happy prince] (Tokyo: Biburosu 2005), 1.

38. Nobi Nobita, "*Yaoi* shōjo no kaibōgaku" [Anatomy of *yaoi* girls], in Irokawa, *Choisir yaoi ronsō gappon II*, 29.

39. Hoshino Lily, *Rabu kue* [Love quest] (Tokyo: Hōbunsha 2006), 34.

40. Ogura Tō, "Gei ga oshieru ningen kankei manaa kyōshitsu" [An etiquette class taught by gays], in *Yoku wakaru gei raifu handobukku* [Essential handbook for gay life] (Tokyo: Takarajima, 1994), 91.

41. Kotani Mari and Keith Vincent, "Kuia seorii wa doko made hirakeru ka" [How expansive queer theory can be?], *Yuriika* 28, no. 13 (November 1996): 80, 82.

42. Satō Masaki, "Shōjo manga to homofobia" [*Shōjo* manga and homophobia], in *Kuia sutadiizu '96*, ed. Kuia sutadiizu henshū iinkai (Tokyo: Nanatsumori shokan, 1996), 166.

43. See Mizoguchi, "Homofobikku na homo."

44. Kurihara, "Shikarubeki hanron no tame no hanron," 25.

45. Kurihara Chiyo, "*Yaoi* ronsō o sōkatsu suru." [A summary of the *yaoi* debate], in Irokawa, *Choisir yaoi ronsō gappon V*, 72–73.

46. Kurihara Chiyo, "'Genjitsu' no jubaku kara kaihō sareru tame ni" [For being liberated from the spell of "reality"], in *Choisir yaoi ronsō gappon III*, ed. Irokawa Nao (Japan: Self-published, 1994), 32.

47. Kojima, *Tonari no 801-chan*, vol. 2, 28.

48. The original series was published as Araki Hirohiko, *Jo Jo no kimyō na bōken* [Jo Jo's bizarre adventure], 63 vols. (1987–1999; Tokyo: Janpu komikkusu, 1987–1999), but, like many such media properties, the narrative is ongoing.

49. In the Japanese original text, "*ore*," which is a masculine first-person pronoun, is used by the female *fujoshi* character. Although this is done in homage to a male character in *Jo Jo*, the gender switching adds to the effect of further camouflaging the subject position of the addresser, Yaoi-chan.

50. Hakim Bey, *T.A.Z.: Ichijiteki jiritsu zōn* (Japanese translation of *T.A.Z.: The Temporary Autonomous Zone: Ontological Anarchy, Poetic Terrorism*), trans. Yū Minowa (1985; Tokyo: Inpakuto sha, 1997), 197–98.

51. Hikawa Reiko, Kotani Mari, and Arimitsu Mamiko, "Kyōraku suru shōjotachi: Shōjo bunka no genzaikei: Dōjinshi/Komikku maaketto/yaoi" [Girls enjoying themselves: The present situation of girl culture: *Dōjinshi*, the Comic Market, and *yaoi*], *Imago* 6, no. 4 (April 1995): 145.

52. Nobi, *Otona wa wakatte kurenai*, 255.

53. Nagakubo Yōko, "Josei-tachi no 'kusatta yume' yaoi shōsetsu: Yaoi shōsetsu no miryoku to sono mondaisei" [*Yaoi* fiction as women's "rotten dreams": Positive and negative attributes of *yaoi* fiction], *Yuriika* 39, no. 7 (2007): 143.

54. Kotani, *Joseijō muishiki*, 249–51.

55. Murota Naoko, "Shōjo tachi no ibasho sagashi: Vijuaru rokku to shōjo manga" [*Shōjo* searching for a place where they belong: Visual rock and *shōjo* manga], in *Vijuaru-kei no jidai: Rokku/keshō/jendaa*, ed. Inoue Takako et al. (Tokyo: Seidosha, 2003), 196.

56. Nakano Fuyumi, "Yaoi hyōgen to sabetsu: Onna no tame no porunogurafii o tokiho-gusu" [*Yaoi* and discrimination: An analysis of pornography directed at women], *Josei raifu saikuru kenkyū* 4 (1994): 134.

57. Fujimoto, *Watashi no ibasho wa doko ni aru no?*, 143.

58. Fujimoto Yukari, "Bunshin: Shōjo manga no naka no 'mō hitori no watashi'" [Alter ego: "Another me" in *shōjo* manga], in *Manga no shakaigaku*, ed. Miyahara Kōjirō and Ogino Masahiro (Tokyo: Sekai shisō sha, 2001), 72–76, 88, 108.

59. Noa Azusa, "Hanasaku otome-tachi no 'misuteri'" [The "mysteries" of flowery girls], *Gendai shisō* 23, no. 2 (February 1995): 251.

60. Murota, "Shōjo tachi no ibasho sagashi," 197.

61. Nobi, "*Yaoi* shōjo no kaibōgaku," 23–29.

62. Nobi, *Otona wa wakatte kurenai*, 274

63. Fujimoto, *Watashi no ibasho wa doko ni aru no?*, 144.

64. Fujimoto Yukari, "Shōnen'ai/yaoi, BL: 2007-nen genzai no shiten kara" [*Shōnen'ai, yaoi,* and BL: From the perspective of 2007], *Yuriika* 39, no. 16 (December 2007): 42–43.

65. Kaneda Junko, "Manga dōjinshi: Kaishaku kyōdōtai no poritikusu" [Manga *dōjinshi*: The politics of communities' collective interpretation], in *Bunka no shakai gaku*, ed. Satō Kenji and Yoshimi Shun'ya (Tokyo: Yūhikaku, 2007), 169.

66. Kotani, "Fujoshi dōshi no kizuna," 32.

67. Nakano, "Yaoi hyōgen to sabetsu," 134.

QUEERING THE COOKING MAN

Food and Gender in Yoshinaga Fumi's (BL) Manga

TOMOKO AOYAMA

Introduction

No one is perhaps more gender-conscious, and more widely acclaimed as such, among leading contemporary manga artists than Yoshinaga Fumi (1971–). Her ongoing work *The Inner Chambers* (*Ōoku*) has been awarded not only major manga awards but also the Sense of Gender Award (2005) and the James Tiptree, Jr., Award (2009), both of which are given to "science fiction or fantasy that expands or explores our understanding of gender."[1] *Ōoku* is not a BL work but a historical fantasy, set in the Tokugawa period (1603–1868), and because it is serialized in a *shōjo* (girls) magazine, it is classified as a *shōjo* manga. However, as Mizoguchi Akiko notes, it is "arguably the most critically acclaimed manga work by an artist who started her career as a BL author."[2] Yoshinaga wrote a number of BL works for both amateur *dōjinshi* and commercial outlets from the late 1980s.[3] Mizoguchi believes that Yoshinaga's examination of "the fundamental questions of sexuality, reproduction, and gender . . . within the framework of entertaining fiction with sexual depictions . . . is the practice cultivated within the BL genre."[4] Yoshinaga, unusually, if not uniquely, among successful commercial manga artists, is "openly feminist," both in her manga works and in other genres and activities such as essays and interviews.[5] Thus, her work exemplifies the cutting edge of what BL can contribute to gender awareness, and vice versa, both within and outside the genre. With her continuous innovation the BL genre has widened in scope and attracted new audiences.

Besides being a feminist, Yoshinaga is also well-known for her special interest in food. Cooking and eating are not only ubiquitous in her manga but play important roles. Just as her background in BL is closely linked to her feminist convictions about diversity of gender and sexuality, food is connected in her texts to issues of diversity and equity. This in itself is not surprising, for food, as Terry Eagleton points out, "looks like an object but is actually a relationship." Eagleton compares food to literature; both are "endlessly interpretable."[6] This chapter demonstrates that Yoshinaga's manga, too, may look like an object but is actually an endlessly interpretable relationship that provides a window on gender and sexuality.[7] Furthermore, I will argue that Yoshinaga is a master chef of manga who prepares wonderful dishes, often with a BL flavor, for a diverse range of textual consumers and connoisseurs. Working within the BL and related genres for both commercial and *dōjinshi* publications, Yoshinaga depicts food, gender, and sexuality in order to affirm and celebrate desires and gratification, while at the same time presenting acute critiques of the kinds of consumption that involve or nurture discrimination against and subjugation of one group of people by another. Her "cooking" highlights various relationships—not only interpersonal ones but also those between group/society and individual, ideal/fantasy and reality, convention and innovation, and many others. By doing so, she subverts phallocentric and heteronormative myths and stereotypes.

In this chapter, I will focus on three of Yoshinaga's popular series produced at different times in her career, with differing degrees and methods of adopting or transforming BL conventions. *The Moon and the Sandals* (*Tsuki to sandaru*), which is regarded as Yoshinaga's first commercial publication, was originally published in the BL commercial magazine, *Hana oto* (Flower sound), between 1994 and 1996, and was subsequently collected in a volume in 1996.[8] Its sequel stories, published originally as *dōjinshi* between 1996 and 1999, were collected as *The Moon and the Sandals 2* (*Tsuki to sandaru 2*) in 2000.[9] While this first work still maintained, and was combined with, some *dōjinshi* characteristics, *Antique Bakery* (*Seiyō kottō yōgashiten*) established Yoshinaga's commercial success.[10] It was originally serialized in the *shōjo* manga magazine *Wings* (*Uingusu*) from June 1999 to September 2002. The manga was also made into a TV drama (2001), an anime series (2008), and a Korean drama (2008). In this chapter, however, I will concentrate on the print media, the four-volume main text and Yoshinaga's own *dōjinshi* version, *Antique Afterwards* (*Sore kara no Antiiku*).[11] The most recent of the three works discussed here is *What Did You Eat Yesterday?* (*Kinō nani tabeta?*), which has been serialized in *Morning* (*Mōningu*) since 2007.[12] *Morning* is categorized as a *seinen* manga magazine, and hence in a sense it is further distanced from BL.[13] However, despite the fact that only *The Moon and the*

Sandals and the *dōjinshi* version of *Antique Bakery* are BL, the other texts effectively use and parody BL conventions.

The protagonists of each series are all male, and at least one partner among the romantic couples or member of the core group in each work is either a professional chef or an excellent amateur cook. *The Moon and the Sandals*, for example, has four gay protagonists—two schoolboys, their history teacher, and his partner, who is a professional chef specializing in Japanese cuisine. Not only this last character but also one of the schoolboy protagonists and the sister of the other boy are good at cooking. In *Antique Bakery*, four men—one gay, one bisexual, and two heterosexual—run a stylish French cake shop, and in *What Did You Eat Yesterday?*, a gay lawyer cooks for his hairdresser partner every day. Yoshinaga skillfully subverts sociocultural conventions and gender stereotypes. In particular, I want to show here how her protagonists transgress just about every characteristic of the male chefs and gourmand protagonists that I have discussed in my previous projects on the "cooking man" and "gastronomic fiction."[14]

Earlier Cooking Man Discourses

Before examining Yoshinaga's texts, let us look at some of the most common and persistent myths regarding food and gender. "Mythologically, food is men's business; woman takes part in it only as a cook or as a servant."[15] This remark by Roland Barthes seems applicable to many cultures at various times, including that of twentieth-century, if not present-day, Japan. Or, to use the notion of *hare* (special, formal, festive, extraordinary) and *ke* (everyday, informal, and ordinary; also, energy), food that belongs to the special, public, ceremonial sphere has often been seen as the exclusive preserve of men, whereas everyday *ke* food has tended to be associated with women, who are also, mythologically and discursively, associated with *kegare* (defilement, exhaustion of *ke*).[16] Feminist writers and critics have described and deconstructed the "mythological" position of women in activities and discourses surrounding food, eating, and cooking.[17] In contemporary texts, the importance of gender-related issues has by no means diminished, but the nature and kinds of issues have certainly changed since earlier times. Instead of describing and protesting against blatant deprivation and discrimination within a patriarchal society, the focus seems to have shifted to questioning and subverting binaries such as male/female, subject/object, self/other, consumer/consumed, internal/external, body/mind and *hare/ke*. Yoshinaga's texts contribute to this general trend.

To understand Yoshinaga's subversion, it is helpful to revisit the "cooking man" discourse of previous periods. In the latter half of the twentieth century, writers such as Dan Kazuo (1912–1976) and Kaikō Takeshi (1930–1989) claimed in their food essays and fiction that men's cooking, supposedly in contrast to women's cooking, is dynamic, muscular, robust, and adventurous. The "cooking man" rejects domestication and formality. He is not tied to one family, one region, or one culture, but engages in constant global wanderings, in which open-mindedness and adaptability are key. He despises cooking instructions, for he relies on his own intuition and judgment. He likes to cook a whole fish, a whole carcass, or at least a large chunk of meat. Notable also is his general liking for entrails, innards, and guts. During his wanderings, the cooking man mingles with all sorts of people, sharing food and drink, and often also a bed. His (hetero)sexual promiscuity is always accompanied by an ultimate solitude, which is an essential part of the construction of the literary cooking man's masculinity. Also indispensable is knowledge and literacy in both Western and East Asian traditions. The link between the two kinds of orality—for food on the one hand, and for speech, language, and literature on the other—is prominent not only in the stories of postwar cooking men but also in prewar "gastronomic" fiction and some contemporary gourmet fiction. It is usually male characters who pursue this double orality that may also be connected to eroticism and sexuality. One of the recurring themes is that taste is not egalitarian, and this is clearly also applicable to gender issues. Some works of gourmet fiction present or imply the commodification of women—as edible, selectable, and consumable. Another common theme is the rivalry and competition among (usually male) peers.

Yoshinaga's cooking men present clear alternatives to these discourses and characteristics of previous cooking man models. I will examine the three texts in reverse chronological order. This is because the older age-setting and the emphasis on everyday life of *What Did You Eat Yesterday?* make the comparison with the earlier cooking men easier and more pronounced. The reverse chronological order also means moving from non-BL to the core of BL in terms of publication forms and outlets. However, I will show that the commitment to diversity has always been in Yoshinaga's texts, regardless of genre, audience, or date of publication.

What Did You Eat Yesterday?

The protagonist of *What Did You Eat Yesterday?*, Kakei Shirō, does not wander the world, but goes to the office every day, does his food shopping after work, and goes home to cook a meal for his partner and himself. There is a clear emphasis on the quotidian or *ke* kind of cooking, shopping, and other domestic work. Instead of dynamic, large-scale, elitist, eccentric, and intuitive cooking, Kakei likes shopping for and cooking with cheap, ordinary ingredients in small quantities for daily domestic consumption. His aim is not to find the ultimate gourmet food but to cook meals that he and his partner can enjoy in their everyday lives without spending too much time or money, and without wasting ingredients or jeopardizing their health. Cooking clearly soothes and revitalizes him after work, and the meals he cooks are not only a source of nutrition but a site for communication with his partner, and at times other people. Unlike the solitary and egotistical cooking man, Kakei cooks not to impress, exploit, or compete, but to enjoy the process itself and to share the taste, energy, and nutrition of his food with his partner. In each episode—about twenty pages long—there is a cooking scene that functions as an illustrated cooking guide, providing not only the ingredients and cooking method but also how to synchronize the preparation of different dishes, how to use the same ingredients in various ways over a few days, and other practical cooking tips. Yoshinaga does not hesitate to include those details that the cooking man despised—namely, "120g of meat," "half a teaspoon of salt," "slice 5 or 6 mm thick," and so on. Ready-made soup stock, sauces, and seasonings, and even MSG are not excluded. The dishes are quite ordinary, and yet the cooking process convincingly demonstrates the protagonist's skills and love of cooking. The manga not only stimulates the reader's appetite but provides hints on preparing the food it depicts. Furthermore, given the context of the main narrative and the sociocultural conventions it parodies, the seemingly ordinary recipes prompt the reader to question various stereotypes and assumptions, in particular those that relate to gender and sexuality.

The domesticity of Kakei's cooking can also be read as a critique of the gourmet boom of the 1980s and 1990s and its cultural and media representations, in which obsessive pursuit of food is often connected to heterosexism and misogyny. Such gendered biases cannot be found in Yoshinaga's texts. To some extent, the gay couple in *What Did You Eat Yesterday?* seems to accord with the two types that Ishida Hitoshi identified in the cultural representations produced in the first half of the 1990s: "gay man as a new type of ideal man who defies conventional gender roles" and "gay man as a woman's best friend (with whom she can identify)."[18] Ishida also found that these two types are usually separate and that the recurring theme is the "ideal man" type choosing the "woman's best friend" type. While it is not impossible to regard Kakei as the new type of ideal man and his partner, Kenji, as the second type, these are by no means the determining or most prominent characteristics. The two protagonists and other gay men are depicted not as reducible types but as characters with many different facets and social roles to play in their home, at their respective workplaces, and with their gay and heterosexual friends and relatives.

In this manga, Yoshinaga consciously makes the couple resident in a mundane world in which certain duties and chores must be performed. Cooking is an everyday pleasure rather than an obligation for Kakei. Kenji usually contributes to the pleasure by appreciating the food, but when Kakei is in bed with a cold, Kenji is excited to demonstrate his love and care through cooking: "You know I'm the devoted type? But my boyfriend can do everything so efficiently that usually he won't let me? I'm soooo happy today because I can take care of him as much as I like ♥" (figure 12.1).[19] The comical element is enhanced by his colleagues' comments and asides, such as "How silly!" and "Why use honorific language [to refer to Kakei]?" Kenji's enthusiasm is followed by nervousness, awkwardness, panic, exhaustion, and a sense of achievement during the actual cooking.

Figure 12.1 Kenji is happy because he can look after Kakei (Yoshinaga, *Kinō nani tabeta?* vol. 4, 43).

Figure 12.2 Kakei and Kenji have dinner with another gay couple (Yoshinaga, *Kinō nani tabeta?* vol. 4, 35).

An interesting comparison can be drawn between this scene and a short story by the acclaimed writer and "literary daughter,"[20] Kōda Aya (1904–1990). "The Sounds from the Kitchen" (Daidokoro no oto), first published in 1962, is a subtle and moving story about a middle-aged, working-class couple and "an elaborate study of food as a relationship and cooking as a lesson."[21] The husband, Sakichi, is a chef, bedridden with a serious illness. He listens to the sounds his wife, Aki, makes as she cooks both privately and professionally in the kitchen. The sounds provide consolation and information for Sakichi, whereas for Aki the fact that he is listening adds to the already great pressure and responsibility she feels. Both stories—even though one is comical and the other serious—depict the relationship between a couple, their verbal and non-verbal communication, and their values and judgments. The sounds Kenji makes in the kitchen, including his panicky soliloquy, irritate Kakei somewhat, but as he is too feverish to comment or to evaluate the dishes Kenji has prepared, he can only thank him, which makes Kenji very happy. Thus, Yoshinaga's story offers an alternative to the "food as a [heterosexual/patriarchal] relationship and cooking as a [one-sided] lesson"—no matter how loving the relationship and how profound and insightful the lesson may be. Even when there are differences in age, skills, and social status

between partners, there is no fixed hierarchy and there are lessons both can
learn.

Unlike most other food-centered stories, *What Did You Eat Yesterday?*
also makes reference to other types of housework, such as cleaning, doing
the laundry, washing the dishes, and managing the household budget. Kakei
loves to save money, which his partner finds rather stingy for a lawyer on a
good income.[22] Kakei responds that he would "rather have a so-so income
and live a balanced life" than "work so hard [he]'d drop dead."[23] So this is an
alternative to the common image of the workaholic man, or the "corporate
warrior" (*kigyō senshi*) of the previous era. At the same time, Kakei presents
a stark contrast to the earlier samurai masculinity that would regard money
as source and symbol of *kegare*. Kakei declares, "Besides, what's wrong with
loving money? As a gay man I can't depend on a child to look after me in my
old age but I can depend on money."[24]

Issues such as money, old age, and parenthood appear in other episodes,
too. In episodes 25 and 26 (vol. 4), Kakei and Kenji have dinner with another middle-aged gay couple (figure 12.2). One of the guests, Tetsu-san, a
businessman who runs several restaurants, talks about his plan to "adopt" his
partner Yoshi-kun (also middle-aged) so that the latter will be able to inherit
all his assets after his death. Under the current laws, even if Tetsu left a will
leaving everything to Yoshi, one-third of his property would still go to his
parents. "This is money I've worked hard to earn over the years. I don't want

Figure 12.3 Kakei imagines the *bishōnen* boyfriend of a newly acquainted man (Yoshinaga, *Kinō nani
tabeta?* vol. 5, 11).

Figure 12.4 Kakei meets the "*bishōnen*" boyfriend in question (Yoshinaga, *Kinō nani tabeta?* vol. 5, 66).

my parents back home to get a cent," says this chubby, balding businessman with a meek smile.[25] The realistic (though comical) representation of the gay couples in this manga is in marked contrast to the *tanbi* (aestheticism)-oriented conventions in BL and earlier forms, in which heroes are all young and beautiful and middle-aged protagonists appear only as admirers/patrons of beautiful young boys. Yoshinaga presents a hilarious parody of the *bishōnen* (beautiful boy): a newly acquainted gay man describes his lover by comparing him to the protagonist of Takemiya Keiko's *The Song of the Wind and the Trees* (*Kaze to ki no uta*) (figure 12.3).[26] When Kakei actually meets the young man in question, he cannot believe the gap between the imagined beautiful boy and the ordinary-looking bearded man in front of him (figure 12.4).[27]

The gap between appearances and truth or reality is an essential ingredient of Yoshinaga's manga. The element of surprise functions as a warning against unwarranted assumptions. While the primary narrative of this manga

deals with domestic scenes and ordinary recipes, the story also canvasses serious issues such as domestic violence, divorce and child custody, mental and
other illnesses, bankruptcy, and aged care. And there is almost always a twist
or reversal.[28]

Antique Bakery

As is evident from these examples, the comic/trivial and the serious are
mixed and mingled, and a didactic message is presented in entertaining ways.
Reflecting this comic/serious mix, Kakei's (and in fact everyone's) physiog-
nomy frequently and dramatically changes, and in the deformed (*deforume*)
version, everyone looks rather alike, with their pentagon-shaped faces. These
faces also appear in other manga by Yoshinaga, including the *Antique Bakery*
series. Each of the four protagonists transforms not only in appearance but
also in personality and attitude (figure 12.5). The device of comic deforma-
tion itself is nothing new in manga, but in Yoshinaga's texts it is used almost
obsessively, subverting assumptions based on age, gender, sexuality, appearance, occupation, education, class, status, and so on. There is no simple, stable, static face or personality. The owner of the cake shop, for instance, looks
forty-three but is actually thirty-three, and appears frivolous and carefree
but in fact still suffers from a traumatic childhood experience. Similarly, the
chef pâtissier, Ono, usually looks shy and quiet but is actually something of
a gay fatale who caused trouble everywhere he worked before the cake shop.
Another character, the tall, muscular Chikage, looks like a yakuza gangster
in his dark glasses, but is really gentle, polite, bashful, and naïve. He wears
sunglasses purely to protect his weak eyes. The youngest man, Eiji (aged
twenty-two), looks sweet but has had a tough and colorful life as an orphan,
and later as a champion boxer, before he was forced to give up the profession
because of a detached retina. There are numerous examples involving other
characters, including women, where first impressions, expectations, and assumptions turn out to be completely wrong or at least incomplete.

The culinary focus of *Antique Bakery* is gorgeous, delicate French cakes,
which may seem to belong to the domain of *hare* rather than *ke*. However,
this manga, too, has *ke* and *kegare* elements. The cakes are not just for *hare*
occasions such as weddings, Christmas, and a department store's food fair,
but are accessible on a daily basis to everyone—from ex-motorbike gang
members to an aging bar hostess, teachers, nurses, police detectives, and so
on. Furthermore, they are the key to a plot that involves the double mystery
of a child abduction from more than twenty years ago and a present-day serial child abduction/murder. For the cake shop owner who was the victim of

Figure 12.5 Constant transformation of the characters (Yoshinaga, *Seiyō kottō yōgashiten* vol. 3, 174).

the earlier case, however, the repressed memory never returns, and the fear still haunts him in the form of occasional nightmares.

Besides this crime-mystery, there are various subplots that relate to each member of the cake shop's staff and their relationships with one another. Just as these characters' depictions are physiognomically unstable, their relationships change constantly. What seems like dependency may turn out to be just the opposite. What one believes to be an act of unforgivable cruelty (for instance, the rejection of love confessed by one schoolboy to another) may have long been forgiven and forgotten. Just as solving a mystery or a crime is by no means the end of a story, neither is a marriage, divorce, or reconciliation the end or goal of a relationship. There is no ultimate solution, but life goes on—as is clear from the cake shop owner's final soliloquy: "Well, let's get something to eat and go and sell some more cakes!" (figure 12.6).[29]

Life goes on, not just for him but for everyone: the absence of conclusion or resolution may also be interpreted as meaning that life can go on despite

Figure 12.6 Life goes on (Yoshinaga, *Seiyō kottō yōgashiten* vol. 4, 228).

all kinds of difficulties and traumatic experiences. As critics have noted, none of the characters expects anyone else to solve or cure their traumas or problems.[30] While there is no easy solution or happy ending, there are things one can do to help oneself and others. BL fiction writer Matsuoka Natsuki finds that Yoshinaga's endings invite deeper readings and greater imagination.[31] Matsuoka is referring to *Gérard et Jacques* and other BL works by Yoshinaga, but this is also applicable to her non-BL texts, including *Antique*.[32] In the main text of *Antique*, BL elements are clearly present but there are no graphic sex scenes. Yoshinaga not only encourages readers to use their imagination to understand various relationships while reading her manga but also produces her own *dōjinshi* stories in which the gay *pâtissier* Ono's past, present, and imagined erotic encounters are depicted.[33] These sexually explicit stories are by no means simple, formulaic pornography. On the contrary, Yoshinaga uses a range of narrative devices to enhance the comic and ironic pleasure. In one episode entitled "Ono Dreams in the Kitchen" (Ono wa chūbō de yume o miru), the apprentice Eiji narrates an erotic story in order to entertain and energize his fatigued master, Ono.[34] The protagonists of this story within a story are Ono and the shy Chikage. In another story, three schoolgirls tell each other improvised BL stories involving the staff of the cake shop while the models listen to them behind the kitchen door.[35] Yoshinaga thus provides entertaining examples of endlessly interpretable relationships and texts.

The Moon and the Sandals

Many of the main characteristics of these two series can also be found in the earlier work, *The Moon and the Sandals*, which, unlike the other two series, clearly belongs to the BL genre. In this manga, too, food and cooking are directly and indirectly connected to various issues of gender and sexuality, and surprises and reversals are everywhere. In the first episode, for example, Kobayashi, the younger of the two schoolboys, is in love with his teacher, Ida-sensei, and often visits his flat and cooks him supper. Ida, however, is worried because his lover Hashizume has been offered a job in a famous restaurant in Kyoto. Will this be the end of their relationship? Here, it is not the teacher but the student who advises, consoles, and cooks for the other. The dishes Kobayashi prepares are ordinary *ke* food, and they are his expression of love and kindness as well as sexual desire (figure 12.7).[36]

Figure 12.7 Cooking as expression of love, kindness, and sexual desire (*Tsuki to sandaru* vol. 1, 15).

However, Kobayashi and Hashizume don't cook for the sake of sexual/culinary competition or conquest. And the story doesn't focus on a search for the ultimate taste. Instead, each of these men is concerned about the feelings of the people they love—not only their romantic/sexual love interest but also their friends and family. Even the older student, Narumi "Jaian [Gian]" Tōyō, who seems aloof and arrogant, turns out to be kind and considerate.[37]

As in other works by Yoshinaga, women are neither neglected nor treated as the second-class citizens of the BL world. Narumi's younger sister, Naru-chan, for example, is gifted not only academically but also in culinary matters. She is kind, brave, cute, popular, and good. As a female character in a BL story, Naru-chan is of course not part of the romance. Even though she is romantically interested in Kobayashi, he becomes her brother's lover instead. The first volume of *Tsuki to sandaru* ends with a cameo of this girl, who, though shocked and wounded, says, "I'll be OK. I'm sure I'll be OK some time."[38] As if in a film, the focus shifts from the girl, crying, to each of the four men in separate frames, and then finally into a street, with the concluding words of Naru-chan's monologue (as in a voiceover), "because each of us will be able to find our own space (*ibasho*)" (figure 12.8).[39] As Fujimoto Yukari pointed out in her pioneering study, the search for one's *ibasho* is the generic theme of *shōjo* manga.[40] Thus, the conclusion of the volume suggests that each character will continue her/his search for self in relation to the others, and at the same time guarantees the reader that she/he, too, will be able to find her/his own space.

In the second volume of *The Moon and the Sandals*, which consists of five stories originally published as *dōjinshi* between 1996 and 1999, Naru-chan and other attractive women add positive elements to the story. Sugita-san works under Hashizume at his restaurant. By the time of this episode, Ida and Hashizume have had their "gay marriage" in Japanese style—that is, Hashizume, some months younger than Ida, has been "adopted" onto Ida's family register. Like everyone else, Ida is impressed by Sugita-san's pleasant personality and ability as a chef but he cannot help feeling jealous. When Hashizume comes home late one night, Ida is in tears. This is followed by about ten pages relating a passionate sex scene between this gay couple, depicted graphically in some frames and yet with almost haiku-like omission and a touch of non-discriminatory humor, ending with the lovers calling each other's name (as in their school days) in ecstasy. After this BL-specific erotic scene, Ida confesses that he was worried that Hashizume might be attracted to Sugita-san. Hashizume responds: "But Sugita-san is a woman."[41] The humor here has no hint of misogyny. As a coda to this episode, Sugita-san's job

Figure 12.8 "because each of us will be able to find our own space" (*Tsuki to sandaru* vol. 1, 216).

interview is depicted. Hashizume frankly and calmly explains, "The name of this restaurant, Ida, is taken from the name of my homosexual partner," and asks her if she would still like to work with him. Sugita-san responds, "Yes, of course!", with her thought bubble saying "a workplace free of sexual harassment."[42]

There is another memorable example in one of the later episodes, involving Gian's boss, Ms. Ōkōchi in the Ministry of Finance.[43] In a conventional discourse, the bespectacled older woman at work could be expected to be a meddling, unpleasant character. Yoshinaga makes her a very positive character, again employing highly economical descriptions. When Gian confides in her about his sexuality, she becomes a strong ally in his plan to come out at work. Unlike in *What Did You Eat Yesterday?*, cooking recipes are not a regular feature of this manga. However, there are some didactic and informative elements. How can inexperienced teenagers find out practical things about sex between men? How best can one come out at school, at home, at work? How should one deal with prejudice and discrimination? These and many other issues are dealt with, at times with pathos but mostly with light, intelligent humor. It is a bildungs-romantic comedy, so to speak, with some serious messages.

Conclusion: Diversity and Subversion within BL and Beyond

In a dialogue with the writer Miura Shion, who is also known to be an avid BL reader, Yoshinaga remarks that *Antique Bakery* is not a BL work but a *shōjo* manga that includes gay protagonists. Many of her readers, however, see it as an unusual BL.

> Being regarded as BL may limit the range of the audience, but there's nothing I can do about it, and more importantly, I want my readers to read as they like. Surely we should be allowed to read manga with whatever dogma and prejudice we like.[44]

Yoshinaga and Miura emphasize the diversity of the BL genre. As one of the reasons for this, Yoshinaga points out that girls have more varied points of repression (*yokuatsu pointo*) and hence more diverse erotic interests (*moe pointo*), as well as more opportunities to think, than boys.[45] This remark has impressed many critics. Fujimoto Yukari could not agree more:

> *Yaoi* and BL provide a massage space where the chains of gender-repression are removed, allowing one to choose and re-adjust gender elements as one wishes. It is like a custom-made massage machine that puts pressure on the exact spots that are stiff.[46]

Psychologist Saitō Tamaki, too, was "deeply moved" by Yoshinaga's insightful remark and her "epoch-making coinage of the term '*yokuatsu pointo*.'"[47] He writes that Yoshinaga has "in effect, made a claim that women are essentially a minority"—not in number but in consciousness—and that they reject simple solidarity.[48]

Yoshinaga demonstrates that it is possible to convey feminist ideas and messages in the commercial media. She does this by employing the BL and wider *shōjo* manga conventions of homoeroticism involving beautiful male protagonists, but at the same time transforming and subverting these conventions. In a sense, she has managed to find convincing recipes that will make her protest against the commodification of women, children, and marginalized people palatable in the popular media.

One final question: does Yoshinaga commodify gay sexuality? She is acutely aware of this issue. In a gourmet-restaurant-guide-cum-diary-like-manga entitled *I Can Live On/Keep Eating Even Without Love* (*Ai ga nakute mo kutte yukemasu*), "Y-naga" apologizes to her "real gay" salaryman friend "A-dō" for earning her living by depicting "fake gays" in her manga without even realizing for years that he is gay.[49] He says that he has never minded it, and that "if a gay man got annoyed with that sort of trifle all the time, he couldn't survive."[50] This is yet another example of empowering critique leading to creativity. The apology within the text does not resolve the issue of what Ishida has termed "*hyōshō no ōdatsu*" (the appropriation of representations);[51] nevertheless, it foregrounds the appropriation and commercialization of gay sexuality. A-dō looks and behaves just like a handsome character from Yoshinaga's more overtly fictitious manga. While eating the sushi Y-naga has treated him to, he cheerfully explains that he was bisexual in his high school and university days but that, when he started working, he "became gay in order to be consistent with the orientation that's more difficult to live by in society."[52] Thus, Yoshinaga manages to subvert the BL genre as well as the genres of restaurant guide and cooking recipes, not by censoring the consuming passion but by using both the motifs and conventions of these existing genres and their critiques.

Notes

1. Yoshinaga Fumi, *Ōoku* [The inner chamber], 9 vols., ongoing (Tokyo: Hakusensha, 2005–). On the Tiptree award, refer to the homepage of the James Tiptree, Jr., Literary Award Council, http://tiptree.org/?see=front_page#TiptreeAward. The Sense of Gender Award (est. 2000) is a Japanese version of this award.

2. Akiko Mizoguchi, "Theorizing Comics/Manga Genre as a Productive Forum: Yaoi and Beyond," in *Comics Worlds and the World of Comics: Towards Scholarship on a Global Scale*, ed. Jacqueline Berndt (Kyoto: Kyoto Seika University International Manga Research Center, 2010), http://imrc.jp/images/upload/lecture/data/143-168chap10Mizoguchi20101224.pdf, 162. See also Hikari Hori, "Views from Elsewhere: Female Shoguns in Yoshinaga Fumi's *Ōoku* and their Precursors in Japanese Popular Culture," *Japanese Studies* 32, no. 1 (2012).

3. The term "*dōjinshi*" originally signified coterie magazines, including highbrow literary magazines. In more recent years, it has been used for self-published amateur manga/fiction magazines, including parodic fiction with sexually explicit themes. See James Welker's chapter in this volume for more information. Early *dōjinshi* works of Yoshinaga include parodies of three extremely popular texts: Ikeda Riyoko's *shōjo* manga, *Berusaiyu no bara* [The rose of Versailles], 5 vols. (1972–1973; Tokyo: Shūeisha bunko, 1994); Inoue Takehiko's *shōnen* manga,

Slam Dunk, 31 vols. (Tokyo, Shūeisha, 1991–1996); and Tanaka Yoshiki's science fiction, *Ginga eiyū densetsu* [Legend of the galactic heroes], 10 vols. (Tokyo: Tokuma shoten, 1982–1987).

4. Mizoguchi, "Theorizing Comics," 163.

5. Mizoguchi, "Theorizing Comics," 163; Hori, "Views from Elsewhere," 79–80.

6. Terry Eagleton, "Edible Écriture," in *Consuming Passions: Food in the Age of Anxiety*, ed. Sian Griffiths and Jennifer Wallace (Manchester, England: Mandolin, 1998), 204–205.

7. An earlier Japanese version of this chapter was presented at Ochanomizu University in December 2009 and appeared as Aoyama Tomoko, "Yoshinaga Fumi no manga ni miru 'shoku' to jendaa" ['Food' and gender in the manga of Yoshinaga Fumi], *Center for Comparative Japanese Studies Annual Bulletin* (Ochanomizu University) 6 (2010).

8. Yoshinaga Fumi, *Tsuki to sandaru* [The moon and the sandals] (Tokyo: Hōbunsha, 1996).

9. Yoshinaga Fumi, *Tsuki to sandaru 2* [The moon and the sandals 2] (Tokyo: Hōbunsha, 2000).

10. Yoshinaga Fumi, *Seiyō kottō yōgashiten* [Antique bakery], 4 vols. (Tokyo: Shinshokan, Wings Comic, 2000–2002).

11. Yoshinaga Fumi, *Sore kara no Antiiku* [Antique afterwards], 2 vols., *dōjinshi* (Tokyo: Ōsawa kaseifu kyōkai, 2005–2006).

12. Yoshinaga Fumi, *Kinō nani tabeta?* [What did you eat yesterday?], 7 vols., ongoing (Tokyo: Kōdansha, Morning KC [Kodansha Comic], 2007–).

13. The term "*seinen*," which was earlier used in a different sense, signifying young men (usually excluding women), is less gender segregated. In the manga context, it is used for a genre whose target audience is older than *shōjo* or *shōnen* (boys).

14. Tomoko Aoyama, "The Cooking Man in Modern Japanese Literature," in *Asian Masculinities: The Meaning and Practice of Manhood in China and Japan*, ed. Kam Louie and Morris Low (London: RoutledgeCurzon, 2003); and Tomoko Aoyama, *Reading Food in Modern Japanese Literature* (Honolulu: University of Hawai'i Press, 2008), chapter 5.

15. Roland Barthes, *The Rustle of Language*, trans. Richard Howard (New York: Hill and Wang, 1986), 253.

16. For a brief introduction to the concepts of *hare*, *ke*, and *kegare*, see Yoshio Sugimoto, *An Introduction to Japanese Society*, 3rd ed. (Cambridge: Cambridge University Press, 2010), 263–65.

17. For detailed discussion of food and gender in works by modern and contemporary Japanese women writers, see Aoyama, *Reading Food*, 24–32, 71–80, 172–203.

18. Ishida Hitoshi, "'Hottoite kudasai' to iu hyōmei o megutte: Yaoi/BL no jiritsusei to hyōshō no ōdatsu" [On the declaration "Please leave us alone": The autonomy of *yaoi*/BL and the appropriation of representation], *Yuriika* 39, no. 16 (December 2007): 121. See also Mark McLelland, "Gay Men as Women's Ideal Partners in Japanese Popular Culture: Are Gay Men Really a Girl's Best Friends?," *U.S.–Japan Women's Journal* 17 (1999).

19. Yoshinaga, *Kinō nani tabeta?*, vol. 4, 43. All English translations of the passages I quote from Japanese sources are mine unless otherwise noted.

20. Kōda was the daughter of the celebrated writer father, Kōda Rohan. See Tomoko Aoyama, "Literary Daughters' Recipes: Food and Female Subjectivity in the Writings of Mori Mari and Kōda Aya," *Japanstudien* 12 (2000).

21. Aoyama, "Literary Daughters' Recipes," 108.

22. Yoshinaga has a law degree from Keiō University. Lawyers and law lecturers and students appear in many other Yoshinaga works.

23. Yoshinaga, *Kinō nani tabeta?*, vol. 1, 15.

24. Ibid.

25. Yoshinaga, *Kinō nani tabeta?*, vol. 4, 36.

26. Takemiya Keiko, *Kaze to ki no uta* [The song of the wind and the trees], 10 vols. (1976–1984; Tokyo: Hakusensha bunko, 1995).

27. Yoshinaga, *Kinō nani tabeta?*, vol. 5, 11–14, 65–67.

28. In episode 7, for example, Kakei handles a domestic violence case. The victim is a sturdy man whose "petite, cute" wife regularly beats him up with kitchen utensils (Yoshinaga, *Kinō nani tabeta?*, vol. 1, 129).

29. Yoshinaga, *Seiyō kottō yōgashiten*, vol. 4, 228.

30. Uno Tsunehiro, "Zero nendai no sōzōryoku: 'Ushinawareta 10-nen' no mukōgawa" [The imagination of the zero-generation: Beyond the "lost decade"], *SF magajin* 29, no. 1 (2008): 95–96. See also Fukuda Rika's comments in Hagio Moto et al. "Yoshinaga Fumi wa suki desu ka?" [Do you like Yoshinaga Fumi?], special feature, *Da Vinci* 166 (February 2008): 158–59.

31. Hagio Moto, et al., "Yoshinaga Fumi wa suki desu ka?," 157.

32. Yoshinaga Fumi, *Jeraaru to Jakku* [Gérard et Jacques] (Tokyo: Hakusensha, 2004).

33. Yoshinaga, *Sore kara no Antiiku*.

34. Ibid., vol. 1, 5–41. The title of this episode is a parody of another (non-BL) work by Yoshinaga, *Kare wa hanazono de yume o miru* [He dreams in the flower garden] (Tokyo: Shinshokan, 1999).

35. Yoshinaga, *Sore kara no Antiiku*, 42–80.

36. See, for example, the episode involving asparagus tempura in Yoshinaga, *Tsuki to sandaru*, 14–17.

37. Nicknamed after the bully-boy character in the popular children's manga/anime *Doraemon*.

38. Yoshinaga, *Tsuki to sandaru*, 214–15.

39. Ibid., 216.

40. Fujimoto Yukari, *Watashi no ibasho wa doko ni aru no?: Shōjo manga ga utsusu kokoro no katachi* [Where do I belong? The shape of the heart reflected in *shōjo* manga] (Tokyo: Gakuyō shobō, 1998).

41. Yoshinaga, *Tsuki to sandaru* 2, 101.

42. Ibid., 103.

43. As always, Yoshinaga's choice of name is impeccable. The episode is in Yoshinaga, *Tsuki to sandaru* 2, 113–49.

44. Yoshinaga Fumi, *Ano hito to koko dake no oshaberi* [Confidential chat with that person] (Tokyo: Ōta shuppan, 2007), 140.

45. Yoshinaga, *Ano hito to*, 143–44.

46. Fujimoto Yukari, "Shōnen'ai/yaoi, BL: 2007-nen genzai no shiten kara" [Shōnen'ai, yaoi, and BL: From the perspective of 2007], *Yuriika* 39, no. 16 (December 2007): 46.

47. Saitō Tamaki, *Haha wa musume no jinsei o shihai suru* [Mothers control daughters' lives] (Tokyo: Nihon hōsō shuppan kyōkai, NHK Books, 2008), 106–107.

48. Saitō Tamaki, *Kankei no kagaku to shite no bungaku* [Literature as relationship chemistry] (Tokyo: Shinchōsha, 2009), 61.

49. Yoshinaga Fumi, *Ai ga nakutemo kutte yukemasu* [I can live on/keep eating even without love] (Tokyo: Ōta shuppan, 2005).

50. Yoshinaga, *Ai ga nakutemo*, 42.

51. Ishida, "'Hottoite kudasai,'" 116, in reference to earlier critical comments by Keith Vincent and Satō Masaki. See also Ishida Hitoshi's chapter in this volume.

52. Yoshinaga, *Ai ga nakutemo*, 37.

REGULATION OF MANGA CONTENT IN JAPAN

What Is the Future for BL?

MARK McLELLAND

Introduction

For anyone whose only knowledge of how sexuality is variously represented in Japanese popular culture is based on reports in the English-language press, the general impression will probably be one of a sexually very open, even unrestrained society. Certainly this is the impression given in the many hyperbolic reports by Western journalists who have penned endless articles about the supposed sexual depravity of Japanese popular culture, particularly manga and anime. A classic exemplar of this genre is *Atlantic Monthly* journalist James Fallows's report tellingly entitled "The Japanese Are Different from You and Me," in which he argues that Japan's "underlying social motif" is one of "low grade pedophilia."[1] Fallows's main evidence for this claim is the apparent youthfulness of many manga and anime characters. There are multiple genres, popular with both men and women, where young-looking characters feature in sexual and violent scenarios that would be problematic in many Western countries where "child abuse materials" legislation has been broadened to capture purely fictional images as well as actual child pornography.[2]

In English-language reports, Japan is frequently presented as failing to comply with "international standards" restricting fantasy sex and violence where young people are involved. Spokespersons for international agencies such as UNICEF have been lobbying Japanese policymakers for the past decade, demanding increased restrictions, not only on what kind of content is judged suitable for minors, but also on the way in which minors themselves are depicted in manga, anime, computer games, and other media.³ It has been argued that the level of sexuality and violence depicted in some manga, anime, and games is unsuitable for their target audience of young teens, and that characters who are, or appear to be, young teens themselves are depicted in violent and sexual scenarios which, if they were depictions of real young people, would be unlawful. UNICEF "goodwill ambassador," singer, and media personality Agnes Chan has been particularly voluble in lobbying Japanese politicians to ban sexualized depictions of young people in manga and anime, arguing that "ultimately, pornography depicting sexual abuse against children is made for a minority of people of a particular 'disposition' who wish to view children as sexual playthings."⁴ However, as discussed below, Chan's claim that the sexualized depiction of "child" characters is a minority interest fails to take into account the active engagement that young people themselves in Japan and internationally have taken in creating and disseminating such images and narratives.⁵ Although the majority of examples of harmful depictions cited in these reports pertain to the fascination for *rori* (Lolita) figures in media directed at boys and men, the increased scrutiny not only of young people's reading material but of the depictions of young people in that material has also placed the spotlight on a sexualized genre popular with girls, that of "boys love" (BL) manga and associated media.

However, despite the fact that in an international context the depictions of male–male sex and romance played out in BL texts between figures who may "appear to be" minors has placed this material firmly in the context of global debates over child pornography, the frame of the debate over the inappropriateness of BL is different in Japan.⁶ In this chapter, I argue that the proposed "harmful" nature of BL depictions needs to be understood in the context of a wide ranging debate over "gender-free" policies in education that has been taking place in Japan since the early 1990s. As will be discussed, conservative politicians, lobby groups, and media commentators have been arguing that Japan's economic woes and, in particular, the rapidly declining birth rate stem from confusion over gender roles created by liberal social and educational policies that are seen as attacking traditional sex and gender roles for men, and particularly women.

In this chapter, I draw attention to the criticism that has been levied at BL texts that specifically emphasizes, not so much the seeming youthfulness of their characters, but their depiction of "inappropriate" and "incorrect" sex and gender roles that are likely to cause misidentification and confusion among their youthful readers. Linking these anxieties to the manner in which BL texts flaunt the conventional sex and gender roles outlined in sex education directives from the Ministry of Education, I argue that female

BL fans self-depiction as *fujoshi*—that is, "*rotten* girls"—has a heightened significance when considered in the context of the official "purity" narratives that are channeled via Ministry directives into the classroom.[7] BL narratives, with their rejection of conventional masculine roles, of heterosexuality, but most importantly of the procreative function of sex, are in direct opposition to sex education narratives rolled out in schools and to increasingly strident government calls for Japanese women to produce more children to address the falling birth rate. Hence, the BL subculture functions much like the girl-oriented zines and Internet sites offering "safe spaces," discussed by Anita Harris, that support "the expression of missing discourses" surrounding youth sexuality.[8]

As Huiyan Fu has pointed out, there exists a "blatant contradiction between formal and informal sectors" regarding the "understanding of sexuality and gender in Japan";[9] and it is no surprise that Japan's "rotten girls" are increasingly coming under official scrutiny. In this chapter, I will look at two specific examples of measures designed to rein in sexual expression in BL manga and other media directed at young people, and at the arguments that were raised against these measures. As will be seen, the context of debates over these contentious materials is different in Japan than in the West. I will first start with a general overview of manga regulation in Japan in the postwar period.

A Brief Outline of Manga Regulation in Japan

As Sharon Kinsella points out, in the postwar period there have been "recurrent bouts of institutional interference in the moral, educational and political content of manga."[10] There has never been an anything-goes policy in Japan regarding depictions of fantasy sex or violence, as is sometimes suggested in alarmist articles in the Anglophone media.[11] Japanese manga, like all other publications, are governed by Article 175 of the Penal Code that prohibits "indecency" (*waisetsu*). Indeed, in 2004 manga artist Suwa Yūji and the publisher Shōbunkan were both successfully prosecuted under the article for extreme depictions of sexual violence in the manga *Honey Room* (*Misshitsu*).[12]

In addition to national legislation prohibiting obscenity, various municipalities in Japan have the power to pass local ordinances (*todōfuken jōrei*), and these have been used to restrict distribution of material deemed "harmful to youth." Since manga are a ubiquitous source of entertainment in Japan sold in convenience stores, train stations, and newsstands as well as bookstores, children have had ready access to them. As Kinsella points out, "in order to avoid legal action and fines . . . retail outlets have tended to refuse to stock manga categorized as 'indecent.'"[13] This has had a wash-back effect on manga producers who have practiced self-censorship so as not to run the risk of losing access to major retail outlets. Kinsella lists a number of popular manga serials that were wound up by the publishers after community concern was voiced that their contents were "unsuitable for children."[14] Where Japanese and Western codes of indecency do differ is in the *degree* of fantasy sex and violence considered permissible. Censors in Japan have tended to apply very specific and technical definitions of obscenity, focusing on such items as visibility of genitalia, pubic hair, and sexual penetration, whereas highly figurative, stylized, or symbolic representations of sex have been overlooked. Indeed, for the judges in the *Honey Room* case, it was the fact that the artist had depicted the sex scenes as "realistically and lewdly as possible" that rendered the manga obscene.[15] More stylized depictions, such as those characteristic of BL materials, have not tended to attract the same attention.

Calls for restrictions on sex and violence depicted in manga directed at young people, often led by Parents and Teachers Associations (PTAs), have gathered pace since 1968, when Japan's most popular boys' manga *Shōnen Jump* (*Shōnen janpu*) began to serialize the story *Harenchi Gakuen* (Shameless school). This wildly successful series (later turned into several movies and a TV show) made explicit reference to the repressed sexuality of a coed school environment and scandalized many parents and educators. However, the most sustained call for reform of manga content followed on from the tragic murder of four infant girls between 1988 and 1989 by serial killer Miyazaki Tsutomu. An investigation of Miyazaki's background and lifestyle revealed that he was an isolated youth who had been an avid collector of "Lolita"-style manga and anime, as well as adult pornography. In press reports, popular psychologists drew a clear connection between his private fantasy life and real-life actions, generalizing beyond Miyazaki to an entire generation of alienated young men "who cannot make the transition from a fantasy world of videos and manga to reality."[16] Following on from the Miyazaki scare, a coalition of PTA committees, feminist groups, and women's organizations lobbied local and national politicians for increased surveillance and regulation of violent and sexualized imagery in manga and anime, particularly those marketed to young people. These groups also lobbied publishers themselves, sending complaint letters about manga that they considered particularly "harmful." One result of this increased vigilance was a spike in 1990 in the number of manga designated "harmful" to youth. As

Kinsella points out, by 1993 "the political regulation movement had largely been internalized within the manga publishing industry," resulting in "a wave of anticipatory self-censorship exercised directly by manga editors and individual manga artists."[17]

However, this self-censoring industry code only applies to official publications released by Japan's major companies and does not cover the extensive self-published genre of original and "parody" manga known as *dōjinshi*. These self-published zines are created either by individual authors or "circles" of writers/artists working together, and they can be highly sexualized. As Sharalyn Orbaugh points out, the widespread popularity of these unofficial manga that are sold at major comics conventions, such as Tokyo's Comic Market, results in "permeable boundaries between the producers and consumers of narratives in Japan."[18] It is not uncommon for talented amateur artists to be recruited by major companies, nor is it unusual for established artists to turn to *dōjinshi* to self-publish "material too experimental or risqué for their regular venues."[19] Hence, it is in *amateur* work, not publications from the major outlets, that the most sexualized content can often be found.

As will be discussed below, anxieties over the potentially harmful effects of sexualized depictions in manga and other media popular with young people have only grown in a convergent media environment where access to these materials has been made ever easier due to the Internet. However, until fairly recently, it was the harmful effects of the sexualized depictions of girls on boys and men that were singled out. Girls' comics (*shōjo* manga) and associated products have largely escaped scrutiny. But this has recently changed and now girls' manga, and BL products in particular, have emerged as sites of concern.

The Sakai Library "Boys Love" Incident

In the past decade, a growing number of complaints from the general public show that BL depictions are beginning to attract mainstream attention and criticism. One notorious incident occurred in 2008, when an undisclosed number of people began a campaign to have BL books removed from public display in libraries in Sakai, a middle-sized city of over 800,000 people, located in Osaka prefecture. The target of the campaign was not BL manga per se, but "BL novels," that is, light fiction depictions of male–male romance, often accompanied by racy illustrations.

The campaign consisted of a series of phone calls and emails sent to libraries and to the local council, inquiring why public funds were being used for the procurement of this "pornographic" genre and asking libraries to account for the actual numbers of BL titles in their collections.[20] As a response, in August 2008 Sakai Municipal Library made the unilateral decisions to remove all existing BL novels from the shelves and place them in a storage facility, to only lend them out on request to mature-age readers, and to refrain from purchasing any further BL titles. The lack of transparency over how this decision was made and the lack of explanation as to why only BL titles were targeted caused concern among other library users. In November of the same year, these moves prompted twenty-eight Sakai city residents and a further twelve persons from around Japan, including prominent feminist academic Ueno Chizuko, to contact the library and request that they reconsider their decision and restore all BL titles to the general collection.[21] This was followed by a complaint signed by forty-one woman city councilors and two gender-related citizens' groups who argued that the library council had exceeded its authority when it unilaterally decided to restrict a particular genre of reading matter based on a small number of complaints and that restricting access to BL material potentially infringed upon the rights of young people to freedom of expression and could even be perceived as a form of sexual discrimination against young women (who were the primary requestors and readers of the sequestered material).[22]

In the meantime the national press had gotten wind of the dispute and was running articles about this "troubling" genre and remarking on the sheer volume of BL titles in library collections. The total number of BL novels in Sakai public libraries was reported to be 5,500 titles that had cost in the region of 3,700,000 yen (over $37,000).[23] Other media reports also made much of the fact that these sexual stories featuring male–male romance were requested by women known as "rotten girls" (*fujoshi*), thus drawing attention to the self-consciously subversive nature of the works' readership.[24]

This issue generated considerable debate on Japan's social networking website *mixi* and on BBS systems set up to "scrutinize" so-called "FemiNazi" attacks on the family, with BL's detractors launching a range of critiques.[25] The main points reiterated by BL opponents were that BL is a pornographic genre and as such should be treated akin to male-oriented pornography and kept away from minors because of its "bad effects." Furthermore, having defined the genre as pornographic, the use of taxpayers' money to acquire BL was "inappropriate." Also, the fact that the genre dealt in male–male sexual relations could be construed as a form of "sexual harassment" toward heterosexual readers who might stumble across it. However, the argument of most interest was that the popularity of BL among female youth was a sign that the "gender-free" policies being implemented by local councils in order to root out institutionalized sexism had gone too far and that the result was young women were confused about appropriate gender roles, causing them to identify with male homosexuals and potentially render them transsexual! This last point seems to have been a major concern since Atsuta Keiko, in an analysis of the list of sequestered items provided by the library, draws attention to the fact that it was only titles dealing with male homosexuality targeted at women that were removed. The discussion of homosexual sex per se seems not to have been a problem, as other "gay literature" titles written by and for gay men were not on the list, nor were titles dealing with heterosexual sex.[26]

Rather than engage with the "BL is pornography" contention or the clearly hysterical anxieties concerning BL's effects on readers head-on, many supporters of BL countered by arguing that libraries had a responsibility to respond to reader demand rather than set their own agenda on what reading materials should or should not be made available. The high demand for BL material indicated a strong interest in the genre among borrowers and it should therefore be the fans of the genre and not its detractors who should be listened to; to do otherwise would constitute unfair censorship. Hence, BL supporters tried to limit the debate to matters of procedure and policy: libraries are publicly funded institutions that have a mandate to make available reading material requested by the public. The corollary of this is that it is inappropriate for one set of readers to limit the reading choices of others based upon their own personal dislike of a particular genre. Furthermore, it was argued that it is not the role of library councils to seek to sway public opinion by supporting or restricting access to particular kinds of information or reading matter.

Although, after consideration of the arguments made by both sides, the Sakai Municipal Library eventually decided to return its BL titles to general circulation, its initial knee-jerk reaction in warehousing the collection is a good indication of the sensitivity surrounding BL and its relation to young readers. Indeed, soon after the resolution of the complaint concerning Sakai library's BL collection, another city council, this time in the city of Kuwana, part of the greater Nagoya metropolitan area, was quizzed about its libraries' BL-acquisitions policy, suggesting that BL may now be emerging as another battlefront for proponents and detractors of "gender-free" policies in employment, education and elsewhere.[27]

It is worthy of further consideration that it is argued by BL detractors that it is not just the "pornographic" nature of BL materials that renders them unsuitable for minors but also the fact that same-sex sexuality is depicted. Indeed, it could be argued that the reason that social concern has only recently been focused on BL material—despite the longevity of its various genres—is because of heightened sensitivities in Japan around the supposed confusion of gender roles due to the rise of "gender-free" policies, particularly in education. Indeed, in an article reflecting on the Sakai incident published in current affairs magazine *Tsukuru* in May 2009, the aforementioned Ueno identified the rise in online "bashing" of feminists, sexual minorities, and "rotten girls" as symptomatic of a wider backlash against the affirmative action policies instigated by many local councils against gender discrimination.[28] Hence, to understand the *specific* anxieties that surround BL in Japan it is necessary to consider the background to the "gender-free" controversy.

Background to the "Gender-Free" Debate in Japan

By the mid 1990s, it was apparent that there were numerous problems facing Japan. The birth rate, on the decline for decades, was continuing to fall, and the economy was in the midst of the worst recession in the postwar period. There was a growing sense that "gender equality was good for business" and that women's increased participation in the workforce would not only help provide greater financial stability for the establishment of families but also increase consumption and help revive the economy.[29]

Japanese legislation relating to women, especially women's employment, has seen a number of revisions in the postwar period. The 1947 constitution, drafted by the Americans during the Allied Occupation of the country, was progressive for the time, outlawing discrimination on the basis of sex. The 1947 Labor Standards Law, however, designed to "protect" women from exploitation and ensure that they had time available for family duties, placed restrictions on the number of hours a woman could be expected to work overtime, and placed limits on holiday work and late-night shifts. Some of these limitations were removed in the 1985 Equal Employment Opportunity Law, but only for women in managerial positions and jobs requiring specialized knowledge and technical skills. Hence, further reform was necessary if women in general were to be able to enter the workforce on an equal footing with men.

The possibility of getting further gender reform legislation through the Japanese Diet was increased in the 1990s due to the splintering of support for the conservative Liberal Democratic Party that had ruled Japan almost uninterrupted since the end of the Occupation period, and the rise of high-profile female opposition leaders who ensured that reform of gender specific legislation remained in the spotlight.³⁰ This confluence of factors resulted in "an unprecedented level of feminist involvement in policy making" during the 1990s, culminating in the passing of the Basic Law for a Gender Equal Society in 1999.³¹

As Osawa Mari points out, increased involvement in policy making by feminist groups helped shift the manner in which gender issues were debated. Until the mid 1990s, "It ha[d] been customary to argue that in Japan, 'gender' is understood in the same context as 'sex'—that is, as being 'natural,' so that differences in social roles are not, in themselves, discriminatory."³² Until this time, the most prevalent Japanese term for what in English would be described as "gender equality" was "*danjo byōdō*," literally "man–woman equality." The idea of gender as a set of culturally framed distinctions between men and women only gained popular currency in the 1990s, the loanword *jendaa* appearing in the *Kōjien* dictionary for the first time in 1991. As Osawa observes, it was not until 1996 that the term "*jendaa*" appeared in an official government report (albeit in parentheses). From this time on, the idea of "natural" role divisions between men and women began to be challenged by a new discourse calling for "a policy focused on 'the freedom from gender,' or 'gender free' society."³³ This new awareness of the constructedness of gender divisions fuelled demands for a "gender-free" (*jendaa furii*) society, and the term "*jendaa furii*" began to be used increasingly by academics and journalists, becoming in the early 2000s "a widely used term in government, education, and mass media."³⁴

Ayako Kano has noted how the use of the term "gender-free" was originally intended to signify freedom from gender discrimination. However, its use was promulgated at the same time as a similar phrase "barrier free" (*baria furii*) was circulating in the media to refer to accessibility for the disabled. As a consequence, for some the term came to connote "eliminating gender" from society—as if gender distinctions in themselves were a barrier—although this was not how it was intended in most feminist discourse.³⁵ However, by playing on anxieties stirred by this misinterpretation, conservative groups in Japan were able to orchestrate a backlash in the media against supposedly "radical" and "fringe" feminist policies that were seen as on the rise across society as a whole. What Hyōdō Chika refers to as "feminist bashing" intensified at the political level with the election of the conservative Ishihara Shintarō as governor of Tokyo in 1999.³⁶

Also of concern to conservatives was the manner in which a supposed "gender-free" ideology was informing sex education in schools where more liberal-minded teachers were discussing contraception, male and female homosexuality, and self-pleasure—topics that are not included in the

curriculum devised by the Ministry of Education. Indeed, until 1965 sex education in Japanese schools was discussed under the rubric "purity education,"
and directives from the Ministry have primarily been concerned with the
need for instilling proper "etiquette" between the sexes through the establishment of "healthy environments" and "wholesome activities" on school
campuses. Since sex was designated as part of the "world of adults," emphasis
has always been placed on maintaining the "natural pureness" of young people and avoiding circumstances that might result in precocious interest in
sexual matters.[37] Hence, until 1992 there was no explicit curriculum provided
by the Ministry for sex education nor were there specially designated sex-
education classes—teachers were expected to follow the general guidelines
provided by the Ministry and address relevant aspects of sexuality in the context of other classes, including biology, the social sciences, and health and
fitness. The introduction of classes specifically branded as "sex education" in
1992 was the result of a number of factors including an increase in teenage
pregnancy, anxieties about HIV infection, and concern over declining fertility rates. The last point reinforces Hu's argument that "the state production
of sex education policy has consistently focused on the control of both the
quantity and the quality of the Japanese population."[38] This can be seen in
the fact that even in the more detailed post-1992 sex-education curriculum,
"unproductive" individual-oriented functions of sex, such as homosexuality and pleasure, are either denied or silenced, and "abstinence only" is still
emphasized over discussion of contraception.[39]

Controversy over the provision of sex education to children is, of course,
not unique to Japan. Many Western nations, in particular the U.S., which
has a strong conservative Christian lobby, have very restrictive sex-education
policies at the local or national level that emphasize abstinence, support
heteronormativity, and only discuss contraception in terms of its failure.[40]
But despite the fact that Japan is not a Christian nation, as Naitō Chizuko
points out, "methods being used by 'bashing' groups in Japan structurally
resemble some of the methods used by American Christian fundamental-
ists."[41] These include an attack on the very notion of "gender" itself as it supposedly denies the natural differences between male and female roles and
thereby undermines the family. It is therefore no surprise that conservative
educators would have been troubled by reports of the large number of BL
materials—which are, after all, defined by their playful subversion of male
and female roles and depictions of "unproductive sex," homosexuality, and
pleasure—made available in libraries.

Concerned about the potential social effects of "gender-free" initiatives
supposedly being rolled out in schools, in 2000 the Liberal Democratic Party

set up a "Project Team for Investigating the Status of Radical Sex Education and Gender Free Education" to report back to the Diet on these dangerous initiatives. These heightened anxieties led to a crackdown in 2003 by the Tokyo Metropolitan Board of Education on "extreme" sex education materials in twenty-two schools "resulting in the punishment of 102 educators and some sex education practitioners," albeit in 2009 the Tokyo District Court ruled that this represented unjust interference in the education process.[42] It was not just schools targeted in this backlash, but some prefectures cut funding to women's centers or acceded to demands that "inappropriate" and "radical" books supposedly attacking traditional family values be removed from public display.[43] Naitō has argued that this escalation in gender bashing is related to Japan's economic troubles and the growing number of men working part-time or who are unemployed who "experience a sense of loss stemming from their lack of identity as full-fledged members of society in possession of male authority."[44]

Hence, it is in this context—general anxiety about the threat that "gender-free" education and social inclusion policies represent to "traditional" gender roles, male authority, and particularly young women's reproductive choices—that debates over the suitability of BL as reading matter for girls and young women emerged. The "gender-free" debate has not subsided but in 2010 re-emerged in the context of a new attempt to restrict young people's access to sexually explicit manga, anime, and associated products, this time spearheaded by Ishihara, whose term as governor of Tokyo ran through 2012. Ishihara is a reactionary figure, infamous for his discriminatory remarks about a range of people, including older women past childbearing age, who he has described as "useless," and gay people, who he claims are "abnormal."[45] Ishihara was the prime mover behind what became known in the press as the "Non-Existent Youth Bill," due to its focus on depictions of purely fictional underage characters depicted in "harmful" ways. The emphasis on "harm" in debates surrounding the bill suggests that it is the threat such material represents to the development of highly normalized notions of "healthy" (that is, sexually innocent but still heterosexual) young people that is driving the legislation.

The Tokyo Metropolitan Authority's "Non-Existent Youth Bill"

As noted above, policies on sex education in Japan have tended to refer only to the reproductive functions of sex in the context of marriage. "Uncontrolled sex" outside of marriage is represented as both physically and morally dangerous, leading to the potential for unwanted pregnancy, disease, and estrangement from family and society. As Fu notes, even today, "sound and healthy societal maintenance features prominently in the sex education curriculum of Japanese schools."[46]

Given this attitude toward sex education in schools in Japan, it is no surprise that young people's access to a wide range of sexual texts and depictions in popular culture has been of concern to conservative politicians and lobby groups. Concerns about young people's exposure to sexually explicit materials and regulations aimed at protecting them are often discussed at the Tokyo Youth Affairs Conference, which is convened regularly by the Tokyo governor to review policies relating to youth residents within the Tokyo metropolitan area. In December 2008 the conference was convened for the twenty-eighth time. The purpose of the conference was to "address the wholesome development of youth in an era where mass media are increasing their spread within society." The conference made a number of recommendations concerning revision of the regulations for the protection of young people, in particular that restrictions be placed on the sale and distribution of manga, anime, and games depicting "non-existent youth" in "antisocial sexual situations." These draft proposals were made public and comments from the public invited.

In February 2010, the Tokyo Metropolitan Government's Office for Youth Affairs and Public Safety proposed a series of amendments to the Tokyo Metropolitan Ordinance Regarding the Healthy Development of Youth that were based on recommendations by the Tokyo Youth Affairs Conference. If adopted, the recommendations would have considerably increased the power of bureaucrats to make decisions concerning representations deemed harmful to young people, particularly around the category of child pornography. New provisions included the installation of filtering devices on mobile phones used by young people, and measures aimed at restricting the availability of imaginary visual representations of sexualized youth. Material featuring pornography or strong violence was already prohibited from sale to minors, but the proposed extension would have included publications featuring "non-existent youth"—that is, purely fictional or imaginary characters who could be "recognized" as looking like or sounding like they were under the age of eighteen and who were "recklessly" depicted in "antisocial" sexual scenarios. The rationale behind the revisions was that such representations "may highly impede the development of a healthy capacity for judgment regarding sexuality" and thereby "impede the healthy development of youth."

Officially known as Bill 156, the bill proposing changes to the ordinance was also referred to as the "Non-Existent Youth Bill," especially by its opponents. As the bill proceeded through various readings in the assembly, opposition mounted. In May, the Tokyo Bar Association issued a statement arguing that the bill was an intrusion by government into issues that were better handled by parents who should have oversight of their children's reading matter. The Japan Federation of Bar Associations also spoke out against the revisions, arguing that the current bill should be replaced with a new bill that placed emphasis on protecting the rights of real children instead of limiting their freedoms. On May 25, nearly 1,500 manga artists and ten publishers publicly protested the bill, maintaining that the wording was too vague and could significantly impede free speech because authors and publishers would be unable to anticipate what may or may not be restricted. On May 31, the Writers Guild of Japan also formally declared its opposition. In June, some of the manga artists, academics, journalists, and other intellectuals who opposed the bill published opinion papers in two books commenting on the debate.[47]

New media, including Twitter and YouTube, were also deployed to publicize the negative effects of the legislation and garner support to oppose it. Many of these interventions made the point that sexualized representations that might "appear to be" minors had become so commonplace throughout Japanese popular culture that contrary to Agnes Chan's assertions that such material appealed only to those of "a certain disposition," ordinary consumers and "regular people" (*ippan no hito*) ran the risk of being caught up by the legislation and branded "sex criminals" (*sei hanzaisha*). People were invited to reflect on their own consumption habits and to look through their collections of manga, anime, games, novels, art works, and music, and screen them for images that might "appear to be" minors and that might potentially be deemed "harmful to youth"—the insinuation being that most people would have some material that could fall into this category, given its ubiquity.

During May, opposition to the bill was also building in the Tokyo Metropolitan Assembly itself. Although the Liberal Democratic Party, the leader of the minority coalition government, supported the bill, it did not have the majority necessary to push through the revisions. The opposition Democratic Party of Japan, the largest single party, eventually withdrew its support for the bill in its current state and was said to be contemplating rejecting the bill outright. The DPJ was later joined in their opposition by the other two opposition parties. However, despite the concerns raised by all the opposition parties, Governor Ishihara continued to claim that the bill may be badly worded but that its intent was good and that the proposal should simply be sent back for redrafting. Despite his protestations, the bill was defeated in a vote before the entire assembly on June 16—the first time that a bill supported by Ishihara had been defeated during his decade-long tenure as governor. However,

Ishihara signaled his intent to reintroduce the bill later in 2010, and a revised version was duly made available for consultation in person at the city hall (but not on the Internet) on November 22. However, as critics pointed out, given that the winter assembly only sat between November 30 and December 15, this left little time for public consultation and debate.

The revised bill attempted to avoid the previous criticisms of vagueness by being more explicit as to which media were to be targeted and what kinds of depictions were to be considered harmful.[48] In the revised bill, the scope of the legislation was reduced—manga, anime, and computer games were specifically singled out for scrutiny, whereas real-life photography and literature were exempted. The original, vaguely phrased text—concerning "non-existent youth" depicted in scenarios liable to be "sexually stimulating"—was rephrased. The new bill targeted any character (irrespective of age) engaged in "sexual or pseudo-sexual acts that would be illegal in real life" or "sexual or pseudo sexual acts between close relatives whose marriage would be illegal" if presented in a manner that "glorifies or exaggerates" the acts in question.

These revisions did little to quiet the concerns of opponents of the bill. If anything, the manga and anime industry, as well as fans, felt that they were being unfairly targeted. Also the removal of the controversial (and much-ridiculed) term "non-existent youth" failed to staunch criticism given that the revised bill actually expands the target to offending characters of any age. In an article published in the May 2010 edition of current-affairs magazine *Tsukuru*, various opinions of critics of the bill were put forward.[49] These included Takemiya Keiko, one of Japan's most prominent and well-respected female manga artists and a key figure in the development of BL aesthetics, who argued that the wording of the bill was so vague that even her own classic manga *The Song of the Wind and the Trees* (*Kaze to ki no uta*; serialized from 1976 to 1984), which deals with homoerotic themes and sexual abuse, could fall under the regulations.[50] Takemiya later published an article which pointed out that it was ironic that *The Song of the Wind and the Trees*, a very popular manga that many of today's mothers had grown up reading, was now in danger of being banned as "harmful" to their children. [51]

Critic and scholar of BL and gender studies, Fujimoto Yukari, also got involved in the debate. Fujimoto christened the new bill the "Non-Existent Sex Crimes Bill" on her blog. As she stated:

> While the last revision was concerned with regulating "non-existent youth," this time the bill is unique in targeting "non-existent sex crimes." So the logic is that any illegal sex acts that would be subject to penalty should be regulated even when they are only drawn on paper.

Why stop at sex acts, Fujimoto went on to ask; why not regulate depictions of all illegal activity?[52]

Fujimoto also drew attention to the potential deleterious effects the bill could have on women's manga culture, particularly the BL genre that frequently engages themes of rape and incest. As she notes, "women, who are often considered to be victims of rape and incestuous relationships, often themselves adopt these themes in their works," going on to argue that

> speech is not always about the representations of objects of desire that exist in reality, nor about compelling parties to realize their desires in reality, but [the ability to engage in narrative speech] also provides to individuals who have the potential to be caught in such [abusive relations], a means of not only simulating and learning how to control such situations, but also helping to heal wounds that were inflicted as a result of such situations.[53]

Fujimoto is voicing concerns held by other feminist media commentators who have argued for the need for girls and young women to "articulate a 'missing discourse of desire'" that is "beyond the gaze of adults, the state and commercial interests."[54] Indeed, missing from this debate entirely were the voices of young people who, after all, are among the main consumers, and among the *dōjinshi* subculture, producers, of this material. In official government discourse, BL and other sexually explicit youth media were only ever positioned as problematic texts that minors should be protected from. However, as feminist academics have argued, the *dōjinshi* subculture and other sexually explicit youth media also give young people agency and are important sites for the development of "sexual subjectivities" that can critique the normative sex and gender roles supported by "official" government discourse.[55]

Despite the raising of these and other similar concerns, Bill 156 was passed by the Tokyo Legislative Assembly on December 15, 2010. Self regulation on the part of publishers was mandated from April 1, 2011, and sales regulation enforcement began on July 1, 2011.[56] Following on from this development, in 2013 the ruling Liberal Democratic Party's Policy Research Council made the recommendation that existing child pornography legislation be brought in line with that of many Western countries and expanded to capture even purely fictional images that "violate the rights of children."[57] This led to an outcry from Tokyo's Comic Market, and representatives from the manga and anime industries who argued that the emphasis on *images* once more meant their products would be unfairly targeted.[58]

Conclusion

As can be seen from the preceding discussion, the context surrounding the controversies generated by BL and other sexually explicit media is rather different from that in many Western societies, where depictions of characters who may "appear to be" under age in sexual scenarios are caught up in child pornography legislation. The production and consumption of this material in the West is therefore an even more serious and morally fraught issue than in Japan, which only introduced restrictions on the simple possession of child pornography materials in 2014. It should be recalled that the "Non-Existent Youth Bill" was never about banning this material altogether but simply restricting its availability to minors in the Tokyo area. However, as opponents of the bill pointed out, the legislation is certain to have an impact on artists and publishers who could lose access to one of their most valuable markets.

The attacks that conservative politicians and lobby groups have launched on sexually explicit media, and on BL specifically, need to be understood in the context of the "gender-free" debate that has been taking place in Japan over the last two decades. Conservative policymakers such as Ishihara seem to believe that Japan's current economic woes and declining birth rate are directly linked to the erosion of traditional values, in particular, clear gender roles for men and women.[59] It is easy to see, then, how BL, which deliberately plays with and subverts male authority and the kind of "wholesome" relations between the sexes inculcated in the sex education system, can be seen as "dangerous to youth." While the "pornographic" nature of manga and other media directed at boys has been a source of concern since at least the late 1960s, girls and their reading matter are now being increasingly placed under scrutiny. As Daisuke Okabe and Kimi Ishida argue, "*fujoshi* culture involve[s] not only the creative reshaping of mainstream fantasy narratives and sexuality but also the playfully undercover subversion of gender expectations."[60] No doubt the thrill of the "transgressive desire" shared among the *fujoshi*'s "rotten friendships" (discussed by Galbraith in this volume) is enhanced because these desires run contra to the normative discourses encoded in state and local government policies that seek to reaffirm differences between the sexes and keep girls "pure" in readiness for their future roles as wives and mothers. As a response to these heightened calls for the "zoning" of BL materials, feminist critics have pointed out how this would amount to discrimination against women's sexual self-expression."[61]

The Tokyo Metropolitan Authority's use of zoning laws to restrict young people's access to sexually explicit manga is, in an age of convergent media, unlikely to be very successful, especially given the highly sexualized nature of amateur *dōjinshi* that freely circulate via the Internet. The very fact that BL fans have themselves embraced the "rotten" signifier also indicates that there is a great deal of active resistance among young people to the manner in which agents of the Japanese state continue to promote fixed, normalized gender roles through educational and other policies. Indeed, as I have suggested, the very embrace of the term "rotten" is given heightened effect when juxtaposed with the "purity" narratives still embedded in official sex education discourse.

Despite the increased controversy that BL narratives have become embroiled in over the last decade, what is encouraging in the Japanese context is the scale of opposition to government attempts to legislate on what constitutes the "healthy development" of youth. As was seen in the Sakai library incident, a broad coalition of female legislators and academics, as well as readers, opposed the removal of BL items from a public facility, and succeeded in having them restored to circulation. Although the "Non-Existent Youth Bill" passed, it did galvanize a wide-based opposition and enabled extensive public debate about the nature of childhood, freedom of expression, and the role of the state in promulgating fixed, normative gender roles. However, as recent moves by the Liberal Democratic Party to further extend the reach of child pornography law to include fictitious images show, BL is likely to remain a controversial and contested form of girls' culture in Japan. In addition, Tokyo's winning bid to host the 2020 summer Olympics is also likely to give conservative legislators the impetus to "clean up" aspects of Japanese popular culture that may be disapproved of by overseas visitors.[62]

The existence of BL subcultures outside Japan is even more perilous. In contrast to the public furor that greeted the "Non-Existent Youth Bill" in Japan, the recent redrafting of "child-abuse publications" legislation in counties such as Australia, the UK, and Canada to include purely fictional characters has largely been overlooked by the media and no concerted opposition from academics, liberal legislators, or indeed readers and fans themselves has emerged to challenge this legislative creep. BL, and Japanese manga and anime in general, are likely to remain key objects of surveillance in Western societies, as the common supposition that they pose a danger to youth goes unchallenged by the media, academia, and fandom alike.

Notes

1. James Fallows, "The Japanese Are Different from You and Me," *Atlantic Monthly*, no. 258 (September 1986): 38; see also Mark McLelland, "Interpretation and Orientalism: Outing Japan's Sexual Minorities to the English-Speaking World," in *After Orientalism: Critical*

Entanglements, Productive Looks, ed. Inge Boer (Amsterdam: Rodopi, 2003), 106, for other instances.

2. Mark McLelland, "Australia's Child-Abuse Materials Legislation, Internet Regulation, and the Juridification of the Imagination," *International Journal of Cultural Studies* 15, no. 5 (2012): 470–71.

3. UNICEF, "Child Rights Advocates Seek to Strengthen Laws against Child Pornography in Japan," March 31, 2010, http://www.unicef.org/infobycountry/japan_53219.html; and Isabel Reynolds, "UNICEF Says Japan Failing to Control Child Porn," *Reuters UK*, March 11, 2008, http://uk.reuters.com/article/idUKT20430220080311.

4. Agnes Chan, "Kids Need Protection from Sex Abuse Porn," *Asahi shinbun*, May 3, 2010, http://www.asahi.com/english/TKY201005020231.html.

5. McLelland, "Australia's Child-Abuse Materials Legislation," 470.

6. Ibid.

7. The Ministry of Education (Monbushō) was in 2001 merged with the Science and Technology Agency and is now known as the Ministry of Education, Culture, Sports, Science and Technology. In this chapter, I continue to refer to it as the Ministry of Education for convenience.

8. Anita Harris, "Discourses of Desire as Governmentality: Young Women, Sexuality and the Significance of Safe Spaces," *Feminism and Psychology* 15, no. 1 (2005): 42.

9. Huiyan Fu, "The Bumpy Road to Socialise Nature: Sex Education in Japan," *Culture, Health and Sexuality* 13, no. 8 (2011): 904.

10. Sharon Kinsella, *Adult Manga* (London: RoutledgeCurzon 2000), 139.

11. See, for example, Stephen McGinty, "Japan's Darkest Secrets: the Dark Side of the Orient," *Scotsman*, August 31, 2002, http://www.highbeam.com/doc/1P2-18749960.html; see also the discussion in McLelland, "Interpretation and Orientalism."

12. Kirsten Cather, *The Art of Censorship in Postwar Japan* (Honolulu: University of Hawai'i Press, 2012), 221.

13. Kinsella, *Adult Manga*, 140.

14. Ibid., 143.

15. Cited in Cather, *Art of Censorship*, 257.

16. Cited in Kinsella, *Adult Manga*, 127.

17. Ibid., 149, 150.

18. Sharalyn Orbaugh, "Girls Reading Harry Potter, Girls Writing Desire: Amateur Manga and *Shōjo* Reading Practices," in *Girl Reading Girl in Japan*, ed. Tomoko Aoyama and Barbara Hartley (London: Routledge, 2010), 177.

19. Ibid.

20. The issue was first raised on the Sakai city local council's "citizens' voice" Q&A page on July 30, 2008. The email and the library's initial response was accessed on December 30, 2008, http://www.city.sakai.osaka.jp/city/info/_shimin/data/5374.html.

21. A copy of Ueno's letter to the library can be found on the blog *Midori no ichi-go ichi-e*, accessed on July 31, 2012, http://blog.goo.ne.jp/midorineto02/e/26c039ea8b73a72bf86188c06 cfbffb4.

22. A detailed step-by-step outline of the developing controversy and various responses can be found on feminist activist Teramachi Midori's blog *Teramachi Midori no uebupeeji* from December 2008, under the title "Jendaa tosho haijo jiken: Sakai shiritsu toshokan & Fukui-ken jōhō kōkai soshō" [Gender publications exclusion incidents: Sakai Municipal

Library and the Fukui prefecture access to information lawsuit], http://gifu.kenmin.net/midori/news/68.html. The controversy is still very much alive at the time of writing, and in October 2012 it was the topic of a lecture by Teramachi at the free speech organization Uguisu Ribbon: see "Sakai shiritsu toshokan BL shōsetsu haiki yōkyū jiken o furikaeru" [Looking back on the Sakai city library BL novels exclusion and reinstatement incident], *Uguisu ribon*, http://www.jfsribbon.org/2012/10/bl.html.

23. "Nayamashii 'Bōizurabu': Sakai no toshokan shōsetsu 5500 satsu" [Troubling "boys love": Sakai library has 5500 fiction volumes], *Asahi shinbun*, November 5, 2008.

24. "BL shōsetsu 18 kin no hazu ga Sakai-shi toshokan ga itten kashidashi kaikin" [BL novels should be limited to those over 18 but the Sakai city library has changed course and lifted its ban], *J-CAST nyūzu*, December 12, 2008, http://www.jcast.com/2008/12/28032951.html?p=2.

25. I followed these debates on *mixi* at the time but since this social networking site is available to members only, I have not been able to list the URLs here.

26. Atsuta Keiko, "'BL' haijo kara mieta sabetsu to sei no kyōju no ishuku" [Discrimination and the decline of the enjoyment of sex from the perspective of removal of "BL"], *Yuriika* 44, no. 15 (December 2012): 186.

27. This information comes from a series of emails passed on to me from an academic gender studies mailing list in Japanese that reported on a meeting of the Kuwana City Council on March 12, 2009, where the issue of BL acquisitions in libraries was challenged. Members on the list pointed to the increased scrutiny of BL in libraries as a "leading case" in the backlash against supposed gender-free policies being employed by local councils.

28. Ueno Chizuko, "Sakai shiritsu toshokan BL hon haijo sōdō tenmatsu" [The circumstances surrounding the controversial exclusion of BL books at Sakai Municipal Library], *Tsukuru* 39, no. 5 (May 2009). This argument is also made by Atsuta, "'BL' haijo kara mieta sabetsu."

29. Osawa Mari, "Japanese Government Approaches to Gender Equality since the Mid 1990s," *Asian Perspective* 29, no. 1 (2005): 159.

30. Ibid., 161.

31. Ayako Kano, "Backlash, Fight Back, and Back-Pedaling: Responses to State Feminism in Contemporary Japan," *International Journal of Asian Studies* 8, no. 1 (2011): 42.

32. Osawa, "Japanese Government Approaches to Gender Equality," 162.

33. Ibid., 161.

34. Kano, "Backlash, Fight Back, and Back-Pedaling," 45.

35. Ibid.

36. Hyōdō Chika, "HIV/AIDS, Gender and Backlash," in *Another Japan is Possible: New Social Movements and Global Citizenship Education*, ed. Jennifer Chan (Stanford, CA: Stanford University Press 2008), 200.

37. Genaro Castro-Vasquez, *In the Shadows: Sexuality, Pedagogy and Gender among Japanese Teenagers* (Lanham, MD: Lexington Books, 2007), 34.

38. Fu, "The Bumpy Road," 906.

39. Ibid., 907; Hyōdō, "HIV/AIDS, Gender and Backlash," 200.

40. Kerry Robinson, "'Difficult Citizenship': The Precarious Relationship between Childhood, Sexuality and Access to Knowledge," *Sexualities* 15, nos. 3–4 (2012): 269–70.

41. Naitō Chizuko, "Reorganizations of Gender and Nationalism: Gender Bashing and Loliconized Japanese Society," *Mechademia* 5 (2010): 327.

42. Fu, "The Bumpy Road," 908.

43. Women's Asia 21, "Unbelievable Events Happening in Japan Motivated by Conservative Politicians," *Voices from Japan*, no. 17 (Summer 2006).

44. Naitō, "Reorganizations of Gender and Nationalism," 329.

45. Japan Civil Liberties Union, Committee on Elimination of Discrimination against Women, "The Third Consideration of Japanese Governmental Report: Proposal of List of Issues for Pre-Sessional Working Group," January 27, 2003, http://www.jclu.org/katsudou/seimei_ikensho/20030127e/03speech.html; "Ishihara's Homophobic Remarks Raise Ire of Gays," *Japan Policy and Politics*, April 3, 2000, http://business.highbeam.com/435558/article-1G1-61635352/feature-ishihara-homophobic-remarks-raise-ire-gays.

46. Fu, "The Bumpy Road," 903.

47. These were Comic Ryū henshū-bu, ed. *Hijitsuzai seishōnen tokuhon* [Non-existent youth reader] (Tokyo: Tokuma shoten, 2010); and Saizō and Hyōgen no jiyū o kangaeru kai, eds., *Hijitsuzai seishōnen kisei hantai tokuhon* [Nonexistent youth restriction opposition reader] (Tokyo: Saizō, 2010).

48. The controversy surrounding the bill, including links to major debates and documents, is detailed in the Wikipedia entry: Wikipedia, s.v. "Tōkyō-to seishōnen no kenzen na ikusei ni kan suru jōrei," last modified July 14, 2013, http://ja.wikipedia.org/wiki/東京都青少年の健全な育成に関する条例.

49. Nagaoka Yoshiyuki, "Manga no sei hyōgen kisei o neratta tōjōrei kaitei meguru kōbō" [Concerning the pros and cons of pursuing reform of local ordinances regulating sexual expression in manga], *Tsukuru* 40, no. 5 (June 2010).

50. Takemiya Keiko, *Kaze to ki no uta* [The song of the wind and the trees], 10 vols. (1976–1984; Tokyo: Hakusensha bunko, 1995).

51. Takemiya Keiko, "*Kaze to ki no uta* wa auto! Aidentiti o mamoru tame ni" [*The Song of the Wind and the Trees* is out! For the sake of protecting identity], *Popyuraa karuchaa kenkyū* 5, no. 1 (2011).

52. Fujimoto Yukari, "Bill 156—The Nonexistent Crimes Bill (Fujimoto's Analysis Translated)," trans. Dan Kanemitsu, *Dan Kanemitsu's Paper Trail*, December 5, 2012, http://dankanemitsu.wordpress.com/2010/12/05/bill-156-the-nonexistent-crimes-bill-fujimotos-analysis-translated/.

53. Ibid.

54. Harris, "Discourses of Desire as Governmentality," 42.

55. Ibid.; see also Orbaugh "Girls Reading Harry Potter," 178, for a discussion of the functions of women's self-publishing and reading communities.

56. "Ordinance Passed against Manga 'Extreme Sex,'" *Japan Times*, December 16, 2010, http://search.japantimes.co.jp/rss/nn20101216a4.html.

57. "Controversy Raging over Revisions to Child Pornography Law," *Asahi shinbun* July 27, 2013, http://ajw.asahi.com/article/behind_news/social_affairs/AJ201307270063.

58. Komikku maaketto junbikai, "Jidō poruno kinshi hōan ni tai suru iken hyōmei" [Declaration of opinion concerning the child pornography law plan], May 29, 2013, http://www.comiket.co.jp/info-a/C84/C84Notice2.html; Nihon manga gakkai, "Jidō poruno kinshi hō kaiseian hantaiseimei" [Statement of opposition to the proposed reform of the child pornography law], May 31, 2013, http://www.jsscc.net/info/130531.

59. Naitō, "Reorganizations of Gender and Nationalism," 329.

60. Daisuke Okabe and Kimi Ishida, "Making Fujoshi Identity Visible and Invisible," in *Fandom Unbound: Otaku Culture in a Connected World*, ed. Mizuko Ito, Daisuke Okabe, and Izumi Tsuji (New Haven, CT: Yale University Press, 2012), 222.

61. Atsuta, "'BL' haijo kara mieta sabetsu," 190.

62. See, for example, Betsy Gomez, "Tokyo Olympics Emboldens Censors," *Comic Book Legal Defense Fund*, September 12, 2013, http://cbldf.org/2013/09/tokyo-olympics -emboldens-censors/.

WORKS CITED

Please note: Original serialization dates for manga later published in independent volumes are provided for manga when known. For ongoing series, the number of volumes published is current as of late 2013.

Commas are not used to separate authors' surnames and given names for publications written in Japanese by Japanese authors or for published translations where the author's name is given in the Japanese order.

Abnorm. *Island*. Japan: Self-published, ca. 1979.

Aida Miho. "Komikku maaketto no genzai: Sabukaruchaa ni kan suru kōsatsu" [The contemporary Comic Market: A consideration of Japanese Subculture]. *Hiroshima shūdai ronshū, jinbun-hen* 45, no. 2 (2005): 149–201.

Aida Saki. *Deadlock*. Tokyo: Tokuma shoten, 2006.

Akisato Wakuni. *Tomoi*. 1986. Tokyo: Shōgakukan bunko, 1996.

Allison, Anne. *Permitted and Prohibited Desires: Mothers, Comics, and Censorship in Japan*. Berkeley: University of California Press, 2000.

Anderson, Benedict. *Imagined Communities: Reflections on the Origins and Spread of Nationalism*. New ed. London: Verso, 2006.

Angles, Jeffrey. *Writing the Love of Boys: Origins of Bishōnen Culture in Modernist Japanese Literature*. Minneapolis: University of Minnesota Press, 2011.

Aoike Yasuko. *Ibu no musuko tachi* [Eve's sons]. 3 vols. 1976–1979. Tokyo: Hakusensha, 1995.

Aoyama Tomoko. "The Cooking Man in Modern Japanese Literature." In *Asian Masculinities: The Meaning and Practice of Manhood in China and Japan*, edited by Kam Louie and Morris Low, 155–76. London: RoutledgeCurzon, 2003.

———. "*Eureka* Discovers *Culture Girls, Fujoshi*, and *BL*: Essay Review of Three Issues of the Japanese Literary Magazine, *Yuriika* (Eureka)." *Intersections: Gender and Sexuality in Asia and the Pacific* 20 (2009). http://intersections.anu.edu.au/issue20/aoyama.htm.

———. "Literary Daughters' Recipes: Food and Female Subjectivity in the Writings of Mori Mari and Kōda Aya." *Japanstudien* 12 (2000): 91–116.

———. "Male Homosexuality as Treated by Japanese Women Writers." In *The Japanese Trajectory: Modernisation and Beyond*, edited by Gavan McCormack and Yoshio Sugimoto, 186–204. Cambridge: Cambridge University Press, 1988.

———. *Reading Food in Modern Japanese Literature*. Honolulu: University of Hawai'i Press, 2008.

———. "Transgendering *Shōjo Shōsetsu*: Girls' Inter-text/sex-uality." In *Genders, Transgenders and Sexualities in Japan*, edited by Mark McLelland and Romit Dasgupta, 49–64. London: Routledge, 2005.

———. "Yoshinaga Fumi no manga ni miru 'shoku' to jendaa" ['Food' and gender in the manga of Yoshinaga Fumi]. *Center for Comparative Japanese Studies Annual Bulletin* (Ochanomizu University) 6 (2010): 153–61.

Aoyama Tomoko, and Barbara Hartley. "Introduction." In *Girl Reading Girl in Japan*, edited by Tomoko Aoyama and Barbara Hartley, 1–14. London: Routledge, 2010.

Araki Hirohiko. *Jo Jo no kimyō na bōken* [Jo Jo's bizarre adventure]. 63 vols. 1987–1999. Tokyo: Janpu komikkusu, 1987–1999.

Asupekuto. *Raito BL e yōkoso* [Welcome to light BL]. Tokyo: Ōunsha, 2012.

Atkins, Paul. "Chigo in the Medieval Japanese Imagination." *Journal of Asian Studies* 67, no. 3 (2008): 947–70.

Atsuta Keiko. "'BL' haijo kara mieta sabetsu to sei no kyōju no ishuku" [Discrimination and the decline of the enjoyment of sex from the perspective of the removal of "BL"]. *Yuriika* 44, no. 15 (December 2012): 184–91.

Awaji Nae. *Kisu mii chokoreeto* [Kiss me chocolate]. Tokyo: Libre, 2009.

Azuma Sonoko. "Mōsō no kyōdōtai: 'Yaoi' komyuniti ni okeru ren'ai kōdo no kinō" [Fantasy community: The function of the love code in the 'yaoi' community]. In *Shisō chizu, vol. 5: Shakai no hihyō*, edited by Azuma Hiroki and Kitada Akihiro, 249–74. Tokyo: NHK shuppan, 2010.

———. "Onna no homosōsharu na yokubō no yukue: Niji sōsaku 'yaoi' ni tsuite no ichi kōsatsu" [In search of the female desire for homosociality: Thoughts on *yaoi* and derivative writings]. In *Bunka no shakaigaku: Kioku, media, shintai*, edited by Ōno Michikuni and Ogawa Nobuhiko, 263–80. Tokyo: Bunrikaku, 2009.

b-Boy. "Suki na mono wa suki!!" Vol. 3 (1992): 75–79.

Barthes, Roland. *The Rustle of Language*. Translated by Richard Howard. New York: Hill and Wang, 1986.

Berlant, Lauren, and Michael Warner. "Sex in Public." In *Queer Studies: An Interdisciplinary Reader*, edited by Robert J. Corber and Stephen Velocchi, 170–86. Malden, MA: Blackwell, 2003

Bersani, Leo. *A Future for Astyanax: Character and Desire in Literature*. 1976. New York: Columbia University Press, 1984.

Bessatsu Takarajima, no. 358. *Watashi o Komike ni tsuretette!: Kyōdai komikku dōjinshi maaketto no subete* [Take me to Komike! All about the giant *dōjinshi* market]. Tokyo: Takarajimasha, 1998.

Bey, Hakim. *T.A.Z.: Ichijiteki jiritsu zōn*. Translated by Yū Minowa. Tokyo: Inpakuto sha, 1997. Originally published as *T.A.Z.: The Temporary Autonomous Zone, Ontological Anarchy, Poetic Terrorism* (Brooklyn, NY: Autonomedia, 1985).

Bhabha, Homi. *The Location of Culture*. London: Routledge, 1994.

Budōuri Kusuko. "Fudanshi fukei jisho nenpyō: Hosokuban for fudanshi nau" [A chronological table of *fudanshi* and *fukei* (rotten older brothers): Supplemental version for contemporary *fudanshi*]. Japan: Self-published PDF. http://p.booklog.jp/book/54367.

Bungei shunjū. "Shōwa no bidan besuto 50" [The 50 most handsome men of the Showa era]. February 2008, 156–66.

Butler, Judith. "The Forces of Fantasy: Feminism, Mapplethorpe, and Discursive Excess." In *Feminism and Pornography*, edited by Drucilla Cornell, 487–508. Oxford: Oxford University Press, 2007.

Carter, Angela. *The Sadeian Woman: An Exercise in Cultural History*. London: Virago Press, 2006.

Castro-Vasquez, Genaro. *In the Shadows: Sexuality, Pedagogy and Gender among Japanese Teenagers*. Lanham, MD: Lexington Books, 2007.

Cather, Kirsten. *The Art of Censorship in Postwar Japan*. Honolulu: University of Hawai'i Press, 2012.

Childs, Margaret H. "The Value of Vulnerability: Sexual Coercion and the Nature of Love in Japanese Court Literature." *Journal of Asian Studies* 58, no. 4 (1999): 1059–79.

Comic Market. See Komikku Maaketto.

Comic Ryū henshū-bu, ed. *Hijitsuzai seishōnen tokuhon* [Non-existent youth reader]. Tokyo: Tokuma shoten, 2010.

Comiket. See Komikku Maaketto.

Corber, Robert J., and Stephen Velocchi. "Introduction." In *Queer Studies: An Interdisciplinary Reader*, edited by Robert J. Corber and Stephen Velocchi, 1–20. Malden, MA: Blackwell, 2003.

———. *Queer Studies: An Interdisciplinary Reader*, edited by Robert J. Corber and Stephen Valocchi. Malden, MA: Blackwell, 2003.

Death in Venice. Motion picture. Directed by Luchino Visconti. Italy: Alfa Cinematografica, 1971.

de Lauretis, Teresa. *Technologies of Gender: Essays on Theory, Film and Fiction*. Bloomington: Indiana University Press, 1987.

Deleuze, Gilbert. *Foucault*. Translated by Seán Hand. Minneapolis: University of Minnesota Press, 1988.

Deleuze, Gilles, and Félix Guattari. *A Thousand Plateaus: Capitalism and Schizophrenia*. Translated by Brian Massumi. Minneapolis: University of Minnesota Press, 1987.

Dollase, Hiromi Tsuchiya. "Ribbons Undone: The *Shōjo* Story Debates in Pre-War Japan." In *Girl Reading Girl in Japan*, edited by Tomoko Aoyama and Barbara Hartley, 80–91. London: Routledge, 2010.

Dostoevsky, Fyodor. *Notes from the Underground*; *The Double*. Translated by Jessie Coulson. Harmondsworth, England: Penguin, 1989.

Doty, Alexander. "Queer Theory." In *Film Studies: Critical Approaches*, edited by John Hill and Pamela Church Gibson, 146–50. Oxford: Oxford University Press, 2000.

Eagleton, Terry. "Edible Écriture." In *Consuming Passions: Food in the Age of Anxiety*, edited by Sian Griffiths and Jennifer Wallace, 203–208. Manchester, England: Mandolin, 1998.

Eng, Lawrence. "Strategies of Engagement: Discovering, Defining, and Describing Otaku Culture in the United States." In *Fandom Unbound: Otaku Culture in a Connected World*, edited by Mizuko Ito, Daisuke Okabe, and Izumi Tsuji, 85–104. New Haven, CT: Yale University Press, 2012.

Evans, Dylan. *An Introductory Dictionary of Lacanian Psychoanalysis*. London: Routledge, 2001.

Fallows, James. "The Japanese Are Different from You and Me." *Atlantic Monthly*, no. 258 (September 1986): 35–42.

Fiske, John. "The Cultural Economy of Fandom." In *The Adoring Audience*, edited by Linda A. Lewis, 30–49. New York: Routledge, 1992.

Foucault, Michel. *History of Sexuality*. Vol. 3. *The Care of the Self*. Translated by Robert Hurley. Harmondsworth, England: Penguin, 1986.

Freedman, Alisa. "*Train Man* and the Gender Politics of Japanese '*Otaku*' Culture: The Rise of New Media, Nerd Heroes and Consumer Communities." *Intersections: Gender and Sexuality in Asia and the Pacific* 20 (April 2009). http://intersections.anu.edu.au/issue20/freedman.htm.

Freud, Sigmund. "'A Child is Being Beaten': A Contribution to the Study of the Origin of Sexual Perversions." In *The Standard Edition of the Complete Psychological Works of Sigmund Freud*, vol. 17, edited and translated by James Strachey, 175–204. London: The Hogarth Press, 1955.

Fu, Huiyan. "The Bumpy Road to Socialise Nature: Sex Education in Japan." *Culture, Health and Sexuality* 13, no. 8 (2011): 903–15.

Fujimoto Sumiko. "Kankeisei kara miru BL no genzai" [Examining contemporary BL works through the concept of matchmaking]. *Yuriika* 39, no. 16 (December 2007): 89–95.

Fujimoto Yukari. "Bunshin: Shōjo manga no naka no 'mō hitori no watashi'" [Alter ego: 'Another me' in *shōjo* manga]. In *Manga no shakaigaku*, edited by Miyahara Kōjirō and Ogino Masahiro, 68–131. Kyoto: Sekai shisō sha, 2001.

———. "*Shōjo* manga ni okeru '*shōnen'ai*' no imi" [The meaning of "*shōnen'ai*" in *shōjo* manga]. *Nyū feminizumu rebyū* 2 (1991): 280–84.

———. "Shōnen'ai/yaoi, BL: 2007-nen genzai no shiten kara" [*Shōnen'ai, yaoi*, and BL: From the perspective of 2007]. *Yuriika* 39, no. 16 (December 2007): 36–47.

———. "Takahashi Macoto: The Origin of Shōjo Manga Style." Translated by Matt Thorn. *Mechademia* 7 (2012): 24–55.

———. "Transgender: Female Hermaphrodites and Male Androgynes." Translated by Linda Flores and Kazumi Nagaike. Translation edited by Sharalyn Orbaugh. *U.S.–Japan Women's Journal* 27 (2004): 76–117.

———. *Watashi no ibasho wa doko ni aru no? Shōjo manga ga utsusu kokoro no katachi* [Where do I belong? The shape of the heart reflected in *shōjo* manga]. Tokyo: Gakuyō shobō, 1998.

Galbraith, Patrick W. "*Fujoshi*: Fantasy Play and Transgressive Intimacy among 'Rotten Girls' in Contemporary Japan." *Signs* 37, no. 1 (2011): 211–32.

———. "*Lolicon*: The Reality of 'Virtual Child Pornography' in Japan." *Image and Narrative* 12, no. 1 (2011): 83–114. http://www.imageandnarrative.be/index.php/imagenarrative/article/view/127.

———. "*Moe*: Exploring Virtual Potential in Post-Millennial Japan." *Electronic Journal of Contemporary Japanese Studies* (October 2009). http://www.japanesestudies.org.uk/articles/2009/Galbraith.html.

———. *Otaku Spaces*. With photographs by Androniki Christodoulou. Seattle: Chin Music Press, 2012.

Giddens, Anthony. *The Transformation of Intimacy: Sexuality, Love and Eroticism in Modern Societies*. Cambridge: Polity Press, 1992.

Goffman, Erving. *Gender Advertisements*. Cambridge, MA: Harvard University Press, 1979.

Graeber, David. *Fragments of an Anarchist Anthropology*. Chicago: Prickly Paradigm Press, 2004.

Greer, Germaine. *The Boy*. London: Thames and Hudson, 2003.

Gregson, Kimberly S. "What if the Lead Character Looks Like Me? Girl Fans of *Shoujo Anime* and Their Web Sites." In *Girl Wide Web: Girls, the Internet, and the Negotiation of Identity*, edited by Sharon R. Mazzarella, 121–40. New York: Peter Lang, 2005.

Hagio Moto. "Jūichigatsu no gimunajiumu" [November gymnasium]. 1971. In her *Jūichigatsu no gimunajiumu*, 3–48. Tokyo: Shōgakukan bunko, 1995.

———. "The Moto Hagio Interview." By Matt Thorn. *Comics Journal*, no. 269 (July 2005): 138–75.

———. *Pō no ichizoku* [The Poe clan]. 3 vols. 1972–1976. Tokyo: Shōgakukan bunko, 1998.

———. *Tōma no shinzō*. 1974. Tokyo: Shōgakukan bunko, 1995. Published in English as *The Heart of Thomas*, translated by Matt Thorn (Seattle: Fantagraphics, 2012).

Hagio Moto, Miura Shion, Kondō Fumie, Toshima Miho, Higashi Naoko, Matsuoka Natsuki, and Fukuda Rika. "Yoshinaga Fumi wa suki desu ka?" [Do you like Yoshinaga Fumi?], special feature, *Da Vinci* 166 (February 2008): 148–61.

Happii fujoshi [Happy *fujoshi*]. Tokyo: Hobii Japan, 2007.

Harata Shin'ichirō. "Vaacharu 'jidō poruno' kisei no ronri to 'moe' no rinri" [The logic of regulating "virtual child pornography" and the ethics of "*moe*"]. *Shakaijōhōgaku kenkyū* 11, no. 1 (2006): 109–120.

Harris, Anita. "Discourses of Desire as Governmentality: Young Women, Sexuality and the Significance of Safe Spaces." *Feminism and Psychology* 15, no. 1 (2005): 39–43.

Hartley, Barbara. "Performing the Nation: Magazine Images of Women and Girls in the Illustration of Takabatake Kashō." *Intersections: Gender and Sexuality in Asia and the Pacific* 16 (2008). http://intersections.anu.edu.au/issue16/hartley.htm.

Hatsu Akiko. "Yaoi no moto wa 'share' deshita: Hatsu kōkai, yaoi no tanjō" [Yaoi started as a 'joke': Public for the first time, the birth of *yaoi*]. *JUNE*, no. 73 (November 1993): 136.

Hikawa Reiko, Kotani Mari, and Arimitsu Mamiko. "Kyōraku suru shōjotachi: Shōjo bunka no genzaikei: Dōjinshi/Komikku maaketto/yaoi" [Girls enjoying themselves: The present situation of girl culture: *Dōjinshi*, the Comic Market, and *yaoi*]. *Imago* 6, no. 4 (April 1995): 136–50.

Honda Masuko. *Ofiiria no keifu: Arui wa shi to otome no tawamure* [The genealogy of Ophelia; Or, playing at death and the maiden]. Tokyo: Kōbunsha, 1989.

———. "The Genealogy of *hirahira*: Liminality and the Girl." Translated by Tomoko Aoyama and Barbara Hartley. In *Girl Reading Girl in Japan*, edited by Tomoko Aoyama and Barbara Hartley, 19–37. London: Routledge, 2010.

Hori Akiko. "Yaoi wa gei sabetsu ka?: Manga hyōgen to tashaka" [Does *yaoi* discriminate against gay men?: Manga portrayals and the creation of "others"]. In *Sabetsu to haijo no ima 6: Sekushuariti no tayōsei to haijo*, edited by Yoshii Hiroaki, 21–54. Tokyo: Akashi shoten, 2010.

Hori, Hikari. "Views from Elsewhere: Female Shoguns in Yoshinaga Fumi's *Ōoku* and Their Precursors in Japanese Popular Culture." *Japanese Studies* 32, no. 1 (2012): 77–95.

Hoshino Lily. *Rabu kue* [Love quest]. Tokyo: Hōbunsha, 2006.

Hyōdō Chika. "HIV/AIDS, Gender and Backlash." In *Another Japan is Possible: New Social Movements and Global Citizenship Education*, edited by Jennifer Chan, 198–202. Stanford, CA: Stanford University Press, 2008.

Ichikawa Kōichi. "Comiket." Interview by Patrick Galbraith. In *The Otaku Encyclopedia: An Insider's Guide to the Subculture of Cool Japan*, by Patrick W. Galbraith, 46–48. Tokyo: Kodansha International, 2009.

Ikeda Michiko. "Danshokuron: Shisutaa bōi no miryoku" [On male homosexuality: The charms of sister boys]. *Fujin kōron* 41, no. 11 (November 1957): 168–73.

Ikeda Riyoko. *Berusaiyu no bara* [The rose of Versailles]. 5 vols. 1972–1973. Tokyo: Shūeisha bunko, 1994.

Ikeda Shinobu. "The Image of Women in Battle Scenes: 'Sexually' Imprinted Bodies." In *Gender and Power in the Japanese Visual Field*, edited by Joshua Mostow, Maribeth Graybill, and Norman Bryson, 35–48. Honolulu: University of Hawai'i Press, 2003.

Inagaki Taruho. *Shōnen'ai no bigaku* [Aesthetics of boy loving]. Tokyo: Tokuma shoten, 1968.

Inoue Takehiko. *Slam Dunk*. 31 vols. Tokyo: Shūeisha, 1991–1996.

Irigaray, Luce. *This Sex Which is Not One*. Translated by Catherine Porter and Carolyn Burke. New York: Cornell University Press, 1985.

Irokawa Nao. "Byōki o idaki tsuzuketai onna ni 'kagaisei' wa jikaku dekinai" [Women who wish to maintain their propensity are incapable of realizing their "malicious intents"]. In *Choisir yaoi ronsō gappon II*, edited by Irokawa Nao, 28–33. Japan: Self-published, 1994.

———. "Tadai na konwaku no ato no awai teinen" [A faint sense of resignation after great confusion]. In *Choisir yaoi ronsō gappon V*, by Irokawa, 46–48. Japan: Self-published, 1996.

Ishida Hitoshi. "Gei ni kyōkan suru joseitachi" [Women identify with gay men]. *Yuriika* 39, no. 7 (June 2007): 47–62.

———. "'Hottoite kudasai' to iu hyōmei o megutte: Yaoi/BL no jiritsusei to hyōshō no ōdatsu" [On the declaration "Please leave me alone": The autonomy of *yaoi*/BL and the appropriation of representation]. *Yuriika* 39, no. 16 (December 2007): 114–23.

———. "Sūji de miru *JUNE* to *Sabu*" [*JUNE* and *Sabu* by the numbers]. *Yuriika* 44, no. 15 (December 2012): 159–71.

Ishida Minori. *Hisoyaka na kyōiku: "Yaoi/bōizu rabu" zenshi* [A secret education: The prehistory of yaoi/boys love]. Kyoto: Rakuhoku shuppan, 2008.

Ishikawa Yū. "Monogatari tekusuto no saiseisei no rikigaku: Yaoi no monogatari ron teki bunseki o chūshin to shite" [The dynamics of reproducing narratives: A narratological analysis of *yaoi*]. Ph.D. diss., Osaka Municipal University, 2012.

Ishiwari Osamu, and Maruo Toshirō. *Tanaka Kinuyo: Nihon no eiga joyū* [Tanaka Kinuyo: Japanese movie actress]. Tokyo: Waizu shuppan, 2008.

Itō Gō. *Manga wa kawaru: "Manga gatari" kara "manga ron" e* [Manga changes: From "manga narrative" to "manga discourse"]. Tokyo: Seidōsha, 2007.

Itō Kimio. *Danseigaku nyūmon* [An introduction to men's studies]. Tokyo: Sakuhinsha, 1996.

Ito, Kinko. *A Sociology of Japanese Ladies' Comics: Images of the Life, Loves, and Sexual Fantasies of Adult Japanese Women*. Lewiston, NY: Edwin Mellen Press, 2010.

Ito, Mizuko. "Introduction." In *Fandom Unbound: Otaku Culture in a Connected World*, edited by Mizuko Ito, Daisuke Okabe, and Izumi Tsuji, xi–xxxi. New Haven, CT: Yale University Press, 2012.

Iwabuchi, Koichi. "Undoing Inter-national Fandom in the Age of Brand Nationalism." *Mechademia* 5 (2010): 87–96.

Jackson, Earl, Jr. "Kabuki Narratives of Male Homoerotic Desire in Saikaku and Mishima." *Theater Journal* 41, no. 4 (1989): 459–77.

Jardine, Alice. *Gynesis: Configurations of Woman and Modernity.* Ithaca, NY: Cornell University Press, 1985.

Jenkins, Henry. *Textual Poachers: Television Fans and Participatory Culture.* New York: Routledge, 1992.

Jin, and Kojima Ajiko. *Tonari no 801-chan: Fujoshi-teki kōkō seikatsu* [My neighbor Yaoi-chan: *Fujoshi*-esque high school life]. 3 vols. Tokyo: Kodansha, 2008–2009.

Josei sebun. "Ima sugoi ninki no shōjo komikku sakka no karei-naru shi seikatsu" [The splendid private lives of currently wildly popular *shōjo* manga authors]. December 3, 1975, 194–99.

Kajimoto Jun. *Unmei na no ni saiaku na kyōshi* [It may be fate but he is the worst teacher]. Vol. 2. Tokyo: Kaiōsha, 2011.

Kajita Yujirō. "Taishō kara Shōwa shoki no aida ni oite no risō no shōnen imeeji no keisei: Takabatake Kashō no te ni yoru *Nihon shōnen* no hyōshie kara" [The formation of the ideal image of the boy from Taisho into the early Showa era: From the magazine covers of *Nihon shōnen* (Japanese boys) drawn by Takabatake Kashō]. *Kyōto Seika Daigaku kiyō* 37 (2010): 110–21.

Kakinuma Eiko, and Kurihara Chiyo, eds. *Tanbi shōsetsu, gei bungaku bukkugaido* [Guidebook to aesthete fiction and gay literature]. Tokyo: Byakuya shobō, 1993.

Kan Satoko, Dollase Tsuchiya Hiromi, and Takeuchi Kayo, eds. *"Shōjo manga" wandaarando* ["Girls' manga" wonderland]. Tokyo: Meiji shoin, 2012.

Kaneda Junko. "Manga dōjinshi: Kaishaku kyōdōtai no poritikusu" [Manga *dōjinshi*: The politics of communities' collective interpretation]. In *Bunka no shakai gaku*, edited by Satō Kenji and Yoshimi Shun'ya, 161–90. Tokyo: Yūhikaku, 2007.

———. "Yaoi-ron, asu no tame ni, sono 2" [*Yaoi* studies for tomorrow, Part 2]. *Yuriika* 39, no. 16 (December 2007): 48–54.

Kaneda Junko, and Miura Shion. "'Seme X uke' no mekuru meku sekai: Dansei shintai no miryoku o motomete" [The world surrounding "*seme X uke*": Searching for the attractiveness of male bodies]. *Yuriika* 39, no. 16 (December 2007): 8–29.

Kano, Ayako. "Backlash, Fight Back, and Back-Pedaling: Responses to State Feminism in Contemporary Japan." *International Journal of Asian Studies* 8, no. 1 (2011): 41–62.

Karatani Kōjin. *Nihon kindai bungaku no kigen.* Tokyo: Kōdansha, 1980. Published in English as Karatani Kōjin, *Origins of Modern Japanese Literature*, translated by Brett de Bary (Durham, NC: Duke University Press, 1993).

Kawahara Yumiko. *Zenryaku: Miruku hausu* [Dispensing with formalities: Milk house]. 10 vols. Tokyo: Furawaa komikkusu, 1983–1986.

Kihara Toshie. *Mari to Shingo* [Mari and Shingo]. 13 vols. 1977–1984. Tokyo: Hana to yume komikkusu, 1979–1984.

Kinsella, Sharon. *Adult Manga.* London: RoutledgeCurzon, 2000.

Kio Shimoku. *Genshiken.* Vol. 4. Tokyo: Kōdansha, 2004.

Kishi Yūko. *Tamasaburō koi no kyōsōkyoku* [Tamasaburō's love capriccio]. 5 vols. 1972–1979. Tokyo: Shōgakukan, 2010.

Kōga Yun. *Kanketsuban Aashian* [The complete version of *Earthian*]. 5 vols. Tokyo: Sōbisha, 2002–2008.

———. *Loveless.* 12 vols., ongoing. 2001–. Tokyo: Ichijinsha, 2002–.

Kojima Ajiko. *Tonari no 801-chan* [My neighbor Yaoi-chan]. 5 vols. Tokyo: Ohzora shuppan, 2006–2010.

———. *Yorinuki tonari no 801-chan* [Selections from my neighbor Yaoi-chan]. Tokyo: Ohzora shuppan, 2010.

Komikku maaketto 84 katarogu [Comic Market 84 catalogue]. Tokyo: Komiketto, 2013.

Komikku maaketto junbikai, ed. *Komikku maaketto 30's fairu* [The Comic Market files—30 years]. Tokyo: Komiketto, 2005.

Konjoh Natsumi. *Mōsō shōjo otaku-kei* [Fantasizing girl, otaku-style]. 7 vols. Tokyo: Futabasha, 2006–2010. The first three volumes were published in English as Konjoh Natsumi. *Fujoshi Rumi*, 3 vols. (New York: Media Blasters, 2008–2009).

Konomi Takeshi. *Tenisu no ōjisama* [Prince of tennis]. 42 vols. Tokyo: Shūeisha, 2000–2008.

Kotani Mari. "Fujoshi dōshi no kizuna: C-bungaku to yaoi-teki na yokubō" [Bonding among *Fujoshi*: C-literature and *yaoi*-like desire]. *Yuriika* 39, no. 16 (December 2007): 26–35.

———. *Joseijō muishiki: Tekunogaineeshisu, josei SF-ron josetsu* [Techno-gynesis: The political unconscious in feminist science fiction]. Tokyo: Keisō shobō, 1994.

Kotani Mari, and Keith Vincent. "Kuia seorii wa doko made hirakeru ka" [How expansive can queer theory be?]. *Yuriika* 28, no. 13 (November 1996): 78–98.

Kotobuki Tarako. *Tonari no shibafu* [The neighbor's lawn]. Tokyo: Biblos, 2002.

Koyama Shizuko. *Ryōsai kenbo to iu kihan* [The standard of good wife and wise mother]. Tokyo: Keisō shobō, 1991.

Kurihara Chiyo. "Tanbi shōsetsu to wa nani ka" [What is *tanbi* fiction?]. In Kakinuma and Kurihara, *Tanbi shōsetsu, gei bungaku bukkugaido*, 325–35.

———. "'Genjitsu' no jubaku kara kaihō sareru tame ni" [For being liberated from the spell of "reality"]. In *Choisir yaoi ronsō gappon III*, edited by Irokawa Nao, 30–33. Japan: Self-published, 1994.

———. "Shikarubeki hanron no tame no hanron" [A refutation for proper refutation]. In *Choisir yaoi ronsō gappon II*, by Nao Irokawa, 20–25. Japan: Self-published, 1994–1996.

———. "*Yaoi* ronsō o sōkatsu suru." [A summary of the *yaoi* debate]. In *Choisir yaoi ronsō gappon V*, edited by Irokawa Nao, 72–77. Japan: Self-published, 1996.

Kuroda Isao. "Uchi naru tasha 'Osaka' o yomu" [Reading "Osaka" as an internal other]. In *Media bunka no kenryoku sayō*, edited by Itō Mamoru, 198–221. Tokyo: Serika shobō, 2002.

Kurumada Masami. *Seinto Seiya* [Saint Seiya]. 28 vols. Tokyo: Shūeisha, 1986–1991.

Laplanche, Jean, and J. B. Pontalis. "Fantasy and the Origin of Sexuality." In *Unconscious Phantasy*, edited by Riccardo Steiner, 107–144. London: H. Karnac, 2003.

Les Amitiés particulières. Directed by Jean Delannoy. France: Progéfi and LUX C.C.F., 1964.

Levi, Antonia, Mark McHarry, and Dru Pagliassotti, eds. *Boys' Love Manga: Essays on the Sexual Ambiguity and Cross-Cultural Fandom of the Genre*. Jefferson, NC: McFarland, 2010.

Liu, Tina. "Conflicting Discourses on Boys' Love and Subcultural Tactics in Mainland China and Hong Kong." *Intersections: Gender and Sexuality in Asia and the Pacific* 20 (2009). http://intersections.anu.edu.au/issue20/liu.htm.

Lunsing, Wim. "*Yaoi Ronsō*: Discussing Depictions of Male Homosexuality in Japanese Girls' Comics, Gay Comics and Gay Pornography." *Intersections: Gender, History and Culture in the Asian Context* 12 (2006). http://intersections.anu.edu.au/issue12/lunsing.html.

Manga no techō [Manga handbook]. No. 8 (summer 1982).

Mann, Thomas. *Venisu ni shisu* (*Death in Venice*). Translated by Saneyoshi Hayao. Rev. ed. Tokyo: Iwanami bunko, 2000.

Massumi, Brian. "Translator's Foreword: Pleasures of Philosophy." In *A Thousand Plateaus: Capitalism and Schizophrenia*, edited by Gilles Deleuze and Félix Guattari, translated by Brian Massumi, ix–xv. Minneapolis: University of Minnesota Press, 1987.

Masuda Yumiko, and Saeki Junko, eds. *Nihon bungaku no "joseisei"* [The "femininity" in Japanese literature]. Tokyo: Nishōgakusha daigaku gakujutsu sōsho, 2011.

Masuyama Norie. "*Kaze to ki no uta* no tanjō" [The birth of *The Song of the Wind and the Trees*]. *JUNE*, no. 36 (September 1987): 55–56.

Masuyama Norie, and Sano Megumi. "Kyabetsu batake no kakumeiteki shōjo mangakatachi" [Revolutionary *shōjo* manga artists in a cabbage patch]. In Bessatsu Takarajima, no. 288, *70-nendai manga daihyakka*, 166–73. Tokyo: Takarajimasha, 1996.

Matoh Sanami. *Fake*. 7 vols. Tokyo: Biburosu, 1994–2000.

Matsui, Midori. "Little Girls Were Little Boys: Displaced Femininity in the Representation of Homosexuality in Japanese Girls' Comics." In *Feminism and the Politics of Difference*, edited by Sneja Gunew and Anna Yeatman, 177–96. Halifax, NS: Fernwood Publishing, 1993.

Matsumoto Temari, and Hodaka Parugo. *Paradaisu e oideyo!* [Come to paradise!]. Tokyo: Kadokawa shoten, 2003.

Matsutani Takayuki, Ikeda Riyoko, Kusano Tadashi, Kawauchi Atsurō, and Morina Miharu. "Tezuka Osamu to Takarazuka Kageki: Myūjikaru fōramu" [Tezuka Osamu and the Takarazuka Revue: A musical forum]. In *Tezuka Osamu no furusato, Takarazuka*, edited by Kawauchi Atsurō, 3–61. Kobe, Japan: Kobe shinbun sōgō shuppan sentaa, 1996.

Maya Mineo. *Patariro!* [*Patalliro!*]. 91 vols., ongoing. 1978–. Tokyo: Hana to yume komikkusu, 1979–.

McHarry, Mark. "Boys in Love in Boys' Love: Discourses West/East and the Abject in Subject Formation." In *Boys' Love Manga: Essays on the Sexual Ambiguity and Cross-Cultural Fandom of the Genre*, edited by Antonia Levi, Mark McHarry, and Dru Pagliassotti, 177–89. Jefferson, NC: McFarland, 2010.

McLelland, Mark. "Australia's Proposed Internet Filtering System: Its Implications for Animation, Comic and Gaming ACG) and Slash Fan Communities." *Media International Australia* 134 (2010): 7–19.

———. "Australia's 'Child-Abuse Material' Legislation, Internet Regulation and the Juridification of the Imagination." *International Journal of Cultural Studies* 15, no. 5 (2012): 467–83.

———. "Gay Men as Women's Ideal Partners in Japanese Popular Culture: Are Gay Men Really a Girl's Best Friends?" *U.S.–Japan Women's Journal* 17 (1999): 77–110.

———. "Interpretation and Orientalism: Outing Japan's Sexual Minorities to the English-Speaking World." In *After Orientalism: Critical Entanglements, Productive Looks*, edited by Inge Boer, 105–122. Amsterdam: Rodopi, 2003.

———. "Local Meanings in Global Space: A Case Study of Women's 'Boy Love' Web Sites in Japanese and English." *Mots Pluriels* 19 (2001). http://www.arts.uwa.edu.au/MotsPluriels/MP1901mcl.html.

———. *Male Homosexuality in Modern Japan: Cultural Myths and Social Realities*. Richmond, England: Curzon, 2000.

———. *Queer Japan from the Pacific War to the Internet Age*. Lanham, MD: Rowman and Littlefield, 2005.

———. Review of *Gay Erotic Art in Japan (Vol. 1): Artists from the Time of the Birth of Gay Magazines*, compiled by Tagame Gengoroh, with English translation by Kitajima Yuji. *Intersections: Gender and Sexuality in Asia and the Pacific* 10 (2004). http://intersections.anu.edu.au/issue10/mclelland_review.html.

———. "The Role of the '*Tōjisha*' in Current Debates about Sexual Minority Rights in Japan." *Japanese Studies* 29, no. 2 (2009): 193–207.

———. "A Short History of '*Hentai*.'" *Intersections: Gender History and Culture in the Asian Context* 12 (2006). http://wwwsshe.murdoch.edu.au/intersections/issue12/mclelland.html.

———. "The World of Yaoi: The Internet, Censorship and the Global 'Boys' Love' Fandom." *Australian Feminist Law Journal* 23 (2005): 61–77.

———. "Thought Policing or the Protection of Youth? Debate in Japan over the 'Non-Existent Youth Bill.'" *International Journal of Comic Art (IJOCA)* 13, no. 1 (2011): 348–67.

———. "Why Are Japanese Girls' Comics full of Boys Bonking?" *Refractory* 10 (2006). http://refractory.unimelb.edu.au/2006/12/04/why-are-japanese-girls'-comics-full-of-boy s-bonking1-mark-mclelland/.

McRobbie, Angela. *The Aftermath of Feminism: Gender, Culture and Social Change*. London: Sage Publications, 2009.

———. "Girls and Subcultures." In *Resistance through Rituals: Youth Subcultures in Post-war Britain*, edited by Stuart Hall and Tony Jefferson, 177–88. 2nd ed. 1976. London: Routledge, 2006.

Meyer, Uli. "Hidden in Straight Sight: Trans*gressing Gender and Sexuality via BL." In *Boys' Love Manga: Essays on the Sexual Ambiguity and Cross-Cultural Fandom of the Genre*, edited by Antonia Levi, Mark McHarry, and Dru Pagliassotti, 232–56. Jefferson, NC: McFarland, 2010.

Miller, Laura, and Jan Bardsley, eds. *Bad Girls of Japan*. New York: Palgrave Macmillan, 2005.

Minagawa Hiroko. *Hanayami* [Blooming darkness]. Tokyo: Chukō bunko, 1992.

Minamikata Sunao. *801-shiki chūgakusei nikki* [Yaoi-style junior high school student diary]. Tokyo: Ohzora shuppan, 2009.

Minegishi Hiromi. "Jūjiro" [Crossroads]. *Fanii* 1, no. 2 (July 1969): 120–36.

Misaki Naoto. "2007-nen no josei-kei parodi dōjinshi no dōkō" [Trends in female-produced parody *dōjinshi* in 2007]. *Yuriika* 38, no. 16 (December 2007): 176–79.

Mishima Yukio. *Akatsuki no tera. Hōjō no umi*, vol. 3 [*The Temple of Dawn. The Sea of Fertility*, vol. 3]. Tokyo: Shinchōsha, 1970.

———. *Kamen no kokuhaku* [*Confessions of a Mask*]. Tokyo: Kawade shobō, 1949.

Miura Shion, and Yoshinaga Fumi. "Miura Shion and Yoshinaga Fumi taidan: 'Feminizumu wa yappari kankeinakunai no yo'" ["A conversation between Miura Shion and Yoshinaga Fumi: It is not unrelated to feminism"]. In *Yoshinaga Fumi taidanshū: Ano hito to koko dake no oshaberi*, by Yoshinaga Fumi, 47–91. Tokyo: Ōta Shuppan, 2007.

Miura Shion, and Kaneda Junko. "'Seme X uke' no mekuru meku sekai: Dansei shintai no miryoku o motomete" [The world surrounding '*seme X uke*': Searching for the attractiveness of male bodies]. *Yuriika* 39, no. 7 (June 2007): 8–29.

Miura Shion, Kaneda Junko, Saitō Mitsu, and Yamamoto Fumiko. "2007-nen no BL kai o me-gutte: Soshite 'fujoshi' to wa dare ka" [About a BL circle in 2007: Who are "*fujoshi*"]. *Yuriika* 39, no. 16 (December 2007): 8–25.

Mizoguchi Akiko. "Homofobikku na homo, ai yue no reipu, soshite kuia na rezubian: saikin no yaoi tekisuto o bunseki suru" [Homophobic homos, rapes of love, and queer lesbians: An analysis of recent *yaoi* texts]. *Kuia Japan* 2 (2000): 193–211.

———. "Male–Male Romance by and for Women in Japan: A History and the Subgenres of *Yaoi* Fictions." *U.S.–Japan Women's Journal* 25 (2003): 49–75.

———. "Sore wa, dare no, donna, 'riaru'? Yaoi no gensetsu kūkan o seiri suru kokoromi" [Whose and what kind of 'real' is it? An attempt at sorting out the discursive space of *yaoi*]. *Image and Gender* 4 (2003): 27–55.

———. "Reading and Living Yaoi: Male–Male Fantasy Narratives as Women's Sexual Subculture in Japan." Ph.D. diss., University of Rochester, 2008.

———. "Theorizing Comics/Manga Genre as a Productive Forum: Yaoi and Beyond." In *Comics Worlds and the World of Comics: Towards Scholarship on a Global Scale*, edited by Jaqueline Berndt, 143–68. Kyoto, Japan: International Manga Research Center, 2010. http://imrc.jp/ images/upload/lecture/data/143-168chap10Mizoguchi20101224.pdf.

Mizuma Midory. See also Tanigawa Tamae.

———. *In'yu toshite no shōnen'ai: Josei no shōnen ai shikō to iu genshō* [*Shōnen'ai* as metaphor: The phenomenon of women's inclination for *shōnen ai*]. Osaka: Sōgensha, 2005.

Mizuno Hideko. *Faiyaa!* [Fire!]. 4 vols. 1969–1971. Tokyo: Asahi panorama, 1973.

Mizushiro Setona. *Nezumi wa chiizu no yume o miru* [Rats dreams of cheese]. Tokyo: Shōgakukan kurieitibu, 2006.

Mori Mari. *Koibitotachi no mori* [A lovers' forest]. Tokyo: Shinchōsha, 1961.

Mori Naoko. *Onna wa poruno o yomu: Josei no seiyoku to feminizumu* [Women read porn: Female sexual desires and feminism]. Tokyo: Seikyūsha, 2010.

Mori Ōgai. *Maihime* [*The Dancing Girl*]. 1890. Tokyo: Shūeisha, 1991.

Morikawa Ka'ichirō. *Shuto no tanjō: Moeru toshi Akihabara* [Learning from Akihabara: The birth of a personapolis]. Tokyo: Gentōsha, 2003.

Morton, Leith. "The Concept of Romantic Love in the *Taiyō* Magazine, 1895–1905." *Japan Review* 8 (1997): 79–103.

Muñoz, José Esteban. *Cruising Utopia: The Then and There of Queer Futurity*. New York: New York University Press, 2009.

Murota Naoko. "Shōjo tachi no ibasho sagashi: Vijuaru rokku to shōjo manga" [*Shōjo* searching for a place where they belong: Visual rock and *shōjo* manga]. In *Vijuaru kei no jidai: Rokku/ keshō/jendaa*, edited by Inoue Takako, Murota Naoko, Morikawa Takuo, and Koizumi Kyōko, 163–205. Tokyo: Seidosha, 2003.

Nagaike, Kazumi. "Elegant Caucasians, Amorous Arabs, and Invisible Others: Signs and Images of Foreigners in Japanese BL Manga." *Intersections: Gender and Sexuality in Asia and the Pacific* 20 (2009). http://intersections.anu.edu.au/issue20/nagaike.htm.

———. *Fantasies of Cross-Dressing: Japanese Women Write Male–Male Erotica*. Leiden: Brill, 2012.

———. "Gurōbaruka suru BL kenkyū: Nihon BL kenkyū kara toransunashonaru BL kenkyū e" [The globalization of BL studies: The transition from Japanese BL studies to transnational BL studies]. In *Josei to manga*, edited by Ōgi Fusami. Tokyo: Seikyūsha, forthcoming.

———. "Matsuura Rieko's *The Reverse Version*: The Theme of 'Girl-Addressing-Girl' and Male Homosexual Fantasies." In *Girl Reading Girl in Japan*, edited by Tomoko Aoyama and Barbara Hartley, 107–18. London: Routledge, 2010.

———. "Perverse Sexualities, Pervasive Desires: Representations of Female Fantasies and *Yaoi Manga* as Pornography Directed at Women." *U.S.–Japan Women's Journal* 25 (2003): 76–103.

Nagaike, Kazumi, and Katsuhiko Suganuma, eds. "Transnational Boys' Love Fan Studies." Special issue, *Transformative Works and Cultures* 12 (2013). http://journal.transformativeworks.org/index.php/twc/issue/view/14.

Nagakubo Yōko. "Josei-tachi no 'kusatta yume' yaoi shōsetsu: Yaoi shōsetsu no miryoku to sono mondaisei" [*Yaoi* fiction as women's "rotten" dreams: Positive and negative attributes of *yaoi* fiction]. *Yuriika* 39, no. 7 (June 2007): 142–47.

———. *Yaoi shōsetsu ron: Josei no tame no erosu hyōgen* [Theorizing *yaoi* fiction: Erotic representations for women]. Tokyo: Senshū daigaku shuppankyoku, 2005.

Nagamine Shigetoshi. *Zasshi to dokusha no kindai* [Magazines and readers in the modern era]. Tokyo: Nihon editaa sukuuru no shuppan-bu, 1987.

Nagaoka Yoshiyuki. "Manga no sei hyōgen kisei o neratta tōjōrei kaitei meguru kōbō" [Concerning the pros and cons of pursuing reform of local ordinances regulating sexual expression in manga]. *Tsukuru* 40, no. 5 (June 2010): 64–71.

Nagayama Kaoru. *Ero manga sutadiizu: "Kairaku sōchi" toshite no manga nyūmon* [Erotic manga studies: Introduction to manga as a "pleasure device"]. Tokyo: Iisuto puresu, 2006.

Naitō Chizuko. "Reorganizations of Gender and Nationalism: Gender Bashing and Loliconized Japanese Society." *Mechademia* 5 (2010): 325–33.

Naka Tomoko. *Hana no bijo hime* [Beautiful flower princesses]. 3 vols. 1974–1976. Tokyo: Shōgakukan.

Nakajima Azusa. *Bishōnen-gaku nyūmon* [Introduction to the study of beautiful boys]. 1984. Tokyo: Shūeisha, 1987.

———. *Komyunikēshon fuzen shōkōgun* [Communication deficiency syndrome]. Tokyo: Chikuma shobō, 1991.

———. *Tanatosu no kodomotachi: Kajō tekiō no seitaigaku* [The children of Thanatos: The ecology of excessive adaptation]. Tokyo: Chikuma shobō, 1998.

Nakamura Keiko. *Shōwa bishōnen techō* [Handbook of Showa era beautiful boys]. Tokyo: Kawade shobō, 2003.

Nakano Fuyumi. "Yaoi hyōgen to sabetsu: Onna no tame no porunogurafii o tokihogusu" [*Yaoi* and discrimination: An analysis of pornography directed at women]. *Josei raifu saikuru kenkyū* 4 (1994): 130–38.

Nakano Hitori. *Densha otoko* [Train man]. Tokyo: Shinchōsha, 2004.

Nakata, Kaoru. "The Room of Sweet Honey: The Adult Shōjo Fiction of Japanese Novelist Mori Mari (1903–1987)." MA thesis, The Ohio State University, 2004.

Natō Takako. "'Niji sōsaku' katsudō to sono nettowaaku ni tsuite" ["Derivative writings" and their networks]. In *Sorezore no fan kenkyū: I am a fan*, 55–118. Tokyo: Fūjinsha, 2007.

Nishihara Mari. "Masu media ga utsushidasu yaoi no sugata: Gensetsu bunseki ni yoru" [A discourse analysis approach to the depiction of *yaoi* in the mass media]. *Ronsō kuiaa* 3 (2010): 62–85.

Nishimoto Masashi. *Naruto*. 66 vols., ongoing. Tokyo: Shūeisha, 2000–.

Nishimura Mari. *Aniparo to yaoi* [*Aniparo* and *yaoi*]. Tokyo: Ōta shuppan, 2002.

Nitta Youka. *Haru o daite ita* [Embracing spring]. 14 vols. Tokyo: Ribure shuppan, 1999–2009.

Noa Azusa. "Hanasaku otome-tachi no 'misuterii'" [The "mysteries" of flowery girls]. *Gendai shisō* 23, no. 2 (February 1995): 246–53.

Nobi Nobita. *Otona wa wakatte kurenai: Nobi Nobita hihyō shūsei* [Adults won't understand us: The critical essays of Nobi Nobita]. Tokyo: Nihon hyōron sha, 2003.

———. "*Yaoi* shōjo no kaibōgaku" [Anatomy of *yaoi* girls]. In *Choisir yaoi ronsō gappon II*, edited by Irokawa Nao, Japan: Self-published, 1994. 28–33.

Oda Ei'ichirō. *One Piece*. 71 vols., ongoing. 1997–. Tokyo: Shūeisha, 1997–.

Ogura Tō. "Gei ga oshieru ningen kankei manaa kyōshitsu" [An etiquette class taught by gays]. In *Yoku wakaru gei raifu handobukku*, 82–91. Tokyo: Takarajima, 1994.

Okabe, Daisuke, and Kimi Ishida. "Making *Fujoshi* Identity Visible and Invisible." In *Fandom Unbound: Otaku Culture in a Connected World*, edited by Mizuko Ito, Daisuke Okabe, and Izumi Tsuji, 207–224. New Haven, CT: Yale University Press, 2012.

Orbaugh, Sharalyn. "Creativity and Constraint in Amateur Manga Production." *U.S.–Japan Women's Journal* 25 (2003): 104–124.

———. "Girls Reading Harry Potter, Girls Writing Desire: Amateur Manga and *Shōjo* Reading Practices." In *Girl Reading Girl in Japan*, edited by Tomoko Aoyama and Barbara Hartley, 174–86. London: Routledge, 2010.

Osawa Mari. "Japanese Government Approaches to Gender Equality since the Mid-1990s." *Asian Perspective* 29, no. 1 (2005): 157–73.

Oshiyama Michiko. *Shōjo manga jendaa hyōshōron: "Dansō no shōjo" no zōkei to aidentiti* [On gender representation in *shōjo* manga: The shape of "girls dressed as boys" and identity]. Tokyo: Sairyūsha, 2007.

Ōtsuka Eiji. *Sabukaruchaa bungaku ron* [A theory of subculture literature]. Tokyo: Asahi shinbunsha, 2004.

———. *Teihon monogatari shōhi ron* [A theory of narrative consumption: standard edition]. Tokyo: Kadokawa shoten, 2001.

Pafu. "Boy's Love Magazine kanzen kōryaku manyuaru" [A complete mastery manual on boy's love magazines]. No. 217 (August 1994): 52–59.

Pagliasotti, Dru. "GloBLisation and Hybridisation: Publishers' Strategies for Bringing Boys' Love to the United States." *Intersections: Gender and Sexuality in Asia and the Pacific* 20 (2009). http://intersections.anu.edu.au/issue20/pagliasotti.htm.

Penley, Constance. "Feminism, Psychoanalysis, and the Study of Popular Culture." In *Cultural Studies*, edited by Lawrence Grossberg, Cary Nelson, and Paula A. Treichler, 479–500. London: Routledge, 1992.

Pentabu. *Fujoshi kanojo* [Fujoshi girlfriend]. 2 vols. Tokyo: Enterbrain, 2006–2007. Published in English as *My Girlfriend's a Geek*, 2 vols. (New York: Yen Press, 2010–2011).

Pettman, Dominic. "Love in the Time of Tamagotchi." *Theory, Culture and Society* 26, nos. 2–3 (2009): 189–208.

Peyrefitte, Roger. *Les amitiés particulières: Roman*. Marseille: Jean Vigneau, 1943.

Prescott, Anna Catherine. "Male Viewers of Soap Operas." *Media and Communications Studies Site*, April 1998. http://www.aber.ac.uk/media/Students/acp9601.html.

Prough, Jennifer S. *Straight from the Heart: Gender, Intimacy, and the Cultural Production of Shōjo Manga.* Honolulu: University of Hawai'i Press, 2011.

Rabu-tan seisaku iinkai. *Rabu-tan: Fujoshi no tame no kiso chishiki* [Love-tan: Basic knowledge for *fujoshi*]. Tokyo: Sandeesha, 2006.

Ravuri. *RAPPORI: Yaoi tokushū gō* [RAPPORI: Special *yaoi* issue]. Japan: RAPPORI henshū jimukyoku, 1979.

Reichert, Jim. *In the Company of Men: Representations of Male–Male Sexuality in Meiji Literature.* Stanford, CA: Stanford University Press, 2006.

Rich, Adrienne. "Compulsory Heterosexuality and Lesbian Existence." *Signs* 5, no. 4 (1980): 631–60.

Robertson, Jennifer. *Takarazuka: Sexual Politics and Popular Culture in Modern Japan.* Berkeley: University of California Press, 1998.

Robinson, Kerry. "'Difficult Citizenship': The Precarious Relationship between Childhood, Sexuality and Access to Knowledge." *Sexualities* 15, nos. 3–4 (2012): 257–76.

Rousseau, Jean-Jacques. *The Confessions.* Oxford: Oxford University Press, 2000.

Russell, John G. *Nihonjin no kokujin kan: Mondai wa "chibi kuro Sambo" dake dewa nai* [Japanese attitudes toward black people: The problem is not just "little black Sambo"]. Tokyo: Shinhyōron, 1991.

Sagawa Toshihiko. "Bungaku to goraku no aida o ittari, kitari" [Going back and forth between literature and amusement]. Interview by Ishida Minori. In Ishida Minori. *Hisoyaka na kyōiku: "Yaoi/bōizu rabu" zenshi*, by Ishida Minori, 325–52. Kyoto: Rakuhoku shuppan, 2008.

Saitō Tamaki. *Haha wa musume no jinsei o shihai suru* [Mothers controls daughters' lives]. Tokyo: Nihon hōsō shuppan kyōkai (NHK Books), 2008.

———. *Kankei no kagaku to shite no bungaku* [Literature as relationship chemistry]. Tokyo: Shinchōsha, 2009.

———. "Moe no honshitsu to sono seisei ni tsuite" [The essence of *moe* and its genesis]. *Kokubungaku* 53, no. 16 (2008): 6–13.

———. "*Otaku* Sexuality." Translated by Christopher Bolton. In *Robot Ghosts and Wired Dreams: Japanese Science Fiction from Origins to Anime*, edited by Christopher Bolton, Istvan Csiscery-Ronay, Jr., and Tatsumi Takayuki, 222–49. Minneapolis: University of Minnesota Press, 2007.

Saizō, and Hyōgen no jiyū o kangaeru kai, eds. *Hijitsuzai seishōnen kisei hantai tokuhon* [Nonexistent youth restriction opposition reader]. Tokyo: Saizō, 2010.

Sakakibara Shihomi. *Yaoi genron: "Yaoi" kara mieta mono* [Phantasmic discourse on *yaoi*: Things seen from a "*yaoi*" perspective]. Tokyo: Natsume shobō, 1998.

Sanrūmu (Takemiya Keiko fan club). *Sanrūmu* [Sunroom]. No. 6. June 15, 1978. Urawa, Saitama, Japan: Self-published.

Satō Masaki. "Shōjo manga to homofobia" [*Shōjo* manga and homophobia]. In *Kuia sutadiizu '96*, edited by Kuia sutadiizu henshū iinkai, 161–69. Tokyo: Nanatsumori shokan, 1996.

———. "Yaoi nante shinde shimaeba ii" [I wish all *yaoi* dead]. In *Choisir yaoi ronsō gappon II*, edited by Irokawa Nao, 1–3. Japan: Self-published, 1994.

Schodt, Frederik L. *Dreamland Japan: Writings on Modern Manga*. Berkeley, CA: Stone Bridge Press, 1996.

——. *Manga! Manga! The World of Japanese Comics*. New York: Kodansha America, 1983.

Scott-Stokes, Henry. *The Life and Death of Yukio Mishima*. New York: Ballantine Books, 1985.

Sedgwick, Eve Kosofsky. *Between Men: English Literature and Male Homosocial Desire*. New York: Columbia University Press, 1985.

Seiya ni muchū! [Mad for Seiya!]. *Seiya dōjinshi kessaku ansorojii*. Vol. 4. Tokyo: Fyūjon puro-dakuto, 1987.

Shah, Nayan. "Perversity, Contamination and the Dangers of Queer Domesticity." In *Queer Studies: An Interdisciplinary Reader*, edited by Robert J. Corber and Stephen Velocchi, 121–41. Malden, MA: Blackwell, 2003.

Shigematsu, Setsu. "Dimensions of Desire: Sex, Fantasy, and Fetish in Japanese Comics." In *Themes in Asian Cartooning: Cute, Cheap, Mad, and Sexy*, edited by John A. Lent, 127–64. Bowling Green, OH: Bowling Green State University Popular Press, 1999.

Shiina Yukari. "Amerika de no BL manga ninki" [The popularity of BL manga in America]. *Yuriika* 39, no. 16 (December 2007): 180–89.

Shimada Masako. *Dorakira* [Dracula Kira]. Tokyo: Biburosu, 2004.

Shimizu Yuki. *Ze* [Yes!]. Vol. 9. Tokyo: Shinshokan, 2010.

Shimotsuki Takanaka. *Komikku maaketto sōseiki* [The genesis of Comic Market]. Tokyo: Asahi shinbun shuppan, 2008.

Shinba Rize. *Fujoshi kanojo* [Fujoshi girlfriend]. 5 vols. Tokyo: Enterbrain/B's Log Comics, 2007–2010. Published in English as *My Girlfriend's a Geek*, 5 vols. (New York: Yen Press, 2010–2011).

Shurato makū gensō [Shurato enchanted sky fantasy]. *Shurato dōjinshi kessaku ansorojii*. Vol. 6. Tokyo: Fyūjon purodakuto, 1990.

Silverberg, Miriam. *Erotic Grotesque Nonsense: The Mass Culture of Japanese Modern Times*. Berkeley: University of California Press, 2007.

——. "The Modern Girl as Militant." In *Recreating Japanese Women, 1600–1945*, edited by Gail Lee Bernstein, 239–66. Berkeley: University of California Press, 1991.

Silverman, Kaja. *Male Subjectivity at the Margins*. New York: Routledge, 1992.

Sontag, Susan. *Illness as Metaphor and AIDS and its Metaphors*. New York: Doubleday, 1990.

Stanley, Marni. "101 Uses for Boys: Communing with the Reader in *Yaoi* and Slash." In *Boys' Love Manga: Essays on the Sexual Ambiguity and Cross-Cultural Fandom of the Genre*, edited by Antonia Levi, Mark McHarry, and Dru Pagliassotti, 99–109. Jefferson, NC: McFarland, 2010.

Sugimoto, Yoshio. *An Introduction to Japanese Society*. 3rd edition. Cambridge: Cambridge University Press, 2010.

Sugiura Yumiko. *101-nin no fujoshi to ikemen ōji: Fujoshi "ren'ai kan" kenkyū* [101 *fujoshi* and handsome princes: Research on the perspectives on love of *fujoshi*]. Tokyo: Hara shobō, 2009.

——. *Fujoshika suru sekai: Higashi Ikebukuro no otaku joshitachi* [Fujoshi-izing world: The *otaku* girls of East Ikebukuro]. Tokyo: Chūō kōron shinsha, 2006.

——. *Kakure otaku 9-wari: Hotondo no joshi ga otaku ni natta* [90 percent hidden *otaku*: Almost all girls have become *otaku*]. Tokyo: PHP kenkyūsho, 2008.

———. "Moeru onna otaku" [Excited female *otaku*]. *Aera*, June 20, 2005, 42–45.

———. *Otaku joshi kenkyū: Fujoshi shisō taikei* [*Otaku* girls research: A compendium of *fujoshi* thought]. Tokyo: Hara shobō, 2006.

Sugiyama Akashi. Research outcome report on "Komikku dōjinshi sokubaikai 'Komikku Maaketto' no bunka-shakaigakuteki kenkyū" [A sociocultural study on comic dōjinshi sokubaikai, "Comic Market"]. Grants-in-Aid for Scientific Research, no. 16330100. Japan Society for the Promotion of Science, 2008.

Suzuki, Kazuko. "Pornography or Therapy: Japanese Girls Creating the Yaoi Phenomenon." In *Millennium Girls: Today's Girls Around the World*, edited by Sherrie A. Inness, 243–67. Lanham, MD: Rowman and Littlefield, 1998.

Suzuki, Michiko. *Becoming Modern Women: Love and Identity in Prewar Japanese Literature and Culture*. Stanford, CA: Stanford University Press, 2010.

Suzuki Takayuki, ed. *Bungaku wa naze manga ni maketa ka!?* [Why did literature lose to manga!?]. Kyoto: Kyoto seika daigaku jōhōkan, 1998.

Takabatake Asako. "Takabatake Kashō no kodomo e ni tsuite no ikkō: Arisu to no dōshitsusei o megutte" [Thinking about Takabatake Kashō's images of children: Concerning similarities with Alice]. *Bigaku bijutsu shi ronshū* 19 (March 2011): 55(452)–80(427).

Takabatake Sumie. "Takabatake Kashō to narushishizumu: Kashō sakuhin no seishin bunseki teki shiron" [Takabatake Kashō and narcissism: A psychoanalytic discussion of Kashō's work]. *Taishō imajurii* 3 (2007): 144–64.

Takahara Eiri. "The Consciousness of the Girl: Freedom and Arrogance." In *Woman Critiqued: Translated Essays on Japanese Women's Writing*, edited by Rebecca Copeland, 190–91. Honolulu: University of Hawai'i Press, 2006.

———. *Muku no chikara: Shōnen hyōshō bungaku ron* [The power of innocence: Literary studies on the representations of boys]. Tokyo: Kōdansha, 2003.

Takahashi, Mizuki. "Opening the Closed World of *Shōjo Manga*." In *Japanese Visual Culture: Explorations in the World of Manga and Anime*, edited by Mark Wheeler MacWilliams, 114–36. Armonk, NY: M.E. Sharpe, 2008.

Takahashi Yōichi. *Kyaputen Tsubasa* [Captain Tsubasa]. 37 vols. 1981–1988. Tokyo: Shūeisha, 1982–1989.

Takamatsu Hisako. "'Teki mikata' ron no kanata e: Miyou to suru koto, mietekuru koto" [Thinking through a perspective of "friend or foe": Things that we attempt to see and that come into view]. In *Choisir yaoi ronsō gappon II*, edited by Irokawa Nao, 3–6. Japan: Self-published, 1994.

Takayuki Yokota-Murakami. *Don Juan East-West: On the Problematics of Comparative Literature*. Albany: State University of New York Press, 1998.

Takemiya Keiko, Ishida Minori, and Shimamoto Kan. "Takabatake Kashō tanjō hyaku nijū shūnen kinen kōden" [Commemorative lecture marking the one hundred and twentieth anniversary of Takabatake Kashō's birth]. *Taishō imajurii* 4 (2008): 46–58.

———. *Kaze to ki no uta* [The song of the wind and the trees]. 10 vols. 1976–1984. Tokyo: Hakusensha bunko, 1995.

———. "*Kaze to ki no uta* wa auto! Aidentiti o mamoru tame ni" [The *Song of the Wind and the Trees* is out! For the sake of protecting identity]. *Popyuraa karuchaa kenkyū* 5, no. 1 (2011): 8–18.

————. "Sanrūmu nite" [In the sunroom]. 1970. In her *Sanrūmu nite*, 5–54. Tokyo: San komikkusu, 1976.

————. *Takemiya Keiko no manga kyōshitsu* [Takemiya Keiko's manga classroom]. Tokyo: Chikuma shobō, 2001.

Takeyama, Akiko. "Commodified Romance in a Tokyo Host Club." In *Genders, Transgenders and Sexualities in Japan*, edited by Mark McLelland and Romit Dasgupta, 200–215. New York: Routledge, 2005.

————. "The Art of Seduction and Affect Economy: Neoliberal Class Struggle and Gender Politics in a Tokyo Host Club." Ph.D. diss., University of Illinois at Urbana-Champaign, 2008.

Tanaka Mitsu. *Inochi no onna tachi e: Torimidashi ūman ribu* [To the women of life: Tearing my hair out women's liberation]. Tokyo: Kawade shobō shinsha, 1992.

Tanaka Suzuki. *Kōfuku no ōji* [Happy prince]. Tokyo: Biburosu, 2005.

Tanaka Toshiyuki. *Danseigaku no shintenkai* [New developments in men's studies]. Tokyo: Seikyūsha, 2009.

Tanaka Yoshiki. *Ginga eiyū densetsu* [Legend of the galactic heroes]. 10 vols. Tokyo: Tokuma shoten, 1982–1987.

Tanaka, Yukiko. *Women Writers of Meiji and Taisho Japan: Their Lives, Works and Critical Reception, 1868–1926.* Jefferson, NC: McFarland, 2000.

Tanigawa Tamae [Mizuma Midory]. "Josei no shōnen ai shikō ni tsuite III: 'Yaoi ronsō kara" [On women's preference for *shōnen' ai* Part 3: From the "*yaoi* debate"]. *Joseigaku nenpō* 16 (1995): 36–51.

————. "Josei no shōnen'ai shikō ni tsuite II: Shikisha no kenkai to, feminizumu ni aru kanōsei" [On women's preference for *shōnen' ai*, part 2: Expert opinions and feminist possibilities]. *Joseigaku nenpō* 134 (1993): 66–79.

Tanizaki Jun'ichirō, *Shunkinshō* [A portrait of Shunkin]. Tokyo: Shinchōsha, 1951.

Tezuka Osamu. *Ribon no kishi* [*Princess Knight*]. 2 vols. 1953–1955. Tokyo: Kōdansha manga bunko, 1999.

Thorn, Matthew. "Girls and Women Getting Out of Hand: The Pleasure and Politics of Japan's Amateur Comics Community." In *Fanning the Flames: Fans and Consumer Culture in Contemporary Japan*, edited by William Kelly, 169–87. Albany: State University of New York Press, 2004.

Thorndike, Robert L., and Florence Henry. "Differences in Reading Interests Related to Differences in Sex and Intelligence Level." *Elementary School Journal* 40 (1940): 751–63.

Tipton, Elise K. "Pink Collar Work: The Café Waitress in Early Modern Japan." *Intersections: Gender History and Culture in the Asian Context* 7 (2002). http://intersections.anu.edu.au/issue7/tipton.html.

Tojitsuki Hajime. *Shironeko* [White cat]. Tokyo: Kaiōsha, 2005.

Torūpaa hana fubuki [Trooper flower blizzard]. *Torūpaa dōjinshi kessaku ansorojii.* Vol. 1. Tokyo: Fyūjon purodakuto, 1989.

Treat, John Whittier. "Yoshimoto Banana Writes Home: Shōjo Culture and the Nostalgic Subject." *Journal of Japanese Studies* 19, no. 2 (Summer 1993): 353–87.

Tsubasa hyakkaten [Tsubasa department store]. *Bessatsu komikku bokkusu.* Vol. 1. Tokyo: Fyūjon purodakuto, 1987.

Tsukumogō. *Saigo no sangatsu* [The last March]. Tokyo: Shōbunkan, 2008.

Ueno Chizuko. *Hatsujō sōchi: Erosu no shinario* [The erotic apparatus: Erotic scenarios]. Tokyo: Chikuma shobō, 1998.

———. "Sakai-shi toshokan, BL hon haijo sōdō tenmatsu" [The circumstances surrounding the controversial exclusion of BL books at Sakai Municipal Library]. *Tsukuru* 39, no. 5 (May 2009): 106–112.

Uno Tsunehiro. "Zero nendai no sōzōryoku: 'Ushinawareta 10-nen no mukōgawa" [The imagination of the zero-generation: Beyond the "lost decade"]. *SF magajin* 29, no. 1 (2008): 90–97.

Vincent, Keith. "A Japanese Electra and Her Queer Progeny." *Mechademia* 2 (2007): 64–79.

Walnuts. *Hi Five Boogie.* Japan: Self-published, 2008.

Warner, Michael. *The Trouble with Normal: Sex, Politics, and the Ethics of Queer Life.* New York: The Free Press, 1999.

Watanabe Tsuneo, and Iwata Jun'ichi. *Love of the Samurai: A Thousand Years of Japanese Homosexuality.* Translated by D. R. Roberts. London: Gay Men's Press, 1989.

Watanabe Yumiko. "Seishōnen manga kara miru yaoi" [*Yaoi* as seen from the perspective of manga for boys and young men). *Yuriika* 39, no. 7 (June 2007): 69–83.

Welker, James. "Beautiful, Borrowed, and Bent: 'Boys' Love' as Girls' Love in *Shōjo Manga*." *Signs* 31, no. 3 (2006): 841–70.

———. "Drawing Out Lesbians: Blurred Representations of Lesbian Desire in *Shōjo* Manga." In *Lesbian Voices: Canada and the World; Theory, Literature, Cinema*, edited by Subhash Chandra, 156–84. New Delhi: Allied Publishers, 2006.

———. "Flower Tribes and Female Desire Complicating Early Female Consumption of Male Homosexuality in Shōjo Manga." *Mechademia* 6 (2011): 211–28.

———. "Lilies of the Margin: Beautiful Boys and Queer Female Identities in Japan." In *AsiaPacifiQueer: Rethinking Genders and Sexualities*, edited by Fran Martin, Peter A. Jackson, Mark McLelland, and Audrey Yue, 46–66. Urbana: University of Illinois Press, 2008.

Williams, Alan. "Raping Apollo: Sexual Difference and the *Yaoi* Phenomenon." In *Boys' Love Manga: Essays on the Sexual Ambiguity and Cross-Cultural Fandom of the Genre*, edited by Antonia Levi, Mark McHarry, and Dru Pagliassotti, 221–31. Jefferson, NC: McFarland, 2010.

Women's Asia 21. "Unbelievable Events Happening in Japan Motivated by Conservative Politicians." *Voices from Japan*, no. 17 (Summer 2006): 39–40.

Wood, Andrea. "'Straight' Women, Queer Texts: Boy-Love Manga and the Rise of a Global Counterpublic." *Women's Studies Quarterly* 34, nos. 1–2 (2006): 394–414.

Yajima Masami. *Dansei dōseiaisha no raifu hisutorii* [Life histories of homosexual men]. Tokyo: Gakubunsha, 1997.

Yamaai Shikiko. *Arekisandoraito* [Alexandrite]. 1992. Tokyo: Kadokawa bunko, 2006.

———. *Nemeshisu* [Nemesis]. Tokyo: Daria bunko, 2010.

Yamada Tomoko. "Pure-'Yaoi/BL' to iu shiten kara: 'O-hanabatake' o junbi shita sakkatachi'" [Perspectives on "pre-*yaoi*/BL": Artists preparing "flower gardens" for their descendants]. *Yuriika* 39, no. 7 (June 2007): 123–31.

Yamagishi Ryōko. *Hi izuru tokoro no tenshi* [Emperor of the land of the rising sun]. 11 vols. 1980–1984. Tokyo: Hana to yume komikkusu, 1980–1984.

Yamamoto Fumiko, and BL sapōtaazu. *Yappari, bōizu rabu ga suki: Kanzen BL komikku gaido* [Indeed, we do love BL: A complete guide to BL comics]. Tokyo: Ōta shuppan, 2005.

Yanagida Ryōko. "Satō-san e no tegami" [A letter to Satō-san]. In Irokawa, *Choisir yaoi ronsō gappon I*, edited by Irokawa Nao, Japan: Self-published, 1994. 13–16.

Yi, Erika Junhui. "Reflection on Chinese Boys' Love Fans: An Insider's View." *Transformative Works and Cultures* 12 (2013). http://journal.transformativeworks.org/index.php/twc/article/view/424/390.

Yonezawa Yoshihiro. "Manga to dōjinshi no sasayaka no kyōen: Komiketto no atacta cikyō" [A small feast of manga and *dōjinshi*: the influence of Komiketto]. In Bessatsu Takarajima, no. 358, *Watashi o komike ni tsuretette!*, Tokyo: Takarajimasha, 1998. 40–49.

———. "Manga/anime no kaihōku, komike tte nani?" [What's Komike, that space of liberation for manga/anime?]. Interview. In Bessatsu Takarajima, no. 358, *Watashi o Komike ni tsuretette!*, Tokyo: Takarajimasha, 1998. 10–25.

———. *Sengo ero manga shi* [A history of postwar erotic manga]. Tokyo: Seirin kōgeisha, 2010.

———. *Sengo shōjo manga shi* [A history of postwar *shōjo* manga]. 1980. Tokyo: Chikuma shobō, 2007.

Yoshida Akimi. *Banana Fish*. 19 vols. 1985–1994. Tokyo: Furawaa komikkusu, 1987–1994.

Yoshimoto Taimatsu. *Fudanshi ni kiku 2* [Interviewing *fudanshi* 2]. Japan: Self-published, 2010.

———. *Fudanshi ni kiku* [Interviewing *fudanshi*]. Japan: Self-published, 2008.

———. "Otoko mo sunaru bōizu rabu" [Men also do BL]. *Yuriika* 39, no. 7 (June 2007): 106–12.

Yoshinaga Fumi. *Ai ga nakutemo kutte yukemasu* [I can live on/keep eating even without love]. Tokyo: Ōta shuppan, 2005.

———. *Ano hito to koko dake no oshaberi* [Confidential chat with that person]. Tokyo: Ōta shuppan, 2007.

———. *Jeraaru to Jakku* [Gérard et Jacques]. Tokyo: Hakusensha, 2004.

———. *Kare wa hanazono de yume o miru* [He dreams in the flower garden]. Tokyo: Shinshokan, 1999.

———. *Kinō nani tabeta?* [What did you eat yesterday?]. 7 vols., ongoing. Tokyo: Kōdansha, Morning KC (Kodansha Comic), 2007–.

———. *Ōoku* [The inner chamber]. 9 vols., ongoing. Tokyo: Hakusensha, 2005–.

———. *Seiyō kottō yōgashiten* [Antique bakery]. 4 vols. Tokyo: Shinshokan, Wings Comic, 2000–2002.

———. *Sore kara no Antiiku* [Antique afterwards]. 2 vols. Tokyo: Ōsawa kaseifu kyōkai, 2005–2006.

———. *Tsuki to sandaru 2* [The moon and the sandals 2]. Tokyo: Hōbunsha, 2000.

———. *Tsuki to sandaru* [The moon and the sandals]. Tokyo: Hōbunsha, 1996.

Yuriika. Special issue, "*Shōjo* manga" [Girls' comics]. Vol. 13, no. 9 (July 1981).

———. Special issue, "BL (bōizurabu) sutadiizu" [BL (boys love) studies]. Vol. 39, no. 16 (December 2007).

———. Special issue, "BL on za ran!" [BL on the run!]. Vol. 44, no. 15 (December 2012).

———. Special issue, "Fujoshi manga taikei" [Fujoshi manga compendium]. Vol. 39, no. 7 (June 2007).

Yūya. *Chikyū no ōsama* [The king of the earth]. Tokyo: Ōkura shuppan, 2008.

CONTRIBUTORS

Tomoko Aoyama is an associate professor in Japanese at the University of Queensland, Australia. Her monograph *Reading Food in Modern Japanese Literature* (2008) was awarded the Asian Studies Association of Australia's Mid-Career Researcher Prize (2010). She edited *Girl Reading Girl in Japan* (with Barbara Hartley; 2010), and guest edited the special issues of *Asian Studies Review* 32, no. 3 (2008) on "The Girl, the Body, and the Nation in Japan and the Pacific Rim," and *U.S.–Japan Women's Journal* 38 (2010) (with Hiromi Tsuchiya Dollase and Satoko Kan) on "Shōjo Manga: Past, Present and Future." She was awarded the Inaugural Inoue Yasushi Award for Outstanding Research in Japanese Literature in Australia (2007).

Fujimoto Yukari is currently an associate professor at the School of Global Japanese Studies, Meiji University, Japan. She also has an established career as an editor at Chikuma publishing; moreover, as a cultural critic, she has actively engaged with such topics as Japanese comic books and gender/sexuality. She is the author of *Where Do I Belong? The Shape of the Heart Reflected in Shōjo Manga* (*Watashi no ibasho wa doko ni aru no? Shōjo manga ga utsusu kokoro no katachi*, 1998), *The Spirit of Shōjo Manga* (*Shōjo manga damashii*, 2000), *The Electric Current of Pleasure* (*Kairaku denryū*, 1999), *Critique of Love* (*Aijō hyōron*, 2004), and *The Edge of the World* (*Kiwakiwa*, 2013).

Patrick W. Galbraith holds a Ph.D. in Information Studies from the University of Tokyo, and is pursuing a second Ph.D. in Cultural Anthropology at Duke University. He is the author of *The Otaku Encyclopedia* (2009), *Tokyo Realtime: Akihabara* (2010), *Otaku Spaces* (2012), and *The Moe Manifesto* (2014); he is also co-editor of *Idols and Celebrity in Japanese Media Culture* (2012). His academic articles include "*Lolicon*: The Reality of 'Virtual Child Pornography' in Japan" in *Image and Narrative* (2011), "*Fujoshi*: Fantasy Play and Transgressive Intimacy among 'Rotten Girls' in Contemporary Japan" in *Signs* (2011), and "Osamu Moet Moso: Imagining Lines of Eroticism in Akihabara" in *Mechademia* (2014).

Barbara Hartley is a senior lecturer at the University of Tasmania. With Tomoko Aoyama, she is the joint editor of the Routledge collection entitled *Girl Reading Girl in Japan* (2010). She has published widely on women's literature in Japan and worked on translations related to this topic. She is also interested in representations of China and the Asian mainland in twentieth century Japanese narrative. Barbara has a particular interest in the cultural production of the interwar period and the commercial artists, including Takabatake Kashō (1888–1966) and Takehisa Yumeji (1884–1934), active during that time.

Jeffry T. Hester is professor of Sociocultural Anthropology in the Asian Studies Program at Kansai Gaidai University in Hirakata, Japan. His research interests include culture and identity in the nation-state system, Koreans, and other minority groups in Japan, and gender, sexuality, and popular culture. Among his publications is *"Datsu Zainichi-ron*: An Emerging Discourse on Belonging among Ethnic Koreans in Japan," in *Multiculturalism in the New Japan: Crossing the Boundaries Within* (2007). His *fujoshi*-related research grows out of an interest in youth engagement in popular culture in the creation of meaningful social worlds.

Ishida Hitoshi received his Ph.D. in Sociology from Chuo University, Japan, and he is the chief research fellow for the Nikkōso Foundation for Safe Society. His research examines the histories of discourses surrounding homosexuality and transgender in postwar Japan. He is the editor of *Gender Identity Disorder: Gender, Medicine and Law* (*Sei dōitsusei shōgai: Jendaa, iryō, tokureihō*, 2008), and is a contributor to *Gender: An Illustrated Guide* (*Zukai zatsugaku: Jendaa*, 2005), *Genders, Transgenders and Sexualities in Japan* (2005), *A Social History of Transgenderism and Homosexuality in Postwar Japan* (*Sengo Nihon josō/dōseiai kenkyū*, 2006), and *Postwar Histories of Sexuality* (*Sekushuariti no sengoshi*, 2014).

Mark McLelland is professor of Gender and Sexuality Studies and an Australian Research Council Future Fellow at the University of Wollongong, and was the 2007–2008 Toyota Visiting Professor of Japanese at the Center for Japanese Studies at the University of Michigan. He has published widely about gender and sexuality in Japan in books such as *Male Homosexuality in Modern Japan* (2000), *Genders, Transgenders and Sexualities in Japan* (2005), *Queer Japan from the Pacific War* (2005), and *Love, Sex and Democracy in Japan during the American Occupation* (2012); and on the global spread of Japanese popular culture, most recently in a special themed edition of the journal *Intersections* on "Transnational Japanese Fandoms and Female Consumers."

Kazumi Nagaike is an associate professor at the Center for International Education and Research at Oita University, Japan. She is the author of *Fantasies of Cross-Dressing: Japanese Women Write Male–Male Erotica* (2012), and has published journal articles, book chapters, and translations in relation to her ongoing analysis of female acts of fantasizing about male–male eroticism, both in literary works and in popular culture materials.

Rio Otomo is professor of English in the Department of Film Studies at the Japan Institute of the Moving Image. She has written critical essays on Japanese novels such as works by Mishima Yukio, Murakami Haruki, and Kanehara Hitomi. Her research draws on feminist psychoanalysis with a focus on the subject formation and its relationship to the body. Her recent publications include "A Girl with Her Writing Machine" (in *Girl Reading Girl in Japan*; 2010) and the Japanese translation of *Mister Pip*, by Lloyd Jones (2009). Her current research focuses on pornography and the act of reading.

Joanne Quimby earned her Ph.D. in Japanese and Comparative Literature at Indiana University, and she is currently visiting assistant professor of Japanese at North Central College in Naperville, Illinois. Her research focuses on contemporary women writers and representations of the body and sexuality, especially performative sexuality and performative gender identities.

Katsuhiko Suganuma is a lecturer in the School of Humanities at the University of Tasmania. His research focuses on contemporary Japanese sexuality politics, queer globalization, and transnational cultural studies. He has published critical essays on gay and lesbian sexualities in contemporary Japan. He is a co-editor of *Queer Voices from Japan* (2007) and the author of *Contact Moments: The Politics of Intercultural Desire in Japanese Male-Queer Cultures* (2012).

Kazuko Suzuki received her Ph.D. in Sociology from Princeton University and is currently assistant professor at Texas A&M University. She was a 2009–2010 Visiting Scholar at the Center for Advanced Study in the Behavioral Sciences and the Center for Comparative Studies in Race and Ethnicity at Stanford University and a 2008–2009 Visitor in the School of Social Science at the Institute for Advanced Studies, Princeton, NJ. Previously, she lectured at the Center for the Study of Ethnicity and Race and Weatherhead

East Asian Institute at Columbia University. She was also an Abe Fellow of the Social Science Research Council and a postdoctoral fellow at the Center for Comparative Immigration Studies at the University of California, San Diego. She specializes in international migration, race and ethnic relations, and gender and sexuality. She is currently working on her second book project, *At the Crossroads of Fantasy and Reality: Yaoi and Post-Male Feminism in Contemporary Japan.*

James Welker is an associate professor in the Department of Cross-Cultural Studies at Kanagawa University, Japan. His research and publications examine female gender and sexual expression in postwar and contemporary Japan, including, most recently, "The Revolution Will Not Be Translated: Transfiguring Discourses of Women's Liberation in 1970s–1980s Japan" in *Multiple Translation Communities in Contemporary Japan* (forthcoming), "Flower Tribes and Female Desire: Complicating Early Female Consumption of Male Homosexuality in *Shōjo* Manga" in *Mechademia* (2011), and "From *The Cherry Orchard* to *Sakura no sono*: Translated Texts and the Transfiguration of Gender and Sexuality in *Shōjo* Manga" in *Girl Reading Girl in Japan* (2010). He is currently completing a monograph examining the transnational engagements of the women's liberation movement, the lesbian community, and readers and artists of queer *shōjo* manga in Japan.

INDEX

CPSIA information can be obtained at www.ICGtesting.com
Printed in the USA
BVOW07*0205060115

382049BV00003B/5/P